ASPECTS OF GREEK AND ROMAN LIFE

ROMAN LIFE

General Editor: H. H. Scullard

★ ★ ★

ISIS IN THE
GRAECO-ROMAN WORLD

R. E. Witt

ISIS
IN THE
GRAECO-ROMAN
WORLD

R. E. Witt

CORNELL UNIVERSITY PRESS
ITHACA, NEW YORK

First published 1971

International Standard Book Number 0-8014-0633-1

Library of Congress Catalog Card Number 72-146278

PRINTED IN ENGLAND

CONTENTS

LIST OF ILLUSTRATIONS

FIGURES

ERRATUM

Page 269, line 10, for 'Bruno's influence . . .'
read 'Pico della Mirandola's influence . . .'

PREFACE

OUR WESTERN WORLD's Graeco-Roman and Christian civilization
has emerged and taken shape out of the cultural melting pot of the
Near East. Historians however have not always acknowledged
how potent a factor in this process was the religion of Egypt.
From Memphis and Alexandria the cult of Isis and her Temple
Associates shed an incalculable influence on other rival faiths,
including even Christianity. A full-scale investigation in a field
which appears neglected is long overdue.

This monograph, planned to present the salient facts, offers a
conspectus of the whole religion in a fresh treatment of the
material first comprehensively studied nearly a century ago by
Lafaye and since then much enlarged by experts in various
branches of archaeology.

Archaeology and its allied disciplines will not automatically
grant us the key to what we may appropriately call the mystery of
Isis. Nevertheless, the deeper the archaeologist delves the mightier
the goddess is revealed to be. She cannot be hidden away completely out of sight. She declines to be brushed aside as effete
because she is old. She may be a virtually forgotten link between
the faraway past and our immediate present. But there she is. As a
result of the present inquiry the greatness of Isis as the Egyptian
forerunner, it is to be hoped, will henceforward be matter for
continued debate among the theologians of the Christian Church.

Some works of real merit have been published during the last
decade by Isiac scholars. Special mention may be made of con-
tributions by Gwyn Griffiths, Tran Tam Tinh, Merkelbach,
Münster, Bergman and Grimm. As far as possible their findings
have been utilized. The many literary references of the Graeco-
Roman period are cited by page and line from Hopfner's source

book, which though now nearly half a century old is still indispensable. The timely appearance of Vidman's *Sylloge* has greatly facilitated the citation of epigraphical references.

With the aid of the illustrations the non-specialist reader for whom this book is primarily intended ought to feel at home as he looks at Isis in the world of Alexandria and Rome, amid the ruins of Delos and Pompeii, confronting Augustus and Paul, Apuleius and Plutarch. Above all else, the author has endeavoured to be succinct yet comprehensive, avoiding as far as possible those technicalities which drive the general reader away.

An author's debt to the work of others cannot always be easily stated. My friendship with Dr Gwyn Griffiths has enabled me to seek his views on important topics. Close contact with Mr Peter Clayton has been of quite inestimable benefit at every point. My son has supervised all the indexing and rescued me from slips of various kinds. My wife has helped as cartographer. Throughout, of course, the editor of the series, Professor H. H. Scullard, has been a tower of strength to me in the fulfilment of a task at once exacting, exciting and irresistible.

Queen Mary College,   R. E. WITT
University of London

CHAPTER I

THE ANCIENT GODDESS OF
THE NILE

MAN'S GODS are very old. To him they have ever seemed to control the world beyond him, his immediate surroundings, and his destiny. He probes outside him and above him in constant need of a saviour to rescue him from hunger and sickness and plague, from sin and from death. Driven by the indwelling force of mind and soul he searches for a First Cause. Divine worship is his means of giving thanks for the crops that feed him, for the health whereby he keeps alive and fit for his tasks, and for all his other blessings. Often he pins his faith on ritual and magic. He does not easily break away from the religious traditions of his forebears. At times he soars theologically into the unknown on the wings of poetry and philosophy, only to hear as it were the Word of God

Then drop into thyself, and be a fool.

We are still no less fascinated than was the Graeco-Roman world by the mysteries of our own beginning, our life here and now, and our end. Few of us can go on for long without a belief in the efficacy of prayer. Mankind hopes that divine intercession will bring such comfort and security as a devoted mother bestows on the child she screens from harm. So our own generation is in just the same case as the ancient Egyptians.

To us in western Europe today the Egypt of the Pharaohs is a strangely remote and lost land. The temples and pyramids, the creeds and cults of the Nile elude our understanding. A modern mind is easily baffled by the apparent confusions and illogicalities of Egyptian religion. For our western world to appreciate the civilization of the Nile is hard—the agricultural way of life instead of an industrialized society, the belief in the king's divinity instead of democracy, the worship of animals and gloating regard for the mummified dead instead of the far more spiritualized faith of Christianity. Factories and machines, swift strides in science and technology, space probes and now the treading of the Moon by astronauts all seem to cut us off from Egypt and its early achievements. Its culture and its gods, we tell ourselves, belong to a past we have long outgrown.

Of course, our occidental society today is firmly founded on long Christian and Graeco-Roman tradition. But this in turn did not arise *in vacuo*. If we look beneath the surface we can find links between our present-day modes of thinking and the wisdom of Egypt.

There, in the beginning was Isis. Oldest of the old, she was the goddess from whom all Becoming arose. She was the Great Lady —Mistress of the Two Lands of Egypt, Mistress of Shelter, Mistress of Heaven, Mistress of the House of Life, Mistress of the Word of God. She was the Unique. In all her great and wonderful works she was a wiser magician and more excellent than any other god (*Pl. 1*).[1]

Egypt for its inhabitants was the Black Land.[2] The name betokened the fertility of the Nile and its dark rich mud. The land was indeed the gift of the River. The hallowed god—*Deus Sanctus Nilus*—was represented in statues carved from dark stone.[3] Revived each year by Isis, the Nile unified the two Kingdoms of Upper and Lower Egypt. The Upper Egyptian even more than the northern dweller in the Delta could observe stark and clear the contrast between the inhospitable red sand of the harsh desert and the teeming black earth which gave him his livelihood. The Two Lands blended geographically, politically and culturally for a quarter distance of the four thousand mile long waterway, like the tall stem of a lotus with the Fayum as the bud and the Delta as the blossoming flower (*Pl. 44*).

Year by year the Nile performed the miracle of inundation. If he was sluggish then men's nostrils were stopped up and breath and life departed.[4] It was popularly believed that during the night

Isis shed tears and that as she sorrowed the Nile began rising. The
river that seemed dead as Osiris was reborn as the living water,[5]
Horus, emerging to rejuvenate the whole land: and the Lord,
the human embodiment in control of it all, was the Pharaoh.
Throughout the 4000 years of Egyptian history every Pharaoh was
the incarnation of the youthful Horus, and therefore was the son of
Isis, the Goddess Mother who had suckled and reared him. At
death the King of Egypt sped away like the spent Nile. Hence-
forth as Osiris he held sway over 'Those Yonder' in the shadowy
kingdom of the dead.

In the land of the living the throne of the Pharaoh was everlasting like the Nile itself. She who bore the Pharaoh, who gave
him his power with her milk (*Pl. 3*), and who was the Mother
Throne, was personified by Aset— ⫟ ⌒ —Isis as she was named
by the Greeks.[6] She was the goddess portrayed in the *Book of the
Dead* with her feet on the prow of the Solar Bark and with
her everlasting arms outstretched, reciting her magic spells.
Already in a *Pyramid Text* she was known as 'the Great Isis'.[7] She
could feel the pangs of grief at the murder of her Brother-
Husband Osiris. She could make him endure and live. Death
itself she never suffered.[8] She was indeed herself concerned with
the resurrection of the dead.[9] One of the most sublime deifications
of Motherhood, and yet in the Osiris Hymn called 'the Great
Virgin',[10] she was *Das Ewigweibliche*, the female embodiment of
the Nile's annual reawakening. Her association with the star
Spdt ⫟ ⌖, Sirius for the Greeks and Sothis when viewed as a
goddess, can be seen from early times.[11] The solemn inundation
festival was celebrated on the banks of the Nile by priests of Isis
with rites that must have existed even in pre-historic days.[12]

Egyptian history begins with the Old Kingdom and can boast
more than thirty royal dynasties. Plato thought of Egypt as
immemorially old.[13] He quotes an Egyptian priest telling Solon
the Athenian that what Greece lacks, in contrast with Egypt, is
ancient tradition, 'science hoary with age'. The reason, we learn, is
geographical. The River Nile is the ever-present saviour of its
land. It rarely sweeps down calamitously from above upon the
fields but keeps, preserves and consolidates the land and the works

of its people. 'And so it is that the culture which Egypt maintains is the most ancient.' From Plato we glean a little about the antiquity of the 'Lays of Isis'—the traditional Lamentations[14] in which the goddess engages in dialogue with her sister Nephthys during the enactment of the Passion of Osiris. These had probably been committed to writing by Dynasty IV, *i.e.* by about 2500 BC,[15] and Plato, an unbounded admirer of whatever struck him as peculiarly old, characterized them as having been preserved by the Egyptians 'for all this long time'.[16]

Plato's fellow Greek, Herodotus, had earlier stayed in Egypt and had written about its religion; he concluded that its gods had been appropriated by the cities of Greece.[17] Herodotus supposed Egyptian Isis was none other than Hellenic Demeter (*Pl. 7*), and so fundamentally a fertility goddess.[18] This identification is not surprising. The richness of the soil in the Delta is stupendous, especially when contrasted with the territory to the east and the west. The whole Nile valley is indeed a huge oasis, a refuge between wildernesses on either side. Its good earth is the product of the annual inundation, the resurrection ushered in by Isis shedding her tears and beating her wings to bring the Etesian winds. She poured the air from the north into the nostrils of the dead Osiris. It was to the loneliness of the marshes in the Delta that Isis fled with her baby Horus.[19] It was her persecutor, hateful Seth, the slayer of Osiris, who presided over the desert as Lord of all foreigners. With its marshes and lagoons the whole region of the Delta is the immemorial witness to the fructifying magic of the River of Egypt, opening the way to life.

For untold centuries in the fruitful fields by the sycamores, the date palms and the persea trees men had sowed corn, had harvested it into sheaves and ground it into flour. Lower Egypt, named *Ta-meh* or 'Flax Land', was the home for spinning thread to make linen garments and weaving canvas. Tradition held that the invention of these skills was due to Isis. The papyrus, feathery-headed and rooted in the river bank, served to make both writing material and the punt-like boats[20] which were borne by their canvas sails up and down the river. From barley the Egyptians brewed the national beverage, beer. Isis herself was known as Lady of bread, of beer, of green fields, and the Egyptian view of heavenly food was eternal bread which could never mould and everlasting beer which could never sour.[21] Men and animals were friends. Dogs and cats had much domestic importance, besides sheep and goats, oxen and geese. In a land bounded on its two sides by desert everything that drew breath—and the breath of life was given by Isis as by the gods generally to the nose[22]—even deadly creatures like the serpent and the crocodile could be held to be sacred. In the religious rites of Egypt reverence for life held pride of place.[23]

> He prayeth well, who loveth well
> Both man and bird and beast.

So those who sacrificed an animal beat their breast in show of sorrow.[24] Much use is made in hieroglyphics of signs taken not only from man and the mammals generally but also from birds, reptiles, fish and even the dung-beetle and the bee (*Pl. 1*). Embalment was regularly carried out on the bodies of the dead. The deity who presided over the mummification of the corpse was Isis' intimate companion and messenger, Anubis, Lord of the Mummy Wrappings, the ferryman of souls to the Other World.

How did the ancient Egyptians picture life after death? It was an exact copy of their earthly experience in field and city, save that the rule of Justice, *Ma'et*, would prevail in the Hall of Judgment.[25] The humblest tiller of the soil could look forward to the fields of eternal ease and the pleasant pools of peace and rest. The Overlord in that Other Kingdom was Osiris. Certainly he could exact from his subjects irrigation service. But they enjoyed benefits also. Through their land ran a broad river with large estates and cattle round about. Sheaves of corn were there and kidney-shaped boats made of papyrus and wickerwork. Up above was a table set with bread, lentils, beer and fine linen. One of the *Pyramid Texts* conveys the fond hope of the black stone bowl of beer.[26] Men knew that on the way to death they were protected from harm by Isis with outstretched wings.

Clearly then Those Yonder followed the same social and economic pattern that they had known during their lifetime. The

only difference was that their perfect happiness was assured by
their just and good[27] king, Osiris. Osiris from this aspect was the
deity of vanished life, whereas his consort Isis, like his Hellenistic
successor Sarapis, was a force which produced living things and
therefore enjoyed immortality,[28] present in the land of the Nile
where every year her son Horus was reborn under the name of
'fresh water'.[29]

The legend of Isis and Osiris is founded on perfect sexual union
and perfect motherhood. Their mating is said to have taken place
in the womb of their own mother Nut, goddess of the sky.[30] Isis
by her very name ⌗ was born to show affection ⌗,
to give the heart, *ib*, to her husband Osiris as she laid hold of her
breasts for her son Horus.[31] As the ideal wife and mother Isis was
pre-eminently the goddess of the family in Egypt and later on
wherever she appeared in the Graeco-Roman world.

Geographically the two divinities were worshipped in the
closest proximity. At Philae Osiris was identified with the Nile
and there he and Isis had temples (*Pl. 12*). One of the god's most
important local habitations was Busiris, in the heart of the Delta.
Less than ten miles away to the north at a place now called Bahbit
el-Higara was a famous cult centre of the goddess whose temple,
built in the fourth century BC, contained dedications to 'the Great
Isis, Mother of the God'.[32] Here, as at Philae, the blending of cults
originally independent was helped by geographical proximity.
From earliest times Isis and Osiris were complementary divinities,
although the theological systematization of a 'Divine Pair'
remained to be achieved by such writers as Plutarch.

As one of the nine great early Gods of On, the Ennead of
Heliopolis, Isis belonged to the cosmogony evolved by the priests
there.[33] In it she was thought to be a child, like Osiris, Seth and
Nephthys, of the Earth-god Geb and the Sky-goddess Nut. As she
appears so often in this context together with either Osiris or her
sister Nephthys[34] she may easily pass (despite her title of the Great
Isis) for a somewhat colourless figure without a firm cult individuality of her own.[35] But in one respect at least she is unique
among pagan deities, for she overflows with affection and compassion. She is invoked as the one who has made her brother

Osiris endure and live, for love of whom she feels joy. She the Great One burns incense for her young child.[36] To Osiris she says 'Behold thou my heart, which grieveth for thee' . . . 'I love thee more than all the earth' . . . 'Thy duck, thy sister Isis, produceth the sweet odours belonging to thee and with thee.' Osiris himself is told 'She dandleth thy son in front of thee, at the head of the south and north' . . . 'She protected thy limbs from all evil.'[37] It was her capacity to feel deeply, and in particular to express so poignantly human grief,[38] 'The still, sad music of humanity', that more than any other factor enabled her to win the hearts of men in the Graeco-Roman world whom the traditional Olympian theology had often quite alienated. It was especially as the kind, warm-hearted wife, sister and mother, nursing her child at home, that Isis appealed to those who embraced her faith.[39]

Later antiquity could think of Isis as the Egyptian soil which the Nile commingles with and fructifies.[40] In her non-terrestrial aspect she could be held to haunt both the Dog Star and the Moon. In the latter capacity she bore an obvious resemblance to the Artemis of Greece and the Diana of Rome. Of Queen Cleopatra we read that she styled herself 'Isis or the Moon'.[41] Isis was indeed a most influential Queen of Heaven. It is not for nothing that the Libyan-born Latin writer Apuleius invoked her as 'The mother of the stars, the parent of seasons and the mistress of all the world'. In Egypt itself a festival was ordained by Ptolemy III throughout the land on the day when the star of Isis, Sothis, arose, this being regarded as New Year's Day. The rising marked three events simultaneously: the birth of a new year, the summer solstice, and the beginning of the inundation.

We can easily see how the cult of Isis came to gain the devotion of the ancient world and inspired such wonderful hymns of praise. She had the gift of universality. Her magic wings could turn into seaborne sails. The Hellenistic and Graeco-Roman *Navigium Isidis* (Pl. 65), the symbol of the extension of her power beyond Egypt, can plausibly be traced back to the procession on the banks of the Nile at Philae as the water begins to rise. Isis, of course, fulfilled many diverse roles. On earth she was the maternal life force, in heaven she reigned as queen. She calls herself 'the great, the god's mother, lady of the House of Life, dwelling in the House Beautiful'.[42] Under her influence, writes Apuleius, the fruit-bearing trees rejoice in their fertility and gay buds.

For Herodotus Isis was apparently no more than a fertility goddess, identical with Demeter (*Pl. 7*). Two centuries later, when she was taken across the 'Great Green' (as the Egyptians called the waters of the Mediterranean) she acquired other attributes as *Isis Pelagia*.[43] Already in the Ptolemaic age she was known at Philae as Isis of the Innumerable Names.[44] Now, however, she was identified with all the purely anthropomorphic goddesses of the Graeco-Roman Pantheon. As the deity of the earth, or rather the soil that the Nile fructified, she could coalesce with the Eleusinian Demeter and her daughter Persephone the Queen of the Underworld. Already identified in Egypt with Neith of Sais, she could be equated with Pallas Athena of Attica.[45] A very early text had shown her expressing delight with what she beholds.[46] Naturally, therefore, she could become Aphrodite and Venus, goddess of beauty and love. She could assume the queenly office of Hera consort of Zeus (himself then identified with Sarapis) ruling as mistress of all three dominions—heaven, earth and hell. As can be seen in the novel by Xenophon of Ephesus she could enter into a peculiarly close union with Artemis, goddess of virginity, the divinity with lunar powers who presided over childbirth and whose light shone upon dead men in the darkness of Tartarus. She could be worshipped as the Great Mother of all Nature. She could be the personification of Wisdom (*Sophia*) and Philosophy. She could be said to establish her son Horus Apollo as the youthful Pantocrator of the world.[47] 'Voilà le culte oriental,' writes Gérard de Nerval, 'primitif et postérieur à la fois aux fables de la Grèce, qui avait fini par envahir et absorber peu à peu le domaine d'Homère.'[48] Isis was all things to all men. This was what made her so formidable a foe to Jesus and oecumenical Paul.

During the formative centuries of Christianity the religion of Isis was drawing converts to it from every corner of the Roman Empire. Her priests were dedicated missionaries like soldiers crusading on hallowed service.[49] In Italy itself the Egyptian faith was a dominant force. At Pompeii, as the archaeological evidence reveals (*Pls. 22–29*), Isis played a major role. In the capital, temples were built in her honour (*Pls. 41–43*), obelisks were set up, and emperors bowed to her name. Women grovelled on their knees in the street in lamentation to her.[50] She took possession of the traditional centres of Greek worship—Delos (*Pl. 14*), Delphi and Eleusis, and she was well-known in northern Greece and in Athens (*Pls. 16, 17, 31*). Harbours of Isis were to be found on the Arabian Gulf and the Black Sea. Inscriptions show that she found faithful followers in Gaul and Spain, in Pannonia and Germany.[51] She held sway from Arabia and Asia Minor in the east to Portugal and Britain in the west and shrines were hallowed to her in cities large and small: Beneventum, the Piraeus, London (*Pls. 19–21*).

The civilization and mythology of Egypt lasted for so long that its religious folklore presented insoluble inconsistencies. Already in the fourteenth century of the pre-Christian era Akhenaten's monotheistic austerity gave a flickering hope that temples would be forever closed and polytheism swept away. But priestcraft struck at heresy as soon as he was dead and the untidy jumble of Egypt's pantheon stayed. Plutarch when he set about writing his essay on Isis and Osiris had the task of weaving a systematic theology out of the odds and ends of Egyptian mythology. That he should have used that as the basis for his own particular Platonic philosophy witnesses to the importance of this African-born faith in the second century AD.

Greek writers such as Diodorus Siculus and Plutarch are fully aware of the enormous antiquity of Isis and her brother-husband. Indeed, the *Pyramid Texts* already in the third millennium BC reveal the divine pair, placed sixth and seventh in the great Ennead of On,[52] as well in the lead. But the emergence of Isis as a universal power in the post-Alexandrian world is not to be explained by simply searching ancient Egyptian texts.

In the fourth century BC two theological experts had been called upon by Ptolemy I to systematize the religious ideas of his kingdom. One was Manetho, himself an Egyptian priest, and the other Timotheus, a Greek. Even for their subtle minds the welter of discrepancies between legends stemming from the sundry tribal sources in which the country abounded was a great stumbling

block. But by what is called *Interpretatio Graeca*, involving a ruthlessly Procrustean handling of Egyptian religion, they achieved
the desired reformation.[53]

From time immemorial Egyptian society had been ruled by a
priestly caste whose duty was to tend the local god or gods. When
the cult of the gods of the Nile spread overseas the order of priest
came to be of much missionary importance. The man whose ideogram in Egypt showed water flowing from a vase as an emblem of
purity—the *w3b* priest—pursued a hallowed ministry. He
sprinkled blest water in the temple of Isis. He resembled the
minister of Mithras and of Christ inasmuch as he performed the
rite of baptism.[54] Wearing now a black cassock and now a linen
surplice he held fixed daily services. His living quarters were the
pastophoria near the temple. He was a man set apart as holy.

The existence of a priesthood much helped to win men to the
faith of Isis. But its popularity was due to other causes also. Here
we may mention one. She was the great sorceress.[55] The art of
medicine was hers. Horus, the child born weak, is named 'son of
an enchantress'.[56] It is to Isis the divine sorceress that the great god
Re is forced to reveal the secret of his name. Her magical nature
renders her potentially hermaphrodite. So she is not bound by the
normal law of sex. She can resuscitate the dead Osiris and by spells
obtain the gift of a son. We learn that she discovered health-
giving drugs and simples as well as the elixir of life. Like Apollo
and Asclepius she was an expert in making men well when they
betook themselves to her temple, where after incubation they
could look forward in hope to gain a cure. Skilful as healer and
discoverer of the mysteries of birth, life and death, she was the
lady who saved. She resurrected. The gates of Hell, besides salvation,
were in her hands.[57]

So it was that in the Graeco-Roman world Isis came to win the
unswerving love and loyalty of countless men and women of
every rank. Her names were infinite[58] and her wisdom immeasur-
able. She did not allow room for any quarrel between science and
religion, for any prudery about sex, for racial discrimination and
segregation according to the colour of one's skin. For Plutarch,
'wise and wisdom-loving' Isis was a 'philosophic' divinity,

sharing in the love of the Good and Beautiful and imbued with the purest principles. She taught her followers to pursue penitence, pardon and peace.[59] Elsewhere she is characterized as being the inventress of all, as having divided earth from heaven, as making the universe spin round and as being triumphant over Fate, Fortune (Pl. 24) and the Stars. Her light was not merely the cold bright beam of physical science. She was tender-hearted as a mother.[60] On the whole human race she could be thought to bestow her love, being its never-absent redeemer and its haven of rest and safety, the Holy One—*sancta et humani generis sospitatrix perpetua*. The friend of slaves[61] and sinners, of the artisans and the downtrodden, at the same time she heard the prayers of the wealthy, the unblemished maiden, and the aristocrat and the emperor. She was ready to associate with other cosmic deities such as Mithras.[62] She won the heart of Roman conquerors like Vespasian just as she had Egyptian Cleopatra. For her sake women could both fast and make merry.[63] She prevailed through the force of love, pity, compassion, and her personal concern for sorrows such as she had herself known, as she sat near the well at Byblos, 'lowly and tearful'.[64]

The cult of Isis had its cradle in north-east Africa, in Egypt and Ethiopia.[65] There from the very dawn of civilization she played her part, whatever cult centres she had, establishing herself as the loving and sorrowing consort of Osiris and the sorceress daughter of Re. To her, the indigenous figure of mother and home, belonged the Nile valley, the land of corn fields, trees and fish ponds, teeming with lotus plants and the blue blossoms of flax and the papyrus reeds which served her so well. When the star Sothis shone bright then the New Year began[66] as the river grew big with the tears of Isis and its waters flooded the land of the Delta. Dynasties ebbed and flowed like the Nile itself (Pl. 44), even if not with the same steady rhythm of annual intervals. Pharaoh followed Pharaoh. As overlords of all that lived they could be hard taskmasters, like Ramesses II.[67] But each of them was at birth as weak as the divine child Horus and each had Isis as his mother to suckle him and afterwards enthrone him (Pl. 3). She always protected the living Pharaoh as the embodiment of her son Horus.

To follow the transformation of what began as a purely African faith into a world religion as Isis became first Greek and then Graeco-Roman[68] is a complicated and yet fascinating task. How the gospel of Isis like that of Jesus found its way into Europe is a question that no historian of civilization can afford to disregard. Isis in the Graeco-Roman world demands our closest attention.

CHAPTER II

ISIS, GIVER OF LIFE

CIVILIZED MAN has long since abandoned belief in the divinity of living things which seem to him below his own level. Already at the outset of Christianity the charge could be brought that paganism had changed the glory of God into the image not only of man (as in Greece) but also of birds, and four-footed beasts, and creeping things (as in Egypt). To understand ancient Egyptian religion at all, and especially the religion of Isis, we must recognize the sacredness of life in all its forms for the whole Nile civilization. This is not easy for us today. As we look at the statue of a Greek god, an Apollo, the message flashes at once to us across the centuries. Its beauty will never be outmoded and fade into nothingness. Then we walk through the Egyptian rooms of the British Museum, or the Louvre, or the Vatican. We gaze at the solar god of Egypt, the falcon-headed Horus. How can we bow down to worship a Nile monster? We remember the classic utterance of the Roman Augustus. He was wont, he said, to revere gods, not bulls.[1]

As we stand in some mysterious temple near the Nile we find it hard to reach back to those far-off days when the quadruped's muzzle and paw were divine symbols, when the beak of a bird, the image of a crocodile, the dung-beetle and the hooded cobra might each have its theological significance. The world of the Egyptian gods teemed from end to end with all living things, even plants and trees.[2] Here we are closer to the African jungle than when we lift up our eyes to the hills in monotheistic Palestine or to Olympus in Greece with its diversified anthropomorphic pantheon. In Egypt from the earliest times non-human forms of life were tended with deep religious care. This must seem odd to the modern churchgoer of our western world. So it did to the Roman

who was sent to the temple of Isis in Egypt to find out why it was
that in that land animals of little worth received the same rank
as gods. The Greek mind too scorned the deification of ibis,
ape, goat and cat.[3] Perhaps an explanation for the apotheosis
of animals in ancient Egypt can be given by present-day geo-
morphology.

At the beginning of the Ice Age the Sahara Plateau achieved
outstanding importance, being in those days bountifully supplied
with meadows and forests. So it became a place of refuge for
myriads of living creatures driven out of their own homes by the
cold. The ensuing drought drove countless denizens of the Sahara
into the fertile gorge of the Nile. Within the long and narrow
compass of the river valley and estuary man and the other animals
had to live side by side as neighbours. To share in the richly vege-
tated land had important consequences. Man very early discovered
that some creatures could be easily tamed and their aid secured for
his own welfare. He learnt the value of the cow and the ox, the
hawk, the sheep, the goat, the dog and the cat. Other species were
by nature just as obviously intractable, and yet were held in
respect and even reverence because of their greater strength or
power to harm and kill. One of the wonders of ancient Egypt was
the sacred crocodile, a creature that could be reared by the priests
in the temple of Isis and that was said to be in awe of her. In the
long history of man's search for God the theriomorphic theology
which is so characteristic of Egypt must receive a prominent
position.

In the development of Egyptian religion the cult of animals
doubtless followed after the worship of sacred trees, such as the
sycamore[4] and the acacia, the date-palm and the persea-tree. In
the persea-tree the Egyptians felt the peculiar power of Isis
'because its fruit resembles her heart'.[5] It was precisely this tree
which, according to Christian tradition, bowed down its head
before the Mother of Jesus when the Holy Family were at
Hermopolis.[6] We see that both fauna and flora could be thought
of as in the power of Isis, whom even the medieval age in western
Europe could call 'the goddess of plants and griffons'.[7]

In ancient Egypt the symbol of life and indeed the word *to live* had unmistakable divine authority as the *ankh* ☥ . The great god Re bore it in his hand as the emblem of stability and living sustenance. Legend declared that the god's daughter Isis had received into her own bosom the god's true name when he grew old.[8] Possessing the magic and supernatural token she too held the *ankh* and in the Graeco-Roman world could be regarded as herself the source of all that lived, 'Lady of the House of Life'.[9] That Isis came to occupy the position of a life-giver and of a divine authority for Egyptian animal worship can be clearly seen from the legend of Osiris' death.

This legend runs briefly thus.[10] Just as the Nile ebbs and flows again and after what seems death restores the land of Egypt to life, so the divine husband-brother of Isis suffers for the love he bears towards his world, is craftily slain by another brother Seth (called Typhon by the Greeks) and in the end rises from death to eternal life, albeit in the realm of the dead. Isis discovers that the body of Osiris has been cruelly dismembered and the torn pieces scattered in sundry places by the evil Seth. According to the tale in Plutarch she visits Byblos in Phoenicia to regain the ark or coffer in which the corpse has been buried. In the end after long search she finds all the missing parts save one—the phallus. Then the loving and grief-stricken wife performs the miracle of reconstituting the body and restoring it to life.

From the writer Diodorus of Sicily, who flourished in the first century BC, we learn that Isis wished Osiris to be honoured by all the inhabitants of Egypt. So she fashioned over each of the fragments the figure of a human body. Then she called the priests of each locality together and asked them to bury the artificial body, made out of spices and wax, in the various districts and to honour Osiris as a god. Each group of priests was to pay worship to whatever animal of their district they chose. 'Therefore even till now each set of priests holds that Osiris has his tomb in their midst and venerates the animals originally hallowed to him and at their death re-enacts in the burial rites the Mourning for Osiris.'[11] Egypt's teacher of religion is Isis herself.

In a land where life was held precious the wanton slaughter of animals could never be the general rule. From time to time, of course, a creature had to be killed. But public sentiment was speedily shocked at the death of an animal that in our own society would hardly stir deep feelings. Diodorus tells about the behaviour of a mob of Egyptians after a cat had accidentally been slain by a Roman, whose life, apparently had to be sacrificed despite his rank.[12] The cat was the sacred animal of the goddess Bast and afterwards, as can be seen at Pompeii, of Isis also. Animals generally were symbols of divinity. According to Herodotus the Egyptian priests deemed it holy to slay only such as were required for ritual sacrifice: sheep, bullocks and calves. The citizens offered supplication not to an actual animal when they bowed down before it in worship but rather to the divine being to whom the animal belonged.[13]

The various gods of the Nile had their own animal emblems. The lion could be associated with Re at Heliopolis. The bull Apis (cf. Pls. 71, 72) was revered at Memphis. The dog and jackal were specifically animals of Anubis (Pl. 46), whose cult centre was Sekhem. The vulture was hallowed to Neith at Sais. The black boar was the symbol of Seth at Avaris. At Hermopolis Thoth had the ibis and the ape as his.[14] Amun of the Libyan desert, like Khnum the wind god, could be shown with the horns of a ram. So also was Arsaphes, sometimes called son of Isis (as also were Dionysus and Heracles) at his own city in the Fayum, where the ichneumon (the mongoose) was equally sacred. The crocodile divinity was Sebek, in whose city was a temple with a lake where tame crocodiles were kept and fed with food and wine like human beings. The wolf-headed deity was Wepwawet, like Anubis a lieutenant of Osiris, leader of the tribal warriors as well as of the mourners. The great sky-goddess was Hathor, the celestial cow with a famous cult centre at Dendera, the Great Mother of all that the Universe embraces, whose functions were such as to lead to her identification with Isis (Pl. 2). Horus, son of Isis, otherwise Harsiesis, a minor tribal god to begin with, dwelt near Buto in the Delta, and like his namesake, Horus the sky-god, was often portrayed in the form of a falcon. To Osiris were consecrated at Memphis the special bulls known as Apis and Mnevis. According to Diodorus the deification of these animals was introduced (at the bidding of Isis) throughout the land of Egypt because of their special help in the discovery of corn and in all the labours of tilling the ground.[15]

In the myth of the death and resurrection of Osiris the god Seth plays an indispensable part. From earliest times Seth was important. In primitive Egyptian religion, however, he was essentially the bitter rival and worsted enemy of his brother Horus the Elder. Lord of Avaris and of Upper Egypt he was worshipped by the Hyksos invaders[16] and like them was at last banished out of the country into the desert, but only after innumerable struggles with Horus. Besides the boar another creature with strange features of uncertain identification was his emblem, usually called the 'Typhonian animal'. It had a curved and pointed muzzle, its ears were high and square, and its tail was forked. In this representation we apparently have the stylized portrait of a tribal deity. The stiff forked tail was the mark of the arrow with which Horus punished his foe before sending him into exile in the wilderness. In later times, as can be seen from Plutarch, this god was deemed to be the incarnation of all that was evil. Among his symbols, besides the boar and his own peculiar creature, were the antelope, the crocodile, the hippopotamus and the ass. In the novel by Apuleius the hero Lucius suffers the misfortune of being transformed into an ass and is only restored from his evil plight to human shape by the intervention of Isis. For her it is Seth's peculiar pet and therefore 'a long since accursed animal'.

One legend about Egyptian zoolatry records that the various deities under Seth's persecution transformed themselves into their animal counterparts. In this account the gods of Greece flee to Egypt, leaving only Athena and Zeus behind. Apollo (Horus) becomes a falcon, Hermes (Thoth) an ibis, and Artemis (Bastet, Bast) a cat.[17] The cat divinity of the Nile, equated with an earlier lioness-headed goddess Tefnut, had become a most important influence centuries before the Christian era. Her temple was at Bubastis, in later times the capital of the kingdom, her musical instrument was the clapper or rattle, and her festivals were celebrated with processions which brought worshippers to her shrine by river in barges.[18] For Herodotus the many festivals during the year in honour of 'Artemis', as he calls Bastet, and of Isis were indistinguishable save for their localization in their respective cult centres Bubastis and Busiris. Bubastis was the city where cats were embalmed after death and buried in hallowed ground, and the cemetery there, where their remains can still be seen, vividly reveals the fondness of the ancient Egyptians for the cat both as a household pet and as Bastet's sacred animal.

In Graeco-Roman times the functions of the cat divinity were taken over by Isis. In the temple of Edfu the mythological list explains that the soul of Isis is present as Bastet and in a well-known Greek Hymn to Isis the introductory epicleses are 'goddess of Bubastis, bearer of the sistrum'. On the sistra found in the Iseum at Pompeii the figure of the she-cat is frequent (*cf. Pl. 39*). As the lioness divinity Tefnut merged into Bastet, so Bastet herself in course of time was identified with Isis in an association which had important results for religion in later days.

The early Isis was imagined along with her sister Nephthys as a mourning falcon. She could also be equated with Hathor, the cow goddess. Seen from this angle the age-old veneration of Mother and Child in the persons of Isis and the Young Horus might have sprung from the worship of a sacred cow and calf at Sebennytus. In Roman times Isis was famous as the Cow Goddess of Memphis where too the Bull Apis, to whose mother Isis a temple was dedicated at Saqqara,[19] had been held in honour from Dynasty I. The bovine portrayal of Isis (*Pl. 4*) enabled her at the same time to be recognized as a moon goddess, a point which is brought out by Diodorus very clearly.[20] The Egyptians, he states, attach horns to the head of Isis, the everlasting and ancient, because of the appearance she presents whenever she is like the crescent moon, as well as because the cow is her hallowed creature among the Egyptians. For the Roman poet also she is characterized by the lunar horns she wears along with the yellow ears of bright golden corn.[21]

It is true that over the centuries Isis acquired the attributes of other Egyptian divinities such as Bastet and Hathor. But at the outset she apparently had no special cult creature of her own.[22] From her breasts sprang forth the milk of life for whatever drew breath.[23] It was she who knew the mystery of birth and could raise from the dead not only her husband Osiris but also her son Horus when his corpse had been found beneath the waters of the Nile. The *Pyramid Texts* already show her as both a funerary figure, along with her sister Nephthys, and a life-giver.[24]

In Egyptian religion there was nothing to prevent any deity from acquiring more than one creature as a sacred symbol. Thus with Seth could be associated both the ass and hippopotamus, the desert antelope and crocodile, with Osiris both the hare and lion, with Horus the Younger both the falcon and goose. But none of the Egyptian deities attracted a more varied assortment of sacred animals than Isis. In the later period of the ancient world her cult creatures could include the falcon, the vulture and the ibis. She could charm the crocodile. The gazelle, the goose and the swallow were hers. On her head she wore the sacred asp or *uraeus*. Each of these living things revealed a particular power of the goddess who in the language of the Oxyrhynchus *Litany* was the diadem of life, by whose command images and animals of all the gods were worshipped and who brought decay on what she pleased and increase to what had been destroyed. Everything that drew breath and whatever held sap could praise Isis. In the Graeco-Roman world her role was the same as that of the Living Aton, the beginner of Life worshipped centuries before by His beloved son Akhenaten.

As can be seen from the remains found at such places as Beneventum and Pompeii a temple of Isis would be provided with a wealth of animal carvings. In Hellenistic times she was especially associated with her three other Egyptian companions, Sarapis/Osiris (*Pls. 17, 18, 33*), Horus/Harpocrates (*Pls. 20, 52, 53*), and the dog-headed Anubis (*Pls. 46, 67*). Moreover, she had by then absorbed the functions not only of other Egyptian goddesses such as Bastet but also of those of Greece and Rome. Her votary could therefore be as eclectic as he wished. An abundance of representations of typical Nile fauna and flora would be visible to her initiates as they made their way into her temple (*Pls. 8-11, 45*). Even in distant Italy could be found the Alexandrian divinities amid the palm trees, the adoration of the mummy of Osiris (*Pl. 25*), the procession of Isis (*Pl. 30*), all portrayed in the Iseum's

mural decorations. At Beneventum there have been discovered
statues of a crocodile, a falcon, a sphinx, a lion, the bull Apis and
the dog-headed Anubis. In the Iseum excavated at Pompeii a
remarkable variety meets us. The cat wears a lotus on its head.
Serpents coil with Nile boats above them. The uraeus, the crocodile and the dog are there. Real and fabulous animals are depicted:
the lion, the black and white ibis, the scarab, the phoenix, the
sphinx and the androsphinx. The Apis bull is adorned with a lunar
crescent on his head. In a large tableau with a mixed group of
animals a monkey holds a serpent between its legs, a sheep and a
jackal spring towards it, and to add to the bizarre effect the artist
has included a mole, a vulture and probably an ichneumon.

Other Pompeian buildings have provided further evidence that
in the cult of Isis zoomorphic symbolism was important. The
faithful Isiac paid his devotions to his divine lady in shrines far
away from the land of the Pharaohs and the waters of the Nile.
But he was vividly aware as he stood in her presence of the pro-
fusion of beasts, birds and reptiles that were sacred in her name.
Even outside the temple he might gaze at strange creatures
reminding him of her power over the animal realm. At Pompeii
there are excellent specimens of terracotta animal figures forming
waterspouts for the roof. In this instance, as in so many others, the
external form of Isiacism as it was practised in the Graeco-Roman
world is a forerunner of what is later encountered in the Christian
tradition. The animal water-spouts at Pompeii foreshadow the
gargoyles of gothic cathedrals. Inside the Iseum at Pompeii can
still be seen a votive offering to Isis bearing the sign of the *ankh*.
Here again is a case of an Isiac symbol prefiguring a characteristically Christian token, the cross. The Tau Cross or the Cross of
St Anthony is the descendant of the hieroglyph for life, stability
and living sustenance, borne by Isis and her consort Sarapis.
Significantly, when the Christians under Archbishop Theophilus
towards the end of the fourth century destroyed the Sarapeum at
Alexandria (*Pl. 68*), the *ankh* was eagerly interpreted by them as
being an unconscious anticipation of the crucifix and of their own
doctrine of a future life.[25]

The firmer the hold that Isis took of the Graeco-Roman world,

the keener became the longing of her worshippers to know about
the sundry local gods of the Nile valley, in their anthropomorphic
but also in their zoomorphic manifestations. The faithful follower
of Isis could take interest, no doubt, in the cult of the ibis at
Hermopolis and of the cat-headed Sun God at Heliopolis[26] as well
as in the Apis Bull at Memphis 'reared with a farmer's symbol
upon him' and the Sacred Cow of Isis in the same city. A Roman
poet, wishing a friend of his who was a Roman general to
succeed in his task of finding out about Egyptian religion on the
spot, could call on Isis 'Queen of Pharos and Deity of the Orient'
to take him to her sacred seaports and inland cities, and to guide
him to understand why Anubis the guardian of the Underworld
tended her altars, what was the meaning of the self-sacrifice of the
phoenix,[27] and what Apis considered to be his proper domain.[28]
Another writer of a somewhat earlier date could make the startling
claim, in Greek, that the birth of zoolatry at Memphis and the
deification of the Bull Apis there[29] emanated from none other than
Moses, whose wonder-working rod had been dedicated by the
Egyptians in all their temples to Isis.[30] In the light of this conception certain words attributed in the Old Testament to Moses—
'The eternal God is thy refuge and underneath are the everlasting
arms'[31]—may be thought curiously reminiscent of the Egyptian
portrayal of Isis. Already in the XVIIIth Dynasty, she had been
represented, like the much later Guardian Angel of Christianity,
as kneeling at the foot of the sarcophagus or coffin to keep the
dead from harm with her outstretched arms or wings[32] (Pl. 1).

Centuries afterwards a writer with a particular interest in the
natural history of Egypt observed that its inhabitants adorned the
head of Isis with a vulture's feathers and carved vultures' wings in
relief on the vestibule door of her temple. Almost immediately
after this we are told that the people of Coptos associated another
creature, the scorpion, with her worship. In that city during the
ceremony known as the Lamentation of Isis the women would
walk barefooted amid these reptiles and yet remain unhurt. The
same passage informs us that at Coptos although the stag antelope
was sacrificed yet the female gazelle was deified and called by the
charming name of 'Isis' plaything'.[33] It was also in this city,

according to the naturalist Pliny, that Isis had a sacred island which at the beginning of spring the swallows surrounded with a dike strengthened with straw to stop it being swamped by the waters of the Nile.[34]

The link between Isis and the cat is clearly defined by Plutarch. He states that on the rim of the Isiac rattle or sistrum (*Pl. 39*) the Egyptians engraved a cat with a human face and below it, under the sound-producing part, on one side the face of Isis and on the other that of Nephthys, the former meaning birth or creation, the latter death or the end. We are also informed that the cat symbolizes the moon.[35] Some twenty sistra of Isis have been found at Pompeii and at least fifteen of these have at the top the figure of a she-cat.[36] Here we see the sign of Isis-Bastet.

Of the other creatures associated with Isis the 'beautiful goose' is mentioned as having miraculous power. The uraeus or sacred asp, the mark of divine majesty and the invincibility of royal power, grew to be one of the goddess' best-known emblems. When Cleopatra applied to her bosom such a serpent, or in Shakespearean language an 'aspic', the 'pretty worm of Nilus', she was using to bring about her death what was both her own queenly emblem and that of the goddess whose name she had assumed in an happier hour. Isis is described as protecting sailors in boats made out of papyrus by inspiring the crocodiles around them with fear and awe. A sacred crocodile was kept in a Libyan Iseum and in one of the legends about Osiris the dead body was brought to his sister by a crocodile. The dog of Anubis could belong to Isis. On the gable of her temple in Rome was erected a statue of her riding upon a hound[37] (*Pl. 42*).

At Praeneste, the modern Palestrina, was the Temple of Fortuna Primigenia, with whom Isis in course of time must have been identified in view of the mosaic found there (*Pls. 8-11, 45*).[38] The artist has achieved a real *tour de force*. The whole map of Egypt has been abridged into a single picture with an astonishing variety of Nilotic fauna and flora. Among the animals real or fabulous are a sphinx, 'krokottas' (perhaps hyena), 'onocentaur' (tailless ape), hawk, cameleopard, water-snake, hog-snouted ape (perhaps baboon), and rhinoceros. The purpose of this mosaic is evident.

Just as nowadays in a Catholic church Christians may gaze at the Nativity tableau, so in the ancient shrine of Isis her devout worshipper could study the sacred animals of Egypt in their natural setting, from the mountains of Ethiopia through Thebes in the middle with its Temple of Ammon down to the city of Memphis with its Temple of Isis. Right in the heart of Roman Italy a single glance would bring to mind the Goddess of Myriad Names, the Life Force dwelling within all those different creatures.

CHAPTER III

OSIRIS—BROTHER, HUSBAND, SON

GEB, THE GOD of the earth, and Nut, the goddess of the sky, had as their firstborn children Osiris and Isis. According to Plutarch these had fallen in love and had mated while still in their mother's womb. Osiris, the *Book of the Dead* informs us, created light and imparted it to his sisters Isis and Nephthys when all were still embryos in the body of their mother Nut. Both Diodorus and Plutarch stress the fact that in the hieroglyph for Osiris—*Wsir'*— one of the elements is the ideogram for 'eye'—*'irt.*[1] Osiris sending forth his rays to every part beholds all land and sea so to speak with many eyes. He is – 𓊨 ☁ –, and Isis is 𓊨 ☁. In both names the 'throne' is the essential element.

Throughout the long history of Egyptian religion Isis and her brother-husband remained complementary deities. In the earliest records the role of Isis was that of the mourner (like that of Nephthys) for the lost Osiris. In course of time the Osirian myth underwent various developments. No doubt it had to be artificially joined to the solar religion systematized by the priests of Heliopolis. Although in the account given by Plutarch Osiris suffered a cruel death at the hands of his foe Seth, yet in an earlier form of the story he died by accidental drowning and his body was brought to the river bank by his two sisters. In the Middle and New Kingdoms the hymns and stories introduce into the theme of the dying god episodes unknown at the beginning. Among these later developments are the compassion shown by Re in sending Anubis to perform on Osiris the rites of embalmment and the resurrection of the latter when the beating of the wings of Isis bestows on him the breath of life.

Plutarch's long and detailed monograph on Isis and Osiris was written some two and a half millennia after the *Pyramid Texts*. We must be cautious, therefore, in seeking from his pages irrefutable proof as to the exact shape of the primitive saga. On the other hand, whatever accretions the original legend, or rather legends, may have acquired over so huge a span of time the fundamental ideas stayed unaltered. Osiris did indeed suffer a sudden death, usually ascribed to Seth, and was greatly mourned by his sisters Isis and Nephthys. Isis scoured the whole land spending many days in fruitless search for the corpse. Eventually Osiris was awarded a new life—at the hands of the gods, according to the *Pyramid Texts*. But before he had risen from the dead the child Horus, Harsiesis ('Har, Son of Aset'), had been miraculously conceived by Isis in a necrophilous union. This was the child who was to continue the struggle against Seth, triumphing in the end against his eternal enemy and mounting the paternal throne. The regal power was magically conveyed to the son by Isis, who could promise that the god who was but an embryo would one day rule the land and become its master.

For the understanding of the story an image of vital importance is the *throne*. In all the Osirian mythology Isis as the *throne* exerts a unifying and steadying influence. Joined with Osiris in sexual union already in the maternal womb, Isis was fast wedded to him in life, and when he was no longer king in this world she was able to perform the miracle of bearing a son without the father's procreative agency. She it was on whose lap the divine child was habitually represented sitting as on a throne (*Pl. 3*). And it was through her unabating help that in the end Horus rose up to the seat of Osiris his dead father, sitting on his throne as the archetype of all the Pharaohs, his (Horus') eponymous descendants.

The myth of the death of Osiris and the search for his body by his widow is one of the most significant in the whole range of Egyptian religion. Its origins are lost in obscurity. Among the aspects of Osiris is that of the all-seeing sun regularly rising and setting. But he is at the same time the power that is resuscitated and regenerated by the agency of his sister-spouse, the vegetation god who dies to be reborn at the inundation of the Nile. The link between the Nile and the earth that it waters is the clue to the meaning of the pre-natal mating of the divine brother and sister.[2] In the well-known *Lamentation of Isis for Osiris* the goddess cries: 'Ho my Lord! There is no god like unto thee! Heaven hath thy soul, earth hath thy semblance, and the Netherworld is equipped with thy secrets; thy wife is thy protection and thy son Horus is ruler of the lands.'[3] Here may be detected an allusion to a struggle between Lower and Upper Egypt in which the former triumphed in a contest which resulted in a fusion of the Two Lands. In the earliest form of the saga the real hero is Horus, son and avenger of Osiris, Horus with whom the ruler of Lower Egypt could identify himself. Whatever the path of development may have been, the relation between Osiris and Isis was constantly visualized as a drama of birth, death and resurrection. And when in the fifth century BC Herodotus dealt with Egyptian religion he had no doubt that the whole population alike worshipped just the two.

About Osiris and his pilgrimages through life and death there was, not surprisingly, considerable disagreement. In the very early days can be distinguished two traditions. In the *Pyramid Texts* the deceased Pharaoh can be deified as both Osiris and Re. Osiris is then a solarized deity, bringing light and food especially to Those Yonder, the denizens of the netherworld, as he makes his nocturnal journey through their midst in his boat. But he was also the resident king of the dead, true of heart and voice, watching with an eye that was never at rest over the rewards of those who came into his realm. This was the chthonic aspect of Osiris. For the Greek writer Diodorus of Sicily at the close of the pre-Christian era there were just two Egyptian gods who were both eternal and primeval, Osiris the sun and Isis the moon. Such an interpretation is the result of the Greek desire to simplify what was felt to be a puzzling and bewildering mass of theological speculations. As Diodorus himself puts it, the Greeks appropriate both the heroes and the gods which are most famous of Egypt. So the same goddess Isis is variously named Demeter, Thesmophorus, Selene, Hera and even all of these, whereas Osiris is Sarapis for some and Dionysus for others, as well as Ammon, Zeus, Pan, and Sarapis, called Pluto by the Greeks.[4]

It is important to appreciate the part played by Isis and her faithful attendant Anubis in the resuscitation of Osiris, as this affected the Pharaonic succession. The dead king Unas, of the Vth Dynasty, could be described as having been made to endure and to live, dying not, because he had been brought back to life: Osiris had been revivified to reign as his own posthumous son Horus. The god of mummification, Anubis, shared in the funerary rites. These were the Opening of the Mouth and the daily Toilet Ceremonies. Isis, depicted as a bird hovering over the king's mummy, held in one hand the billowing sail 𓊝, the hieroglyph for the wind or breath of life, and in the other the *ankh*, ☥. The resurrection of the dead Osiris was the result of Isis breathing into his nostrils the breath of life by flapping the air with her wings. He himself can be seen in the *Book of the Dead* rising to life in the shape of a great falcon, having been rejuvenated as Horus. In another version of the Osirian legend the dead god is described as being borne down the Nile until Isis and Nephthys espy him and undertake the care of him. Horus at Busiris enjoins them to preserve the floating body from drowning. They fetch him to land. He steps inside the secret portals into the magnificent place of the lords of eternity and enters the brotherhood of the gods.

In the literature of the Graeco-Roman world no mythological topic was ever more carefully handled and with greater wealth of information than the Egyptian saga by Plutarch in his *Essay on Isis and Osiris*, dedicated to the Isiac priestess at Delphi. Born in AD 45, Plutarch lived during a period when mankind's yearning for an oecumenical faith was deepening in the widespread empire established by Rome. During his lifetime all those writings that constitute the canon of the New Testament had been completed and Christianity carried far and wide by such preachers as Paul of Tarsus. Among pagan writers of the early Christian era none showed a keener longing for piety and holiness than the Platonist of Chaeronea[5] in his erudite and penetrating study of Egypt's gods.

Isis and Osiris presents the ancient Nile myth with many embellishments such as are to be expected of an author steeped in Plato and the syncretistic philosophy which had germinated out of the Platonic writings. The feelings and religious needs of the ordinary men and women of the day were as well understood by Plutarch as by Paul. Isis and Osiris rouse the pagan philosopher as 'Christ crucified' does the convert Rabbi.

Plutarch stresses the cultural achievements of Osiris and the help received from Isis in training mankind to respect the laws and revere the gods. Osiris is represented as going on a kind of missionary journey. He preaches goodness. He is the prototype of Orpheus, preaching the platonic gospel of the good life, culture and music. All this arouses the jealousy and enmity of his brother Seth at whose hands he suffers death. The corpse (as Plutarch tells the story) is thrown into the Nile and is carried out into the Mediterranean across the waters of which it goes to Phoenician Byblos. There, after patient search, the sorrowing widow at last finds it. She bears it back to Egypt and hides it in the swamps at Buto, where afterwards she rears the young child Horus.

When Seth lights upon the body, dismembers it and scatters the fragments far and wide, Isis again starts off to regain them and with one exception does so. Then, having pieced them together with the magical skill which is peculiarly hers, she raises Osiris from the dead and bestows upon him eternal life. Along with the son who has been born she dwells in the marshes of the Delta until he is of age to avenge the death of his father. Horus engages in repeated combats with Seth. On one occasion he lays hands on his own mother and wrests the royal diadem from her head. In the end there is a happy dénouement. The child who has been so utterly weak at birth, especially in his nether limbs, is rescued from all his perils by the sorcery of his mother. Before the tribunal of the gods he establishes the legitimacy of his birth in face of the charge of bastardy brought by his uncle Seth. Seth is found guilty. Horus is justified. The victor enters into his heritage as ruler of the two Egypts, entrusted by Geb to Osiris to lead them into prosperity.

The Osirian legend retained its importance throughout the Dynasties. Already in the second millennium BC the folklore of the New Kingdom reveals the importance of Isis as clearly as we can see it in the late dynastic epoch which ends with the arrival of Alexander. Plutarch, with his serious interest in discovering the philosophical import of the story, in interpreting it as the clue to 'the nature of the blessed and imperishable', leaves out those elements which for his purpose are unprofitable and superfluous, such as the dismemberment of Horus and the beheading of Isis. Wherever we look we find that it is the goddess who is the magic life-giver, the indefatigable sorceress who secures for her son Horus the final victory in his perpetual struggles with the arch-enemy Seth. Thus when the question of the son's paternity is challenged by Seth she transforms herself first into an old hag, then into a beautiful damsel, and lastly into a bird. In this form she almost wins the votes of the tribunal who are trying the case. In another version are found personifications of Truth and False-hood and the marriage of the former with a noble lady and the birth of a son. The mother soon grows tired of her blind husband and divorces him but through pity makes him the doorkeeper. The child grows in strength and virtue. One day he comes back home in tears because his school-mates have taxed him about his paternity. The mother reveals to him the secret that Falsehood has been allowed by the tribunal of the gods to pluck out the eyes of Truth, his father. Thereupon the son swears to avenge his father.[6]

In this kind of fairy tale a writer like Plutarch would have observed the main ingredients of the traditional myth, as well as certain awkward discrepancies. Isis in the Graeco-Roman world was above all else the faithful wife and indeed the divine patroness of family life and instructress in such domestic arts as weaving and spinning. The Isis whom Greece and Rome came to know was far from having divorced her husband. She was esteemed as the model spouse. She was hymned as upholder of the marriage covenant. It was her ordinance that parents should be loved by their children and that in the wedding service of the Egyptians the husband should make a solemn contract to be obedient to his wife.[7] The tale of Isis and Osiris, whatever the discrepancies of detail, con-tained just those elements which for later antiquity could serve as the pattern of family bonds of affection.

In the *Pyramid Texts*, as in later documents such as the papyrus with the title *The Lamentations of Isis and Nephthys*, Osiris is bewailed by the pair of his sisters. In course of time the bitter dirges came to be the sole province of Isis. According to Herodotus

the Sorrowing Wife and Mother was shown in pantomime by
female mummers in their tens of thousands, men and women
alike beating their breasts.[8] This took place at Busiris, where the
cult of Osiris had been long established and where in the heart of
the Delta Isis had a very large temple. Such rites, however, were
not peculiar to worshippers of Isis and Osiris in Egypt. Similar
scenes could be witnessed at Eleusis in the name of Demeter and
Persephone/Kore or at Byblos in Phoenicia during the com-
memoration of the death of Adonis. Diodorus records that at
harvest the first fruits of the earth, discovered by Isis and cultivated
by Osiris, were dedicated according to ancient custom, the reapers
standing by the sheaves they had cut and smiting their breasts
as they called upon the name of Isis, whom they were
commemorating.[9]

A similar ritual of lamentation inside the Isiac temple is known
from the Roman poets. Tibullus writes about young people from
foreign parts who are wonderstruck before the god they have
chosen, Osiris, and strike themselves in grief for the cow-headed
goddess of Memphis.[10] According to Firmicus Maternus worshippers lacerated their own bodies. Such behaviour is the butt for
Juvenal's sarcasm. He has a poor opinion of the priest as he scurries
along wearing a 'dog's head', the mask of Anubis, and scoffing at
the congregation around him with their linen surplices and
tonsured heads and hands that beat their chests in grief. For
another poet, Lucan, yielding to such feelings of sorrow reduces
the divine to the merely human: 'Osiris, by your mourning
proved a man.'[11] The passion of a dying god, so deeply stirring
the hearts of Isiacs and afterwards of Christians, was found to be
utterly irrational by one who had been steeped in the traditional
philosophy of the Greeks.

In seeking to blend the myths of the Osirian cycle the moralist
Plutarch was guided neither by ethnology nor by anthropology.
He did not raise the question about the part played by the priests
of Heliopolis in assimilating the tribal cults of Osiris with their
own solar religion. He did not conceive the attack on Osiris by
Seth as a theological reconstruction of a political struggle in
primitive times. His approach was that of the Hellenic syncretist.

Three interesting points are made by Plutarch.[12] (1) On her journey in search of her husband's corpse Isis meets Anubis and it is this dog-headed god who accompanies her and assists in the rites of embalming when at last the dead Osiris is found. Anubis, inventor of the embalmer's craft, became a strong competitor of Horus/Harpocrates for a place in the so-called 'Alexandrian triad' whose other members were Isis and Osiris/Sarapis. (2) Wherever Isis regains a portion of the body that Seth has dismembered she builds a tomb. This detail is obviously introduced on aetiological grounds lest the cult of Osiris in so many different places such as Busiris, Abydos and Philae should be found puzzling. (3) Lastly, when the coffer containing the corpse is carried over the sea Isis follows it to Byblos in Phoenicia. Byblos, where Egyptian antiquities have been unearthed,[13] was a point of economic and religious contact between Phoenicia and the Nile country. It was there that Osiris was assimilated to Adonis (Thammuz) and Isis herself into Astarte (Istar, Ashtaroth).[14]

It is not to be expected that the Greek treatment—*interpretatio Graeca*—of Egyptian mythology should clear away the many bewilderments or that it should disclose the deeper meaning which the Egyptologist today seeks objectively. In the view of a well-informed Greek writer there was a determined hellenization of Egyptian gods and heroes, which was generally recognized, and which enabled Osiris to be called Dionysus by some, Pluto by others, Zeus by some, and Pan by others.[15] We must remember also that in his own country Osiris underwent identification with Ptah, Sokar and Re. Another significant fact is that Osiris was always portrayed with human features. From these circumstances we can see how in the post-Alexandrian period a new idea of the consort of Isis could be evolved—the oecumenical Sarapis.

The subtle complexities of the personalities of Osiris and Isis and their interrelations are bound to startle a modern mind. We seek for a logic which at least superficially seems to be missing. What we need to remember is that Egyptian religion was undergoing developments over an enormously long span of time and that sometimes there exists deep down beneath the apparent theological discrepancies a core of unity. When, for example, Osiris was regarded as 'the Great Black'[16] he was himself the dark slime of the Nile marshes and the brackish Bitter Lakes. When he was called 'the Great Green'[17] he was the life-giving fresh water of the River and under this aspect even the salt water of the sea. As with other gods of Egypt he could be addressed as a bisexual being: 'You are Father and Mother of men. They live from your breath and eat of the flesh of your body.' The parable of life arising out of death was eloquently conveyed by the fable of the phoenix, identifiable with the *bennu* bird which was revered at Heliopolis as the soul of Osiris,[18] as well as by the sight of his ithyphallic mummy (*Pl. 25*).

As resurrectress of her brother-husband, Isis could be held responsible for both aspects of impregnation in a most miraculous way, for she could characterize herself as a woman who turned herself into a male.[19] The conventional familial kinships seem here to a modern mind to have been muddled to the point of irrationality. But such nomenclature, extraordinary though it may be to later ages, is not peculiar to just these two divinities of Egypt, for the ithyphallic Amun can also be called 'the husband of his mother'. Moreover, the Neoplatonist Porphyry, in writing about the chthonic and heavenly powers of Osiris,[20] does not find it illogical that the god should be indissolubly tied to the goddess by birth, wedlock and parentage. 'Isis who according to mythology commingles with Osiris is the land of Egypt and in virtue of this achieves equality and conceives and brings forth the fruits of the earth. And this is why tradition has made Osiris her husband, her brother and her son.' So too in palaeochristian thinking Mary was Christ's 'sister, mother, consort'.[21] The regenerative powers of the River Nile and the earth he waters are matched in hermaphrodital union. Just as the god of the inundation, Hapi, has the breasts of a woman though otherwise he is male, so Isis and Osiris as fertilizing forces reach full sexual equality.

The position assumed by Osiris in the Egyptian trinity of Father, Mother and Son can be still better grasped from studying the theogamous birth of the Pharaoh. The Pharaoh even while an embryo in the womb of his mother was the child Horus. Son of Isis (*Pl. 3*), Ruler of the Living and Protector of Osiris his father—

so he remained till the day he died. His kingly divinity was marked by what modern society stigmatizes as an incestuous marriage with a sister and by his sitting on the throne that Isis had made for him, and *was*. When he had ended his earthly life he himself became an Osiris and rose to a new life in the World Yonder. The royal relationship in Egypt typified and *was* that of Osiris and Isis, the Osiris killed by Seth and the Isis responsible for the resurrection of her husband-brother by the birth of her child Horus.

Osiris, although worshipped as especially god of the dead, in his resurrected form shared the life-giving power so well wielded by his wife. Even before the time of Akhenaten a hymn had been written in his honour praising him for making with his hand the land of Egypt, its water and air, its vegetation and cattle, its birds and creeping things, and the beasts of the desert.[22] This view of Osiris anticipated by many centuries the Hellenistic and Graeco-Roman conception of Sarapis. The henotheism there displayed brings it into line with what Akhenaten was to declare about his Sole God and with what Hellenistic aretalogists were to hymn in their panegyrics to Isis.[23] The Living Aton, as portrayed by his 'beloved son' Akhenaten, was the sun-disk, capable of personification as Re, yet unknowable. 'Thou art remote yet thy rays are upon the earth. Thou art in the sight of men, yet thy ways are not known.'

The Aton sun-disk, as with Osiris in the earlier hymn, could make and bring forth the Nile waters to sustain Egypt 'even as thou hast made them live for thee . . . the Lord of every land'. The Aton sun-disk like the Graeco-Roman Isis spreads his powers even beyond Egypt. 'All distant foreign lands also, thou createst their life.' He has fashioned 'all men, all cattle great and small, all that are upon the earth that run upon their feet or rise up on high flying their wings'. The great Aton-hymn brings to light the heretical Akhenaten's repudiation of the cult of Osiris as the god of the dead. But it accords perfectly not only with the pre-Amarna Hymn to Osiris already quoted, where praises are bestowed on his sister-wife, but also with what Apuleius writes[24] about Isis in terms that would have delighted both Akhenaten himself and the earlier author of the Hymn to Osiris.

CHAPTER IV

THE SPREAD OF THE EGYPTIAN FAITH

WHEN ALEXANDER of Macedon conquered the kingdom of the Pharaohs in 332 BC the last of Egypt's thirty-one dynasties came to an end. After an enormous span of almost 3000 years the lands of the Nile were to be swallowed up into foreign empires. But the religious beliefs, far from suffering setback, gained a reputation and an influence never seen before.[1]

In the expansion of Egyptian religion a most important part was played by the god Ammon, the Amun whose power had been firmly established in the XIIth Dynasty, relatively late, at Thebes on the Upper Nile. His famous shrine at the oasis in the Libyan Desert was resorted to by pilgrims from every part, including Greeks, who knew also another temple of his at Aphytis in the Pallene peninsula of Macedonia.[2] Even in the heart of Greece Zeus-Ammon had his devotees. The poet Pindar in his home town of Boeotian Thebes dedicated an image and composed an ode in the god's honour. Ammon was identifiable with Osiris in the minds of the Greeks.[3] Writing at the very end of the pre-Christian Era Strabo could declare that the Oracle of Ammon had been wellnigh abandoned.[4] But certainly some three hundred years earlier it had been visited by the greatest of all who had ever gone there, the conqueror who was to be hailed by the High Priest as 'Son of Ammon' and still in the radiance of youth was to make it his goal to show respect for Egypt's ancient civilization and the shrines of its old gods.

Alexander lost no time in making his way to Memphis. There he sacrificed to the Bull Apis and was hailed as the new Pharaoh. There too according to one report he was enthroned.[5] The

Macedonian conqueror had something in common with Napoleon centuries afterwards. He brought with him learned men to help in the understanding of whatever the culture of the Nile had to bestow. As the pupil of the great Aristotle he himself began eagerly to apply his mind to the economic and political advantages of his position as heir of all the Pharaohs. It was not for nothing that he was said to have wished to be portrayed wearing the horns of Ammon,[6] whether or not he seriously held a belief in his own divine birth. The religious faiths which he found in Egypt were of obvious value to him in his great aims.

When Alexander returned to the coast we are told he sailed about twelve miles along it westward from the Canopic mouth of the Nile until he reached the 'Marian Lake' where he disembarked. Here it seemed to him was the finest site for the city he was planning to build, a city which should be great and prosperous, the economic entrepôt and the religious metropolis of the world. Arrian, who tells the story, ascribes the lay-out of the city to Alexander himself. In the plan besides a commercial quarter were included temples for the various gods, both those of Greece and of 'Isis of Egypt'. The specific mention of the Egyptian goddess is a reminder of the importance of Isis Pharia, whose shrine was to arise on the island famous also for its lighthouse in the Bay of Alexandria (Pls. 13, 60–62).[7]

The choice of such a site for the capital of a new empire showed consummate skill and imagination. Lying at the very heart of a domain that stretched from the upper reaches of the Nile in the south to the Danube in the north, Alexandria was immediately able to become not merely the world's trading centre but also the spiritual emporium of science, philosophy and religion. From the harbour where the Pharian goddess held sway, ships were to sail forth, some bearing her name, to the most distant parts of the Alexandrian Empire, helping in the world-wide diffusion of the Egyptian seaport's material and cultural wealth. Furthermore, even when a swift political break-up prepared the way for other empires, yet the process of disseminating what the city poured forth never ended.

Alexander's untimely death raised to the throne of the Pharaohs

a Greek whose theological ideas were moulded in the pattern laid
down by his predecessor. The first Ptolemy, son of the Macedonian Lagus, took the deepest interest in the religious beliefs of
the land where fortune had given him the sceptre and where the
neglect of them might have undermined his throne. Ptolemy,
styled both 'the Great' and 'the Saviour', aimed at making his
capital the most splendid city and the most deeply cultured home
of learning in the world. Holding not just Egypt itself but also
Palestine and the south-western shores of Asia Minor at the end of
the fourth century BC he was lord of an Egyptian Empire which
bestowed on him all the traditional characteristics of an oriental
despot. His capital was certainly colonized by Greeks and Mace-
donians. But in his kingdom the freedom of the city states of
Greece and the right of the citizens to democratic voting was
replaced with a genuinely Egyptian theocracy.

In both the political and the religious sense the Ptolemies were
Pharaohs. Ptolemy II, called Philadelphus, did not hesitate to wed
his own sister, Arsinoe,[8] who was indeed the widow of his first
wife's father, and who was herself depicted sometimes as Isis. It
was due to the Ptolemies that the eastern Mediterranean became
for a time virtually an Egyptian sea, that the gods of the Nile
appeared along the shores of Asia Minor and in the Aegean, and
that splendid temples were built on the holy island of Isis with its
Abaton at Philae. The Ptolemies explored the Red Sea and,
ultimately, like the Venetian Doges of a later age, sent their ships
into the Indian Ocean. Trade links were established with the
growing power of Rome through an important route from Alexandria to Puteoli. The faith of Egypt was thus effectively carried
far and wide throughout the Mediterranean and even beyond.

The missionary work was helped both by ordinary traders and
by professional priests. The faith of Isis and the gods associated
with her had to be ready to adapt itself to the religious climate of
the locality. It had to compete likewise with other expanding cults
born in the Middle East. Sometimes, as in Macedonia, the land
whence the Ptolemaic dynasty had sprung and where Zeus
Ammon had been for long fervently revered, the reception was
by no means unfavourable. Elsewhere opposition might be

encountered. Delos provides an example. There the faith had been brought from Memphis well before the end of the third century BC by a certain priest named Apollonius. One of the priests who followed, perhaps Demetrius Telesarchides, built a temple for the practice of the cult, which became the object of a law-suit (*Pl. 14*). The opponents, however, were defeated.⁹ Here, as afterwards in Rome at the end of the Republic, we have a seesaw, yet finally successful movement.

Alexandria was built to be a Greek city on Egyptian soil. Here in the famous Museum and Library founded by Ptolemy I were to flourish all those liberal arts and sciences which had been so keenly studied in the various centres of Greece and over which in Egypt Isis traditionally presided. In religious matters the Alexandrian attitude was conservative: a respect for Egypt's immemorially long past combined with the natural desire (found earlier in Herodotus) to achieve an exact equivalence between its gods and those of Greece.

In other spheres, however, the spirit of original research, enterprise and invention was felt very strongly. Science and religious belief went hand in hand and between them there could be no conflict. Diodorus tells of the popular identification of Isis' son Horus with the Greek Apollo: 'the benefits he has bestowed on the human race through oracles and medical treatments spring from the lessons his mother gave him in healing and divination.'¹⁰ In the Sarapeum built by Ptolemy I at Alexandria was established a hospital where medical students went to gain clinical experience and where Ptolemy Philadelphus gave permission for anatomical dissection.¹¹ Alexandrian doctors consequently discovered the existence of the nerves as well as the function of the brain as the centre of the nervous system. It was widely accepted that the collections of books in the Library were priceless.¹² In Alexandria Jews and Greeks could meet and philosophize together against an Egyptian or rather a cosmopolitan background.

The Museum was the home of the religion of Isis and Sarapis, Anubis and Horus, as well as the centre of scholarship, as exemplified by Aristarchus, and the scene of scientific research, as we see it in the physician Erasistratus and the geographer Eratosthenes.

Here for centuries flowered the spirit of research, enterprise and invention, presided over by Isis. The glory of Alexandrian culture was that all spheres of human inquiry were held to be interrelated and knowledge religious and scientific seemed one and inseparable.

The Ptolemies, though tracing their descent from Macedonia, thought about kingship not as the Greeks did but as the Egyptians. Alexander himself as a pupil under Aristotle might well have pondered hard about the vicissitudes of monarchy as exhibited for instance in the *Oedipus* of Sophocles. Yet Alexander perhaps had no qualms about accepting the deification proclaimed for him by the priests of Ammon in the Libyan Desert, while tradition even alleged that he liked being called 'Son of Ammon' and being modelled by sculptors wearing a pair of ram's horns. He could indeed allow that in his veins ran not the ichor of a god but the blood of a man. Nonetheless the story could later circulate that some of his soldiers who declined to flatter him with divine honours were severely punished.[13]

By any Athenian of the Periclean age the idea of worshipping a king like Alexander as ram-headed Ammon or like Ptolemy IV as Dionysus would have been utterly scorned.[14] In the post-Alexandrian age things were different. The Rhodians having been delivered from siege by Ptolemy I consulted the Libyan oracle and were led thereby to hail him as 'Saviour' and greet him as god. Before that the theocratic and traditionally Egyptian character of his dynasty had been ensured by his being eulogized at his coronation with all the familiar titles of divinity assumed by the Pharaohs of old. So he was called the god Horus, the incarnation of the crown prince of Upper and Lower Egypt, the Horus who had triumphed over Seth and evil, the King of Upper and Lower Egypt, and the Son of Re. The Ptolemy who as Horus defeated Seth was obviously dependent for his divine birth on Isis. The apotheosis of the king in Ptolemaic Egypt and of the *princeps* afterwards in imperial Rome was greatly assisted by the practice of the Isiac faith. Cleopatra, the last of the Ptolemaic queens, regarded herself as the incarnation of Isis and appeared (as Shakespeare long afterwards wrote) 'in the habiliments of the goddess'.

Isis was favoured by Roman rulers. Caligula and Otho were her worshippers. Vespasian, who wrought miracles in the name of Sarapis, practised incubation along with Titus in the Roman Iseum (Pl. 42). Later on in the capital Domitian built another Iseum and a Sarapeum. Hadrian adorned his villa at Tibur with Isiac scenes. Commodus took part in the rites of Isis and wore the mask of Anubis. At Thessalonica Galerius held Isis as his divine protectress. Emperor worship and the Egyptian faith stood together hand in hand.

Alexander through an untimely death had to leave to his successor in Egypt the problem of religious syncretism. The divinity of the king could in the end be justified on an Hellenic basis of heroization. What was not so easy was to harmonize the pantheon of Hellas with the strongly localized gods of the Nile. The sky dwellers of Macedonian Olympus could not readily transform themselves into Nile denizens, whatever their riparian rights were alleged to be. To take but one example, the identification of Apollo with Horus, which is at least as old as Herodotus, involved some harsh and Procrustean treatment.[15] In classical Greece Apollo was the one unchallenged Sun God, his position precisely defined as were his typically anthropomorphic features, invariably of the one type. In the Olympian hierarchy Apollo was not supreme, for his father was Zeus. Delos and Delphi worshipped him as brother of Artemis through the mother Leto. In Egyptian solar theology there was no higher divinity than Re. Re was the Sun God and the supreme overlord, equivalent to Zeus. With Re could be identified Harachte-Horus, Amun, Sobek and Khnum. In the morning the sun could be Khepre, at noon Re himself, and in the evening Atum. The heretic Pharaoh Akhenaten could attempt to replace the Heliopolitan Re-Atum with his own monotheistically conceived Sun Disk, the Aton. Moreover, to the Egyptian mind there was no incompatibility between an Osiris who ruled in the shadowy realm of the dead and the all-seeing solar eye reborn each day as Osiris in the brilliance of dawn. Amid all this solar polytheism of Egypt the Greek Apollo appeared almost an overseas intruder. If he was to be, in particular, Horus the son of Isis, how could the finely chiselled face of a handsome man take on the beak of a hawk and how were Leto his mother and Artemis his sister to be dealt with when the former was identified with the snake goddess Buto of Khemmis and the latter with the cat goddess Bast of Bubastis? Here were some theological puzzles for the experts whose help was sought by Ptolemy I.

The king's choice fell on two priests, one an Egyptian and the other a Greek from Athens. Manetho, the Egyptian, had been born at Sebennytus in the Delta close to the famous shrine of Isis.[16] He specialized in Egyptian history and from the sources provided by him can be gleaned much that is valuable in a field where other evidence is sometimes meagre. The second priest was Timotheus. Born a member of the Athenian Eumolpid family of sacerdotal settlers from Egypt, he was linked with the mystery rites of Demeter and Persephone at Eleusis and he well understood the chthonian side of Hellenic religion, which whether directly derived from Egypt or not finds obvious parallels there. Ptolemy chose well.

Manetho was steeped in the lore of his native land whereas Timotheus not only claimed an Egyptian pedigree but also knew at first hand such venerable Greek shrines as Eleusis and Delphi. Neither of them saw how to escape entirely from the inevitable confusions of their respective polytheisms. But as professional priests and even king's counsellors they sought to establish a divine hierarchy with oecumenical authority that would appeal to the contemporary world. The priestly ritual of the Nile would be maintained. The piety and the inner content of the new theology, the result of a unifying and simplifying process, would display a characteristically Greek spirit.[17] Their reformation would mean the suppression of such elements of Egyptian mythology as did not fit in with a divine triad (or less accurately tetrad) expressible in Hellenic terms as Zeus (Pluto, Dionysus, Aesclepius), Hera (Demeter, Aphrodite, Athena, Artemis), Apollo and Hermes. The Alexandrian gods were the traditional Mother and Child, Isis and Horus, the cynocephalous Anubis, Guardian and Guide, and an almost transfigured Consort of Isis, an immanent as well as transcendent Pantocrator, Ruler in Hades, Earth and Heaven, Sarapis. Sarapis was a Father Figure whose features could be discovered in Pluto and Ammon, Zeus and Osiris, Adonis and Dionysus, and even the Jewish patriarch Joseph.[18] His oracular description of himself could be: 'My head is the firmament of heaven, my belly the ocean, my feet constitute the earth, my ears are set in the sky, and my far-seeing eye is the bright light of the sun.'[19]

The origins of Sarapis have been much debated.[20] Little doubt now remains that his cult was first established by Ptolemy Soter,[21] as an extension of that of the Apis Bull at Memphis, the sacred animal whose immaculate mother was Isis herself and into whose body the soul of Osiris always passed after the god's death. The tales about Sarapis and his connection with the Black Sea Greek colony of Sinope bring out the fact that Sarapis, unlike his great consort, was theologically a novelty for Egypt. Equally he was Zeus and Poseidon. He was linked in popular imagination especially with Pluto, a colossal statue of whom is said to have been fetched at top speed from Sinope to Alexandria,[22] and with Apollo and the Eleusinian chthonian divinities of central Greece. Nor is this surprising. We must remember the part played by Ptolemy's theological experts in spreading the cult abroad. Manetho had been arch-priest at On, that City of the Sun where centuries earlier another high priest had given his daughter in marriage to the Hebrew Joseph,[23] a place where everything shone bright and clear in the unfailing light from heaven. Timotheus had his own intimate experience of Eleusis, where the mystic drama of Demeter and Kore was enacted in the silence and the darkness of night. The two priests represented the two streams of thought that chiefly influenced the new attitude towards the consorts of Isis.

Osiris was so much the god of his own African river that he needed a permanent revitalization before he could take his seat as Zeus on the peak of the Thessalian mountain and from there rule the Graeco-Roman world as Zeus-Sarapis, no longer just the shadowy god of the dead but of the living also. Along with his consort Isis, whose functions, as Aristides shows us, he could share, the transfigured Osiris knew no bounds to his territorial expansion.[24] In the second century of the Christian era, a period when admittedly Isis was gaining ascendancy over him,[25] he could be invoked as the god who travels over the earth by day and decides for the living his unseen judgments by night, himself a saviour and guide of souls. For Julian the Apostate, the formula 'One Zeus, one Hades, one Sun Sarapis'[26] was a means of conveying Plato's philosophy: Sarapis was not just the Hades of the *Phaedo* but also the Intelligible World 'whither he declares ascend the souls of those whose lives have been most virtuous and righteous'. Yet for all his transcendence Sarapis was not remote from mankind.[27]

The dead over whom Osiris was the traditional ruler in Egypt needed no healer to keep them alive. Sarapis shared with Isis the task of curing the sick. His consort had been long renowned in her native land as the discoverer of many health-giving drugs and as a most experienced physician. Sarapis appeared as another physician, a therapeutic mage whose hands could likewise touch and heal those with ailing bodies. He took over the role of the divine healers of Greece, Apollo and Asclepius. Like the latter, he was believed to effect miraculous cures when the patients had undergone 'incubation', *i.e.* after they had slept within the temple precincts. Of the Sarapeum at Canopus we are told: 'Because it was much hallowed and did produce cures, people of the highest renown had faith and slept within it.'[28] Elsewhere Sarapis was deemed worthy to be publicly proclaimed not just at religious festivals but at all other seasons also as the Guardian and Saviour of all mankind. Like Isis he protected human life. Addressing the citizens of Alexandria the emperor Julian could mention King Sarapis as the city's protector in company with Isis, Queen of all Egypt, the maiden sitting at his side.[29] The two were saviour divinities: the first Ptolemy could have desired no higher title than that of Soter. In the Egypt of the time of the emperor Hadrian those who called themselves bishops of Christ are recorded to have devoted their souls to Sarapis.[30] The link between the two faiths was the gospel of salvation.

Of the temples erected to Sarapis in Egypt itself, according to a writer of the Imperial Age forty-two in number, the most famous was the colossal structure at Alexandria. The most venerable, however, was at Memphis, into which neither stranger nor priest might enter before the burial of the Apis Bull. At Abydos, the age-old cult centre of Osiris, the traditional name continued in use among the Egyptians whereas the Greeks adopted *Sarapis* to mark what for them was the transformation of an ancient idea. Outside Egypt Sarapis spread his dominion over the Mediterranean and then travelled further afield. Wherever he went he was joined and often preceded by his consort.[31] Whenever a temple was built for him, Isis had her own chapel or altar inside it. The pair, sometimes joined by Anubis and Horus/Harpocrates, as *Synnaoi Theoi* (Temple Associates) were invoked with dedications and *ex-voto* offerings much as in Christian churches today.

Sarapis was deliberately created by the Ptolemaic theologians for export abroad. He had powers of assimilation to the leading gods of Greece and in time won international acceptance. Isis, too, became increasingly cosmopolitan. In the Nile valley, however, she remained true to her ancient tradition. Her statues there were of conservative native type and her temple at Alexandria was built in Egyptian style. Local associations were retained through distinctive epithets, which as time went on gained international currency—Isis of Pharos, Isis of Memphis, Isis of Paraetonium, and so forth. Her iconography was indigenous. In her hands she might be holding the Egyptian timbrel or *sistrum*, the breast-shaped pail or *situla*, and the long-spouted *hydreion* filled with water from the Nile. On her head there would probably rest a crown of stars with a crescent moon, or the Egyptian *uraeus*, or a diadem of leaves and choice flowers with a lotus on top in sign of purity, or ears of corn as the mark of plenty. Her vesture of fine linen—a robe of many colours—would be tied with a girdle formed into the 'Isiac' or 'mystic' knot. At her feet might be resting a crocodile. The total effect of all this was unmistakably Egyptian. Among the Greeks and the Romans she came as a victress in the foreign dress of the Nile.

Her features underwent some change. In her own land she had been sometimes identified with Hathor, the Cow Goddess (*Pl. 2*). Hence a Roman poet could write about Isis as the Cow of Memphis, and as the Heifer of Pharos.[32] But in the Hellenistic

1 Find-spots of Isiac material within the Roman Empire. Concentrations are seen in areas, 1-3, Germania (Rhine and Danube lands); 4-6,

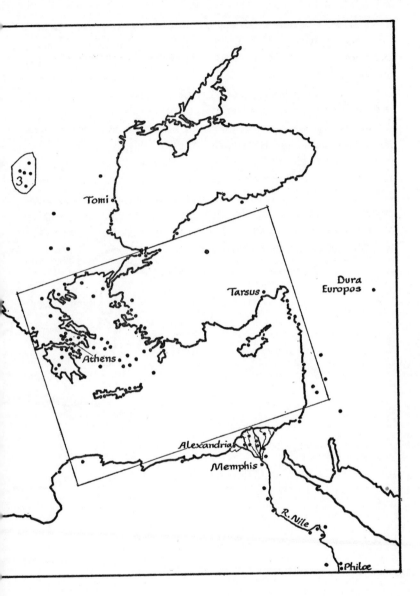

Cisalpine Gaul; 7, Central Italy; 8, Sicily and South Italy. The inset map area appears in detail on pp. 264–5

period, as we can see from the mural paintings at Pompeii
(*Pls. 24, 27*), artists took to portraying the face of Isis in an idealized
iconography. Her features gained a sweetness combined with a
gravity for which her dwelling in Greece might well have been
responsible and a grace blended with her traditional majesty was
achieved suggesting that her lineaments were suffused with the
beauty of Aphrodite, the majesty of Hera, the warrior temperament of Athena, and the chastity of the Virgin Artemis. All this,
however, was closely related to the Egyptianizing background,
the exotic symbols that she bore. After the time of the Emperor
Hadrian the Nilotic style of treatment became increasingly
strong. The gravity, the living charm and the strange mystery
were abandoned in favour of a conscious striving for archaism
and the freshness and warmth were lost.

CHAPTER V

IN THE HOUSE OF ISIS

IN A POPULAR Hellenistic aretalogy, a hymn of praise to Isis, the goddess has this to tell about herself in Greek: 'I have revealed to mankind mystic initiations, I have taught reverence for the gods' statues, I have established the gods' temples.'[1] Clearly in the Graeco-Roman world Isis was due to become the acknowledged founder of religious observances and inventress of temple sculpture and architecture. She was to be the champion of whatever Christianity was to stigmatize and attack as idolatry. She laid claim to the temples of pagan antiquity and never failed to make herself at home amidst her polytheistic surroundings.

On the banks of the Nile the idea of a temple connoted that of a house or home. Both notions are covered by the hieroglyph *pr* ⊏⊐,[2] which is also the determinative in such names as the *Great House* or *palace*, the actual designation of the Pharaoh himself as time went on, as well as the national shrines of Upper and Lower Egypt. Isis herself indeed could be called in Greek 'the house of Horus', and associated with 'the house of Hephaestus', doubtless the temple of Ptah at Memphis. An early Egyptian text invokes her thus: 'Be established in thy house.'[3] Here the term *pr* has several overtones: palace, temple, dwelling place, Isis herself and her own bosom. She found an abode easily. In the minds of her worshippers it was her prerogative to rear gods and kings and walls of temples and palaces. Like the Mother of God whom Christianity later came to venerate, Isis could either have a house of her own or have a share in one.

In Egypt itself two Isea of considerable importance existed at Busiris and Memphis. Elsewhere Isis dwelt in temples along with cognate deities: Min at Coptos, Hathor at Dendera, Horus/Harpocrates at el Fayum, Amun and the Elder Horus at Edfu,

Sarapis in Alexandria and Rome, and Apollo and Artemis at Megara. Rome and Pompeii were richly provided with private chapels in her honour, where side by side with her Egyptian figure could be seen the traditional features of the Italian family Genius, the Lares and the Penates. At el Fayum a domestic shrine was built in her name by an official styled Isionomus. As in Christian churchyards, Isiac tombstones could be reared.

In the temple of Hathor at Dendera the emperor Augustus appears in the company of a divine group including Isis. Ramesses II, whom we may plausibly identify with the Old Testament's 'king which knew not Joseph', the bitter taskmaster of the Israel-ites, appeared at Coptos in a red granite triad between Isis and Hathor.[4] At Coptos the same Pharaoh was also shown along with Nebnachtef, his overseer of works, on the temple wall, where the text shows that already in the thirteenth century BC, just as in the Graeco-Roman period, doxologies were uttered to Isis at set times: 'This humble servant reached his city to give praise to Isis, to glorify the great goddess daily.'[5] According to Herodotus the Iseum built by the Pharaoh Amasis in the sixth century BC at Memphis was a great tourist attraction.[6] The citizens in the time of Lucian could boast of the Hair of Isis as a hallowed relic, much as the Ark of Osiris was on display in the Iseum at Byblos in Syria. King Juba of Mauretania, a man who seems to have been a keen follower of the Egyptian cult and who is known to us for his interest in odd names such as 'Hair of Isis' and 'Cross Flute of Osiris', dedicated in the Iseum at Caesarea a crocodile which was still to be seen alive in the first century AD.[7] Here any spectator could witness for himself that the creature sometimes delineated at the feet of Isis lived indeed under her power and in awe of her. Was it not the crocodile that had fetched her the dead body of her brother-husband? And was it not she who kept it from harming those who sailed their papyrus boats amidst the marshes of the Delta? In an Iseum a crocodile was not out of place.

The Roman satirist Juvenal was probably using hyperbole when he wrote about the Isiac enthusiast bringing water from the remote reaches of the Nile to Rome.[8] Yet the picture, however fanciful, is not wholly inaccurate. In the Campus Martius, between the present Church of S. Maria sopra Minerva and the Piazza Sant' Ignazio, there existed a famous Iseum (together with a Sarapeum) which did indeed 'rise next-door to the old Sheep Market' and which had above its gable the figure of the goddess riding on a hound (Pls. 41–43).[9] Inside this House of Isis priests undoubtedly sprinkled holy water on the congregation from the vessels they held in their hands. What is not so certain, however, is the special journey which we are told was made to 'scorching Meroe', an 'island' on the borders of Egypt and Ethiopia, a centre where Egyptian and African cultures blended and where a figure of a late first century BC king named Teritegas standing before Isis has been discovered.[10] The fervent zeal of Juvenal's Isiac is not in dispute. In Rome, however, as in even more distant parts of the Empire, the *situla* or pail of Isis could not constantly be filled from the Nile. The local waters seen with the eye of faith were as good.

Some four hundred miles north of Meroe, not far from the First Cataract at Assuan, Isis possessed another sequestered haunt, the city and island of Philae, where she could be told by the devout, 'The Nile sprang forth under your feet'.[11] The island was called Abaton, for its holy ground was not to be trodden by the profane. Here it was that according to one legend Isis had buried Osiris. Here she was pre-eminently the goddess of countless names and bore the special titles 'Queen of the South' and 'Queen of the Southern Peoples.' Here where she dwelt the silence of the sanctity must not be broken.[12] The island was not large—less than a quarter of a mile from north to south and not even half this even at its widest. Up till now the Assuan Dam projects have not utterly shut out the admirable view at certain seasons of the Ptolemaic temples and the Roman colonnades amid the date palms (Pl. 12). The most important temple is the Iseum.

Although it is called the Great Iseum its modest dimensions cannot compete with the size of St Peter's in Rome: the length is some hundred feet and the frontage two-thirds of this. The cult of Isis apparently never inspired the erection of huge temples in her sole name. At Philae she was associated especially with Hathor and Osiris, sharers of her buildings. At Alexandria the colossal

Sarapeum could accommodate her as the queen consort (*paredros*) of the eternally revitalized Osorapis. The alliance between her and Sarapis in Hellenistic and Imperial times was inevitably so close that in his temples a lady chapel could always be found for her.

Pilgrims who went to Philae in the imperial age, on landing from the south-east, were confronted with the west colonnade, through the pillars of which, even now a striking feature of the landscape, they would go into a courtyard with the still surviving Nile Gauge on their left as a reminder of the local Festival of the Inundation. Passing a terrace and climbing some steps they would emerge into the forecourt of the Great Iseum, the orientation of which had a symbolic and essentially cosmic significance. On the west side lay the Chapel of Osiris and behind them was another Iseum, the Birth House or Mammiseum. Had they walked about they could have looked at other shrines, some for such indigenous deities as Hathor, Arnuphis[13] and Mandulis, and two built by the local community in honour of the Roman emperors Augustus and Trajan. But probably the first thought for a visitor to the island fastness after the difficult crossing through the mudbanks and reed-covered marshland would be the sight of the image of the Queen of the South in her main dwelling place.

Even as late as the fifth century of the Christian era Philae was the scene of an important ceremony.[14] In fulfilment of an age-old tradition representatives of a tribe called the Blemmyes would ascend to the House of their Lady and take her hallowed image aboard their boat. They would ferry it over to the other shore for their great festival in the hills. The procession would gather to acclaim the one who brought with her the hope of the harvest and whose statue would afterwards be restored to its resting place in the *cella* of the temple. Nowadays this kind of *pompe*, although not unknown in Christian practice, is hard to visualize when the Nile waters are dammed up and the yearly flooding which the ancients gladly attributed to the Divine Mother and her Child has been virtually obviated. Beneath the river where of old the husband-brother could be thought to suffer drowning the sacred buildings of the Abaton are for months submerged from view, just as were the temples and the other relics of Isis for long centuries at Pompeii and Herculaneum under the lava of Vesuvius.

Of peculiar interest at Philae is the House of Incarnation,[15] sometimes called the Mammiseum, the building of which was due to Ptolemy VII in the second century BC, additions being made in later Roman times. Entrance into it was impossible without purification by means of water and incense. On its walls were representations of incidents which in one way and another manifested traditional Egyptian ideas about a Divine Birth and its importance for the Pharaonic succession. Isis herself sits on her throne holding her new-born babe in her arms. In the inner vestibule among the birth scenes Amun-Re is shown with Isis on a couch. In the sanctuary the goddess suckles the young god. The king offers the crown to Osiris, Isis and Harpocrates/Horus. Horus can be seen standing as a hawk in a clump of papyrus and is suckled in the same setting by his mother, worthy to be called Isis *galactotrophousa*.[16] On the exterior walls two Roman emperors may well surprise us with their deference to Isis and her Holy Family. A shrine with Isis *galactotrophousa* is opened by none other than Augustus, who offers her the gift of myrrh. In another scene Tiberius presents the Divine Triad with milk and incense, and makes various gifts to Isis: a collar, geese and gazelles. The Nativity Story of Egypt, writ large on the walls of the Mammiseum, is of course unmistakably polytheistic in its ramifications. What must strike us at once is the deliberate link between the first two Roman emperors and the native divinities, especially Isis and her son.

On the Abaton other situations are represented involving Augustus and Tiberius. The former makes offerings of wine to Isis and beer to Hathor and stands, with sceptre and club, as 'the beloved of Ptah and Isis'. From Tiberius Isis receives a rattle, mirrors and a breast amulet. In the sanctuary of the goddess is a very moving scene. Tiberius before a group of divinities, in an age-old Egyptian scene, is slaying prisoners of war, who vainly invoke his pity with hands outstretched in a suppliant gesture worthy of Dürer. Elsewhere a procession comes before Isis and in it is Augustus 'bringing all good things'. But even before the Roman Emperors the Pharaohs pay their devotions to Philae's

Lady of the South and Queen of the Southern People.[17] Ptolemy
Philadelphus prostrates himself before her, honours her with a
hymn, with linen, a necklace and eye-paint, and from her receives
life. Material from the temple buildings is visible in the Coptic
church erected in later times near to the temenos wall in honour
of the Christian Mother of God by the Abbot Bishop Theodore.
On a block built into the wall of this church is a representation of
the Egyptian goddess of Justice, Ma'et, offered seemingly by
Augustus to the Divine Triad with the Horus hawk on the altar.
An inscription still survives to let us know that the cross has been
and always will be victorious. This is an obvious tilt against
Christianity's bitterest foe, Isis Victrix, whose magic name was for
long centuries reputed to charm evil away, as can be observed on
an amulet bearing the words, 'Isis is victorious'.[18]

One of the most famous sights on the island is said to have been
the tomb of Osiris.[19] As the burial place of the god the island was
called the Holy Field. The tomb was venerated by all the priests of
Egypt in common. Round about it were set jars filled with milk
by the priests appointed for the purpose who performed this daily
ritual and sang the office of a dirge to the gods, naming each in
turn. There was a libation bowl for every day in the year. The
Abaton, therefore, was as hallowed a spot for the Isiac pilgrim as
in later times Jerusalem has become for the Christian and Mecca
for the Muslim. Here were the most convincing reminders of the
two main dogmas of the faith of Isis: the death of the Brother-
Husband and the birth of the Child. In Roman times much care
was taken over the burial rites at Philae. Thus the priest charged
with the task of pouring out the daily libation of milk (*choachytes*)
might also share in the preparations for embalming and burying
the dead (*entaphiastes*). In ancient Egypt there was no stronger
oath than that 'by Osiris who rests at Philae'.

The body of the dead god was buried without the privy
member, which Seth had cast away into the Nile. Isis made copies
of the phallus, which she caused to be worshipped in the rites and
sacrifices accorded to her spouse, ithyphallic images being exposed
with all the fruits of the field to crown them in front of the temple
portals. In other words, the death of Osiris entailed his rebirth as

Horus through the agency of Isis. Believers could think of Isis as a human queen[20] who had passed away in a kind of Assumption or Falling Asleep and declare that, like her husband, 'she had met with immortal honours and had been buried' either at Memphis or at Philae.[21] But all the circumstances demanded that Isis should not die but live, in order to perform the miracle of resurrecting the dead god.

Along the Nile valley Isis had her wayside shrines and her home in the dwellings of companion gods. At Oxyrhynchos and Sais she accommodated herself with Neith/Athena, at Bubastis with Bast/ Artemis, and at Dendera with Hathor/Aphrodite. At Alexandria the Sarapeum was hers by obvious divine right, and to her as Isis Pelagia was dedicated the lighthouse on the Island of Pharos (Pl. 61), one of the Seven Wonders of the World. Such in post-Alexandrian times was the position of Isis in Egypt.

During the same period Isis gained much power over Greek lands, both along the coast of Asia Minor, on the islands of the Archipelago, and on the mainland itself.[22] Buildings of hers have been discovered at Delos, one of Apollo's famous homes, and at Eretria in Euboea, the cult centre of Artemis Amarusia. Pausanias mentions a statue of Isis in the Temple of Apollo at Aegira on the Gulf of Corinth,[23] and Isea in the Peloponnese, one at the citadel of Corinth dedicated to Isis in her two names 'Pelagian' and 'Egyptian'.[24] At least half a dozen others stood within a radius of thirty miles, among them the one made famous by the novelist Apuleius as the setting for the dream of Lucius and the miraculous transformation vouchsafed to him. Geographically the gods of Egypt found the passage easy to the southernmost islands of the Cyclades, Ios, Astypalaea and Thera, and the Peloponnese itself. Pausanias also points out that from the very first the Spartans had apparently been readiest among the Greeks to consult the oracle of Ammon in the Libyan Desert.[25] The southern peninsula of Greece was indeed receptive towards the religious ideas of north-east Africa. From the Peloponnese Egypt's faith spread across the Gulf of Corinth to the district of Phocis where Isis was to find herself near Delphic Apollo by the side of Mount Parnassus. Here as at Delos her assimilation to Artemis was inevitable.

It was at Chaeronea only a few miles from Delphi itself in the very heart of Greece that a young virgin is recorded in an inscription to have vowed herself to Isis for the whole of her earthly life.[26] It was also to the Isiac priestess there that Plutarch dedicated his celebrated treatise on Isis and Osiris. On the outskirts of Tithorea, close to the Delphic home of Apollo and his sister Artemis, Isis had a sacred shrine which was reputed to be 'the most hallowed of all the Greeks have built for the Egyptian goddess', and which only the Tithoreans themselves were permitted to enter, and then only when Isis herself summoned them there through a dream. We are told about a certain stranger who, acting profanely and with rash curiosity, went inside and found the whole place to be full of ghosts. On returning to the town to talk about what he had seen he dropped down dead.[27]

Pausanias spends some time over the local details. Every year a festival was held, one in spring and one in autumn. The sanctuary itself was purposely built in an uninhabited region and about a quarter of a mile away there was a special burial place into which were thrown all the remains of previous sacrifices. On the first day of the festival the ceremonial cleansing of the temple was carried out in some secret way and with the utmost thoroughness. On the second day preparations were made for a fair, the traders' stalls being erected from whatever material came to hand. On the third and last day the morning was spent in the secular business of selling slaves, beasts and clothing. On the afternoon of the third day there began the religious sacrifices. Oxen and deer were the oblation of the well-to-do, whereas people of smaller means offered geese (a favourite gift to Isis) and guinea fowl (a creature specially linked with Artemis).[28]

According to Egyptian custom, we learn, the sacrificial victims were wrapped in linen bandages and so taken away in procession. One band of worshippers escorted the victims into the shrine, while the rest set fire to the booths erected outside and hastened away at top speed. This odd behaviour witnesses to the fact that in the Tithorean ceremonies associated with the shrine of Isis is something very like the ritual of Delphic Apollo and Laphrian Artemis known as the Stepterion, the flight and slaying of the dragon. After what Pausanias says, and in the light of the assertion in one of the Hymns of Isis that the two characteristically Delphic epicleses were 'best' and 'fairest', the assimilation of the Egyptian goddess with the Grecian Artemis,[29] a significant advance in the history of religion, cannot be in doubt.

Between Delphi and Athens lies Eleusis, the home of Demeter and her mysteries. According to Diodorus, a writer who does all he can to establish the Egyptian descent of the Athenians (their Eumolpidae are derived from priests of Egypt and their 'Preachers' from Egyptian 'Pastophoroi'), the ritual of the Eleusinian mysteries was itself imported from the land of the Nile, and Isis bore a greater resemblance to Demeter than to any other Greek goddess.[30] How deeply Isis penetrated into the precincts of Eleusinian Demeter in later antiquity remains uncertain.[31] We know that an Isiac priestess named Paulina was initiated at Eleusis to Bacchus, Demeter and Kore;[32] and it is of course true, as Diodorus tells us, that the rites of Dionysus and Demeter bore the closest resemblance to those of Osiris and Isis.[33] But possibly to more than a few Greek minds with conservative religious beliefs Isis was an unwelcome and foreign upstart.

In Athens an Egyptian temple existed in the third century BC. In the region below the north-east slope of the Acropolis going down from the Law Court a Sarapeum was built in the reign of Ptolemy Philadelphus. Both in the city of Pallas Athena and in its seaport the Egyptian cult gained ground and won public recognition by the first century AD. For the Athenians an association between their own city patroness and Isis was simple enough. The link was the androgynous warrior divinity Neith of the Saite nome in the Nile delta. At Sais according to Plato the people were especially friendly towards the Athenians and 'in a sense their kinsfolk'.[34] The statue in the famous temple of Neith at Sais was regarded as representing equally Athena and Isis, with its celebrated inscription: 'I am all that has been, and is, and shall be, and my robe has never yet been uncovered by mortal man.'[35] So as time went on, Athens became familiar with Egyptian religion. In the city which the Christian missionary Paul saw as 'wholly given to idolatry' Isis with her myriad names and her own

temple was thoroughly at home, outvying as elsewhere her consort Sarapis. 'In the great city of intellectuals', it has been well said
with reference to the early centuries of the Christian era, Isis 'out-
distances not merely her partner but all other foreign gods'.[36] Yet
the temple of the autochthonous Virgin of Attica, the Parthenon
high on the Acropolis could in more than one sense look down
not only on the Jewish preacher on Mars' Hill but also on the
lowly Sarapeum (Pl. 17), where the Egyptian priest was indeed in
Pauline language just 'a setter forth of strange gods'.

From Alexandria with its trade links northwards to such ports
as Therme (Thessalonica) and Neapolis (Cavalla)[37] the pre-
dominant Egyptian religion was exported across the Aegean.
Significantly in the Cyclades Isis was blended with Artemis, goddess of triune nature.[38] Sarapea were constructed both at Delos and
at Thessalonica, and an Iseum at Eretria on the Island of Euboea.
Because of navigation ties between Neapolis and Alexandria the
cult of the Egyptian gods, particularly Isis, underwent an expansion and here, once more, Isis and the local Artemis were brought
into complete inter-connection, as they were also at Beroea.[39]

On the island home of Apollo and Artemis at Delos Isis and
Sarapis firmly established themselves in Hellenistic times (Pl. 14),
as can be proved from over two hundred inscriptions, the oldest of
them witnessing to the dedication of an altar to Isis by one of her
priestesses. As at Thessalonica[40] so at Delos attempts were made
from outside the Sarapeum to stop the foreign faith: the same
behaviour was to be shown later on in Rome towards the end of
the Republic. Demetrius Rhenaeus prevailed on the Roman
Senate to stop Athenians ousting Sarapis.[41] Despite protests the
Egyptian gods succeeded in surviving, albeit in somewhat strange
guise. In the so-called Sarapeum C the Athenian people, around
the middle of the second century BC, raised a small Lady Chapel:
its measurements are about five metres by twelve and its style is
Doric. Some twenty years afterwards a colossal marble statue of
Isis was installed there. The chiton makes it unmistakably Greek
instead of Egyptian. But Isis on Delos is even more than an
Egyptian turned Greek. For besides her identification with
Aphrodite, Tyche, Nike, Hygieia (as at Epidaurus), and Artemis,

she is also invoked as Astarte of Phoenicia, as the Mother of the Gods, and as the Great Mother.[42]

During the first world war excavations at Eretria on Euboea revealed the existence of an Iseum which, from the numismatic evidence, is dated to the second century BC. With its ritual pit, its not very deep well, its aqueduct, and its outside vestibule and inner sanctuary, it is a good example of a temple built in the Egyptian style and in honour of Isis, a house of hers. A sphinx, a crocodile and an ibis find representation and marble statues of Isis-Cybele and Aphrodite-Adonis have been unearthed, besides terracotta lamps. It is hardly an accident that Eretria, as a centre for the cult of Artemis Amarusia, drew Isis to it also.

CHAPTER VI

TO THE SHORES OF ITALY

WHEN PTOLEMY PHILADELPHUS in 273 BC sent an embassy to the Senate of Italy's leading city state, political relations were formally established between Alexandria and Rome. These might suffer fluctuations, but the commercial links that made the Nile flow into the Tiber became ever stronger. For one thing, Egypt was a main granary for a Rome that could starve for lack of bread, so that the identification of Isis, discoverer of the crops, with Italian Ceres seemed peculiarly fitting. Well before the beginning of the Christian era Rome's seaport, Ostia, like the Piraeus, the harbour of Athens, began to feel the influence of Egyptian religion, and for similar reasons.[1] Along with trade came the gods. Wealthy shipowners, whose merchandise had safely sped in little more than a week to Ostia and Puteoli from the city of Sarapis with his mighty temple and of Isis with her miraculous Pharos lighthouse (Pl. 13),[2] must have been responsible for establishing the Sarapeum which has been unearthed at Ostia and which imitated the finest example of its kind in the world at Alexandria.

At Puteoli, where the crowd on the pier could stand, we are told, and joyfully descry the fast Alexandrian mail-boat out at sea from the topsail on the foremast,[3] not only could all the wealth of the Levant be received with what seemed lightning speed but also the natural springs could help to create suitable conditions for the reception of a cult bound up with the Nile. Alexandrian ships themselves carried names reminding onlookers of the divine protection that saved them from the time they sailed away from the Pharos. Paul was taken to Puteoli in a vessel named the *Dioscuri*. The Dioscuri were 'made saviours' by Isis.[4] We read about a vessel with a figure of a little goose, a creature sacred to Isis, painted in gold on the stern and with the name of the goddess on either side of the prow. Another ship of which there is record at Ostia had 'Isis of Geminius' inscribed on it, and a trireme named *Isis* existed in the Misene fleet.[5] Along the shore of Campania and Latium in Hellenistic and Imperial times the Alexandrian faith and the name of Isis, especially Isis whose name embraced the whole world and who was the Saviour of the seafarer, were widely known and revered.[6]

Not merely these two important trading centres but also places further inland were to become familiar with the Alexandrian cult, which can be proved from the archaeological evidence to have taken firm hold amid the novel surroundings of central Italy,[7] the faithful looking not at the Nile and the Pyramids but at the Tiber, Vesuvius and the Apennines. In AD 79 the priests of Isis at Pompeii must have gazed at Vesuvius like stupefied animals caught in a trap. Did they pray to Isis to save their lives when all else had failed them? Or to Vulcan,[8] or to his Egyptian counterpart Ptah? Did their faith give them undaunted courage? At any rate they were resolute in fetching forth from their temple the images, the plates, the other holy vessels and treasure of the goddess who, alas, in this desperate crisis as they were about to learn, could not work one of her unexpected miracles. Seventeen hundred years after their death the interrupted meal of eggs and fish was to be brought to light, burnt to cinders but otherwise laid out intact on their triclinium tables (*Pl. 29*). Today the mural decorations and other finds from the lava under which the Iseum was buried seem to arouse little enthusiasm among a generation for whom the faith professed by those priests is outworn.[9]

Frescoes belonging to the other city overwhelmed by Vesuvius, Herculaneum, vividly reveal various aspects of Isiac ritual (*Pls. 23, 26*). The use of the *sistrum* is striking. Both this and the *situla* or pail can be seen in the hands of a priestess, the one in the right and the other in the left. A choir of both sexes is ranged in four rows antiphonally to take part in the ceremony in which one of the priests in the midst is fanning the flame on the altar. Living ibis roam about. In *Pl. 26* a person wearing a mask and with a lotus flower crowning his hair executes a dance just like David girt with linen at the recovery of the Ark of Jewry. All these Egyptian scenes look very odd in the staid surroundings of Campania. Just as strange, however, must be thought to be the Egyptianizing mosaic at the ancient city of Praeneste (now Palestrina) in Latium (*Pls. 8–11*), or the statue of the bull now in the Square at Samnite Beneventum, or indeed the obelisks linked with Ramesses II and the temple of Isis adorning squares in Rome.

Isis and Sarapis did not arrive in Italy to oust all rivals. Theirs was a peaceful penetration, as in so many other regions of the Graeco-Roman world. The situation at Ostia was no doubt typical. Certainly the Capitoline Triad of Jupiter Optimus Maximus, Juno and Minerva played an important part and clearly in this geographical setting the might of Vulcan was tremendous. The native patrons of war and the sea, Mars and Neptune,[10] never lost their power. Men prayed to Father Tiber, *Pater Tiberinus*. Pagan polytheism permitted a theological alliance between the purely Italian cults and those imported from the eastern Mediterranean, including Syria (to say nothing of Persia) as well as Egypt.[11] Towards the end of the pre-Christian era, like many other centres of religious syncretism, Ostia grew accustomed to the peaceful co-existence of strangely assorted faiths. The process was helped by the presence of the great oecumenical and co-ordinating influences, especially that of the Egyptian goddess known as Panthea at Pompeii, 'in her oneness everything', Isis 'of countless names'.

How many goddesses had secured entry into Central Italy from abroad at the end of the Republic we can estimate from the archaeological evidence in Rome itself and at its seaport.[12] The Great Mother had come in from the Aegean, Cybele from Phrygia, Atargatis from Syria and Tanit from Carthage. With all of these Isis could be plausibly identified.[13] In like manner her consort could be assimilated to the various exotic solar gods, including Mithras.[14] By the end of the fourth century AD Sarapis 'serene Zeus of Egypt' was identifiable with Cronos and Phaethon as well as with Mithras.[15] But, as both Pompeii and Ostia plainly indicate, Isis gained ascendency over all others, even over Sarapis himself. Thus, for example, on one of the frescoes from the Pompeian Iseum she is shown seated in all her majesty almost in

1–3 Three aspects of the goddess Isis. *Right*, kneeling on the sign for gold (*nbw*) and with her hieroglyph on her head, carved on the end of the sarcophagus of Amenophis III in his tomb at Thebes. *Below*, a Hellenistic statue assimilating her with the goddess Hathor and, *below right*, in her aspect as mother, of Ptolemaic date, suckling an infant Pharaoh

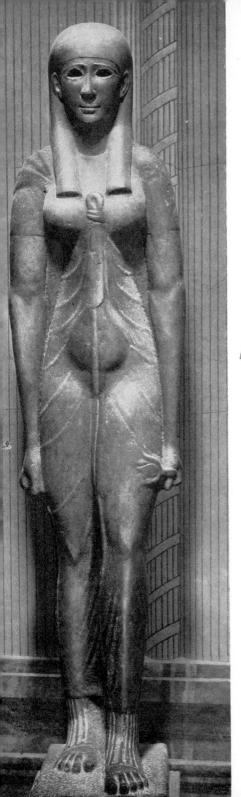

4 The style of portraiture of these two statues of the goddess Isis betrays Hellenistic influence. This composite piece is curious. The face is Greek except for the eyes, which, like the emblems, are Egyptian. The bust has a bull's head carved on the back, the horns can be seen, assimilating it with Apis

5 The Isis knot here conforms to ancient Egyptian tradition. The mantle with the fold on the right shoulder is typically Greek. The left foot advanced in front of the right is well-known in both Egyptian and Greek tradition

6, 7 The statue, *above left*, shows Isis with her typical attributes, sistrum and hydreion. *Right*, she has been assimilated with Demeter and here holds corn ears in place of the sistrum

8 *Overleaf*, mosaic from the Temple of Fortuna Primigenia (identifiable with Isis, goddess of fertility), at Palestrina. All Egypt from Ethiopia to the Delta, with Thebes in the centre, is portrayed in a zoological map of the Nile valley at the moment of inundation

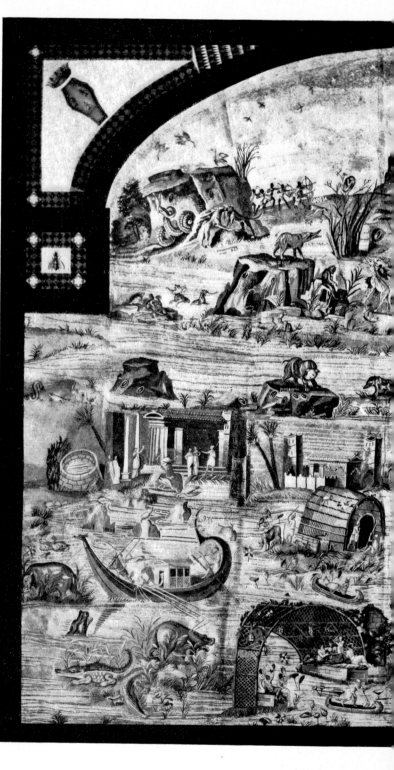

9 Detail of the Palestrina mosaic (see Pl. 8, *lower right*). We see a small shrine on the river bank with a procession passing through it, carrying the cult statue

10, 11 Details of two temples from the Palestrina mosaic (see Pl. 8, *left* and *right*). *Above*, the temple (of Ammon at Thebes?) takes a typically Egyptian form, note the pylons at the entrance. *Below*, a temple more in the Greek idiom, but Egyptian influence is still apparent in the two standing obelisks before its portico

12, 13 *Above,* a late addition, Traianic, to the Temple of Isis at Philae. *Below,* a colossal statue of Isis, weighing 18 tons, recently found in the Bay of Alexandria

the centre of the scene with Sarapis on her left as a kind of prince consort.[16] On a lamp found at Puteoli shaped like a ten-beaked ship (a reminder of the ceremony called the Voyage of Isis, probably performed locally every year in March) she stands a queenly figure between Sarapis and Harpocrates (*Pl. 37*). One of her Pompeian titles is Augusta, a title borne out by her hair style.[17] The word is charged with meaning, for we can be sure from evidence elsewhere that her cult bore a close relation to that of the Roman emperors, themselves worshipped at Ostia. Significant again is the fact that at Ostia a priestess of Bubastis (Cultilia Diodora 'Bubastiaca') dedicated an Altar to 'Isis Bubastis'.[18] By traditional 'Greek interpretation' the Egyptian Bast of Bubastis had been labelled Artemis in the Graeco-Roman world. The dedication therefore is one more sign of the syncretism which leads to the fully blended Isis-Artemis.

Just as striking is the mention of Isis and Sarapis with the Italian homeland deities, 'holy' Silvanus and the Lares.[19] The former had as his main task the clearance of wooded land for tilling. He guarded the herds of his native Latium and like Diana/Artemis protected wild life. He may at first seem a strange companion for Isis, already well provided for with Anubis/Mercury, and even a somewhat parochial divinity in comparison. In northern Greece, not far away from her, we find him at the Roman colony of Philippi. For an Isis with the functions of the Greek goddess of wild life in the woods and fields Silvanus turns out to be a fitting partner. The Lares, too, blend in well. In their plurality these are the typical protectors of agriculture in Italy, like Isis in Egypt. The name Lar in the singular is the symbol of house and home. We need not be surprised, therefore, that indigenous Italian cults such as these should undergo syncretism with that which had been brought out of Egypt, whatever opposition there might have been from time to time.

Nothing from classical antiquity which has survived the wreck of the years has more to tell us about Graeco-Roman Isis in her public, domestic and private cult than Pompeii.[20] Here we can walk amid the columns of the Iseum itself (*Pl. 22*). Admittedly it has been stripped of its artistic ornaments. These, however, we may look for at the Museum in Naples. In the bakehouse at Pompeii we can pause in front of a vaulted niche where the painter has created a group and Isis-Fortuna identified with Luna stands with the globe at her feet.[21] In the House of the Marriage of Hercules we can peer at the much-worn representation of a scene which has as the main theme an Isiac procession. We can halt in the street outside Isis' Temple and read a kind of poster with the names of the election candidates for whom her priests are asking us to vote. We can fancy ourselves taking part in the service and rattling those Isiac timbrels which are surmounted with the figure of the she-cat (Pl. 39).[22] We can admire the Apis Bull with the lunar crescent on his forehead. On the second column of the temple peristyle we can still read the name of a pilgrim, Theophilus, which he has scrawled there, leaving it for us as his memorial mark 'in the presence of the Lady'. We can grimly try to bring back the awful moment[23] when the stream of burning lava overwhelmed streets and buildings and the fire of Vulcan forever incinerated the worshippers of a goddess to whom paeans of praise had been uttered till then as the one who could rescue the apparently doomed. We call on Isis and she fails to hear us.

The Iseum buried by the eruption of Vesuvius was not the first, for one had been destroyed by an earthquake seventeen years earlier.[24] The importance of the Egyptian cult at Pompeii can be judged from the area of the temple and from its position. It stands in the public quarter near the triangular Forum and close to it are the theatres, the Wrestling School, and the temples of Asclepius and Neptune. The name of six-year-old N. Popidius Celsinus, the Iseum's rebuilder, is on a white marble plaque above the entrance. There it is also recorded that for this act of generosity the Decurions of Pompeii admitted him to their order, an honour like that of becoming a senator at Rome. Clearly, the Iseum was regarded as very important for the official life of the city.

Judged by the dimensions of a modern Christian church the Pompeian Iseum is small, hardly more than the chancel.[25] As you walk right round the columns you see eight on each side of the length, seven at the south-west side and six at the north-east. The pronaos, the vestibule or front hall, is less than thirty square

metres in area. The visitor following the Isiac of long ago climbs
up the stairway of seven steps and goes through the pronaos into
the cella, the inner chapel, where can be seen two small pedestals,
doubtless for statues of Isis and Sarapis. Inside the building are
altars and niches, and outside a small detached edifice, an underground chamber or crypt ('the Megaron') reached by a stairway,
doubtless for the use of those who were to be initiated.[26] What
our eyes miss is the pictorial decoration of the temple walls, now
set aside in Naples, including cult scenes, portraits of priests, a
remarkable picture of the reception of Io from Greece by Isis in
Egypt, the adoration of the mummy of Osiris (Pl. 25) and the
discovery of the god by means of a pair of barques.

From niches of private houses, the so-called Lararia, we can
judge how strong the attachment of certain Pompeians could be
to Isis. Thus in the House of Acceptus and Euhodia we can enter
the kitchen on the south-west corner and find a painting of Isis-
Fortuna done on a rough rectangle of white plaster with a red
border. Here is our goddess standing with a wreath of leaves on
her head, on her brow a lotus flower, her dark hair falling over
her shoulders. She wears a yellow chiton and a blue mantle. In her
left hand she bears a cornucopia and in her right a yellow rudder which rests upon a globe. The picture is bordered with large
shrubs having red flowers and with decorative fillets.[27]

In the vaulted niche belonging to the bakehouse a very similar
effect is achieved, although two other figures are introduced,
Luna and Cupid. Both female figures have the upper part of the
body nude.[28] Around the lower limbs of Luna is wrapped a
saffron robe, whereas that of Isis is violet. The latter has large
green wings and on her head wears the crescent moon (redundant
though it may appear), the lotus and the star, all three of which
are characteristic emblems. Her right elbow rests on a pillar with
a sistrum on top. Her right foot is placed on a blue globe. In this
painting again she holds the cornucopia and the rudder, but now
they have changed hands. Luna is seated on a running horse which
she is able to guide as she raises a lighted torch, as does the green-
winged Cupid in flight near Isis. Conspicuous in the zone below
the niche are the bearded and crested serpents in confrontation

at the altar, which is furnished with egg and pinecone.[29] Above the niche are bunches of grapes.

In these two paintings the Isiac worshipper could observe some of the symbolism of his faith. The Egyptian origins are made clear by the sistrum, the lotus and the star of the Nile. The abundance of the gifts of the goddess is manifested by the cornucopia and the festooning grape bunches. The serpents indicate that she is the dynamic life force. She is closely associated with the moon and the lunar torch because she is a light to a world in darkness. The rudder proves her to be Isis Pelagia, mistress of the waves. The globe is a token of her universality.

For the expansion of the cult of Isis at Pompeii there must have been a variety of reasons. Campania was bound to Egypt through the trade that reached its seaports from Alexandria. The nautical motif in the House of the Labyrinth shows that Isis like Aphrodite exerted her sway over both land and sea. In the House of the Dioscuri the owner, probably a wealthy merchant P. Nigidius Vaccula, revealed his devotion simultaneously to the two Heavenly Twins and to their acknowledged coadjutress by erecting a shrine to Isis at the bottom of his garden. The Pompeians viewed her as Panthea, mistress of all.[30] She gave them their daily bread.[31] She offered them salvation in their spiritual darkness. She did not ruthlessly stamp out those gods who had dwelt in the land before her arrival. She did not make war on the Capitoline Triad. Hercules was ready to yield her the precedence.[32] Hers was a peaceful infiltration at Pompeii, whatever might happen in Rome. She was the invincible queen, whose emblem was the Egyptian cobra, the *uraeus*. Artemis and Isis could coalesce in the Aegean, and so could Diana and Isis at Pompeii, as the House of Loreius Tiburtinus reveals. Both Isis and Artemis/Diana could wear the *uraeus*-crown and both were famed for taking just vengeance on the guilty.

All in all, the Isis whom Pompeii received with open arms brought them security. From her they could hope confidently for health of body and of mind. As a saviour she could appeal not just to the affluent citizen who had made his fortune in shipping but even to the man of lowly birth and the down-trodden slave. The mystic initiation into her service was inspired by the belief in the resurrection of Osiris: and in the painting from the south-west wall of the Ecclesiasterion, the adoration of the god's mummy (Pl. 25), we can discover his *bennu* bird, the phoenix emblematic of his immortality, whose head is crowned with the Isiac symbols of the uraeus, the solar disk and the lunar crescent.[33] The Egyptian faith promised a life after death for its believers. Through the irony of history the tokens of Isis at Pompeii have won an immortality not from heaven but from the molten rock of the earth.

Pompeii provides proof of the existence of two contrasted elements in the cult of Isis, the spiritual and holy and the frankly erotic. The Egyptian tradition has phallic worship as its core[34] and a Christian writer can even allege that on her visit to Tyre Isis played the harlot for ten whole years.[35] So too the Roman poet Juvenal writes about the shrines of 'the bawd of Isis', a reminder that the shrines at Pompeii are not far from the brothels.[36] This side of Isiacism must neither be minimized nor judged too harshly. On a phallus, as a fertility emblem, a prayer could be written.[37] In the scene where the mummified Osiris receives adoration is included an ithyphallic idol, a crude but typical symbol of the doctrine of Life in Death. In another panoramic scene the temple of Isis is depicted with a statue of Priapus before it. This again can be treated as the cult's fertility emblem, like the maypole in Christian England.[38]

For any ancient worshipper of Isis, sex was not just dirt. One might seek redemption from sexual errors, like Lucius supplicating Isis at Cenchreae in the novel by Apuleius. But the sexual side of life was not utterly taboo, as it seems to be in Pauline Christianity. In the Egyptian quarter at Delos silver images have been discovered of wombs and genitalia as suppplicatory offerings to the nativity goddess.[39] At Pompeii itself the purity of Isis as ruler of home and family can be inferred, and her chastity is stressed when she is associated with the Italian equivalent of Artemis, Diana. Yet there also Isis can embrace Venus/Aphrodite as she did Hathor in Egypt.[40] Consequently Isis at Pompeii shows her other side, the side which allows assignations near and within her very temple.[41] What the ardent lover in Rome says to the guardian of his girl friend—'Don't ask what can happen in the Temple of linen-clad Isis'—could have been said with the like implications at Pompeii.[42]

Leaving aside for the present the chequered career of Isis in Rome, we may again consider her position at the ancient city of Praeneste. From an inscription at Delos it is clear she was identified already in the year 115/114 BC with Tyche/Protogeneia,[43] in Latin *Fortuna Primigenia*. The identification must have been known at Praeneste, although the date of the mosaic associating the two cults cannot be established with certainty (*Pls. 8–11*). What could more firmly grip our minds than this in our search for Egyptian religion in Italy? Apart from the mosaic itself there are Phoenician bowls from the city on which illustrations appear of Isis wearing over her forehead a winged disk of the sun. In the mosaic at the top are the mountains of Ethiopia and Egyptian Sudan at the moment of the Nile inundation (*Pl. 8*). The lower part affords a *coup d'oeil* of Egypt, especially the Delta. In the centre is Thebes with the Temple of Ammon (*Pl. 10*). At the bottom is Memphis with the Temple of Isis.[44] The general interpretation is that of Isis who brings the flood and so the fertility of the plains. The Egyptian *fauna* add much to the exotic effect. We can say with truth that the whole map of Egypt has been combined into one picture. Here for the eyes of the faithful is not Father Tiber but the Holy Nile of Egypt.[45]

Another old city of Italy was Beneventum. It was on the Appian Way at one of the most important nodal points in southern Italian road communications. The finds from the Iseum at Beneventum leave no doubt that the Egyptian religion was a dominant influence thriving there in full vigour. The temple, in which were figures of Minerva, Juno and the Apis, may have been founded or perhaps reconstructed and enlarged by Domitian in AD 88. On an Egyptian obelisk in the cortile of the Museum is an invocation to 'Domitian living for ever'. The Emperor known for his Isiac propensities, is exhibited in Egyptian dress. Figures of priestesses have survived, one carrying a Canopic jar, others genuflecting.[46] We can see riding on the waves the Boat of Isis in white marble with the characteristic impression of two bare human feet.[47] Among Nilotic creatures are sphinxes, falcons and lions. Cynocephalic statues and peacocks are there as well. A fine example of the *cista mystica* adorned with lunar crescent and sacred serpent has been preserved.[48] Its shape is cylindrical and on its top is represented a coiled serpent, and on its side a horned moon. Here, therefore, as at Pompeii, are abundant tokens that the cult of Isis and her cognate deities had a firm hold over people in Italy during the first century of the Christian era.

At Rome the Iseum Campestre was as important as the Christian St Peter's. The *Mensa Isiaca* preserved at Turin probably belonged to it and four of the existing obelisks in Rome were placed within it. From the Iseum various finds have been assembled in the Capitoline Museum. Among these are two basalt lions, as well as a crocodile and sphinxes. A portrait statue of a priestess of Isis and one of Harpocrates indicate that its ornamentation was like that at Beneventum.

The obelisks formerly belonging to the Iseum Campestre are now in the Squares called Pantheon, Dogali, Minerva and Navona. The first two are datable to the reign of Ramesses II. Another of the same period was brought from the Iseum of Campidoglio[49] and placed in the grounds of the Villa Matthaei. Despite his aversion to Egypt on political grounds, Augustus was not unwilling to remove two obelisks of the XVIII and XIXth Dynasties from Heliopolis.[50] About the time of his curbing the renewed growth of Isiacism in 23 BC he erected the obelisk which now stands in the Piazza del Popolo, a 'petrified ray of the Sun' virtually unable to enlighten the modern tourist in the heart of Rome about 'the Nine Gods of Heliopolis' and of its High Priest's son-in-law, the Hebrew Joseph. How many visitors to Rome nowadays stop to think even for a moment about Rome's reception of Egyptian culture and stone obelisks of ancient heliolatry? According to Hermes Trismegistus, it was the intention of the Egyptians to carve on their columns and obelisks whatever succeeded in benefiting mankind.[51] So these tapering monolithic shafts were indeed worthy to be set up in an Iseum with all their attendant implications.

The *Mensa Isiaca* is considered by Scamuzzi to be an authentic work of antiquity, not indeed from Pharaonic Egypt but from the atelier of an Egyptianizing Greek engraver named Neilos in the reign of the Emperor Claudius. It is a copy of Egyptian art, but an ancient one, and herein lies its value. In the very centre is Isis herself, flanked by serpents with crowns. The Apis and Mnevis Bulls are in the left and right panels respectively. We see the cynocephalous Thoth, the winged solar disk, and Isis Luna. In the Third Zone Ptah appears twice: in the Fourth Group he is seen with Anubis and Bast. The Table is richly decorated with zoological exhibits. Neilos the engraver, like Aelian the writer, obviously had some knowledge of the gods and animals of Egypt, enthusiastically studied in Italy.[52]

CHAPTER VII

THE HOLY SERVANTS OF ISIS

IN THE MINDS of the Egyptians the concepts of priest and purification through water were inseparable. The ordinary priest was recognized as the person who cleansed, and the verb *w3b* whereby this meaning was conveyed had as its ideogram a vase from which flowed water: ⌷. A priest was washed clean and hallowed by the Holy River. The Nile gave him his purity and his power to fulfil a vocation which passed from sire to son. The Vision of God (Horaseia) was transmitted and kept in the family.[1]

Serving the gods in Egypt was a learned calling, for the outward forms and ceremonies needed the trained knowledge of a superior kind of witch-doctor, of a sacerdotal magician inspired by the power of Isis herself[2] with the deep understanding of medicine, skilled in mathematical science and mystic theology including at the outset an initiation into the phallic mysteries[3] as well as in the utterance of such spells as are to be found in the *Book of the Dead*. The intricacies of the ritual demanded histrionic ability. Different places gave their priests different names. Here we find 'servants of the god' and there 'the god's father'. At Memphis the great Ptah possessed his own High Priest. In Amun's temple at Karnak, 'Most-select-of-Places', were the Prophets. At Heliopolis the priests were known as Great Seers, who according to strange and unaccountable tales numbered Moses with his 'staff of Isis' among them and had been taught astrology by Abraham and geometry by Joseph.[4]

All the priesthood of Egypt had one common characteristic. The ultimate source of sacerdotal power was the life-giving Nile. The Roman Vitruvius tells us: 'When in accordance with pure religion the water is brought to the sacred edifice in the urn, then as they raise their hands to heaven and kneel on the ground they

offer thanks to the goodness of the god for the water's discovery.'[5]
Here we must carefully mark both the Egyptian Jubilate, so
striking in Hellenistic Isiacism, and the phrase, so natural in Latin
'pure religion'. The Roman's mother tongue at once gives him the
word he wants, *religio*. In the classical period of Greek literature
the only equivalent noun, *threskeia*, never occurs.[6] Applied by
Herodotus specifically to the religion of Egypt, it stays out of
sight in the great works of the Greek genius and reappears after a
long gap in the writings of Christianity. The Greek rationalist in
the age of Pericles, like the earlier Xenophanes,[7] might have
scorned the emotionalism of a priest-ridden Egypt, well knowing
that in his own *polis* the very word *religion* if used at all had a most
outlandish sound.

Incontestably, the custodians of the civilization of Egypt were
its priests. The omniscient Aristotle acknowledged that the leisure
they enjoyed enabled them to originate the mathematical
sciences.[8] It is recorded by Plutarch that they received in audience
such distinguished Greek philosophers as Thales and Eudoxus,
Pythagoras and Plato, not to mention statesmen like Solon and
perhaps Lycurgus.[9] In the hands of the priests were the medical
cures which were the special concern of Isis. It is interesting,
therefore, to speculate about Euripides having met with her power
if we believe the story that he was restored to health by the priests
in Egypt through treatment at the seaside.[10]

The Egyptian priesthood required highly specialized training
and conferred the highest rank. It demanded 'holy living'[11] and
probably celibacy for the Apis priest.[12] A chief priest or a prophet,
with all his knowledge of philosophy and astronomy, would be
fit to talk with the Pharaoh. His office was indeed royal service,
and one of his tasks was to stand in the presence of the king and to
recite the state prayers in a loud voice.[13] We see the continuation
of this practice in the imperial age when the 'sacred scribe' mounts
the pulpit in the temple of Isis at Cenchreae and from his hieroglyphic prayer-book recites intercessions on behalf of the emperor
himself, the senate and equestrian order, as well as the whole
Roman people, sailors and ships.[14] For the priestly vocation in
general close acquaintance with the hieroglyphic texts must have

been indispensable. In the cult of Isis the rich symbolism and the conduct at her services must have been carefully mastered by her ministers. From the pages of Apuleius we gain a good picture of Lucius' 'father in god' giving spiritual guidance, possessing the title of the highest Mithraic grade and *called* Mithras.[15] The priest has to deal with the mysteries of the faith: the cleansing of the soul by baptism, whereby the initiate gained admission into the sacred band,[16] the seven washings, the soul's death unto sin and rebirth to a better and purer life, the impatient wait in the darkness of the Megaron cell and the worshipper's apotheosis by sanctification into a resurrected Osiris.

In the priestly life there was no room for dirt.[17] Circumcision was strictly practised.[18] According to Herodotus the whole body was shaved once every three days.[19] The priest was clothed in linen and wore sandals made of papyrus.[20] He used neither wool nor leather, as being animal products. He washed in cold water thrice every day and twice every night.[21]

The daily routine was strenuous. The first of the four services started before dawn when the temple was opened by the priest[22] attended by acolytes all clad in their proper linen garments. A hymn (reminiscent of the ancient acclamation 'Awake in peace, Eastern Horus')[23] which we may perhaps cite as 'Awake thou, Sarapis'[24] was sung by the precentor, who opened the Sarapeum by hallowing it with fire and water.[25] The fire was the symbol of the beginning of another day, the fire which likewise represented the arrival of the equinox in Egypt and inspired the tradition there of smearing with red earth such things as sheep and trees.[26] In the cult of Sarapis and Isis the use of incense typified the fire of salvation and fulfilled the purpose of fumigating the temple.[27] Isis like Sarapis was tended with love and care at early morning. Her sacred image was unveiled[28] and exposed to the eyes of the faithful. It was dressed in its holy garb, adorned with jewels and vulture's feathers, and then venerated.[29] It might be gazed at for a period with longing devotion by bystanders in silence.[30] The congregation would have already performed the ceremonial ablution for themselves at the entrance into the temple by turning on the water there provided in the special vessels called *perirranteria*,[31] analogous to stoups in Christian churches. The priest himself would offer libations actually or reputedly from the Nile. He would go around sprinkling the faithful ('circumrorans')[32] with the 'cold water of Osiris' whose life-giving power resided therein.[33] The service would continue (as we can see from the fresco at Herculaneum) with sacred dancing and music, doubtless amid a strange concourse of Nilotic creatures and to the repeated clang of the timbrel. When the holy flame had been lit on the altar, prayer would be made to Isis. She would also listen to the songs of praise, prominent in her cult.

In the afternoon another service would be held for meditation. The general practice of Egyptian priests was to sing hymns to the gods four times each day, dawn, noon, the late afternoon, and evening.[34] In the worship of Isis a woman friend of the poet Tibullus is said to have had to let her hair down twice daily and 'say lauds'[35]—which must indeed have made her conspicuous among the congregation. The respective parts played by priest and layman cannot be ascertained. Probably all joined together as the Iseum re-echoed with antiphonal singing.[36] At the end of the day the statue of the goddess would be disrobed and the sanctuary curtains pulled together for the night. During the hours of darkness, however, when special seasons came round services for which the priests must have been responsible could take place, as they sometimes do in the Christian church today. So the poet Propertius laments that his friend Cynthia should spend ten successive nights at services in the Iseum.[37] At those times lighted tapers could be used in scenes of jubilation of music making and of dancing by the young nobility. The 'lights of Isis' were well-known.[38] In the so-called Calendar of Philocalus, a Latin compilation of the fourth century AD, the *Lychnapsia* or Festival of Lights, is put on 12 August. On this and other festal days, which foreshadow the Candlemas Day of Catholicism, Isis was represented seeking her spouse in the darkness by torchlight, and her processions resembled those of Neith at Sais and of Bast at Bubastis, as well as what Plato at the beginning of his *Republic* tells us took place at the Piraeus in honour of the local Athena and of the Thracian Artemis Bendis.[39] At certain times the temples of

Isis must have seemed wholly ablaze with the flame of tapers and lamps, some of which have survived until today (*Pls. 37, 38*).[40]

The elaborate ritual of the Isiac cult inevitably entailed division of duties and the number of priestly orders was therefore large.[41] The distinctive names give some idea of the special tasks. Some were 'holders of the keys'. Others were in charge of the goddess' wardrobe. We read about the *neocori* of Isis,[42] a title assumed at Ephesus in the cult of Artemis, and theirs was the duty of keeping the temple clean. Certain ministers may have guarded the sacred fire, as in the cult of Vesta.[43] Important were the 'interpreters of dreams' and soothsayers.[44] Women carried the basket with the sacrificial firstlings and the ritual cake inside (*canephoroi*) and others sang the liturgy (*paeanistai*).[45]

Guilds of 'pastophors' existed in whose hands were carried small replicas of Isiac shrines when they walked in procession.[46] Their duties were less exacting and their mode of life less ascetic than those of the chief priests. They learnt by heart the six medical treatises of the encyclopaedic *corpus* called after the god Thoth: hence they understood anatomy, pathology, surgery, pharmacology, ophthalmology and gynaecology—every single branch of the physician's science, the science which according to theological tradition Horus was taught by Isis.[47]

A procession of Egyptian priests is vividly described by a Christian writer and his description seems to fit the archaeological evidence for what was done in the Isiac ceremonial.[48] We see the Precentor advancing at the head with the symbols of music. He has to learn the hymns and the 'reckonings of the king's life'. Following him comes the Astrologer with his characteristic tokens. Next in the procession we have the strange spectacle of the Sacred Scribe with wings on his head and writing implements in his hands.[49] He is an expert in hieroglyphics, besides cosmography and particularly the geography of Egypt and the Nile. He specializes in the sacred ministry, the sacred centres and the sacred rites. Such a sacred Scribe according to Herodotus lived in the Sais district and talked about the source of the Nile as one possessing exact knowledge. It was the prerogative of this priestly order to recite to the king every morning the achievements of former

Pharaohs from the sacred books where the record had been com-
piled. To the same category were ascribed gifts of clairvoyance,
which may explain why the Jewish patriarchs Joseph and Moses
were reputed to have belonged to it.

Two more bring up the procession, the Keeper of the Robe and
the Prophet. The Keeper of the Robe holds the cubit of justice and
the cup for libations. He is familiar with all the details of training
for the ministry and the ritual of sacrifice, and other aspects of
worship such as first-fruits, prayers, processions and festivals.
Followed by a train of attendants with the issue of loaves in their
arms there walks the Prophet himself. Holding the water-vase in
full view, he does not touch it directly but only with the folds of
his mantle (*Pl. 30*).[50] He is the protector of the temple, knows the
ten 'hieratic books', and controls all the revenues. The Egyptian
Prophet reminds us of the Hegoumenos or Abbot in the monasteries of eastern and western Christendom. Furthermore, at the
very time when the Graeco-Roman world was choosing Jesus
instead of Isis, her Prophets were still to be met with among the
Blemmyes beyond Philae, where also an inscription tells us about
a contemporary visitor with the outlandish name of Smetchem
who had gained this same sacerdotal honour.[51]

The mode of life prescribed for the higher priestly orders was as
austere and rigorous as the discipline later on prevalent in Christian
monasticism, in its origins closely bound to Egypt.[52] We cannot
be sure of every detail about their food and drink and sleep nor
can we always reconcile the discrepancies in our various sources.
The general picture is clear enough. The priests were in the habit
of eating little and were ascetic even when they slept.[53] Our
source of information, the Stoic writer Chaeremon, dealing with
Egyptian priesthood as he knew it in the early Roman empire, is
reliable as a guide to the way of life followed by those who professed themselves servants of Isis. The picture is doubtless idealized.
The scandal which led Tiberius to close the Roman Iseum and
cause the priests of Isis to be crucified belongs to Chaeremon's
own day, and even if we treat it as quite out of keeping with their
general behaviour it shows what dangers there were for those
living abstemiously, but not always taming their fleshly appetites.

Chaeremon's readers are expected to admire the combination of religious ministry and scientific inquiry. The priest covets nothing. His training fits him to control his feelings. As a pillow to sleep on he places a well-polished half-cylinder of wood under his head.[54]

Chaeremon stresses the contemplative side of the priesthood. The temple was the chosen place for the pursuit of philosophy in which the priest was free to engage undisturbed when not occupied with services. He need mix with the laity only at festivals. At other times it might be hard for them to meet. The sacred ministry set its holder apart. He had to undergo strict purification and suffer many privations. Despite lapses (the lapses which characterize all perfectionist religion) the discipline of the Egyptian priesthood with its emphasis on bodily and spiritual purity won the praise even of the critical Christian Tertullian. Writing a century or two afterwards the Neoplatonic Eunapius contrasts the young priests of the holy Sarapeum, the guardians of earth's fairest things due to be enslaved by 'a fabulous and formless darkness', with the infiltrating Christian monks and their 'swinish way of life'.[55]

In the imperial age the Egyptian priesthood seems to have been well organized. The priests of Isis, like those of other oriental gods, were trained professionals. The holders of the higher ranks interceded with the deity. The more practical tasks were shared between such priests as the Pastophori and the sacred guilds of lay folk: Isiaci, Sarapiastae and Hermanubistae. For all who held the faith there was work, for women in the Graeco-Roman world as well as men.[56] We have no evidence of any compelling central authority and so we must regard the wide-spread network of Isis and her cognate deities as loosely knit. For instance, the Iseum in London might have had on its staff of priests someone from Alexandria. No doubt when the priest took stock of local conditions he thought of the great Sarapeum and of Isis Pharia at Alexandria as the source of the standards he was trying to follow. In this sense the priest upheld the unity of the faith.

The island of Delos, for centuries as thriving a centre of trade for the Greek world as Ostia and Puteoli were for the Roman, and the sea-girt home of Apollo and Artemis, in post-Alexandrian times became no less surely a focal point for the expanding religion of Egypt. From the archaeological remains we can judge what the hierarchy was there. At the top came the Priest of Sarapis, a person of quality chosen and sent out by the Athenians as long as the island was under their control. This priest held the office for a bare year and at the end of his time he might enter the ministry of Artemis, Apollo or the Dioscuri,[57] all of them to become intimate associates of Isis. During the period in question, towards the end of the second century BC, the priestly title was official rather than professional. The emissary of the nobility of Athens was virtually a government representative.[58] The Athenians, well-known for their belief that their own religious observances were the same as those of Egypt, expected the priest of Sarapis, despite his Egyptian name, to avoid all that to the Greek mind would have been fanatical. His main task was to sacrifice at Delos on behalf of his fellow-countrymen, to offer up their state prayers, and to conform outwardly, as when one named Sosion dedicated a chapel to Isis-Nemesis and venerated the Isis of Taposiris.[59] The priesthood of Sarapis, we can see, could be transmitted at Delos as in Egypt itself from father to son. Thus the priest named Apollonius was succeeded by Demetrius, his son. The former, a member of the sacerdotal caste, had come to Delos from Egypt. He reached the remarkable age of ninety-seven, and the son at his death was merely sixty-one. The succession passed from Demetrius to his son, Apollonius II.

The chief priest at Delos always bore the name of Sarapis. Besides him there was the *cleidouchos*,[60] 'holder of the key', again an Athenian of noble birth. His duty was to open the shrine at daybreak and to expose to view the divine image locked up in the *naos* during the night. Among the others with priestly duties were the sacristans, technically called *zakoroi*, but they were neither Athenians nor of noble birth. The baskets containing sacred food were handled by the *canephoroi*, Athenian girls of good family who were probably under a special vow to Isis.[61] Among the soothsayers, the 'interpreters of dreams', was a Cretan named Ptolemy. In addition to his main function he held two other offices. He catalogued the divine praises and he chanted these and

the divers miracles in the *Jubilate*. But this 'aretalogical' aspect of
the cult during the early stages of its development at Delos was
relatively unimportant.[62]

More significant were the two quasi-priestly brotherhoods, the
Wearers of Black (*melanephoroi*) and the Guild of Servers (*thera-
peutai*). The latter group, with a name at once reminiscent of
classical Greek religion and Jewish mysticism,[63] were keen laymen
and laywomen whose enthusiasm set them to work on improve-
ments in the temple. The Synod of the Wearers of Black (the
'Cassock Group') paid particular devotion to Isis as 'the black-
robed Queen'.[64] Another such group existed at Eretria. References elsewhere to Isiac worshippers in glistening robes of white
linen may make us wonder whether the members of the Group in
Black could have donned the surplice over the cassock. Presumably not all their time was spent in chanting dirges and celebrating
the passion of Osiris. They could hardly have missed the gladness
of his 'discovery', which was an essential feature of the saga. But
theirs was a specialized ministry. The dark gown showed them as
intrinsically mourning, like Isis herself.

In the Egyptian cult is to be seen a class of worshipper, whether
priest or layman, that anticipates the mendicant friar of the
medieval epoch. We read about the proscription of the aedile
M. Volusius just before the battle of Philippi.[65] We may presume
that Philippi even then had become what it certainly was afterwards, the home of Isis, for Volusius succeeded in escaping to the
camp of Brutus by dressing up as an Isiac in a long robe that fell
down to his feet and wearing the dog's-head mask of Anubis. He
walked along the road asking for alms but not revealing his identity to anybody. We are not told about his having shaved off all
his hair. This we may assume he did—unless, of course, he was
already bald.

The dietary regimen of the Egyptian priests may well have
much varied from age to age and from rank to rank. From one
source we gather that if engaged in ceremonial observances they
used no bread at all. According to Tertullian the priest of Isis (as of
Apis and of the Great Mother) had to practise abstinence and
chastity by eating only dry food.[66] Diodorus states they were

allowed to eat veal and goose and to drink a modicum of wine. At
Delos, on the contrary, wine was forbidden.[67] On the reliable
testimony of Plutarch a priest had to abstain from such creature
comforts as woollen clothing, pork, (save once a year, when eaten
sacrificially), fish and wine, nor was he at liberty to consume
much in the way of vegetables.[68] At Pompeii the Isiac diet was a
spare one: eggs, lentils and nuts (*Pl. 29*). Yet as with other religious
ascetics in history the priests of Egypt were not made martyrs by
abstinence, but famed for their good health and long life.[69]

It was not only inside the temple precincts that the servants of
Isis fulfilled their many duties. As we learn from a vivid description by Apuleius the outdoor procession every year on 5 March
brought the priest and the layman together on their way to the
seashore for the Sailing of the Ship of Isis. The scene is set at
Cenchreae near Corinth, but similar festal processions of the
Sacred Vessel of the goddess must have been celebrated wherever
her cult was practised along the shores of the Mediterranean, the
Aegean and even more remote coastlines. It must have taken place
at or near Byzantium and at Ostia and the pattern would have
been the same as at Cenchreae. The symbols of the goddess were
borne by the chief priests, arrayed in white surplices. One held a
lamp in his hand with a bright flame in the middle. Another
carried the 'altars of help' the name of which (*auxilia*) commemorated the 'succouring Providence of the supreme goddess'. After
him there followed a priest lifting up a gold-leafed palm branch,
as well as the wand of Hermanubis.[70] Next came a priest who
stretched out the fingers of his left hand and displayed the 'sign of
Righteousness' (a favourite attribute of Isis) as well as a golden
vessel from which there flowed forth milk. A fifth proffered a
gilded winnowing fan thick with bay leaves. A sixth held up a
jar of wine. All these priests formed part of an immense throng of
men and women in robes of glistening linen. To bring up the rear
of the procession advanced a priest displaying a timbrel for the
goddess and a garland of roses (*Pl. 49*) for Lucius, flowers which
were the miraculous means of his restoration to human shape.[71]
The spectacle of the procession from start to end was a wonderfully variegated panorama of sacerdotal pageantry.

Another outdoor ceremony performed by the priests of Isis is of some interest in the history of religious practices. At Philae on the day of the inundation of the Nile their custom was to throw into the channel around the Abaton coins and gifts of gold.[72] The practice has apparently survived in Islam. For on the day of Arousat-el-Nil, it is recorded, a clay statue representing the Bride of the Nile was thrown into it, as a legacy from ancient times when the river received not merely coins but also a young girl.[73] An obvious parallel in Christianity is the throwing of the silver cross into the sea by the priest of the Orthodox Church on the Feast of Lights or Epiphany, 6 January. These facts should serve to remind us that the religious views and practices of the Egyptians, so much steeped in the Nile, can be linked sometimes with those of a later era. The priest who spent his days in service to Isis provided plenty of examples for future generations to follow.[74]

CHAPTER VIII

TELLING FORTH HER PRAISES

IN THE HISTORY of Egyptian religion doxologies are as important as the decalogue and the psalms in Judaism or the liturgies and the creeds in Christianity. The praise of gods and kings has its own word, *hnw*, and the word has the figure of a man performing the rite associated with it as the determinative: 𒀭. The same determinative appears also in the word *hy-hnw*, the *Jubilate* of which we have examples in the hymns to the Nile, to Osiris,[1] to Amen-Re, and in the magnificent hymn of Akhenaten to the Aton or Solar Disk. As for Isis, in early times her name inspired dirges whatever praises she might have sung to her. The Graeco-Roman world, however, was introduced to an Isis who aroused in the minds of her followers as much jubilation as the Solar Disk had done in Akhenaten's. Nothing else brings out so well the nature of her gospel, her claim to universal supremacy, the rule of her laws, her gift to men of their daily bread, her championing of the mysteries and of idols, her mercifulness, and her almighty control of Destiny. The faith was spelt out in the words of the hymn, the hymn of praise composed in Egypt but intended for Greece.

The two chief centres for the development of the reformed theology of Egypt in the Ptolemaic age were Alexandria itself and Memphis. The newly built seaport was the fitting home for the Osiris whom Hellenistic influence had revitalized as Sarapis and for the Isis whom Alexandrian ships were to carry as *Pelagia*, sea-borne, around Mediterranean shores.[2] But without the conservative elements provided by Memphis the religion of the Alexandrian Sarapeum and the Pharos of Isis could never have flourished.

The economic importance of Memphis may have waned after the time of Alexander and the emergence of his splendid new city and capital. Its traditional importance, however, as the place where Isis and Osiris had 'passed from among mankind' was never lost, and the shrine of the goddess was pointed out to Hellenistic tourists in the temple precincts of the god Ptah.[3] It was from Memphis that the Ptolemies introduced the cult of Sarapis into Alexandria. At Memphis the Apis Bull whose divine Mother was Isis herself was the object of peculiar veneration as 'the renewal of the life of Ptah',[4] besides being regarded as the incarnation of Osiris and his transformation thereby into Sarapis.[5] In Egypt's ancient capital was apparently achieved the welding together of local and Hellenic elements which is often (not quite correctly) styled 'Alexandrian' syncretism.

The new theology, of course, profited from the Alexandrian outlook. The Isis of the doxologies is not earth-bound to the Delta but has taken control, and is the Lady of rivers, winds and ocean. She is mistress of the weather and of all seafaring. She can change the navigability of the seas as she pleases. She can raise islands from out of the depths. Still, she remains well aware and very proud of her Egyptian origins. As queen of Egypt she wears linen garb. She rejoices in Bubastis, the city that she specifically declares 'was built for me', so claiming as her own the cult centre of the cat-headed goddess of Lower Egypt identified by the Greeks with Artemis. This city, where 'the timbrel is carried', she couples with Memphis, 'joyful with its fields that bear the sheaves of corn'.[6] She it is who has caused righteousness to prevail and the oath a man takes, to be his most sacred bond: two ethical principles very dear to the Egyptian mind. She is the goddess who rises in the star of Sothis. She stresses her dual position as Osiris' wife and sister. She has invented hieroglyphics and given them their esoteric value. The pattern of the Hellenistic doxology or aretalogy of Isis is developed from the traditional theology of the Nile valley centred at Memphis with accretions which may have been introduced from Alexandria. As if to avoid any mistake about the provenance of Isis, the *Andros Hymn* begins with the word 'Egypt' and ends with the word 'Nile'. Nevertheless, the whole treatment is Hellenic in expression and in spirit. The aretalogy is for export to Greece.

Memphis, the old capital of the Pharaonic kingdom, although ousted from its position with the growth of Alexandria retained its religious importance. In particular, it was one of the main centres of the cult of Isis. There it was that traditionally she had been equated with Hathor. So Isis could be regarded by the Romans as the sacred 'cow of Memphis'.[7] As a pair of her abodes she could be said to have 'Memphis and palm-bearing Pharos'.[8] From Memphis her image, we read, was taken to Antioch, a city which was to become increasingly important as one of the world's centres of trade, art and science and from which there have been preserved mosaic pavements illustrating a ceremony of Isis and the House of her Mysteries (*Pls. 34, 35*).[9] With its Iseum, built by the Pharaoh Amasis and a century afterwards seen and admired by Herodotus, Memphis must have been the longed for Mecca for many an Isiac pilgrim. Its priests were in a good position to help in the dissemination of the reformed Egyptian faith, a task in which others who had settled there of Greek descent could have a share. In this connection we may recall that the priest Apollonius who established his shrine to Isis at Delos made his way there from Memphis.[10]

What is obviously a stereotyped litany for worshippers beyond the confines of Egypt has survived in half a dozen variant forms. In one of the versions the dedicant, after uttering his prayer to Isis, declares that the words have been copied 'from the column at Memphis standing near the Temple of Hephaestus (*i.e.* Ptah)'.[11] Accepting this statement as authentic, we can think of the texts we have as emanating from the one Memphitic source. That in the course of transmission the original should have been embroidered and expanded is very natural. The best example of this is the version in the *Oxyrhynchus Papyrus* 1380, where the grammatical structure suggests as a title *Te Deam*, and where the patriotism of the Egyptian compiler drags in every possible deity with a net that stretches from the Egyptian Nile to the Indian Ganges and from the coast of Palestine to Italy and Rome.[12] Imaginative, no doubt, are some of the details; the whole picture, however, is convincing, whether or not we swallow all the geography; and phrases at the beginning—'In the House of Hephaestus' and 'art

called Bubastis'—as well as towards the end—'thou at Memphis'
appear to have the ring of truth. The suggestion has plausibly
been made that this papyrus version was itself composed by one of
the Isiac priests at Memphis. Additional support for the view that
our *Te Deam* springs from Egypt's ancient capital is provided by
another aretalogy on the verso of the same papyrus. This is in
praise of the deified medical sage Imhotep, worshipped in Graeco-
Roman times as Imouthes-Asclepius along with Isis, and owning
his main temple on the edge of the desert near Memphis. The
papyrus which gives the Isis *Litany* bears double witness to the
importance of the Memphitic locality for writing religious
propaganda.

The strength of the aretalogical tradition in Egypt itself must
have helped the production of Isiac hymns for foreign export.
Even before the inspired henotheist Akhenaten had told the praises
of 'the living Aton, beginner of life', Osiris could be invoked as
the god of multiple names, with mysterious ceremonies in the
temples, for whom plants grow, to whom were entrusted cattle,
birds, worms and beasts protected by Isis.[13] In this early hymn the
functions of Osiris are curiously similar to those of Isis in the
Graeco-Roman age, although before the end we learn that 'his
sister has taken care of him: she has made light with her wings'.
The Hymn by Akhenaten supplies even more examples of arrest-
ing parallels with the praises which were to be uttered long afterwards to Isis. Thus the Sole God of the heretic Pharaoh achieves
transcendence and immanence through his extended beams, like
loving hands let down from heaven: 'Thy rays embrace the lands
to the full extent of all that thou hast made. . . . Thou art remote
yet thy rays are upon earth.'[14]

Isis does not identify herself with the solar disk: but she does
assert that she has ordained and accompanies the course of the sun
and that she exists in the sun's rays. Just as the Aton divides the
races of men so that each utters its own speech so Isis has drawn up
the Greek and non-Greek 'dialects'. The rays of the Aton are in
the midst of the great ocean: when He shines, the ships have the
way open to sail up and down stream. So Isis presides over
shipping and rivers, winds and sea. The theology of the Aton,

promulgated many centuries before Isis became an international divinity, never took root officially. But in Egypt an ancient tradition once established finds it hard to die. As late as the Coptic period the name of the heretic Pharaoh lives on in the Christian church, where we come across 'St Apa Aknaton'. As to the Hellenistic view of Isis, all that can be claimed is a general resemblance, confirmed here and there by detail, between the Aton-theology of Akhenaten and what we meet in the aretalogies composed in her name and particularly in the paean of praise she receives from Lucius in the novel of Apuleius.

The Aton rules over night, day and mankind. The Aton rises, and is greeted by all that lives, the cattle, the trees and flowering plants, and the birds that flutter over the marshes. The Aton has made all that is on the earth and is in control of the seasons. Such is the doctrine of the great el-Amarna Hymn. Sophisticated Christians steeped in centuries of monotheistic thinking may easily underrate the theological achievement of Akhenaten and dismiss the ideas as commonplace. If we take all those ideas together as a single creed, then the historical importance of the hymn is incontestable. Still more remarkable is the fact that Egyptian religion had to relapse again into the old familiar polytheistic beliefs for more than a thousand years before another reformation was attempted.

Akhenaten had invoked his Sole God as 'the mother and father' of all created things. So if he had known the Isis of Lucius he would certainly not have found him unsympathetic towards her. He could have endorsed every word. 'Thou who art the holy and eternal saviour of the human race . . . worshipped by the powers above and honoured by the powers beneath, thou who dost set the earth revolving in its orbit, source of the sun's light and Ruler of the Universe . . . art obeyed by the stars and makest the seasons return, thou joy of the gods and mistress of the elements. At thy behest the winds blow, the rains bring forth the food, and the seeds take root and turn into sprouting plants.'[15]

To make out lists of the blessings which men are thought to owe to the gods, to utter their glorious deeds, wonders and miracles, and to show forth their praise have been favourite occupations for the devout throughout human history. Examples of such aretalogy can be found, for example, in Homer, besides the Bible. Egypt, however, specialized in this form of religious utterance, and the Isis Hymn can properly be said to be in the long line of descent from the Hymns to Osiris and the Aton. In spite of the claim that unity exists in all the diversities of utterance[16] the form laboured from its verbal diffuseness and the multiplicity of its conceptions. Loosely embodying assorted statements of faith, it lacked the close precision of the Christian creeds evolved in somewhat later times at Councils of the Church.[17] In order to discover genuine parallels in the liturgy of Christendom we must turn not to the creeds but to the *Magnificat*, the *Benedicite* and the *Te Deum*, as well as the *Akathist Hymn* of Greek Orthodoxy and the *Regina Caeli* and *Ave Maria Stella* of Roman Catholicism. In the Old Testament the Lord's praises are told over and over again. We need but remember such psalms as 104 (so strikingly similar to the *Aton Hymn*), 100 (the *Jubilate*), and 150, where everything that breathes is called upon to utter the Lord's praise by every means, including the timbrel and dance. As to the New Testament, at least one hint can be found[18] that the early Christians accepted the convention of an Aretalogy in lieu of a set creed. They are told they are a royal priesthood and holy nation, to show forth their God's praises and goodness (*aretai*). In the first century AD worshippers, whether pagan or Christian, would profess their loyalty not by publicly declaring 'I believe' but by their acquiescence with the formula of divine acclamation.[19]

In the extant versions of the Isis Hymn the case usage is flexible. We hover between nominative, vocative and accusative. At the start of the *Andros* version Isis is invoked as Egypt's Queen, but half-a-dozen lines afterwards she settles down to talking about herself in the first person, as she does in the versions from Cyme and Ios. In the Oxyrhynchus *Litany* a long series of epicleses in the accusative merges into an address to Isis in the second person. In the versions by Isidorus from Medinet Madi (an ancient site just outside Memphis) the technique of invocation is unswerving. The different employment of the cases is only one illustration of the freedom which the various adapters allow themselves in their treatment of what is obviously in the end a single common source, the Memphis stele. But whatever the elaborations, the main themes are clear. These we can discover by turning first to a passage in Diodorus and then to the longer versions of the text on steles from Cyme and Ios.

Diodorus offers us the bare skeleton of an aretalogy and the vagueness of his introductory words casts doubt whether the place he names in Arabia was ever of the same importance as Memphis.[20] The inscription from Cyme is complete and is ostensibly a copy of that at Memphis itself. More than fifty clauses are set forth, each being introduced by Isis herself with the first personal pronoun. Parallels for almost all of them have been discovered in Egyptian texts.[21] The total effect, however, is unmistakably Greek. As a piece of religious propaganda it has the virtue of being clear and straightforward and forms one of the best epitomes of Isiacism in the Graeco-Roman world. The other versions help to supplement it.

Isis does not minimize her role as female divinity. She names her father (in Greek), her husband-brother and her son. She declares: 'I am she called God among women.' She has coupled woman with man. She has ordained that a woman shall bring forth a babe into the world after nine months. She has decreed that parents should be loved by children, and has enjoined punishment on parents who show no affection. She has made women to be loved by men and has invented the marriage covenant.

Isis is also the champion of Justice, like Demeter Thesmophorus.[22] She has established laws that shall never be broken. She has caused what is right to prevail. She has destroyed the empires of despots, and has made righteousness stronger than gold and silver. She has established the overriding sanctity of the oath. When one person forms a plot unjustly against another, then Isis hands the perpetrator over to his intended victim. She assigns vengeance on those who deal unjustly. With her the right prevails and like Demeter and Persephone she is the 'Law-giver'.

The most important aspect, however, is the omnipotence of Isis on a cosmic scale. She has separated earth from heaven. She has revealed the paths of the stars. She has invented seafaring over which she presides, as she does over fresh and sea water, and over winds[23] and the thunder. The waves of the sea she can calm and she can raise. Nobody receives praise unless she thinks fit and whatever she decides will be accomplished. All things bow to her. She frees the prisoner. As if to clinch the question of her invincibility, she ends with the two statements: 'I overcome Fate. To me Fate hearkens.' She is indeed Almighty.

The *Andros Hymn* is a highly wrought recasting in epic hexameters of the original prose catalogue. The Homeric basis of the verse form is evident especially in the choice of epithets: but the poet's taste is for the Doric dialect. In comparison with the *Aton Hymn* or Psalm 104, not to mention such products of Christian inspiration as the *Akathist Hymn* or the *Dies Irae*, the example of Isiac hymnography from Andros is conspicuously artificial. The preciosity of the diction matches the shallowness of the feeling. How different it is from the simplicity of Lucius' invocation to Isis in Apuleius! Lucius, like St Francis of Assisi, sings from his heart and happily escapes the dangers that beset the earnest versifier of the Alexandrian age. The prose invites a metrified rendering as Lucius bursts forth with these words:

> The birds that through the heavens take flight
> The beasts that roam the hills thy might
> Do dread, and things on earth that creep
> And creatures swimming in the deep.

The temptations to which our anonymous poet succumbs can be illustrated in the passage where Isis tells of her interest in the sea and in men's sailing across it. The original statement is simple enough: 'I invented seafaring.' This plain unvarnished utterance gives rise to the following treatment in the *Andros Hymn*. In the style so typical of Alexandrian literature allusions are made mythologically to the Mediterranean, the Nile and the Aegean Islands. The personifications are female. Amphitrite, Poseidon's wife, represents the Sea.[24] Tethys is Mother of the rivers, with the Nile particularly in view. The Greek Archipelago is the domain of 'the daughters of Doris', *i.e.* the Nereids whose father's special haunts are the depths of the Aegean Sea. Isis has a very Greek and female company of divine helpers as she rides the waves. 'When the weather was clear it was possible for vessels to sail across Amphitrite, their prows blackened with the drought of winter, after I had opened wide the grey arms of Tethys with a smile and a blush on my gay cheeks. Over the navigable depths I drove my pathless way when my heart moved me. Speeding in every direction with dark roar the ocean gave deep bellow from its inmost shrine, amid its profound caverns. I was the first to guide the keel of the swift ship, its sails billowing, as I rode on its planked deck above the swell. The beautiful family of Doris started their winding dance as the sea was brought under control by swift vessels of pine. Their minds trembled with amazement as they gazed and gazed on the crew their eyes had never known.'[25] The rhetorical extravagance of all this may be excused perhaps as the fault not of the Isiac hymnographer but of the period to which his composition belongs. But the passage must in the end stand or fall in comparison with utterances elsewhere: verses from Psalm 104 about the great and wide sea, the ships and the leviathan, or the various hymns of Christendom inspired by the New Testament exclamation: 'Even the winds and the sea obey him!' The picture of Isis Pelagia, seen in such a light, is pretty, but the feeling shallow.

Early in the *Andros Hymn* Isis declares: 'I have discovered and carved with chisels the secret hieroglyphs of inventive Hermes, engraving for my initiates the awe-inspiring Sacred Word.' The Sacred Word, *Hieros Logos*, is a term with important overtones in Egyptian religion. Traditionally in the mythology of the Nile Thoth was 'Lord of Holy Words' and the chief of magicians. In the *Pyramid Texts*, though not a member of the Osirian family, he is named immediately before Isis, whom he could assist as did Anubis in other accounts.[26] In the eclectic religion of the Hellenistic age Isis and Thoth/Hermes grew to be more and more closely associated, and the outcome of all this can be observed in the 'Hermetic Books' at the end of the second century AD. Whether the goddess or the god is theologically the more venerable is sometimes hard to make out. According to one view, as we can see in the short version of our Hymn, Isis could be regarded as Thoth's pupil. Yet according to old tradition she had discovered the Sacred

Name from none other than Re himself, and this by means of her womanly cunning and magic.

The eminence of her position in Egypt and the claims she was making to a world supremacy far beyond Egyptian territory hardly permitted her to be subordinate to any other deity. Along with Sarapis, whose praises could be told like hers in 'a Sacred Word',[27] she held the rank of a royal consort obedient to no other superior authority, and from this point of view any dependence on the god Thoth, however venerable he had been, was a theological anomaly. The 'Greek interpretation' of the *Andros Hymn*—Re, Aset and Thoth converted into Kronos, Isis and Hermes—serves only to bring out the inconsistency. When the hierophant of Isis initiated the neophyte into her mysteries 'the awe-inspiring Sacred Word' was surely uttered in her name.

The versions of the Hymn from Medinet Madi supply other interesting features of Isiac faith. Isis is the great inventress, giver of the arts and of all that makes life comfortable and worth while. She bestows the blessing of children. When in any kind of trouble —the pain of sleepless nights, the loss of the way when abroad, the storm and the shipwreck at sea—her suppliants are always rescued. Her festivals give rise to a continuing gladness. Yet as she stands and listens to the prayers of her worshippers full of mercy she appears wearing her robe of black (*Pl. 6*).[28]

In the Oxyrhynchus *Litany* the topographical details about the cult of Isis and the associated gods must be read with caution. What is certain is the belief of our informant that the Egyptian cult found itself at home throughout the Levant. Of particular interest is the claim that Isis held sway along the shore of Palestine and Syria. Specific mention of Byblos is absent, even though its connection with Isis was of the closest and Giblite civilization there 'was born when Isis disembarked'.[29] The names of Berytus and Petra appear, and for Petra there is archaeological confirmation.[30] We also meet the name of Ascalon. Here the statue of a goddess has been found wearing a crescent moon and holding a cornucopia, like the portraits of Isis at Pompeii.[31] The identification of Isis with Astarte of Sidon and 'the Syrophoenician goddess' is not surprising.[32]

A tantalizing reference is made to 'the fifteen commandments'. We also observe how Isis (like the Aton of Akhenaten) brings the sun from rising unto setting 'and all the gods are glad'. The gladness of her worship appears again when she is said to have created every day for joy. She has made her youthful son Horus Apollo the Lord of the whole world. She is the glory and the tender love of the female sex and she has made 'the power of women equal to that of men'. She brings the flood waters to the Nile (and the Eleutherus, and the Ganges). She has dominion over rain and spring and dew, over winds and thunder, lightning and snow. The Dioscuri of the ocean owe to her their power. She is responsible for religious tradition. Those who invoke her name in faith can enjoy the vision of her. In short, she promises her believers the satisfaction of their deepest needs. There is no end to their telling the praises of their almighty mistress, Isis, the name above every name. Queenly as Hera, mystic and fructifying as Demeter, comely as Aphrodite, victorious as Athena and pure as Artemis, she embraces within her the functions of all.[33]

CHAPTER IX

THE ONE WHOSE NAMES
CANNOT BE NUMBERED

FOR MANY CENTURIES now the shores of the Mediterranean and western Europe have never heard the formal gospel of polytheism, particularly as this was preached with conviction and even fanaticism by those who believed in the ancient gods of Greece and Rome and of Egypt, led by Isis and Sarapis. Today the view prevails that religion has moved forward to a higher stage of development and has been purged of primitive errors. Admittedly Catholic Christendom invokes many saints in its polyhagiodulia but it is our custom nowadays to think of such religious beliefs and practices as we find in the zoolatry of Egypt and the anthropomorphic cults of Greece and Rome as outworn, crude and childish falsehoods. The Christian formulates his creed as a conviction about the existence of one God and one Lord Jesus Christ. The faith of the Muslim is pivoted on one God, Allah, and his one prophet Mahomet. The test of orthodoxy in either case is a monotheistic belief. Long ago Christian theocracy destroyed the Sarapeum of Alexandria (Pl. 68) and by this act officially stamped out the polytheistic ideas so long prevalent in the Graeco-Roman world and there preserved in the last and greatest stronghold. Till then, despite occasional monotheistic utterances such as we have in the *Aton Hymn* of Akhenaten or the *Hymn to Zeus* by the Stoic Cleanthes,[1] the attitude of pagan antiquity had been conservative towards the traditional cults. From now onwards the doctrine, so jealously held in Palestine, that there is but one God was to dominate the western world.

The aretalogies or encomia of Isis derived from the Memphis stele all make clear her championship of time-honoured polytheism. She herself was the epitome of it. In her own country she had a strongly marked individuality, revealed through her love for her brother-husband, her power to bring about the Nile flood, her knowledge of healing, and her control of the crops. But when she underwent Hellenization, the richness of her personality enabled her to take in all the characteristic qualities of the Greek goddesses. The purpose of all her hymnographers was to let the worshipper know she was 'the goddess of many (or countless) names'. We do not read about any public recitation of 'belief in Isis', a matter which would have involved the theologians in the task of precisely defining her relation to Sarapis/Osiris. We can assume, however, that ordinary men and women who learnt about her power from what was written in her hymns were not much worried about monotheistic niceties. As for the more philo-sophically minded, Isis was an all-accommodating lady. So Plutarch, sure as he is that 'Isis and the gods associated with her' are familiar to the contemporary world and are international property, considers the meaning of her unique title 'the one of countless names' (*myrionymos*). It is a title found in inscriptions of the second century AD from Nubia and Upper Egypt, besides from Cyrenaica, Italy, Dacia, Germany and northern France and created, no doubt, by the wide variety of the local epicleses.[2] Plutarch brings the title forward in proof of the identity of Isis with the material substrate which he discovers in Plato's *Timaeus:* she is the female principle of Nature and as such is the passive receptacle for every kind of shape and form.[3] To many of the unlearned proletariat and slaves who in the age of Plutarch so readily yielded their hearts and minds to the tender and merciful Lady[4] this metaphysical depersonalization would have seemed an unpalatable doctrine. An intellectualist was robbing them of one of their most dearly held beliefs, that their Almighty Redeemer suddenly intervened in their lives with drastic strength. Yet in the end neither the philosophical nor the popular interpretation of traditional ideas was out of keeping with what the cult meant. It is well-known that in the higher religions, as for instance Christian-ity, the central figure undergoes kaleidoscopic transformations according to the standpoint of the individual believer.

14, 15 *Above*, the small Temple of Isis in the Sarapieion C at Delos built by the Athenians about 150 BC. At the back of the *cella* is a colossal cult statue of Isis. *Left*, the marble dedicatory plaque to Isis Lochia, from the Church of St George at Beroea, is a votive offering from Bruttius Agathophorus and his wife Eleutherion for their daughter Meilesia after childbirth. Note the sistrum in relief underneath

16–18 Isis and Sarapis in the eastern
Mediterranean. *Left* and *above*, lamps from the
Athenian agora, one in the form of a wrapped
mummy, the other showing the Temple of Sarapis
and Isis on its *discus*. *Below*, a relief from Xanthos
showing the two deities holding cornucopiae

19–21 The spread of
the cult of Isis in
western Europe. *Above,*
an enthroned statue of
the goddess found in
the Church of St
Ursula at Cologne.
Above, right, a small
silver statuette of
Harpocrates, bound
with a golden chain
and with his forefinger
under his chin instead
of the more usual
gesture to his lips,
found in the Thames
at London in 1825.
Right, jug with graffito
LONDINI AD FANUM
ISIDIS dug up in Tooley
Street, Southwark in
1912, but not
necessarily from the
Iseum

22 The *cella* of the Iseum at Pompeii. This, the largest known Iseum in which all the architectural details can be studied, was built on the site of another, destroyed by an earthquake seventeen years before the eruption of Vesuvius in AD 79. The mixed style of architecture, blending Egyptian and Hellenistic principles, accords with the syncretism of the cult. Neither its modest dimensions nor its mural decorations compare with the Alexandrian Sarapeum

23 Wall-painting of an Isiac ceremony. Before the temple door a
priest with cropped head holds Nile water in the sacred vase inside
his robe. At right is a priestess with sistrum and situla. Another priest
fans the sacred fire. A choir of both sexes participates, ranged in four
rows. Note the ibis roaming about, the sphinxes adorned with the
lotus, and the palms on either side of the temple, bordered with other
trees, in place of stone pillars

24, 25 Isiac wall-paintings from Pompeii. *Above*, Isis Fortuna, from a latrine corridor wall. *Below*, the Adoration of the Mummy of Osiris, from the Ecclesiasterion of the Iseum

26, 27 *Above*, Divine Service, with sacred dance, at Herculaneum.
Below, the Reception by Isis of Io into Egypt. Seated near Isis is the
infant Harpocrates. From the Iseum at Pompeii

28–30 The worshippers of Isis. *Above left*, a votive statue attired in contemporary fashion and, *right*, remnants of the Isiac priests' meal, both from the Iseum at Pompeii. *Below*, relief of a procession of priests and priestesses holding the sacred symbols

Certainly for any pagan theologian used to the syncretistic method current in the Graeco-Roman world Isis *myrionymos* was an inexhaustible treasure. The title was significantly even wider than *polyonymos*, 'many-named'. This epithet could be applied to Isis herself.[5] It was borne by certain members of the Greek pantheon—Aphrodite and Apollo, Helios and Hermes and it was besought as a gift from Zeus by Artemis, who held the title with the same special rights as Isis, with queenly powers on earth, in the underworld and in the sky. Isis, however, was the only divinity whose epiclesis marked that the number of her names was not merely large but even infinite. It was in this endless diversity that her uniqueness rested. It was the source of her strength, and weakness. She alone claimed an infinity of divine titles: and became all things to all men. She could be 'chaste' and yet raise high the phallus. She could banish life's storms by her calm, and yet be the Roman goddess of war.

Lucius is told some of the important names when Isis visits him. In a remarkably fine periodic sentence[6] where the danger of a bare aretalogical list is avoided by the rhetorician's skill, the goddess achieves the climax by keeping 'Isis' till the very end. She is the mother of Nature, the mistress of the elements, the first beginning of all generations. She represents the fully assembled pantheon of Greece and Rome. Queen of the underworld and first lady of heaven, she is a single shape with the features of all the gods and goddesses. She controls the vault of heaven, the blasts of ocean and the silent realm of the dead. She is the one and only divinity worshipped by all the world, despite the local peculiarities of her ritual, the variations in her ceremonial and the complexity of her names. The Athenians know her as Minerva (Athena), the Cypriots as Venus (Aphrodite), the Cretans as Dictynna Diana (Artemis), the Sicilians as Proserpina (Persephone), and the Eleusinians as 'the age-old goddess Ceres' (Demeter). Here she is Juno (Hera) and there the War Goddess. Some call her Hecate, others Rhamnusia (Nemesis). But to her own peoples in Ethiopia and Egypt she is unmistakably known by her true name, Queen Isis.

The transformation of Isis into Greece's most typical goddess Athena, as we have already seen, was an easy step after the introduction of the Saite divinity Neith into the Osirian myth. Neith had become the protectress of Lower Egypt from the middle of the seventh century BC and was honoured in her temple at Sais on the one hand as Athena—warrior and weaver—and on the other as Isis—male as well as female, guardian of the dead, and patroness of medicine. With Neith was especially associated the Festival of the Lamps, the *Lychnokaia*, which like that of the Lamps of Isis, the *Lychnapsia*, lasted all through the night.[7] Isis and Athena were also pre-eminent for their wisdom and subtlety, which they could exert in their dealings with the King of the Gods. But not all the mythological details could be squared in the 'Greek interpretation' (to say nothing of the five Minervas current in Roman interpretation),[8] for fundamentally Isis was a sister-spouse and Athena a chaste unmarried virgin, the one peaceably staying at home and the other warlike rushing into battle. Diodorus, writing at the turn of the first century BC, has much to tell us about the hellenized Egyptian religion of his day. He specifies the Athenians as followers of it: their Eumolpidae and Heralds have been imported from Egypt and the Athenians 'alone among the Greeks swear by Isis and show the greatest resemblance to the Egyptians in their usages'.[9] This ought not to mislead us into imagining that the goddess of the Nile ever took possession of the temple built by Pericles for the virgin protectress of his city. In Athens Isis was never fully naturalized.[10]

Perhaps the assimilation of Isis to Athena's Roman counterpart, Minerva, was easier. The hold that Isis won over the Romans arose from her control over warfare, generalship and victory. Already in the third century BC a gem from Campania could show an Isis-Victoria of Alexandrian type with a palm branch in her hand, and according to the Oxyrhynchus *Litany* Isis in the Saite nome was known as Athena (*i.e.* Neith) 'the victorious'. The 'Roman interpretation', as we can see from Apuleius, identified the goddess who came in triumph from Egypt equally with Minerva and Bellona, the national War Goddess. Bellona, as sister, wife and daughter of that most Roman god Mars, himself originally the vegetation divinity Silvanus, bore some resemblance in Rome to Isis in Egypt. Along with Minerva, the Italian

counterpart of Athena, the Roman Goddess of War[11] merged into
the Panthea from Egypt among whose countless titles were
'triumphalis' and 'victrix', the *triumphant* and *victorious*.[12]

Other evidence can be found that in the Roman mind the links
were close between Minerva and Isis. Thus the Iseum of the
Campus Martius was part of a complex of buildings and near its
northern side to the west stood the Temple of Minerva Chalcidica. On the site today stands the Church of S. Maria sopra
Minerva, with part of the Iseum beneath it (*Pls. 41–43*).[13] We
may notice also that in the Roman calendar the dates of the Quin-
quatria, the Greater Holiday of Minerva, were from 19–23 March,
but that on the second of the five days an Egyptian Festival was
interposed called Pelusia the theme of which was fundamental in
the cult of Isis—securing the annual inundation of the Nile by
sympathetic magic.[14]

It is the glory of classical Greece to have portrayed gods with
human features. The Greek pantheon was anthropomorphic.
Hellenic sculptors did not carve Athena as though she were a
vulture, or Artemis as a cat, or Apollo as a falcon,[15] or Aphrodite
as a cow. The zoolatrous mythology of Egypt and the whole
tradition of its religious art created very serious problems when
the time came for their Hellenization. It is sometimes held[16] that
Isis herself underwent a complete transformation into a Greek
goddess and that after her voyage over the waters she acquired an
entirely new personality, with a radiantly youthful countenance
borrowed from Aphrodite. This is part of the story, but not the
whole of it. For one thing, the Egyptian divinity whom the
Greeks had for long regarded as Aphrodite was Hathor, the great
heavenly cow. Hathor had much in common with Isis.[17] She too
could suckle the Pharaoh and nourish living creatures with her
milk. As the Good Cow she could help the dead when they
entered the World Yonder. Like Isis she was a guardian of the
female sex. Her statue too was exposed for veneration at sunrise.
Hathor resembled Isis at Pompeii in that as her bovine emblem she
often wore the crescent moon or had a woman's head with two
horns and the solar disk as a crown above.[18] Hathor's principal
sanctuary was at Dendera. There she and Isis enjoyed the closest

friendship. As far back as the thirteenth century BC Ramesses II could be portrayed with each of the two on either side endowing him with life. Before the end of the pre-Christian era complete assimilation enabled Isis to absorb Hathor and sometimes to wear the head of a cow, the animal sacred to both goddesses, after the name of which she could be called as Isis/Io by Roman writers.

The task of Alexandrian syncretism was not easy. The agricultural piety of the Egyptians had created the national goddess of love and joy in the shape of a sacred cow. The time had now come to establish harmony between this bovine conception and the Greek ideal of beauty, the apotheosis of lovely womanhood, Aphrodite. How could the perfect features of Aphrodite be disfigured with the ears of a cow? Moreover, Hathor was essentially a sky-divinity, whereas the Greek goddess of love in popular belief was the offspring of ocean, arose from its foam as Aphrodite Anadyomene, and was borne from Cythera over the waves to Cyprus, a voyage which was to be emulated by Isis Pelagia.[19] In the equation of the Egyptian and Hellenic goddesses certain further awkward problems emerged. However hard it tried, Greek interpretation could discover nothing in the legends about Hathor and Isis analogous to Aphrodite's wedding with the lame blacksmith fire-god Hephaestus and her liaison with Ares, god of war, an episode which had once shocked the moral sentiment of Plato and ill-accorded with the view of Isis as steadfast to her husband and watchful of her family.

From the death of Alexander until the absorption of the land of the Pharaohs into the Roman Empire, a Macedonian dynasty, the Lagidae, ruled with absolutely divine right. The Ptolemies and their wives received all the traditional Egyptian adoration that belonged to kingly godhead. The political and religious climate was that of the Nile, but those who governed the country were Greeks. Of course, they thought not as fifth-century Athenians but as Alexandrians—and they thought in Greek. The free thinkers of Athens never dreamt of accepting Pericles as an Oriental despot and worshipping him with divine honours, as Egypt treated the Ptolemies. Yet the statesman whose vision was to make the Athenian Acropolis the most beautiful place in the world was separated by the gap of only a single century from that other genius of the Greek spirit whose goal was to build a pan-cosmic Hellas with its centre at his own eponymous city of Alexandria.

Alexander and his Ptolemaic successors, like Pericles, had Greek as their mother tongue. It was natural, therefore, that with an increase of settlers from Greece the Hellenization of Egypt and in particular of its religion, should proceed apace. We see this happening in various ways. The names of famous cult centres acquired a Greek look. *On*, the ancient city of the sun, was already known to Herodotus as Heliopolis, and *Wnw*, the city of Thoth, as Hermopolis. The renaming of other cities can be exemplified with Heracleopolis, Letopolis and Aphroditopolis, each called after the Hellenic divinity who seemed to fit the local cult best. Parallels to this procedure can be discovered if we turn to a modern gazetteer and search the continents for place-names having some derivational link with the Latin *sanctus* or with the Biblical *Maria*.

The Greeks who took up residence along the banks of the Nile looked for reminders of their homeland and of their colonial exploits and chose names evocative of their own religious tradition. To the west of Memphis was a plateau in the area of Saqqara, proved by present-day archaeological excavations to be one of the key sites,[20] and here were the tombs of the dead Apis bulls. To this hill the Greeks gave the name of Sinope. The name was borne both by the daughter of Asopus in Greek mythology and by the flourishing Greek colony on the Black Sea which, whatever significance it had for the birth of the Sarapis cult, was clearly the abode of a colossal statue of Hellenic Pluto.

At Memphis Herodotus went to see the temple 'of the foreign Aphrodite', the goddess Astarte worshipped by the Phoenicians from Tyre who dwelt in the vicinity.[21] This 'Aphrodite' Herodotus informs us he inferred to be the same as Helen daughter of Tyndarus. His regular practice is to hellenize the names of the native mythology. Not only is Hathor Aphrodite, but Isis is Demeter, Osiris Dionysus, Amun Zeus, Bast Artemis, and Ptah Hephaestus. According to Herodotus, the names of almost all the

Egyptian gods have been imported into Greece, although he cannot find the equivalents for Poseidon, the Dioscuri and Hera.
The Alexandrian theologians solved this conundrum by con-
verting Hera as the queen of the Olympian pantheon into Isis,
and by granting Isis in addition the omnipotence of Poseidon over
the ocean and ultimate responsibility for the deliverance of sailors
by her agents, the Dioscuri. The Greek expert Timotheus
summoned by Ptolemy Soter to be one of his religious advisers
was only carrying out professionally what many of his com-
patriots had tried to do in Egypt, to reach a rational synthesis.

When Greek exegesis interpreted Egyptian mythology's picture
of the goddess of love, Isis was the obvious choice.[22] The Ptolemaic queens who were to be accorded divine honours and worshipped for their womanly beauty could not appear as Egyptian
Hathors, with horns and bovine ears. The only acceptable
apotheosis was that which identified Isis with Aphrodite and
granted them, at least in name, the ideal loveliness of Greece. So
Berenice I, the wife of Ptolemy Soter, was deified as Aphrodite,
and had a city called after her in that style. Arsinoe II, wife of
Ptolemy Philadelphus, was worshipped simultaneously as
Aphrodite and Isis.[23] When Isis appeared in this form, Hellenistic
convention struck out on a new path. Here the sister-wife of
Osiris, the sorrowful Isis of the *Pyramid Texts*, was but barely
visible through the Egyptian tokens that were revealed on her
head. Otherwise she was a completely nude young woman, like
an Aphrodite by Praxiteles or Scopas. The iconography must have
been evolved in the Ptolemaic age in an important centre such as
Alexandria or Memphis. The type is that of a goddess who
presides over physical love, marriage and the fruitfulness of
women. In the manner of Greek sculpture the figure is almost
always undraped. Very seldom the body is covered with the
Greek chiton or himation with the Isis-knot on the breast.[24] One
aspect of this identification of Isis with Aphrodite is strongly
Egyptian. Figures with the dual name have been found on gems,
bronzes and terracottas buried in graves, a fact which indicates
that hellenized Isis could still be treated as a 'bride of the dead'.[25]
The bold Hellenistic treatment of the Isis-Aphrodite identification

can be observed in passages from the Hymns. Thus Isis is described (like Aphrodite) as having been born 'by Uranus the son of night on the gleaming waves of the sea' and as bearing the titles 'fire of Hades, the Underworld's wedding song, and the loves of the goddess of Cyprus'.[26] Both archaeological and epigraphical evidence, therefore, supports the view that Isis merged herself successfully into the Greek Aphrodite and the Roman Venus, the Venus who confronts us, for example, in the famous exordium of Lucretius' poem *On the Nature of Things*.[27]

We are not told by Apuleius what speech Isis used in her address to Lucius. Language would have presented no problem to one who was held to have arranged all the different tongues of Greeks and barbarians. At Cenchreae she might have been expected to talk in Greek, though Latin names are put into her mouth by the author. She certainly did not puzzle Lucius with spoken hieroglyphics, for she was talking as Isis *myrionymos*, with a list of identifications of which the whole Graeco-Roman world was well aware. The list introduces the Mother of the Gods, the Magna Mater of Phrygia. Then Isis enumerates the Graeco-Roman triad, Athena-Minerva, Aphrodite-Venus and Artemis-Diana. Here again, as we have so often seen, in Artemis are to be found characteristic qualities that bring her into line with Isis. But the detailed discussion of this topic must be reserved for the present. We need only notice that the Cretan Artemis with whom Isis identifies herself was a Mother-Virgin, Dictynna-Britomartis.

Next in the title catalogue we meet 'Stygian Proserpine' and 'ancient Ceres', *i.e.* Demeter and her daughter, Kore-Persephone.[28] Union with Demeter is much easier to understand than with Artemis. Indeed, we meet this identification constantly in Greek writers, and the resemblances spring to the modern mind at once. We find Herodotus writing 'Demeter' for 'Isis'. At the end of the fourth century BC Leo of Pella, author of a work *On the Gods in Egypt*, stresses the identification and still later Diodorus remarks that of all the Greek goddesses he mentions the one who comes nearest to Isis is Demeter.[29] The affinities are at once evident. Both were goddesses of the crops and givers of men's daily bread.[30] Both were protective deities of the departed. Each had suffered bereavement and had been driven to set out on a long journey in the search for a lost relative. Each could be said to have known grief. Even when Isis was carved by the Greek sculptors as a figure of love and joy, one of her emblems was still the sistrum, and the sistrum could spell mourning.[31] Here indeed we touch upon an apparent discrepancy. Isis-Aphrodite conveys the fresh joy of the spring and glow of life, whereas Isis-Demeter portends decay of vegetation in the autumn and winter and gloom of death. Such seeming inconsistencies were pointed out even in ancient times. So the rationalist Eudoxus queried the equation of Demeter with Isis[32] on the ground that the former was not involved in the affairs of the human heart, whereas (like Aphrodite and her son Eros) Isis certainly was.[33] But this kind of objection was pooh-poohed by popular piety. The fertility symbols, the grain measure or *modius* and the ears of corn, could be worn just as well by Isis as by Demeter and her daughter Persephone (*Pl. 7*).

In her homeland Isis could assume the role of Mā'et,[34] who though the personification of Truth, Righteousness and Justice was a shadowy abstraction. Far more graphic was the Hellenistic portrayal of Isis under the title which was peculiarly Demeter's: *Thesmophorus*, 'the lawgiver'. When viewed in this guise she was known as 'the Rhamnusian goddess' in the Latin of Apuleius and in Greek as Themis and Nemesis, both champions of justice at Rhamnus, a coastal town not far from Athens. Isis now typified divine anger, retribution for the evildoer. Upholder of the moral law, she could be lauded as having made Nature distinguish things fair and base, as the divine queen 'whose eye sees everything everywhere on the face of land and sea', and as 'Mistress of all things for ever'.[35] From Isis Thesmophorus sinners could not escape. As Nemesis she was inexorable and as Adrasteia inevitable.[36]

In comparison with Athena and Aphrodite, Artemis and Demeter, Hellenic Hera under her own name tends to seem un-important for the evolution of Isis Panthea.[37] In Egyptian mytho-logy, as Herodotus pointed out, no ready counterpart existed for Hera, though a later Greek writer could declare Osiris had built a temple for his parents 'Zeus and Hera', *i.e.* Geb and Nut.[38] It was as Queen of Heaven that Isis replaced Hera. Instead of the name

Hera/Juno she generally preferred to be styled 'Queen'[39] or 'Lady', 'Mistress' or 'The Almighty', *Pantocrateira*.[40] After this with her untold wealth of titles she could take the one that pleased her best. She could assume the eagle of Zeus and dolphin of Poseidon, the lyre of Apollo and tongs of Hephaestus, the wand of Hermes, the thyrsus of Bacchus and the club of Heracles.[41] It can hardly have been an accident that Hadrian built his Pantheon to replace Agrippa's in the Campus Martius not far from the home of Isis Panthea.

From the foundation of Alexandria till the official acceptance by Constantine of Christianity as the state religion of the Roman empire, ancient polytheism strove hard to survive by readaptation. Under the influence of Isis it experienced a remarkable transformation. She integrated it. She claimed to break down national barriers. Whatever deities the nations worshipped were only manifestations of herself. Having founded their temples and taught men to adore their statues[42] she came as the champion of polytheism. Yet even more strongly she asserted she was herself the one True and Living God.

CHAPTER X

THE ALL-LOVING MOTHER

IN THE HISTORY of Mediterranean civilization the worship of a Divine Mother is of great antiquity. We have seen that in Egyptian mythology Isis and Osiris were not themselves primordial. Both were represented as the offspring of Sky and Earth. Isis was also fundamentally inseparable from her brother, as the two were born to be together. But in the world of the Aegean where the religious ideas of the Greeks took shape, the All-Mother was much more ancient than the All-Father.[1] We see this both in Asia Minor and in Crete, itself the centre of Aegean civilization and the great entrepôt for cultural exchange between Egypt, the Asiatic coastland east of Greece, and the western Mediterranean. Cybele, the Phrygian Mother of the Gods, and the Cretan Universal Mother,[2] whether called Rhea or Dictynna, were omnipotent long before any male divinity had evolved from a purely tribal totem into a universal father figure. Asia Minor provides us with proofs that already 6000 years BC Neolithic man was worshipping the Mother of All Living, who is portrayed in shrines excavated at Çatal Hüyük, in the area south of Phrygia proper and not far distant from the cult centre of Cybele at Pessinus, the burial place of her beloved Attis.[3]

Before Lucius is told by Isis at Cenchreae what are her Graeco-Roman names he hears her call herself 'Mother of the Gods',[4] a title which she informs him the Phrygians use, being a primordial people and attaching it to Pessinus. The next moment Lucius learns that Isis is also Artemis/Diana of Mount Dicte in Crete. The writer Apuleius clearly intends his readers to regard the Egyptian goddess as indifferently the Asian Mother of the Gods at Pessinus[5] and the Cretan Great Goddess at Dicte. In these theological combinations no problem arises. The Hellenistic world was familiar with Cybele, the *Magna Mater* of Pessinus, who had been welcomed into Rome at the end of the third century BC and given an abode on the Palatine.[6] Cybele possessed all the attributes of the Universal Mother in Crete: for Greek and Roman eclectics the two were one. Both Phrygia and Crete had a Mount Ida, and on their crests and in their caverns the orgiastic worship of the Mother Goddess could be carried out at Pessinus by the Corybantes and in Crete by the Curetes. It was natural enough, therefore, that Isis as she became a pancosmic figure should fuse with the primordial Divine Mother of Asia Minor and Crete,[7] as indeed she did with the Ishtar of Assyrian and Babylonian mythology. Already in the year 131/130 BC an Alexandrian priest, *hieropolos*, is found as the minister of 'Isis the Great Mother of the Gods' and the double title is assumed by Cleopatra. At Delos a dedication is offered to 'Isis, Mother of the Gods, Astarte'.[8] In Italy a priest at Brundisium and another at Ostia served both Isis and the Mother of the Gods and at Ostia in like manner a single minister officiated at either's shrine.[9]

Cybele of Phrygia and the Universal Mother of Crete were fertility goddesses. They personified Nature as the source of life, a conception of divinity which as the figures from Çatal Hüyük so well reveal had taken hold of the human mind even in the Neolithic period. The Egyptian idea of Isis came much nearer to the observed facts of human motherhood, in all the multiplicity of its manifestations. For Cybele a handsome young paramour Attis was invented, as Tammuz in Babylonia for Ishtar and Adonis in Phoenicia for Astarte. Isis had a blood-brother as husband. To him and the son in whose person lived the father Isis was forever faithful. The rites associated with Cybele, wearing the turreted crown and carrying the whip, where her Galatian priests in their riot turned themselves into eunuchs, were altogether foreign to Isis of the Nile. Mountaineering orgies belonged to other mythological traditions. Isis loved the family and home.

A human mother seldom exhibits to her children a steady and unswerving uniformity of behaviour. The same is true of Isis. In the *Pyramid Texts* she rejoices for love of Osiris as he impregnates her. But as she laments him the sweat pours from her body. She can appear as a great and kindly protectress: yet there is also 'her evil coming'.[10] In the *Lamentations* her heart grieves for Osiris, whom she loves more than all the earth, and whom she avenges before Horus. We can be sure, therefore, that the view of Isis as a wife and mother with deep human feelings was immemorially old, and probably predynastic. What is so striking is the naturalness of her emotions, judged by ordinary human standards, the strength of her loyalty, and the purity of her character in the family setting.[11]

Clearly the figure of Isis showed strong contrasts. Of her it could be stated in the Oxyrhynchus *Litany* not only that she loved war but also that she loathed hostility. She could be either tenderhearted and loving or stern and angry. Just as in her family conduct she could maintain strict chastity so outside the home she might (like the Mother of the Gods) indulge in what from the Christian point of view is gross obscenity. She would burst into sobs at the death of her husband, but would not hide her maternal happiness as she suckled her babe at her breast. In course of time the picture of Isis was enriched with ever more detail drawn from non-Egyptian mythology and often transformed out of all recognition. The danger to theological coherence was real. For Isis to become all things to all men was to risk losing her oneness. It is remarkable that in spite of this she should have so deeply captivated her world. Ordinary people yielded to the charm of her endless variety and faith abolished the more glaring intellectual anomalies. Parallels may be sought for in Christian iconography. For example, the stern and forbidding Pantocrator[12] of the Monastery at Daphni stands in flat defiance of Holman Hunt's gentle Saviour in *The Light of the World*. In the same Monastery the Panaghia, her weary eyes swollen with sorrow, is an utterly different Mother of God from the untroubled and serenely girlish Sistine Madonna of Raphael.

For thousands of years, as the evidence in Asia Minor indicates, men's religious needs were best answered by their adoration of a Mother Figure. Even in the strictly patriarchal religion of Jewry her presence can be glimpsed as an influence at work in the background of the Diaspora. So Jeremiah, addressing 'all the Jews which dwell in the land of Egypt', complains that they have slipped back to practices known even 'in the cities of Judah, and in the streets of Jerusalem', as they have 'burned incense to the queen of heaven, and poured out drink offerings unto her',[13] the women making ritual cakes for her worship in which their husbands have joined.[14] In this passage we may consider Ishtar rather than Isis to be the appropriate goddess. The fact remains that in the Oxyrhynchus *Litany* the existence is asserted of cult centres either of Isis or some local and comparable goddess right along the shore of Palestine and Phoenicia: at Gaza, Askalon, Caesarea, Dora, Berytus and in general Syrophoenicia. Even in the land which it is customary to regard as indisputably Yahweh's the belief in an omnipotent Mother Goddess seems to have exerted strong attractions. From the passage of Jeremiah it is clear that such a deity was revered as a fertility figure: when the Jews in Egypt offered her their cakes, then they had 'plenty of victuals'.

Isis, by identification with the Mother of the Gods, became without question the Life Force, indwelling Nature, wherever she gained adherents. She was conspicuous now, not merely on the banks of the Nile, but all along the shores of the Mediterranean and further. In her homeland she had been said to be mighty on the earth and great in the Underworld, to make the Nile flood to swell and to embrace and fructify the field, creating all that exists.[15] Now she performed all these functions on a pancosmic scale. We find Isis praised with awe and wonder by Apuleius as Venus is by Lucretius for giving life to all things dwelling in the air, amid the sea and on the ground, fauna and flora. Her power controls the winds, the seasons, and the revolution of the heavens. From her springs the light of the sun. When Lucius falls down flat before her image and presses his tear-stained face against it, calling on her through his broken sobs, his utter abasement bears witness to his feelings of insignificance and unworthiness before the divine majesty. It is a direct encounter between a human wretch and the Almighty Lady.

Yet Lucius, awed as he is, has never abandoned hope of a personal talk with his loving Mother. His opening words set the keynote. 'Hallowed and everlasting Saviour of the human race', he exclaims, 'Thou dost always bestow thy dear love on wretched men in their mishaps.' We must remember that at this moment he has stayed for several days in silent contemplation of the statue of Isis, to whom he is pledged because she has shown him a kindness he can never hope to pay back. His hymn of praise marks the climax of a continuous communion with the affectionate Mother who is ready to save and redeem him. Clad in his linen robe with a torch in full flame held in his right hand and a garland of white palm leaves wreathing his temples, Lucius is brought into full view as the witness of an unswerving faith in the goddess. She who (as Plutarch describes her) has herself endured contests and struggles and in her most hallowed mysteries has blended ideas and representations of her own sufferings in order that ordinary men and women in the grip of similar misfortunes may learn godliness and find comfort from her.[16] His faith is founded on a person in whose love and ability to understand suffering he can pin his deepest hopes.

There were, of course, other saviour divinities in pagan antiquity.[17] They reveal themselves, as Isis does, in the mysteries. The Mother of the Gods can be worshipped, just like Isis, as one who is tender and gracious and who bestows calm and salvation on those who submit to her cleansing initiation. Artemis is conspicuous as a saviour. Isis is the acknowledged champion of those who most direly need help. At times of greatest hazard she steps in when all natural means of rescue seem impossible just like the stock *deus ex machina* at the end of a Greek tragedy. Isis is the one divinity to whose higher authority Fate (*Heimarmene*) has at once to bow. Lucius pays homage to his august Mother because she can unravel the web of Destiny, so twined and twisted together that no other hands than hers know the secret of disentanglement, can tame the storms of Fortune, and can check the harmful ways of the stars. In the list of her praises from the Oxyrhynchus *Litany* we read in succession the titles 'giver of favours', 'gentle' and 'affectionate'; yet she is afterwards magnified as one to whom 'the spirits' (the *demons*, or as Apuleius calls them 'the elements') have to show obedience. True to the tradition of her native Egypt, where the peasant in the fields was never idle, Isis toiled without rest on behalf of her beloved human family, sheltering them on land and sea, banishing the storms that beset their lives, and stretching out to them the strong right hand of a Saviour.

In her service is perfect freedom. Lucius is told by the priest who is concerned with his conversion: 'Having begun to be the servant of the goddess, you will afterwards feel all the more the enjoyment of your freedom.'[18] The compassionate Mother will prove to her faithful children that her yoke is easy and her burden light. Indeed, she will show men their salvation while they are fast asleep with their physical eyes closed. So it is said that 'she stands beside the sick in their dreams providing remedies for their illnesses and if they declare to her their obedience then they regain their health contrary to all expectation.'[19] What is required is faith. It is faith that inspires Lucius during his period of fasting. It is faith that leads Isiac pilgrims to practise incubation in the Sarapeum at Canopus. Certainly, Isis gives her children the sure hope of eternal salvation: but in return she demands of them unquestioning, even blind obedience, just as she subjects them to the most gruelling tests before they reach the haven of their rest. The lesson is an old and perhaps trite one which meets us in epic poetry, but in the religion of Isis it becomes almost a dogma. The faithful must sometimes toil for long without reward before the everlasting arms of their Mother are suddenly reached out to rescue them. Theirs must be a faith that is held blindly, just as their bodies dream blindly when they sleep. Isis was renowned for making those who angered her lose their sight and make public confession that they had done wrong and earned punishment, though if she chose she could help them to see again.[20] She gave her support to those who trusted her.

The saviour divinity of the mystery religions was personally involved in the well-being of mankind.[21] Experience of human suffering, and even the sharing in it, were characteristic. The *mystes* looked to a divine power by whom his prayers would be directly heard and his salvation eternally assured. Isis in her aretalogy boldly asserted that she had been responsible for revealing the mysteries to men. To her indeed they appealed in their distress more than to any other, for all were embraced within her, in the sure hope of consolation and comfort. 'Isis,' they can be thought to have cried, 'In thy black robe have mercy upon us.'[22] The initiate was alone with his Mother. He talked confidentially. She listened compassionately. How different it was from trying to climb Mount Olympus! There dwelt the exalted but remote hierarchy of the Greek pantheon in splendid isolation. They seemed like the gods envisaged by Lucretius in the *intermundia*, fictitious creatures in unknown regions of outer space, quite unconcerned with ordinary human affairs. In the post-Alexandrian world where men and women were so often shaken and disillusioned by the spectacle of crumbling or fallen political edifices small comfort was to be expected from the Olympians. Millions of people at that time must have yearned for a personal colloquy about their hopes and fears with those august and heavenly aristocrats—but all in vain. Isis hearkened to them. Time might pass before she intervened: but she hearkened. Under this aspect she was known like Sarapis as *Epekoos*, a title borne by other pagan redeemers such as the Mother of the Gods and the Healer Asclepius.[23] Here a parallel is provided for us by Christianity. In the nomenclature of the Greek Orthodox Church the Mother of God is ever 'swift to hear'.[24] In ikons the Panagia is found as *Gorgoepekoos*. The name is reminiscent of Isis *Epekoos* and of the 'speed (*gorgotes*) and power' shown on a certain occasion to the ancient Aristides as he was walking out through the vestibule of the Iseum at Smyrna after performing sacrifice.[25] Isis and the Panagia are characterized as being the very reverse of deaf.

Vitruvius, an authority on Roman architecture, contrasts the siting of temples to such Olympian deities as Jupiter, Juno and Minerva with those to Isis and Sarapis. The traditional champions of city-states have their dwelling high on an acropolis, whereas the Egyptian pair are worshipped in a market place.[26] This clear distinction made by an expert observer brings out the relative standing of the old conservative religion and the freshly imported Alexandrian faith, culturally and symbolically as well as topographically. Isis and her companion gods from Egypt gain a foothold in Italian cities by a readiness to take a comparatively low rank. She enters as the friend of the masses. She makes her home hard by the business and trading centre where she can be near and dear to the common man. She is in the fullest sense Love. Looked at from below in the *forum* the Lord and Ladies of the Capitoline Triad can seem aristocratically aloof to the lowly folk who need divine help at their own level (*Pl. 17*).

Such then was the contrast which existed in public worship. In the life of the family, as Pompeii well reveals, the Egyptian cult easily blended with the native household guardians, the Genius, the Lares and the Penates. Domestic Isiacism flourished in a completely eclectic atmosphere. A Pompeian Lararium has yielded bronze statues of Isis-Fortuna surrounded by the Olympians. Isis in this guise has been found in association with Jupiter and Hercules, as well as with Venus Anadyomene and the ophio-morphous Agathodaemon.[27] A bizarre mural of Isis-Fortuna in the corridor leading to the latrine depicts two sacred serpents, incarnations both of Agathodaemon and of the Genius of the family, warning a naked young man about coming to harm when he empties his bowels there (*Pl. 24*).[28]

The Isiac cult, of course, was only one of several exotic arrivals which set a new fashion in the spiritual life of Italy even before the end of the Republic. The Great Mother Cybele of Ida, as the ostensible giver of victory to the Romans over the most stubborn foe in their history, was granted a home high on the Palatine. Sulla introduced the fertility goddess Ma. Foreign recruits in the Roman army conveyed their own religious imports. Thus the Syrians were responsible for the appearance of Baltis and Atargatis. Jupiter Dolichenus, Sabazius and the Yahweh of Jewry were respected Levantine immigrants.[29] The soldiers who fought Rome's battles on her eastern borders were active in assimilating to the occident the sun god of Persia, Mithras. His central rite of the *tauroctonium* (like the *taurobolium* of Cybele) fascinated the pagan mind as the eucharistic meal did the Christian. His highest grade of 'Father' and even his name could be held by a priest of Isis.[30]

The welter of foreign faiths in the Roman world made the task of a final victory of one over the others a long and hard war of relentless attrition. Isis stood her ground well. In the public life of the Italian city her votaries had a certain advantage of locality, for the market could overhear the sound of her praises or on special occasions witness her image brought forth as they walked forth in procession. Of course her religion had also its secret side, as with Mithraism and the other cults in which a mystery was enacted. But, to use a Pauline phrase which if out of context is here surely applicable, Isis of the market place was never 'far from every one' and her abode was always a landmark. Odd facts confirm that this was general. At Pompeii the priests of Isis placarded their temple with an election notice.[31] In London a jug found near the Thames at Southwark bore as its determinative inscription 'At Isis' Temple'[32] (Pl. 21). In Rome Plotinus the philosopher was taken to the Iseum as 'the one unsoiled spot in Rome'.[33] But for baser folk in the Italian capital the same temple could mean little else than a brothel. So Roman poetry regards Isis not as the chaste and loving wife and mother but as a lady of easy virtue, countenancing the sexual enjoyments and love-making. It was this moral looseness which we are told by Josephus led to a scandal in the very shrine of the goddess. A noble lady was seduced by her lover dressed up as Anubis and the offence sternly punished by Tiberius, who shut the temple, split the statue to smithereens, and crucified the priests *en bloc*.

From these anecdotes it cannot be doubted that Isis personified love throughout its spectrum. In her the believer could discover the warm affection of the bereaved wife, the tenderness of the mother suckling her baby as Isis the *Kourotrophos*, the concern of the midwife for the safe delivery of women in childbirth, the sexual passion symbolized by the erect phallus and by the legend that she had played the harlot for ten years at Tyre, and eternal kindness towards those whom she embraced in life and sheltered after death. To many critics the picture may seem riddled with contradictions. But the evidence that Isis is mutilated by the removal of any of these elements is irrefutable.

How widely different popular and metaphysical interpretations of Isis as mother can be is visible by such illustrations as the following. A Roman poet invokes her as one who 'made her stable in a cavern at Argos' (*i.e.* as Io, transformed into a cow).[34] Plutarch, however, cites as Isiac doctrine the identification of the goddess with the Moon, regarded as mother of the world and yet with powers both male and female as she not only undergoes impregnation from the Sun but also emits generative forces of her own.[35] As a mean between these two extreme representations we may take the finely detailed description given by Apuleius. Here 'the Mother of all things in the universe' whom Lucius can feel to be his own as he afterwards kisses her feet is brilliantly portrayed both in colour and in detail of form—'dazzling light in the likeness of the moon shone above her forehead', she wore 'linen shimmering first with pure white, bright yellow like the colour of saffron, and then flaming red as a rose . . . on the surface scattered stars were glistening and in their midst the moon was shedding forth a flaming glow . . . in her right hand she held a rattle of bronze . . . from her left hand hung a ewer of gold . . . a serpent rose upwards rearing its head with wide-swelling throat' —and much else in a gorgeous and richly wrought characterization rounded off imaginatively: 'breathing spice-laden odours of Araby the blest'.[36]

Egyptian religion never emerged into a lasting monotheism. In its history antilogies lay buried that could not be uprooted. Even after the Ptolemaic reformation it could not produce out of its depths a complete answer to the fundamental problems of theology: creation, the balance between divine immanence and transcendence, man's freedom of action, and the immortality of the soul. Its primitive creation story started with an act of masturbation.[37] The weakness in the position of Osiris, transcendently secure though he was, was his impermanence in the world where men lived. The individual's moral responsibility never occupied the mind of Egypt as it did the philosophers of Greece. The Egyptians again differed from the Greeks in that they were interested less in the immortality of the soul than in the resurrection of the body.

Isis, being of Egyptian parentage, faced an impossible task when she set out to make the world forever her own. Sarapis and Isis could assume in Greece the title of 'the Great Deities'[38] but even with the help of an Osiris reconstituted as Sarapis Isis could not in

the end conceal her African pedigree. She was ineffectually
groping her way towards the impregnable security of a creed
that would have said no other gods existed and was seeking to
formulate the commandment 'Thou shalt have none other gods
but me'. In spite of all these difficulties, however, Isis for long
remained the world's almighty mistress in the minds and hearts
of her countless votaries. In her all-loving motherhood can be
seen the source of her power. Towards the world of which she
was in charge she was pleased to show the tenderest maternal
affection and personal care. If western civilization could have
somehow developed on a matriarchal basis, Isis might have been
too stubborn a mistress to dethrone.

CHAPTER XI

GREAT ARTEMIS-ISIS

ARTEMIS is at first sight a puzzling figure in Greek mythology. On the one hand we meet the young virgin of the chase and the forest, Hellenic Artemis Agrotera, vowed to perpetual chastity and filled with loathing for sex even when it is exercised within the marriage bond for the propagation of the human species. No less indubitably, however, there stands before us an Artemis ripe for motherhood, a fertility goddess from Asia Minor with her main cult centre at the Greek city of Ephesus. The ardent votaries of this Artemis are the Amazons. The Amazons (said in the Oxyrhynchus *Litany* to worship *Isis* as 'warlike')[1] do indeed indulge, once yearly, in sexual intercourse, but then simply for one reason, to produce girl descendants. They keep only their female children, who are brought up to emulate Artemis Agrotera[2] in hunting and their own mothers in pursuing warfare. Divine blending of Virgin and Mother contradicts human experience, for bringing forth a child means, for a woman, the loss of maidenhood. How are the two views of Artemis to be reconciled?

The secret seems to lie in the religious thinking of the Mediterranean world as early as the Mycenaean age. The Great Goddess was revered both as virgin and as mother. Kore the daughter and Demeter the mother were one person looked at under two aspects. Of the goddesses of the Greek Pantheon none is more obviously both virginal and maternal than Artemis. As the patroness of the woodlands she sets herself implacably against wedlock,[3] though she is ready to help married women in childbirth, and considered in this guise upholds the ideals of chastity and virginity. Artemis Agrotera symbolized the belief that for women there was a nobler state than being mated with a husband. It was this characteristic which endeared her to those who worshipped her on the Greek mainland. For the Greeks of Ionia, however, another Artemis was the Great Goddess, the Artemis who at Ephesus was the Lady of Fertility endowed with far more than her proper complement of breasts. Either view of Artemis was derived from roots that belonged to a much older period. The fact that in neither of the two aspects did the goddess mother a child of her own exhibited her absolute freedom from the ties that would have bound her to the male sex.

Artemis was recognized by the Greeks, as was her counterpart Diana by the Romans, as holding sway over the entire universe in its three separate realms: the heavens, the underworld, and the world where dwelt all those living things over which as Agrotera she presided:

> Through heaven I roll my lucid moon along;
> I shed in hell o'er my pale people peace;
> On earth I, caring for the creatures, guard
> All [things] that love green haunts and loneliness.

The name of Artemis was revered throughout Greek lands from the Pillars of Hercules to the Crimea, in the Peloponnese and Thrace, along the coast of Asia Minor and on the Aegean islands. She was the most popular of all the Greek goddesses. Her epicleses were many and her functions complicated. She presided over birth and growth. Wild nature was her peculiar joy. Sometimes, therefore, her features were theriomorphic. She ruled over the animal and vegetable kingdoms. She merged with Hecate to hold power equally in heaven and under the earth. Men paid honour to her both in association with her musician brother Apollo at the famous cult centres of Delos and Delphi and in combination with Hecate at crossroads as lunar and infernal divinity. Above all else, however, Artemis was the divine symbol of chastity and its particular guardian.

In the Hymn by Callimachus acclaiming her virtues the first gift for which she asked was perpetual virginity. Then she desired as many names as her brother and his power to draw the bow and bring shafts of light into the world. She would have sixty youthful maids of honour, would spend most of her time roaming the mountains, and would find just a single city enough for her. In the end Zeus granted his daughter cities in plenty both on the Greek mainland and in the Archipelago and made her the guardian of roads and harbours. Artemis then went to Mount Ida on Crete and from there to the ocean to select a large retinue of maids of honour. Having visited the Cyclopes in their island home north of Sicily she proceeded to Arcadia in southern Greece and thence to Mount Haemus in northern Thrace. Her first torch was cut from a pinetree on the mountain slope south of the Sea of Marmara.[4] Her sway was wide. No other member of the Olympic pantheon knew the mountains, the sea and the islands so typical of the geography of Greece better than Artemis.

How soon Artemis and Isis amalgamated cannot be known with certainty. The Oxyrhynchus *Litany* shows us that Isis was invoked as Artemis both in Crete at Dicte and in the Cyclades as the goddess 'of threefold nature'. We may think at first of an apparent stumbling-block, the declared resolve of Artemis to remain a virgin. But this virginal aspect, as we have seen, is but one of two, for at Ephesus she personifies female fruitfulness. Nor is Isis without another guise in her Egyptian setting. She and her sister Nephthys can be mimed in a piece of religious pageantry by two women, brought on to the scene 'with pure body' and each of them *virgo intacta*.[5] So also a Christian writer alludes to women who are 'singular for their chastity' as worshippers of Isis in her homeland. In the Roman calendar she gives her name to 'days of chastity', *puri dies*,[6] with which we may perhaps compare the ember days of the Christian church. The Isiac votary Lucius mentions 'the abstinence which the ascetic rites entail'. Examples occur in Latin poetry where Isis like Diana (Artemis' Roman counterpart) insists on continence. Thus the Delia of Tibullus in scrupulous fulfilment of Isiac rules washes herself, and clean in body and in soul sleeps by herself in an unstained bed. Cynthia, laments Propertius, must be absent from him in service to the goddess[7] night after night. How important sexual abstinence eventually came to be in Egyptian religion can be inferred also from the existence in the Sarapeum at Alexandria of special cells, *pastophoria*, occupied by those bearing the name of *hagneuontes*, 'pursuers of purity'.[8] Clearly Isis in the Graeco-Roman world could demand that sex be tabooed with the same stern authority as Artemis in Greek lands or Diana in Italy. We find Propertius bidding his Cynthia when released from peril to perform the rites of chastity. After her salvation from peril by day she must join those who dance in honour of Diana and for ten long nights she must keep vigil in the temple of Isis.[9] To each of them she owes it to remain pure.

Besides this there are other fundamental resemblances between Greece's great goddess of many names and Egypt's. Their cumulative effect strongly supports the view that when the time was ripe the identification was made easily. Paradoxically, both Artemis and Hellenistic Isis not only led men and women to abstain from sexual intercourse but also presided over birth and growth. Each goddess was almighty in the animal and vegetable kingdoms. Each had a peculiarly close association with the moon. Both were mighty queens in the underworld, where they cast light upon the dead in their darkness. Both rejoiced in processions and in festivals of lights. Both delighted in possessing manifold names. Hellenistic Isis like Artemis assumed the character of 'lady of the ocean'. Like Artemis *Limenitis*, *Limenoscopos*, she had a particular regard for harbours. Like her she could control the winds that blew upon the waters. Like her she was renowned for sudden interventions in human affairs when all other means of salvation had failed.[10] Lastly, Artemis/Diana both in classical and in prehistoric times could acquire a pancosmic significance, which at once united her with Isis *Pantocrateira*, 'all-ruling'. The identification is historically more important than any other and needs to be more deeply stressed than has been done in the past. In the Egyptian religion there existed the theocratic doctrine of Mother and Child. In the final stages of development the Mother Figure was reshaped by devout belief to assimilate the Greek divinity who more obviously than any other championed virginity.

The union did not happen all at once, nor was it necessarily accepted as Isiac dogma. For one thing, not all those whom the faith attracted were spiritually minded. A divine power with the myriad names of Isis made an infinitely varied appeal. The religious needs of worshippers of little intellect and sometimes perhaps even less moral conscience differed much from those of philosophers and theorists. In general, too, the view of Isis taken by women dwelt on the refining and feminine qualities whereas for at least some male adherents the cult was an excuse for unashamed libertinism. The girl who at Chaeronea vowed herself as a virgin to Isis for the remainder of her life[11] anticipated the Catholic nun and the Haghiorite monk. The figure of the chaste wife and mourner, of ancient Egyptian descent, foreshadowed the Panagia and Madonna of Christendom. Coarser interpretations, however, stressed the link with the fertility goddesses.

Isiacism suffered from the lack of a systematic theology. The brief sketch by Plutarch stands alone. What Egyptian religion never produced was an Origen or an Augustine who might have taken up the task begun by Manetho and Timotheus and have introduced bold and drastic changes in Greek and Roman 'interpretation'. There can be no doubt that well before the beginning of the Christian era the assimilation between Isis and Artemis had been achieved. The Oxyrhynchus *Litany* indicates that Isis was widely acclaimed like Artemis in the islands of the Aegean as 'triple-natured' and in Asia Minor as goddess 'of the cross-roads'.[12] At Delos an Athenian who was twice priest of Sarapis seems clearly to have equated 'holy Artemis' with Isis.[13] In Macedonia, where Artemis is shown by the numismatic evidence to have been held in the highest honour, she and Isis were closely linked. Thus at Philippi in the first century BC Isis Regina and Bendis-Artemis were worshipped in the same sector.[14] At Beroea a marble dedicatory plaque formerly used as part of the Holy Table in a church exhibits Isis with the sistrum in her hand under the epiclesis of Lochia.[15] Here she is evidently both the city's patroness and the protectress of women in childbirth, exerting the function traditionally assumed in Greece by Artemis. She is the same Isis to whom the poet Ovid appeals, identifying her with Diana, as his mistress Corinna hovers in labour between life and death.

Seen in the light of the Christian dispensation which followed the downfall of paganism, the fusion of Isis with Artemis has historical significance, but it marks a departure from a Greek interpretation which seems to have been traditional. Herodotus specifically distinguishes Isis from Artemis by conflating the one with Demeter and the other with Bast. The natural consequence is for him to identify Horus with Apollo. The goddess of the Delta and guardian of Lower Egypt, Edjo, is hellenized as Leto, who in Greek mythology, of course, is mother of both Artemis and Apollo. So Herodotus, using Greek names except for Isis, can cite as the Egyptian view that 'Apollo and Artemis are children of Dionysus and Isis, for whom Leto became nurse and saviour.[16] The impossibility of reaching a strict equation between Egyptian and Greek myth is made clear by Herodotus and Pausanias, who quotes the poet Aeschylus on the subject as declaring that 'Artemis is Demeter's daughter, not Leto's'.[17]

One thing is certain. Greek Artemis, when she 'fled to Egypt' along with the rest of the Olympians, assumed the features of the cat-headed Bast.[18] This must be borne carefully in mind when we hear Juvenal exclaiming rhetorically that in Egypt the whole population 'worship cats in one city, and the dog in another, but none worships Diana'.[19] In a certain sense Artemis was always missing from Egyptian theology. The virgin huntress who haunted the wild mountainside and sea-girt territory of Greece was a foreigner to the banks of the Nile. Juvenal's Diana, therefore, regarded as the Italian counterpart of Artemis Agrotera was in truth an outsider. Yet as we can see from Herodotus, though the point is not made by Juvenal, it was exactly in the city of Bubastis, where the cat was the sacred animal, that the Greeks could find the Egyptians worshipping 'Artemis'. The assimilation and subsequent identification of Isis with Artemis could not have taken place without the goddess of Bubastis. Bast was the intermediary when the process of theocrasia began. Bast, like Isis and Artemis, protected maternity and childbirth, presided over growth and nature, and rejoiced to be honoured with outdoor processions. It was through Bast that the mythological discrepancies about the parentage of Artemis were eventually smoothed away. Greek interpretation was seeking to find the most logical path. It is one of the ironies of the history of religion that the pagan figure of the Virgin Mother resulting from the fusion of

Artemis with Isis should have owed its first beginnings to the mediation of a goddess with the features of a cat.

Greek interpretation characteristically made Egypt the scene for the transfiguration of the gods of Olympus from anthropomorphic to animal shapes. According to this view Artemis and all the rest except Zeus and Athena had been terrified by Typhon and had escaped from Greece, Artemis acquiring the head of a cat. The Isis whose sistrum is so often found crowned with the figure of a she-cat (*Pl. 39*) was already conflated in her homeland with Bast/Artemis and the instrument which she herself was held to have invented was adorned at the top of its circumference with the figure of a cat with a human face and underneath the features of Isis and Nephthys. Plutarch, who tells us this, explains that here the cat symbolizes the moon, although he candidly admits that some of the comparisons he draws are fanciful. The Egyptian cat of Bast links Isis with Artemis.[20] Outside Egypt they can be likened to each other as lunar divinities. In Dacia Sarapis and Isis were called respectively Jupiter-Sol and Luna-Diana.

Plutarch, who is well aware that Artemis is a moon goddess, quotes with apparent approval the view of those who see the moon as none other than Isis. 'The statues of Isis which wear horns are representations of the crescent moon, and her black raiment is a sign that she can be overshadowed and obscured as in her yearning she seeks the sun. This is the reason for invoking the moon in love affairs, over which, according to Eudoxus, Isis presides.'[21] Elsewhere she is unmistakably adored as a lunar goddess. For in a magic spell the injunction is given to offer sacrifice to the moon and to utter the words: 'I call upon thy name, Lady Isis.'[22] When Antony and Cleopatra were aping the ancient gods of Egypt, they were painted and sculptured side by side, he as Osiris/Dionysus and she as the 'new Isis', or 'the moon'.[23] Isis, just as surely as Artemis, was the one who brought light to men in darkness, especially to those in the shadow of death, and who was therefore accorded 'phosphoros' as a favourite epiclesis. It is not an accident that when Lucius at Cenchreae is granted the vision of Isis, she appears to him in the light of the full moon rising above the waves of the sea, and is invoked as 'Queen of Heaven and Sister of

Phoebus'. Here all trace of Egyptian zoomorphism is significantly absent.

Of all the identifications which Isis underwent, that with Artemis offered the greatest hope for those whom the traditional forms of polytheism so strongly antagonized and who sought in paganism a God worthy to be worshipped with all the powers of their minds and hearts. Isis, of course, was handicapped. Again and again, as we can see from references in Latin literature, she was openly called the young cow and transformed into the Greek Io, wearing the horns. This difficulty, however, was to be faced later on by Christianity. The Christian Mother of God would indeed be the Queen of Heaven and acquire a lunar association. But she too, like Isis/Io, would be greeted by the faithful as 'the heifer, who didst bring forth the spotless calf'. All such zoomorphic ideas must be repugnant to theistic thinkers, such as the pagan philosopher who condemned his contemporaries for making statues of Osiris and Isis, whether in human or animal shape, and calling divine material objects that could be destroyed. 'It is impossible to mould an image of a nature which is incorporeal, invisible, incomprehensible and immaterial.'[24] When religious minds ceased to treat the things they saw near them as gods and turned their gaze upwards to locate their Isis and their Artemis in the moon, then paradoxically they came closer to the monotheism of the philosopher.

Isis in her aretalogy consciously fulfils the function performed in Greek religion by Artemis-Eileithyia of aiding women to bring forth children: 'I have brought forth the new-born babe at the tenth orbit of the moon—fit light for the deed that is consummated.'[25] Here again we see a lunar amalgamation. In their capacity of deliverers both Isis and Artemis carry the torch symbolizing the light of the moon, present to save mother and child in their darkness. Each as a heavenly midwife is peculiarly ready to hear and to save: *epekoos* and *soteira*. In Greek mythology 'torch-bearing Hecate', originally of Thrace, and renowned for her powers of necromancy, could be merged with Artemis. This aspect was important when Isis entered the field. Hecate was by origin a moon divinity. She bestowed wisdom and gave men

victory. She knew magic, and helped sailors. All these characteristics she shared with Isis as known to later antiquity. Wherever
Artemis/Hecate held sway, particularly in northern Greece, in
Thrace, all around the shores of the Propontis and especially at
Byzantium, the Egyptian Lady of Countless Names found herself
at home immediately. She could represent herself as Selene
Dolorosa, as 'holy Artemis', as Io, whose name began the history
of Byzantium, and as Hecate, magically powerful on earth, above
it and below.[26]

The Christian missionary who is recorded to have been present
at Ephesus when uproar arose because the sale of the silver
replicas of the Temple of Artemis had fallen off, must have been
struck with the prolonged shouting: 'Great is Artemis of the
Ephesians.'[27] As a citizen of Tarsus and a frequent traveller
through Asia Minor he might easily have heard the name of Isis
being invoked according to a similar formula: we read of this
being done before the Iseum at Rhodes. These utterances are not
empty platitudes. Like the Islamic cry 'Allah is great' they present
the infidel with the challenge of their worldwide authority. Isis is
queen everywhere. Artemis is the one 'whom all Asia and the
world worshippeth'. Asia Minor made public confession of the
greatness of Isis-Artemis.

At the date of Paul's visit to Ephesus the explicit identification
of the two ecumenical goddesses may not yet have been achieved:
but it was only a matter of time.[28] Paul, himself a citizen of one of
the chief cult centres of Isis, might easily have seen Isiac *pastophoroi*
carrying small silver shrines like those made for Artemis by the
Ephesian Demetrius. Ephesus bore as its civic title *neocoros*, as the
town clerk who spoke in Paul's defence was careful to point out:
and this name, reminiscent of the Egyptian *w3b*, was borne by
one of the orders of Isiac priests. Lucius invokes Isis as 'Thou who
art worshipped in the shrine at Ephesus'.[29] Throughout the novel
by Xenophon of Ephesus it is tacitly assumed that Artemis and
Isis perform interchangeable roles. Lastly, writing at the beginning
of the fifth century AD Macrobius describes the figure of *Isis* as
having 'the whole body thickly covered with nipples joined
together'.[30] Obviously contemporary art has overtly transformed

the Egyptian mother goddess into the *Diana multimammia* of Ephesus. Macrobius provides no further details. We may be sure, however, that Isis like the polymast Artemis whose statues have come down to us possessed a supernumerary complement of ovate breasts and without any detriment to her Egyptian origin wore as emblems on her dress such things as bulls, griffons, sphinxes, chimaeras and lions. The total effect was that of Great Artemis/Isis as a fertility figure, personifying birth and growth.

Other literary and archaeological evidence can be brought forward testifying that the two goddesses were regarded in later antiquity as one. Sometimes, as at Tibur, a local goddess was ready to help with mediation.[31] Iamblichus, the fourth century Neoplatonist, ascribes to 'the Pythagoreans' the naming of the Dyad as 'Isis-Artemis'.[32] Somewhat earlier Heliodorus, the bishop and romance-writer, portrays his heroine Chariclea as coming out of the temple of Artemis with burning torch in hand and with raiment on which appear the attributes both of Artemis (bow and quiver) and of Isis (the red colour and the knot).[33]

From the same source we learn that people in Egypt spoke about 'Artemis or the native Isis'.[34] Among the material remains where identification can plausibly be discovered is the well-known Boscoreale patera (*Pl. 36*). Here, apart from other deities associated with Isis, including the Dioscuri,[35] the right hand of the figure which is clearly conceived as African if not as Africa itself, holds the *uraeus* and an Isiac crescent surmounts a cornucopia with a sistrum emerging on the extreme left. But from behind the right shoulder appear the bow and quiver of Artemis.[36] Schefold has drawn attention to examples where the cults of the two goddesses are unmistakably blended: Artemis-Tyche meaning Isis-Tyche, the link revealed on a silver beaker, and in a mural of the House of Livia on the Palatine Hill at Rome.[37] At Pompeii the fusion of Isis and Artemis is not boldly attempted. But we find Artemis (along with Actaeon) on the door of the chapel of Isis in the House of Loreius, and elsewhere a landscape reveals features suggesting Diana/Artemis in combination with the Isiac *vannus mystica*.[38] The Pompeian painters follow tradition. They are more interested in the reception of horned Io into Egypt by Isis (*Pl. 27*), or in the mummy of Osiris (*Pl. 25*), than in elaborating Egyptian and Greek mythography as the much later Macrobius finds it treated by artists in his day. Clearly, however, syncretism was bringing Isis and Diana/Artemis closely together even before the destruction of Pompeii. In a niche of one of the houses there near the lararium of Isis and Bacchus have been found statues of Diana together with the torso of a female figure with the *modius* of Isis on the head.[39] Moreover, at Pompeii Artemis/Tyche and Isis-Tyche are the same.

Artemis was not the only member of the Olympian pantheon who could be addressed as 'Virgin'. Apuleius in his novel, even before Lucius invokes Isis, makes Psyche pray to Juno/Hera as 'great sister and wife of Jupiter', who holds the shrines of Carthage, worshipping her as a virgin. Apuleius is introducing a view of Juno which is intended to fit in with all that his last book will reveal to us about Isis. Juno is indeed Isis.[40] Why then, it may be asked, should Artemis be rated higher than Hera, Diana than Juno, when we are considering Isis as Mother and Virgin? The answer is that Hera/Juno, in spite of her obvious resemblances to Artemis (her virginal aspect, her chastity, her celestial authority) and to Isis (her sister-wife relation to Zeus/Jupiter, her regard for marriage and maternity, her championship of women) was never 'received' into Egypt as Artemis was. In the opinion of Herodotus the Egyptians did not know Hera. Isis and Artemis were temple associates far more than any other pair of goddesses. Always bearing in mind, therefore, that Isis had limitless powers of assimilation, we may affirm with confidence that no other identification was more important than that with Artemis.

CHAPTER XII

MYSTERY AND SACRAMENT

RELIGIOUS MYSTERIES were certainly known in ancient Egypt.[1] As being the great wonder-worker the Pharaoh himself was head of the mysteries which grew out of the Osirian saga[2] and which Isis was supposed to have invented.[3] The old ritual texts mention the secrets that nobody knows, that are neither seen nor heard, and that are handed down from father to son. The word *šst3* with the meaning of making secret, mysterious and inaccessible develops the sense which *mysterion* has in Greek. From it is compounded a term *hrysst*, 'he who is over the secrets', the ideogram of which can be the Anubis jackal, either alone or recumbent on a shrine 🛐. Anubis, Hermanubis as he was often called in Graeco-Roman times, was represented at the mysteries as helping in the search for things supernal and infernal. He was the sleuth hound who, in later tradition, taught Isis the way in her search for Osiris' corpse.[4]

For the Mediterranean world where Orphic and Eleusinian rites had long flourished the mysteries in later antiquity did not lose their importance.[5] There were the public religious dramas such as those of the Phrygian Magna Mater.[6] In the Isiac ritual an emperor like Otho or Commodus might openly take a part. There were also the traditional secret *orgia* as a never-failing attraction.[7] Hadrian went through two ceremonies at Eleusis, first an initiation as *mystes* and then the second degree as *epoptes*. Nero before him had shrunk from the ordeal. The importance of Hellenistic mysteries for Christianity is evident when we turn to the Pauline interpretation or to the use of the term for the knowledge that only the disciples had,[8] or to what the Fathers write about baptism as a *mysterion* or enlightenment (*photismos*) and about a creed as a *symbolon* (a password).[9]

Whatever the word *mysterion*'s etymology may be, there can be no doubt that from the time when Herodotus wrote of the rites of the Cabiri in Samothrace or of Demeter at Eleusis, it always meant gaining esoteric wisdom after the endurance of ordeals, some of which might be painful. Whether the initiate was seeking Demeter and Kore at Eleusis, or Orpheus in Thrace, or the Cabiri in Samothrace, or Dionysus and the exotic oriental gods in the Hellenistic cults, he had to learn the same lessons. He had to wait for enlightenment in a state of darkness. He had to undergo the training of silence, patience and perseverance. He had to steer a middle course between fear on the one side and rashness on the other. If he followed the cult of a sun-god like Mithras then he could deem himself a serving soldier and as the god's liegeman and devotee would swear the military oath, the *sacramentum*. Throughout he was guided by blind faith. He knew he would suddenly be granted to see and hear ineffable secrets. He would be 'reborn' if Isis appeared as his loving Saviour.[10] Then he would join the sacred band of the chosen, the Hierophoroi and Hierostoloi to whom she disclosed the Divine Mysteries,[11] those who had been privileged to enjoy a personal meeting with the god. Such is the cumulative experience of initiation into the Graeco-Roman mystery cults.

Herodotus, in dealing with 'what the Egyptians call mysteries', distinguishes the rites in which is enacted a nocturnal Passion (obviously of Osiris) on a lake next to the Saite temple of Neith/Athena and the ceremony of Isis/Demeter 'which the Greeks call thesmophoria' and which according to this account 'the daughters of Danae conveyed out of Egypt and taught the Pelasgian women'. About all of these rites Herodotus assures us he is going to preserve the silence ordained by religion.[12]

Clearly, therefore, the Hellenistic aretalogies of Isis were repeating an older view when they put forward her claim to have taught men initiation into the mysteries.[13] Plutarch, writing with expert knowledge and sympathetic insight, stressed that Isis in her most holy mysteries portrayed the trials and tribulations she had herself endured, the deep distress which had humanized her soul. Thus it was that ordinary men and women in the clutch of similar mishaps could look up to her for comfort and encouragement, a woman of sorrows and acquainted with grief, who would not allow her wanderings and all her deeds of wisdom and bravery to be forgotten. From her they could learn to triumph over evil and to hope for immortality.[14]

From the aretalogies it is clear that in Hellenistic times the northern Aegean and Thrace had become acquainted with Egyptian Isis. We are told that the Thracians identified her with the Mother of the Gods.[15] At Tenedos she is said to have taken an heliolatrous title 'name of the sun' and at Samothrace to have been 'bull-faced'.[16] In the Troad she was well established and all along the shores of the Hellespont was known as Mystis, 'Lady of the Mysteries'.[17] Clearly in that part of the Greek world where the traditional *orgia* of Orpheus and Bacchus and of the Cabiri were especially popular Isis and her associates were no strangers.

The association of Isis with the Cabiri is a fascinating problem. The Cabiri were originally demi-gods, sons of Hephaestus, who could themselves share in the chthonic rites of Demeter and Kore.[18] They were especially powerful at Thessalonica, as is abundantly testified by the evidence of coins. They could even become like Isis and Sarapis 'the Great Gods'.[19] Thessalonica accepted them as its tutelary deities. But their main haunts were Lemnos[20] and Samothrace. Herodotus, identifying the Greek Hephaestus of Lemnos with the Egyptian Ptah of Memphis, was convinced that the great Egyptian fire god and Architect of the Universe had the Cabiri as his sons and that they were natives of Egypt. He specifically names their temple in Memphis, Ptah's own city.[21] This was adjacent, no doubt, to their father's where, according to Diodorus Siculus, Isis had been buried. The bonds between the goddess and the fire god of Memphis grew to be close in the Ptolemaic age. In a demotic text of this period the two are respectively the Lady and the Lord of Semenmaa't.[22] Hard by Ptah's temple was the stele on which was engraved the original version of the aretalogies of Isis found at Andros, Ios, Cyme and Thessalonica. In the Oxyrhynchus *Litany* Isis is brought into immediate connection with 'the House of Hephaestus', *i.e.* the Temple of Ptah (*Fig. 2*).[23]

2 Isiac inscription in the Church of St John the Divine on Ios, second–third century AD. Its content is pre-Christian.

The theology of Memphis during the later dynasties established a family relationship between the Lady traditionally joined to Osiris as sister-wife and the Lord to whom all the epicleses of Osiris could be applied.[24] The link was provided by the Apis Bull. Isis was 'the Mother of the God', the Apis: the Apis could be called 'the living son' of Ptah.[25] In this way the goddess became the consort, *paredros*, of Ptah, as she afterwards did of Sarapis. But her antiquity and traditional greatness, the magic of her name, gave her the dominant position and she grew more and more the active partner.[26] In the first century BC Cicero can describe Ptah as 'the Guardian of Egypt' and Diodorus ascribe to him the hegemony of this land owing to his having been the first to discover fire.[27] The Memphite theology, by closely linking Isis and Ptah, prepared the way for the cult of the Egyptian gods to enter into an alliance with the Greek mysteries in such centres as Lemnos and Samothrace. At Thessalonica also, where civic honours were accorded to the Cabiri, Isis was enabled, by means of the reformed theology of Memphis, to establish herself securely well before the end of the third century BC.[28]

Greek interpretation, by identifying Ptah's son Nefertem with Prometheus, could prove Isis to be of Ptah's lineage. The view which according to Plutarch was 'expressed by many writers' was already current in the third century BC that Isis was 'daughter of Prometheus'.[29] But this pedigree was historically less important than the link, clearly visible towards the end of paganism, between Isis and Imhotep. Imhotep, whose Greek name was either Imouthes or Asclepius, was indeed known as 'Son of Ptah'. Not a mere figure of myth but a great genius of history, he had been High Priest and chief architect of Saqqara as Vizier to Zoser in the Third Dynasty.[30] Eventually he supplanted Nefertem as the Divine Son in the Triad of Memphis and even won precedence over Ptah himself. The Oxyrhynchus Papyrus which shows us the *Litany of Isis* contains also, on the verso, a Hymn of Praise to Imouthes, in which appears the significant statement: 'Every person who is Greek shall worship the Son of Ptah [sic], Imouthes.'[31] From other evidence also—the dedication of a temple at Epidaurus to Isis/Hygieia and Imouthes/Asclepius, and the theology of the Hermetic writings[32]—we can be sure that the deified sage who was so much devoted to medicine and the occult sciences, and whose death was so much mourned by his father Ptah, had entered into the closest ties with the goddess who was herself so deeply occupied with the same medical and occult pursuits.

In the world today there exists a great organization with a ritual and a code of conduct which entitle it to be called the direct descendant of the mysteries of later antiquity. Freemasonry justly claims to be a system of morality. Within it allegory and symbolism play an indispensable part. The affiliation of freemasonry with the rites of Isis and Osiris was recognized years ago by the percipient genius of Mozart in *The Magic Flute*.[33] When Tamino and Papageno are led within the temple for their initiation into the mysteries of Isis they must be thought of from two standpoints. They typify modern freemasonry. They also follow in the steps of their ancient brethren, the Cabiri, and Isis who went in search of the slain Osiris, or met the same god, no longer a corpse but resurrected as Ptah, the Lord of Life, opening and closing the day, creating 'with his heart and tongue', superintending architects and masons at the building of temples and pyramids, ordaining that the house should be established firmly, and holding the *djed* column as his emblem of stability.

In Ptolemaic and Roman times Ptah and Isis (already from evidence outside Egypt forming a trinity with Horus)[34] must have seemed to the esoteric worshipper virtually joint manifestations. The royal epiclesis 'chosen of Ptah', which is frequent in the Ptolemaic period, is applied to Isis at Philae, where he was clearly worshipped in her temple, 'he with the beautiful face, the great god'.[35] Like him she brings the sun from rising unto setting. Like him and his son Imouthes she is skilled in calculations and inventive. Ptah is the lord of fire. Isis, whose tomb is stated to have been in the Temple of Ptah,[36] is the lady of light and flames, and fire of Hades.[37] In an age when the sun was so often worshipped as the divine source of all, men found the Egyptian heliolatry especially congenial. The personal name did not greatly matter. In the mysteries they sought light—and this meant the sun, personified

by a resuscitated Osiris, a Ptah or a Sarapis. At Tenedos, as we have
seen, Isis herself could be adored as 'name of the sun'. The Egyptian gods, therefore, well suited the mystic scene in which light
dissolved darkness.

If we assume the existence of close contacts between the Egyptian gods and the Cabiri in such centres as Samothrace, Lemnos
and Thessalonica, then modern freemasonry has inherited much
from these mysteries. Their general pattern is strikingly similar.
In the ancient Cabiric rite a brother suffers actual death at the
hands of brothers, as indeed does Osiris at the hands of Seth. Freemasonry follows the ethical precepts of the old mysteries, and
inculcates the great virtues of brotherly love, relief and truth. Like
Mozart's stage characters, freemasons of the twentieth century
stand in the line of such Isiacs as Lucius. They take the three
degrees in their 'craft', swear their solemn oaths of inviolable
secrecy, receive the benefit of tokens and passwords which open
the gates to hidden truth, have their own cherished methods of
walking,[38] pass from darkness to light, have some resemblance to
the Horus initiates, sons of widowed Isis, and gain a symbolic
victory over death. Does any system in our world today better
preserve the outlook of the Isiac and kindred mysteries than
freemasonry?

From the pages of Apuleius we can gain much invaluable
knowledge of the main features of Isiac initiation as it was practised in the imperial age. Night after night at Cenchreae Lucius
has been bidden by Isis in dreams to undergo the tempting ordeal
but has procrastinated through certain fears. At last when his
hopes have been pledged by the goddess he talks to the High
Priest and begs for initiation 'in the mysteries of the hallowed
night'. Lucius' spiritual father, whose name 'Mithras' has an
eclectic ring,[39] answers that he must await the call patiently and
undergo a period of ten days' abstinence. On the appointed evening after the uninitiated have been told to leave, Lucius, wearing a
new linen garment, is conducted into the inner chamber of the
very sanctuary. At this point in the tale 'the curious reader' is
warned that exactly what was said and done during the ceremony
cannot be disclosed because the candidate was obligated to

secrecy.[40] 'Ears and tongues would suffer harm alike for rash inquisitiveness. . . . Listen then. But have faith also in the truth. I made my way to the verge of death, I trod the threshold of Proserpine,[41] I travelled through all the elements, and I made my return. At midnight I beheld the sun ablaze with brilliant light, I had a face to face meeting with the gods both of the world below and of the world above, and I worshipped them intimately.' Then, as if to keep the reader still guessing, and following the Egyptian initiate's 'I do not tell it to anybody',[42] Lucius concludes his account of the first degree with the tantalizing words: 'You see I have reported to you what must remain hearsay that you cannot understand.' The ceremony is followed by a banquet and then three days afterwards by a solemn breakfast.[43]

Lucius is not yet a fully fledged *epoptes*. His goddess therefore commands him to take ship for Italy and to proceed to the Iseum in the Campus Martius of 'the Holy City'. He reaches there in mid-December, surprised because he fondly supposes he has already been fully initiated. His priestly adviser, however, assures him that he must be admitted to the degree not only of Isis but also of Osiris, even though these two are inextricably commingled both in theology and in ritual. So Lucius spends another ten days fasting and is again granted illumination. He is admitted this time into the nocturnal rites, or *orgia*, of 'invincible Osiris', *i.e.* the Osiris who as Ptah or Ammon or Horus or Zeus/Sarapis or Horus/Apollo or Dionysus is the Lord of Life, the all-seeing eye, the Ruler of the greatest gods.[44]

Soon now another vision bids Lucius take his third degree. This puzzles him even more. What can have been left out that must be delivered to him in yet one more revelation? A divine message comforts him. He must not mind if his religious pilgrimage is made in three stages. Besides, his former vestments, his old regalia having been laid aside in Greece, he must don a fresh outfit. After another period of abstinence Lucius pays the dues required for him to go through the ceremony.[45] He is not then sorry. For Osiris in his own person appears in a dream as 'the highest among the greatest and the greatest among the highest' and during this intimate encounter tells Lucius face to face about his forthcoming rise to office in the priestly college of the Pastophors, a promise which is not long in being fulfilled.

Lucius enjoys what seems to him a personal intimacy in the first degree with Isis, and in the third with Osiris. He is 'alone with the Alone'.[46] Possibly a statue of the god was exhibited or the god's role was played by a priest, suitably attired: but the effect on the worshipper's mind was like that of the *unio mystica* as described by Plotinus. Indeed, from a celebrated passage of the great Neo-platonist, himself born in Egypt and taught by the African-named Ammonius, we may visualize the kind of experience Lucius enigmatically portrays. The secret of the mysteries, we read, must not be revealed to any one who has not himself had the good luck to see it. The beholder and the beheld are not two but one. Absolute quiet and stillness prevail. We enter the inner chamber of the sanctuary and leave behind us the statues in the temple, which are the first things we see when we emerge from the vision we have experienced within and our intercourse there. This, holds Plotinus, was not with an idol or an image but with the very object of our worship. It is not so much a vision as another kind of seeing, a yearning for contact. In the mystical language of Plotinus, it is the flight of the alone to the Alone. These are the words of an inspired thinker, whose mystical temperament and Egyptian upbringing must surely have created a special interest in the mysteries of Isis and Osiris.[47] Let us remember that the Iseum where the fictional Lucius took his second and third degrees was a place where the Neoplatonic philosopher 'readily consented' to go, along with an Egyptian priest.

Elsewhere Plotinus informs us that when we ascend to the mysteries of the sanctuary we must undergo purifications and strip ourselves of all clothing before going in naked.[48] Certainly in the Isiac mysteries, as in those of Mithras (not to mention Christianity) a preliminary baptism was indispensable.[49] Lucius at Cenchreae, even before his first silent prayer to the Queen of Heaven, symbolically cleansed himself by bathing in the sea and ducking his head seven times under the waves,[50] though still possessing his asinine features and hairy face. Before he was admitted to the first degree he went to the nearest baths with the priest, bathed in the usual way, and was then sprinkled by him with holy water to the opening prayer for divine pardon. But in this account no reference is made to complete nudity as a pre-requisite to initiation. On the contrary, the stress falls on what clothing Lucius wore before and afterwards. Prior to the cere-mony he was invested with a fresh garment of linen and after it he came out as an ordained votary wearing the twelve vestments of the degree. These stoles, on which no doubt were depicted the symbols of the twelve 'regions' or 'zones' through which he would have passed, were in due course laid up in the temple and as we are specifically told they were not considered the right cloth-ing when Lucius was a candidate for the third degree in Rome. Clearly the donning of regalia (not to mention the cost) had its importance. But in the mysteries of Isis the question may be posed, was the body ever naked?

Archaeological evidence from Herculaneum, from the Iseum of the Campus Martius, and from Antioch-on-the-Orontes proves Plotinus correct as regards nudity in the Isiac cult. The priests of Isis are represented often with at least a half-naked torso.[51] More important still, in a mosaic from the House of the Mysteries of Isis at Antioch (Pl. 34) appears the figure of a man who is obviously an initiate and whose body is naked except for a red cloth on his left shoulder. On his left stands Isis, not wearing her usual royal headdress but having a torch. The man seems to have stopped suddenly with his eyes turned back towards the goddess. On his right appears Hermes holding out his magic wand, the kyrekeion, in an effort to touch him, and himself virtually nude. Behind Hermes is the opening of a door. In this scene is graphically represented the crucial experience of the mystes. He is literally 'at death's door', for the door behind Hermes opens to the chamber of death and death is what he has now reached of his own free will and accord—mors voluntaria[52]—although he prays to Isis in hope of a salvation which is not in his own hands—salus precaria. Hermes, of course, is the hellenized Anubis of Egypt, who in Apuleius holds the wand as psychopompus and who tradi-tionally assists in the search for things supernal and infernal. Hermanubis, the interpreter of the will of Isis, is the fittest of all the gods to conduct the candidate to the threshold of death. Symbolically they are both approaching it naked.

The Isiac mysteries were traditionally thought to entail secrecy: from antiquity, we are told, the priests have taken the death of Osiris to be among the unmentionable subjects.[53] In time, however, some of the details became known. What is particularly hard to be sure about is the nature of the ceremony of Osiris' resurrection. In the Egyptian tradition the resurrection of the god was celebrated by a small group of priests in rooms where none of the uninitiated were allowed to enter.[54] So central a rite must have been enacted esoterically for as long as the faith of Isis and Osiris was practised. According to the third century Christian writer Hippolytus the ceremony had simply a sexual basis. 'The Egyptians have the mysteries of Isis, holy and august and not to be talked about with the uninitiated. But these mysteries are simply the lost *pudenda* of Osiris for which she of the seven stoles and black robe goes in search.'[55]

From the account given us by Plutarch it is clear that the 'Seeking and Finding' (*zetesis* and *heuresis*)[56] of the body of Osiris, annually commemorated for a week at the end of October and beginning of November, was in his day not so much a hidden mystery as a public performance. Certainly the priests carried out certain gloomy ceremonies, such as shrouding a golden calf with a black linen veil as an emblem of mourning Isis. But they went out of the temple and down to the sea on the final night. It was a public occasion, marked in the Roman calendar with the name Hilaria. 'Osiris has been found'—so the crowd shouted for joy, while various ministers brought forth the god's sacred ark.[57] Another variation of the formula was 'We have found, and rejoice'. Even though the ceremony did not take place in daytime it was open to view, just as when a show was arranged on the night before the death of the Emperor Caligula and in it Egyptians and Ethiopians gave a quasi-Isiac representation of the Underworld. We may plausibly believe that the ritual of the 'Seeking and Finding' was elaborated in the Ptolemaic age in conformity with the closer associations between Isis and Demeter. We must remember, however, that it was not conducted in strict secrecy, for it was an undisguised pageant of the resurrection of Osiris performed by Isis, a drama out of doors.

In guarded language Lucius informs us that before he came back from the chamber of death he had been 'borne through all the elements'. These we are to be told shortly afterwards are under the control of Isis. They are, indeed, the same as the Pauline 'weak and beggarly elements',[58] the pantocrators of heathen darkness, the heavenly powers ranged under the twelve signs of the zodiac.[59] A second century source indicates that a zodiacal explanation could be sought for the manifold divisions in an Egyptian temple. What Lucius means, therefore, is that in the ceremony of his initiation he was conducted from one temple chamber to another, doubtless to the total number of twelve, receiving a fresh stole in each. To the crowd of the uninitiated who saw him walk forth at dawn he must have seemed a remarkable figure, clad perhaps in a mantle with an astrological map of the world.[60] As he climbed up into the pulpit for all to fasten their eyes on him he was carrying a lighted torch in his hand and was crowned with palm leaves looking just like a halo. But the most striking feature of all, perhaps, was the ankle-length mantle which fell from the shoulder behind the back. On it were marked in different colours the figures of the sacred animals of his faith. Similar characters had attracted his unlearned eyes just before initiation when the priest had read to him from a service book written in hieroglyphics. These signs were now connected in his mind with his recent zodiacal progress. He is careful to tell us at a later stage[61] that the dream in which Isis commanded him to take his second degree occurred when the sun had fully encircled the zodiac. Up there in the wooden pulpit Lucius was displaying to the gaze of a fascinated congregation as diverse a zoological troupe on his so-called 'robe of Olympus'[62] as we can see when we turn to the Palestrina mosaic.

Quite apart from the animals, the Palestrina mosaic (*Pls. 8–11*) adds its own testimony to the importance of the mysteries in the worship of Isis *Protogeneia, Primigenia*. Viewed panoramically, it marks the providential power of the goddess to grant fertility to the plains of Egypt through the Nile inundation. Considered in detail, it reveals ritual preparations which Lucius would have been well able to appreciate. At the bottom is portrayed the temple of Isis at Memphis. At other points we can observe a kind of baptismal font,[63] two votaries greeting each other with a hailing sign, and scenes where animal symbolism, though mysterious to us, is strongly felt.

Lucius candidly states that the day on which he completed his first degree and which he describes as his Birthday in the Faith of Isis was a very happy occasion, with a delightful banquet. The convivial aspect of the ceremony of initiation must be always remembered. The sacramental meal marked the culmination of the service. Thus after the performance of more ceremonies on the third day a solemn breakfast was celebrated to mark the proper consummation of the mystery. The room used for this purpose in the Iseum at Pompeii was the *Ecclesiasterion*. The pagan Eucharist[64] of Isis and Sarapis was integrated into the pattern of worship, as Lucius makes clear, and it is in this religious context that we must interpret a phrase in a papyrus: 'a meal in honour of Lady Isis'. At the same time, however, we can reasonably assume that a meal in the temple precincts did not always mean that the banqueters had arrived there straight from a religious service. Isis herself could (somewhat exceptionally) fulfil the Bacchic role of 'having provided wine to begin with in the festivals of the gods', according to the Oxyrhynchus *Litany*. Isis the convivial certainly now had a much alive spouse who appreciated the value of a good cuisine in his temple. Several references are made in the papyri to club banquets of the Lord Sarapis. We can be sure that in spite of the abstinence and fasting and other ritual disciplines there was scope in the cult of Isis and Sarapis for pleasant social intercourse and conviviality. The Lucius who obeys the command of Isis to enrol himself as a soldier in her hallowed company and endures the ascetic trials of initiation into her mysteries still has more than a trace of the old hedonism left in him and can appreciate the excellent catering arrangements of the temple restaurant.[65]

CHAPTER XIII

THE PROCESSION TO THE SHIP

WATER, for the ancient Egyptian, constituted life itself, and its source was the Nile. Osiris, reborn as Horus, was the river's living power and in this sense as a Christian writer tells us the Egyptians could 'speak of Osiris as water'.[1] In the Isiacism of later antiquity the idea expressly stated in one of the *Pyramid Texts* of the 'cool water' of Osiris persisted in mottoes on graves conveying the hope of everlasting life: 'May Osiris grant thee the cold water', and 'May Isis bestow on thee the holy water of Osiris'.[2] When the Blemmyes, in accordance with a practice which must have belonged to a remote past, bore the image of Isis from her temple at Philae by boat across the river and after their festival in the hills brought it back again to its wonted home, they were indeed undertaking a processional ceremony hallowed by their pilgrimage over the Nile water.[3] The procession from bank to bank at the time of the inundation is the prototype of the sailing of Isis' ship (*Ploiaphesia, Navigium Isidis*) as known to the Graeco-Roman world.

Herodotus states that the first people to institute festivals, processions, and religious presentations were the Egyptians— 'and the Greeks have got their knowledge from them'.[4] Here is a clear recognition of the great antiquity of the pageants of the Nile. Already in the XVIIIth Dynasty, in the reign of Tutankhamen, scenes such as we find so vividly described by Apuleius were familiar holiday spectacles: the sacred barges, the incense and the timbrels, the flowers and the libations, the models of the shrines, and the return by river from Luxor to Karnak eleven days after the setting out.[5] The launching of Isis' ship was a

natural development in a religion which was never land-locked.
It drew its warrant from the processions in honour of Isis at such
centres as Philae and Busiris. Isis 'of the Sea', Isis *Pelagia*, was
essentially the goddess whose tears yearly filled the Nile, the
Isis who in a *Pyramid Text* held the forward cable of the Sacred
Bark;[6] the Isis, moreover, who on discovering that the Ark of
Osiris had been cast up by the Mediterranean in the region of
Phoenician Byblos went across the sea to find it, and then shipped
it back with her to Egypt.[7] According to the mythographer
Lucian a miraculous head sailed once a year on a seven-day
voyage from Egypt to Byblos, and only to Byblos.[8] This head
he declares he has himself seen in the city and adds that some of the
inhabitants regard it as a proof that the Passion and Mystery of
Adonis belong really to Egyptian Osiris. Whatever the date when
the voyage to Byblos became important in the evolution of the
Osirian saga, we can be sure that it is analogous both to the Nile
procession of ancient Egypt and to the launching of Isis' ship in
the Graeco-Roman age.

For our Isiac Lucius the procession down to the beach at
Cenchreae was no ordinary festival, for during the midst of it
his heartfelt prayer was answered through his transfiguration
back from an ass to a man. The miracle is not now our concern.
What is beyond doubt is this. However far-fetched other elements
in Apuleius' novel may be, the details of the procession are all
true to the ordinary experience of an ancient reader. We can
share Lucius' gladness in the spring sunshine which ushers in a
day to be the most memorable of his life, feeling ourselves to be
there as amused spectators among the carnival crowd. Isis no
longer mourns. She smiles upon her universe.[9]

At the head of the great procession walk various people all
dressed up for the parts they have to play. One man wears the
belt of a soldier, another is in fancy dress as a huntsman, and a third
impersonates a woman, wearing fine silks and jewellery as well
as a wig and gilt sandals. We have the gladiator, the magistrate
and the philosopher. Bird-catching and angling[10] have their
representatives with reeds. The tame bear, the monkey and the
donkey walking beside its aged rider are all there to raise a laugh.

We can regard these as the advance party, figures of fun to usher in the long train of the actual religious performers, 'the extraordinary procession of the Goddess who Saves'.[11]

Women in shining white dresses, themselves garlanded with spring blossom, strew flowers all along the route. Some carry polished mirrors and combs which they apply to the hair of their divine Queen. Others make the path smell sweet with the perfumes they sprinkle. A large throng of both sexes seek the goodwill of her 'from whom the stars of heaven stem' by carrying lamps and torches, wax tapers and lights of other kinds. We can listen to the advancing choir of young singers in company with a reed and flute band in a hymn 'which by the grace of the Muses a gifted composer has written and set to music'. Our ears ring too with the cry 'Make way for the procession!' What are these we meet now? They are a great multitude of Isiac initiates, men and women of all ranks and ages, clothed with white linen robes.[12] We can detect the gloss on the women's pomaded hair beneath the gauze veil. The men have no hair, for their heads are completely shaven. Their tonsured crowns are 'stars on earth of the great religious system'. We hear the shrill sharp tinkle of the timbrels they shake[13]—of brass and silver and sometimes even gold.

Into our view now come the priests, clad likewise in white linen.[14] In front of them they hold the appurtenances of the Almighty Divinities, namely Isis and Sarapis, and each of the five has charge of his particular exhibit. The first dazzles our eyes with the brightness of his lamp.[15] It is 'not so much like those which glow at our evening meals but rather one of gold made in the shape of a boat, sending up a small flame from a hole in its middle'.[16] The next priest with both hands elevates a high altar in miniature. He is followed by one carrying the replica of a palm with a gold foil covering, as well as the magic wand of Hermanubis. The fourth lifts up the modelled emblem of Justice, a left hand with the fingers extended, which owing to its lack of the right hand's cunning and craft seems 'better fitted to fairness than the right'. In his charge also is the golden pitcher with a mastoid curvature from which he is pouring out a trickle of

milk.[17] The last of the five priests shows us his branched winnowing fan, *vannus mystica*,[18] all of gold, and he is assisted by a
man with a wine jar. At this point we leave the ministerial
appurtenances and gaze at those gods 'who deign to walk in
procession on human feet'. Hermanubis and Isis, with her bovine
features resembling Hathor or Io, are to pass by us immediately.
In a few moments Lucius will be wriggling his way forward to
nibble at the bunch of roses dangled before his asinine mouth by
the priest (*cf. Pl. 49*).

Here now is the well-known 'Anubis', the 'go-between' of
Heaven and Hades. Of him we must stand in awe. Half of his
uplifted face is black as night and half gold as day and although
he wears a dog's head[19] yet he lifts his neck upwards (*Pl. 46*). Him
we can recognize as Hellenic Hermes also from his herald's
wand, which he holds in one hand and with the other waves
green palm leaves. Walking in the wake of Hermanubis is one of
the Isiac ministry with the statue of a cow on his shoulders. How
lively are his movements and how happy is his gait! The image
rests there as a fertility emblem. We have already heard the
anthem of Sarapis played by the pipers who have moved ahead.
But of that god in this part of the procession there is no sign at all.
Nor in this theophany is Horus, son of Isis, a participant. The
two characters in the drama are Isis and her herald.

The miracle of the transfiguration of Lucius is over. His jaws
have crunched the rose garland as the sistrum tinkles in his ears.
He joins the pageant as it descends to the seashore. There the
images are laid out in due form. A ship can be seen with an
extraordinary variety of hieroglyphics painted upon it. On its
glistening white sail we can read the message (if we can understand the signs), a prayer to Isis for the successful conduct of the
new season's navigation. The high priest holds a lighted torch,
an egg and some sulphur, with which he symbolically cleanses
the vessel and after uttering the most solemn prayers names and
dedicates it to Isis. We watch the pine spar rising up, the mast-
head unmistakable, and the stern twisted like a goose and overlaid
with gilt plate. The whole keel shows us a glistening polish,
being made of pure citrus wood. Now all hands, both the initiated

31–33 *Above*, two tombstones of priestesses of Isis, each holding their ritual sistrum and situla, from Athens *left*, and Naples *right*. *Below*, a pantheistic relief from Rome, showing Isis and Sarapis in company with Jupiter Dolichenus, Juno and the Dioscuri

34, 35 The cult of Isis seen on mosaic pavements from Antioch. *Above*, the *mors voluntaria* and the crowning moment of initiation are depicted in the House of the Mysteries of Isis. *Below*, in the panel of the Isiac ceremony the central figure is Isis with *palla contabulata*, showing her appropriate emblems of stars and moon

36 The tondo of a silver patera from the Boscoreale treasure reveals the assimilation of Isis with Artemis. In addition to an assortment of emblems of other deities can be seen the uraeus and sistrum of Isis, along with the bow and quiver of Artemis behind the right shoulder

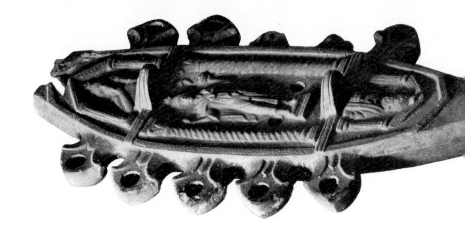

37, 38 Two Roman
lamps relating to the cult
of Isis. *Above*, a boat-
shaped lamp with
multiple wick-holes from
Puteoli. Isis is seen in the
centre within a shrine and
a bust of Sarapis,
similarly enshrined, is at
the bow. *Left*, Isis is seen
in company with
Harpocrates, his finger to
his mouth (*cf*. Pl. 20) and
Anubis with his jackal's
head

39, 40 *Right*, a bronze
sistrum found in the
Tiber at Rome. The loop
is surmounted by a
couchant cat and a very
Romanized version of the
goddess Hathor appears
at the juncture of the
handle and loop. *Far
right*, is a multiple-wicked
and boat-shaped lamp
from Puteoli, showing the
Dioscuri in the centre
and, above them,
Sarapis being crowned
by Isis

41, 42 The monumental entrance to the Temple of Isis in Rome is seen, *above*, in a detail from the relief of the Hatteri in the Vatican. The Temple itself is represented, *left*, on a coin of the Emperor Vespasian. The cult statue appears between the columns and in the pediment is a representation of Isis Sothis (*cf.* Pls 63, 64)

43 The location of the Iseum-Serapeum complex in Rome on the Severan marble plan between Saepta Julia in the west and Porticus Divorum with Temple of Minerva Chalcidica (below *S. Maria sopra Minerva*) in the east

44, 45 Nilus and Nilotic scenes were popular in Roman art. The statue of the god, *above*, has sixteen children, representing the cubits of the Nile, climbing over him. *Below*, a typical Nilotic scene from the Palestrina mosaic (see Pl. 8)

and the undedicated, stow aboard the cargo needed for the launching, winnowing fans laden with sweet spices and other suchlike oblations. On top of the waves a thick compound of milk is poured. The good ship *Isis* has now been loaded to her full capacity with votive gifts to bring her luck, including the picture of a cow.[20] We need not ask whether her sails have been set or her rudder lashed to stop her sheering around. At a given signal she slips down into the water when the cables are cast off and under a light following breeze glides out to sea with no crew to guide her as she disappears towards the horizon.[21]

If we stand on the beach at Cenchreae today with an offshore wind blowing we can visualize the scene so graphically described by the miraculously transfigured Lucius. Although his words belong to fiction we cannot doubt the possibility of the procession of Isis just here. The setting fits. Pausanias specifies a sanctuary of Isis as existing at Cenchreae along with those of Asclepius and Aphrodite (deities closely linked with her) and a statue of Poseidon (a god for whom no parallel was possible in Egypt but whom Sarapis came to embrace and with whom Isis/Aphrodite the Giver of a Good Sailing, *Euploia*, came into obvious association).[22] Here also, we may remind ourselves, the missionary Paul is reported to have been involved in an incident which looks peculiarly Isiac when we recall the shaven heads of the priests seen by Lucius in the procession. Either Paul himself, or his co-religionist Aquilas, is described (in a phrase with an Isiac sound) as having undergone a complete tonsure *in fulfilment of a vow*.[23]

The ship *Isis* has sailed away. Her whereabouts must have appeared as strange to Lucius as he gazed here where we are now standing as the modern mystery of the *Marie Celeste* must remain. But we may at once turn our minds to what lies here before us. Beneath the surface of this very bay, only within the last five years, have been discovered archaeological remains which unmistakably betray Egyptianizing style. On a thin sheet of glass are represented ibises walking about among lotus and papyrus plants. Unmistakably African also is the crocodile ridden upon by a man.[24]

The *Isis* has now been lost to sight. The priests who have taken down the holy symbols of their faith to the shore gladly return to the temple each carrying his own exhibit and all walking with the same dignity as before in their procession. There is now no need to follow them back with Lucius. He will listen to the state prayers as well as a special litany for sailors and ships, read out from the liturgy by the Scribe. The temple rites will end with the dismissal formula *ploiaphesia*: 'The ship has been let go.' Then the congregation will raise a shout of joy. The official glad tidings have been communicated to all that a new season of navigation has started. On the temple steps a silver idol of the goddess has been set up. The people will kiss her feet. Then they will gather up some of the floral decorations and the greenery and joyfully make their way to their homes.

The *ploiaphesia* is well attested. In the region of Byzantium three centuries before this city became the capital of the eastern empire, the Ship of Isis was launched by its symbolic captain, a certain Artemidorus.[25] In Eretrea of Euboea the ceremony was in existence by the first century BC. We have the interesting names of 'captains' in a long list, including two men named Socrates and women called Isigenea, Parthena, Isidora, Theopompis ('the lady of the sacred procession'), Isias (twice), Demetria and Paedeusis ('the lady professor').[26] At Ephesus an Ark Mariner of Isis (*naubates*) bore the very Roman name of M. Pomponius Latinus.[27]

The writer John of Lydia, who was born at Philadelphia not far from Ephesus and who had links with the emperor Justinian, assures us that the Voyage of Isis was still being performed in his day and specifies that the date was 5 March. It is called *ploiaphesia*, he tells us, in honour of 'ancient Isis, or the Moon'.[28] The Egyptians pay her due worship at the commencement of their sea voyages 'because by her nature she presides over the waters'. Himself belonging to an area where the great goddess of Ephesus had for long been omnipotent, our authority treats Artemis as the first-born of all the Greek pantheon, Apollo's elder sister, and implicitly identifies her with Isis by assimilating each with the Moon.

For a votary of Artemis the Isiac *ploeaphesia* would have been a welcome spectacle. Artemis enjoyed waterside processions as much as Isis. This is clear from what Socrates at the beginning of the *Republic* narrates about the spectacle of Artemis-Bendis and her pageant for which the Thracians were responsible at the Piraeus. The tame bear that Lucius noticed at the head of the big procession at Cenchreae would bring to mind Artemis the Brauronian goddess of Attica, to whom the bear was sacred. To Artemis 'the overseer of harbours' and Greece's coastal guardian, the *ploiaphesia* could hardly have seemed out of place.

The evidence of Roman coins from the reign of Diocletian to that of Valentinian II in the fourth century AD, vividly reveals the hold of the Alexandrian religion over the Late Empire (*Pls. 62, 65–67*). On the obverse appears the imperial head and on the reverse the legend *vota publica*, *i.e.* state vows for the emperor's health and good fortune. Throughout the period the power of Isis as a maritime deity is emphasized.[29] We see her side by side with Sarapis/Neptune. She is shown with the sistrum and her sacred vessel in her hands (*Pl. 65*). On a coin of Constantine, whose conversion to Christianity changed the world's religious pattern, Isis has gone aboard her ship and is looking forward towards the sail which she grasps with both hands as a following wind blows on her mantle (*Pl. 62*). On the anonymous coinage with the figures of Isis and Sarapis on the obverse minted in the same century we come across Isis *Faria* (*i.e. Pharia*) repeatedly, the goddess who like Artemis takes care of harbours. On one of these she is depicted with her dress exactly as described by Apuleius stretching from the left shoulder to the right armpit. In another she stands up in the *tensa*, the chariot or car for the parade of her image (*Pl. 66*). She is also represented as *Pelagia* reclining with a large cornucopia in her hand and leaning on an urn from which water is pouring forth. On these fourth century *vota publica* coins are to be found other Egyptian types: Isis *kourotrophos/galacto-trophousa*, Isis seated on the Sothis dog (*cf. Pls. 63, 64*),[30] the recumbent Nile, the Sphinx, Harpocrates with forefinger on mouth, and Anubis with the *caduceus* and a palm-branch or a sistrum (*Pl. 67*). Here we have the strongest numismatic witness to the pagan renaissance in the latter half of the fourth century led by such men as Symmachus and Flavianus and opposed by Ambrose and Augustine. Rome and her mints especially could provide anti-Christian propaganda. The boat of Isis launched again and again with every fresh issue of festival coinage declared open war on the church of Christ.

Nor did the struggle end when Theodosius I caused the destruction of the Sarapeum at Alexandria (*Pl. 68*) and the official degradation of the festivals of paganism. In the next century Isis was still being acclaimed as the inventress of navigation and her boat was still sailing forth on 5 March. A writer in the reign of Theodosius II expressly informs us: 'The anniversary of the start of the sailing season is celebrated with the wonted rivalry and as a public pageant in many cities.'[31]

Isis was an insidiously dangerous foe for Christian theologians because she was believed to give her worshippers their daily bread. With the Dioscuri as her subordinate ministers she granted the corn-fleet immunity from storms and let it safely enter the port of Ostia. It is in the light of this that we can understand the deeper meaning of an inscription quoting an order made by the emperors Valens, Gratian and Valentinian for the restoration of the Iseum at the port of Ostia, probably in AD 376, 'the superintendent of the work being Sempronius Faustus, the minister for the year's corn supply'.[32] The port of Rome must have been the scene for many brilliant processions down to the shore in honour of the goddess who sent out the ships to bring the food. We may surmise that often these grain ships bore the name *Isis*.

Did the Procession to the Boat and the *ploiaphesia* take always the same pattern? To find the answer we must consider how often the *Isia*, the Festival of Isis, occurred in the year. We have only to glance at the Roman Calendar of Philocalus to ascertain that besides the *Isidis Navigium* in March the six-day ceremony of the Search and Discovery (*zetesis* and *heuresis*) took place in October, ending with the *Hilaria* on 3 November. We have already seen that this ended with a procession down to the seashore by night. Between the daytime pageant such as Lucius witnessed and one carried out by torch light in wintry gloom there was obviously room for differences of procedure, although exactly what these were we cannot be sure. A search that lasted nearly a whole week must have involved an elaborate ritual. We know that its performers showed no moderation in the grief they exhibited, that they beat their breasts, and that (as in the procession on 5 March) the image of a cow was carried as a fertility emblem but on this occasion having its gilded features covered up with a black linen shroud.[33] At the end, when 'Osiris has been found' had been shouted, the priests would pour out holy water into a stoup and would use it and a mixture of fertile earth, sweet spices and frankincense to fashion a small image in the shape of a crescent moon. This was the November rite. It foreshadowed winter and in Egypt itself the hope of a successful Nile inundation afterwards. The March festival, on the other hand, inaugurated summer and the sailing season.[34]

The *ploiaphesia* itself was enacted not only in March but also at the beginning of January. This was the occasion for combining the rites of Isis with the naval pageant of the Happiness of the Emperor. Probably a link between the two cults had been established early in the second century. Isis in January, of course, did not give her sailors the signal to launch their ships. This was a festival of preparation, and of greeting to the imperial sovereign. The *vota publica*, so well attested numismatically and in Apuleius characterized as 'solemn' (*maiora vota*), were expressions by the populace of devotion to the state as well as of loyalty to the traditionally deified emperor, side by side with a proper regard for Isis who ruled the waves.[35] It was her priest in her own temple whom Lucius heard reading out the prayers of joy and felicity (*fausta vota*), first for His Imperial Majesty, then for senators and knights, and lastly for all sailors and ships wheresoever they sailed throughout the Roman world. On a coin we can still see Christianity's convert Constantine crowned with a wreath of bay leaves but on the reverse side supported by Isis, looking forward from her ship with the inevitable motto engraved around her, *vota publica* (Pl. 62).[36]

We must never forget the Nilotic origins of the *ploiaphesia*

of the imperial age. Right up to the overthrow of paganism Isis
held fast to her greatness as the ancient goddess of the Nile.[37]
We may adapt to her the language of the *Apocalypse* and call her
'a woman carried away of the flood' (*potamophoretos*), for she was
freely transported over the inland waterways of Egypt. But from
the Nile estuary she could take ship for Byblos in search of her
husband. Legend also reported that in seeking her son Horus/
Harpocrates she first invented the sail.[38] The Nile sent Isis out
of her own country to roam the shores of the Mediterranean as
Pelagia. We see this all the more clearly when we think of the
position she and her consort Sarapis held at Alexandria. Here an
annual procession in honour of the Nile's overflowing was bound
up with the cult of the Lighthouse Goddess (Isis *Pharia*) and the
God of the Sarapeum. The pageant must have gone down shore-
wards like that at Cenchreae. But here the special exhibit was the
Cubit Measure of the rising waters of the Nile, normally kept in
one of the chambers of the Sarapeum but now carried on parade
to a place some distance away (probably with the name Philae)
and afterwards restored to its proper place.[39] Significantly
Constantine, about AD 325, enjoined that the Patriarch Alexander
should superintend the removal of the Cubit from the Sarapeum
into one of his newly consecrated churches.[40]

In a detailed account of Egyptian religion Diodorus of Sicily
records that the abodes of men in this life are merely 'resting
places' in contrast with their tombs after death, which are their
'eternal homes'.[41] The conception of human existence as a halt,
a momentary pause, at a resting place or a 'mansion' had its
importance in the ritual of the procession. From the account in
Apuleius we learn nothing about specific 'stations' on the way to
the shore. But we can infer that in some processions they were
observed with as much devotion as the Stations of the Cross in
Christianity. *Pausarii* of Isis existed at Arles. Others at Rome
built her a 'halt'.[42] The Emperor Commodus was so much
addicted to the faith of Isis that, besides shaving his head and
carrying an image of Anubis, he 'fulfilled all the pauses'.[43] The
pause in its literal sense meant a stop at stated intervals for the
singing of hymns to the goddess. Interpreted figuratively it could

acquire a deeper significance. After all his tribulations Lucius begs the Queen of Heaven to grant him 'rest' (*pausa*) and peace.[44] Here we are involved in the symbolism of the Isiac faith, an extension of earlier ideas, that human life is a pilgrimage or voyage over the sea of life and a return, after pausing at many *mansions*, to the haven of final rest, typified by Alexandria with its Sarapeum and its Lighthouse.[45] The Isis of the *Pyramid Texts* who stands on sentinel duty at the tomb has become the Isis who guides the sailor throughout his travels by land and sea and after all the vicissitudes of life and all its storms brings him safely to his rest at home.

The carnival of medieval and modern times is the obvious successor of the *navigium Isidis*. The ship-carriage, prominent in carnival-processions of Italy and the Rhineland, has descended from the *tensa* of Isis. The name itself may be derived from the expression *carrus navalis*, the carriage of the ship.[46] This does not specifically feature in the account we owe to Apuleius. On the numismatic evidence, however, we can be sure that it could be included in the pageantry. In the carnivals of our own day survive features of the Procession of Isis. Men on these occasions dress up as women. Flowers are strewn in the festival at Nice and elsewhere. The bands still play and the choirs still sing as they once did at Cenchreae and indeed on the banks of the Nile in the days of Tutankhamen. The grotesque characters with animal heads, sometimes painted in different colours, are a reminder of the bear and the monkey, the donkey and the dog of Anubis that fascinated Lucius as he stood, himself a donkey, waiting for a miracle to happen. There are modern parallels to the Isiac women who were mistresses of the wardrobe and in the procession attended to the toilet of their goddess with mirror and comb. At Catania in Sicily remarkable resemblances have been detected between the local Feast of 'St Agatha' and the Isis Festival, the Saint's victorious Veil being received to the sounds of tambourines such as would have pleased Isis' ear.[47] Whatever the etymology of the word *carnival* may be, the festivities which it denotes can be convincingly traced back to those brought by Isis out of Egypt.

The Festival of Isis on 5 March has ecclesiastical as well as secular parallels. The common source is surely the religious processions of the Nile in ancient Egypt. The Epiphany Festival of the Eastern Church termed that 'of the Lights' (*Ton Photon*) at which the holy silver cross is thrown into the sea and afterwards three times retrieved involves a procession of priests and marching choir down to the water's edge. Margate, in Kent, now sees it, like the Piraeus in Greece. The spirit of the ceremony, however, is exactly the same as that we have observed in the rites of Isis. In the Orthodox liturgy can be found a service called 'the Blessing of the Waters of the Nile'. In it occur the words, with reference to the Inundation, 'By God's providence and command (rise) up, O Nile'.[48] The ritual of the Christian Church owes a considerable and unacknowledged debt to the Egyptian religion that preceded it in the Graeco-Roman world.[49]

CHAPTER XIV

HEALING THE SICK

A BITTER STRUGGLE had to be waged before the Graeco-Roman world at last accepted Jesus instead of Isis. Among the reasons for the keenness of the conflict none was more important than the claim made by the upholders of the Egyptian faith that their goddess was the wonder-worker with the gift of healing the sick. Christianity worshipped its Lord as healing all manner of sickness, and its sharpest ancient critic, Celsus, found fault with Jesus on the ground that He had gained 'certain powers' from a stay in Egypt and from these had derived his divinity.[1] Such magic powers were the prerogative of the goddess who in Egypt had made the Lord of Heaven teach her the hidden name and spell, who had brought her brother-husband back to life, whose sorcery had guarded her son from all dangers, and whose skill was trusted to cure the manifold diseases of those who daily thronged her temple after beholding her visions during the night. Isis could be arraigned before any synod of Christian bishops as a dark old Egyptian devil: but all the same she was a most redoubtable devil. Hers was certainly a name to conjure with.

The rivalry between the two religions can be detected when we turn to the account of an act of exorcism performed by Cyril, who was Archbishop of Alexandria early in the fifth century. As one of the leading Christians in Egypt Cyril must have been familiar with the Gnostic view, there strongly held, that Isis and the Virgin Mary shared the same characteristic,[2] a view he could not have ignored when he was energetically championing the official adoption of the dogma of Panagia Theotokos—the All-Holy Virgin Mother of God—at the Council of Ephesus in 431. Cyril was certainly not blind to the hold that Isis still maintained over Egypt.

What this 'divinely ordained shepherd of Christ's intellectual flock' chose to do at Menouthis, two miles from the east side of Canopus, not far from Alexandria, is recounted in strangely guarded language by one of his successors.[3] Cyril, like any Isiac, obeys a divine order which reaches him in a dream. We learn that 'a dark Egyptian devil used to appear assuming a female form. . . . After virtually all the Greek oracles had been wiped out and the one remaining, that of Asclepius, had been burnt down . . . the odious demon went on deceiving and leading astray a large number both of the infidels who were fully attentive to its biddings and of the faithful who bore the tokens of Christ, persuading them to sit down near its altar in the hope of regaining their health or of receiving a message from heaven.' Accordingly, the good shepherd of Christ, perceiving the guile of this devil and observing the harm done to the faithful, entreated the Saviour and besought Him to bring the scandal to an end, to ban the diabolic apparitions and to grant the people a full understanding of the truth. Cyril, in fact, was bent upon destroying the temple of *Isis Medica* at Menouthis.[4] His aim was to cast out the devil, the evil spirit of Isis, by re-inhuming on the same site, where she was indeed known as 'the Truth', the bones of two Christian saints, reputedly 'Cyrus and John',[5] and by building a church which was to be a sure landmark for ships sailing in and out of Alexandria. Thus a visible proclamation to them because of the votive gifts of salvation that it was helping them on their voyage.[6] Here is the typical transformation of an Iseum into a Christian shrine. Here also is the significant silence about the identity of the hated goddess. All we are allowed to know is that the bishop exorcized 'the powers at work in the idol of female form and of many guises'. Cyril's behaviour is a clear proof of his awareness of the strength of *Isis Myrionymus*.

The medico-magical tradition in Egypt, with which the name of Isis is inseparably linked, goes back more than fifty centuries. To draw a hard and fast line between magical methods and scientific medicine is impossible when we survey the papyrological documents. We hover between the African witch-doctor's jugglings and the technique which the modern physician has acquired from the empirical and rationalist medicine of Greece. Over each aspect, however, Isis can be seen presiding. She is the spellbinder, the 'mage' of immemorial antiquity.[7] In the medical papyrus named after the Egyptologist Ebers and dated not later than the sixteenth century BC she is invoked as follows: 'O Isis, thou great Mage, heal me, release me from all things that are bad and evil and that belong to Seth, from the demonic fatal sicknesses—as thou hast saved and freed thy son Horus.'[8]

Isis does not always act the doctor on her own. In the *Pyramid Texts* she comes with healing in her wings along with her sister Nephthys.[9] Thoth, who also appears there as a healer, becomes her close collaborator when he joins the Osirian company although not himself a member of the Ennead of Heliopolis. In one account it is Thoth who, in answer to Isis' entreaty, uses his magic powers to save her child and utters the spell which restores Horus to life.[10] In the final stages of paganism he is the sorcerer who teaches Isis his art.[11] The syncretistic theology of Manetho converts Thoth into 'the first Hermes'[12] and Thoth/Hermes through his omniscience and wisdom can even be represented as Isis' father, though she can be his mother. But their family relationship is then fictitious. More important is their team work in company with Imouthes/Asclepius in the profession of medical magicians[13] possessing mighty powers.

The Mediterranean world knew the land of the Nile as the scene for the enchantments performed by 'the wise men, the sorcerers and the magicians.' Egypt was the home of thaumaturgy and theosophy, and proverbial for its secret theological 'wisdom'.[14] It is significant that in the Egyptian language *Power* is personified as a deity: $S\underline{h}m$. It was the *power* of Isis that caused the Nile to rise.[15] When Lucius was restored to his human shape the amazed bystanders saw manifested the *power* and the glory of Isis. A priestess of hers in the Imperial age took the name of Dynamis.[16] We learn about a 'sacred scribe' at Memphis who to gain the wisdom and culture of the Egyptians lived in a subterranean shrine for a period of twenty-three years and acquired his magic powers from Isis. The idols in the Sarapeum at Alexandria which the Christians finally destroyed held miraculous powers.[17]

It is against the background of Egyptian religion that the Christian apologist Justin discusses the question, so important for the pagan philosopher Celsus, whether the wisdom and the powers ('mighty works') of the Founder, which figure so largely in the Gospels, are due to the possession of 'magical skill': was Jesus indeed a 'mage'?[18] We do well to remember the widespread influence of Egyptian theosophical beliefs in their Hellenistic shape when we encounter the Pauline statement that Christ is the 'power' (*dynamis*) of God and the 'wisdom' (*sophia*) of God.[19] Power and wisdom are the very gifts claimed by the mages of the Nile in the wonders they work either through the *oral* or the *manual* rite.[20] One of the so-called Hellenists at the dawn of Christianity, the martyr Stephen who in the fullness of power did great wonders and signs, and so bore some likeness to Simon, the founder of Gnosticism,[21] freely granted that his predecessor Moses had been 'learned in all the wisdom of the Egyptians' and had exerted power in words and deeds.[22] Not long before this a Jewish source in a discussion about the miraculous rod of Moses which had awed the priests 'beyond Memphis' had reported its being held sacred in all Egyptian temples to Isis.[23]

The hieroglyphic texts which deal with the medico-magical practice of Egypt as well as the Greek magical papyri reveal the strength of the belief that diseases were evil, demonic powers which the mage could harangue and drive out sometimes simply by spells and sometimes by charging an image such as an amulet with magical properties and fastening it to the patient's body. The prescription of drugs was combined with these other procedures. Casting out devils, or else the works of devils, from sufferers whose bodies they had possessed was characteristic of the healing art in Egypt. The very behaviour of the Christian Cyril in exorcizing Isis at Menouthis proves his outlook to have been thoroughly Egyptian. In a peculiarly applicable New Testament phrase, the medical practitioners of Egypt worked according to the theory of 'wrestling against powers'[24]—a fight to find out which power would prove to be the strongest.[25] In all these magical treatments no power of Egypt was greater than that of Isis. Already in the Metternich Stele she is acclaimed as the Great

Sorceress who heals.[26] In later times she is described as the discoverer of the elixir of immortality and as her divine son's medical
teacher. To him she talks in the *Hermetic Literature* about 'philosophy and magic' as sustaining the soul just as medicine cures the
ailments of the body.[27] For the Greek mind the main tenets of
Egyptian religion are that Isis has invented many healthful drugs,
is an expert in medical science, and so takes pleasure in healing
mankind.[28] She affords her own special help and comfort through
visions. According to her own believers this can be proved not
through myths in the manner of the Greeks but through her
evident acts. Her epiphany, the manifestation of her glory, is
witnessed all over the world in the mighty acts and the cures she
performs.[29] Isis does not dwell in the clouds on top of Olympus
far away from the everyday ills and sorrows of men and women.
She unites with them when they are asleep. She can save them
when their lives are despaired of by their own doctors. Those who
obey her can be suddenly restored to health. At her hands the
maimed are healed and the blind receive their sight. Her name
has magical virtue and power, for she is sorceress, apothecary and
physician.

Sarapis, Isis' Hellenistic consort, shared in her medical functions.
He would visit those who slept in his temple and give them advice
in dreams. He was reputed to have restored sight to Demetrius of
Phaleron, who composed hymns of praise for this.[30] He saved the
body by giving it health. He was known for levitation and
'could convey men wherever he pleased without vehicles and
without bodies'.[31] The magical aspect of his godhead is emphasized
by the philosopher Numenius, who declares that the idol in the
Sarapeum at Alexandria was made not simply by sculptors but
with the additional help of mages and potions and demons that
they bound under their spell. According to this view Sarapis,
himself the great wonder-worker, was *achiropoietos*, 'not made
with hands'.[32] All this is in harmony, of course, with traditional
Egyptian magic. But Sarapis, just as obviously as Isis, was the
divinity who presided over the medical school that arose at
Alexandria inspired by the empirical science wrought there by
practitioners from Greece. The great Sarapeum, where the sick

resorted in hope of cure, was an ideal training hospital for physicians.

Next door to the Alexandrian Sarapeum was the great University: the cult of Sarapis and the establishment of the Library and the Museum were alike due to Ptolemy I. The Library was to overflow into the Temple and the links were to remain inseparable till the final onslaught by the Christians. We know that in the Temple there existed 'pastophoria'.[33] These were the quarters of the pastophors whose task was to master the medical texts and all the traditional magical lore of Egypt. Included in their programme were physiology and pathology. In these studies they must have felt the influence of such celebrated anatomists as the immigrant Greeks Erasistratus and Herophilus. A medical revolution was indeed achieved at Alexandria early in the Ptolemaic period when royal permission was granted for the dissection of the human body.[34] It was in this way that age-old medical superstitions were empirically dispelled and the discovery clinically achieved of the arteries and of the nervous system centred in the brain.

The Alexandrian pastophors who worshipped Isis and Sarapis, Anubis and Imouthes lived in an enlightened atmosphere. Greek medical science had arrived to overhaul the treatment of sickness and doubtless to purge away some of the crudities of Egyptian thaumaturgy. When a member of the medical profession was selected to be head of the University he must have followed the path of the historical Hippocrates and Aristotle's grandson Erasistratus with only an occasional side-long look at 'Imouthes'. This does not mean, however, that any quarrel arose in Alexandrian circles between science and religion or that medicine was strongly opposed to magic. If a professional doctor could preside over the University so could the Pontiff of all Egypt, Lucius Julius Vestinus, an Isiac who also took charge of 'the Latin and Greek Libraries in Rome'.[35] Conditions in the Alexandrian Sarapeum, the world's centre for cures of every kind and equally for medical research, must have resembled those seen today in the shrines of the Blessed Virgin at Tenos and Lourdes where pilgrims still practise incubation.

The Temple of *Isis Medica* which Archbishop Cyril destroyed at Menouthis was not far from Alexandria and belonged to a district famous for magic cures. Thus there was at Canopus a most hallowed Sarapeum in which according to a Christian source the priests performed sorcery of every kind in the name of 'Egyptian literary studies'. It was virtually 'a public school for training *mages*'.[36] Men of the highest eminence were reported to show faith in its miraculous cures and to sleep inside it whether for their own sake or for that of others. Paganism believed this to be a favourite area for the mighty deeds wrought by Sarapis 'the Lord' (*Kyrios*) and Isis 'the Lady' (*Kyria*). The 'St Cyrus' reputedly buried by Cyril at Menouthis has a name remarkably like that of the pagan *Kyrios* and *Kyria*, whose influence may survive in today's place-name, Abou*kir*.

The practice of incubation, common to Isiacism and to Catholicism both eastern and western, breaks down all social barriers and brings together within hallowed precincts the strangest assortment of believers. Ptolemy IV and his queen, like Propertius' Cynthia, trust in Isis' power to haunt her temple by night and to declare herself to them in dreams. At Delos the aretalogue Maiistas, like the fictional Lucius at Cenchreae, sleeps within the precincts of the shrine to hear the divine bidding.[37] In the year 141 BC at Kerkeorisis a suppliant laments: 'While I was staying in the great Iseum here for a cure because of the illness that encompassed me, the minister Horus beat me with his rod.'[38] In the Iseum of the Campus Martius at Rome, as the result of a deception, the matron Paulina keeps vigil and undergoes a 'sacred wedding' with Anubis. In the same temple, after their capture of Jerusalem, Titus and Vespasian celebrate their triumph by one night's rest.[39]

In the words of the Oxyrhynchus *Litany*, 'those who call upon Isis in faith' claim that they do indeed behold her in her manifold epiphanies. As the convert Lucius learns for himself, the fruition of the godhead through incubation demands ritual purity and absolute faith. Filled with the same faith Aristides, when suffering from illness, dreams that a light shines upon him from Isis as well as other untold portents of salvation while on the same night he has a vision of Sarapis and Asclepius, each like the other in beauty and size.[40]

Asclepius was Greece's renowned god of health. Apollo, who according to one legend was his father, was responsible for his learning the skills of medicine. Like the Egyptians the Greeks regarded light and fire as the source of healing. The most famous temple of Asclepius was at Epidaurus, but he was also worshipped elsewhere, as on Cos. In each of his cult centres the practice of ritual purification by bathing, fasting and incubation attended the growth of medical science. Clearly, therefore, the functions of Asclepius were exactly the same as those of *Isis Medica*. The prevailing view in late antiquity is thus summed up by a Greek writer: 'Men say that she is the giver of health, as we declare Asclepius is.'[41] Greece's acceptance of Isis the Healer can be well illustrated at Epidaurus itself. Here in the second century AD a temple was erected by a local senator 'to Hygieia, Asclepius and Apollo under their Egyptian names'.[42] The dedication, therefore, was to Isis/Hygieia, Sarapis/Asclepius and Horus/Apollo. A triadic relationship may have been intended with the divine family healers as Mother, Husband and Son. But in Greek mythology Hygieia was the *daughter* of Asclepius. Again, therefore, we see the problem of achieving exact equivalence by the method of 'Greek interpretation'.

One of the associates of Asclepius in Greek mythology was Telesphorus, the god of convalescence. It is at Philippi that we can observe how closely Asclepius, Telesphorus and Hygieia were linked with Isis. This Roman colony at the time when it was visited by the Christian missionary Paul had accepted the Egyptian gods, among whom Isis with her own priests seems to have been most important.[43] After the great battle the Romans installed columns entrusting the city entirely to the guardianship of Isis as the colony's Queen and Saviour, *Kourotrophos* and *Linopeplos*.[44] It was in her role of healer that she ruled as patroness of Philippi. To her were addressed the prayers, the offerings and the devotions of the faithful. A shrine is known to have been dedicated to her in honour of 'the Imperial House' by a doctor called Q. Mofius Euhemerus, whose name is Jewish ('Moses') in a Latinized form.[45] The goddess of healing has transcended all ethnic barriers and is accepted by the Jew of the Diaspora as readily as by the Roman colonist and the Greek. The religious atmosphere at Philippi is no less favourable to Isis than at Alexandria and along the estuaries of the Nile.

The mighty works of 'the queen and restorer of health' were done through the magical virtue of her name. Her name was hallowed in Egyptian legend because the great god Re, who had made the heavens and the earth, had once been made to yield up his to her. When the holy god had grown old, she gained knowledge of him 'in his own name' through a stratagem. Out of the spittle which fell from his dribbling mouth she kneaded clay and fashioned it in the shape of a holy serpent, which she caused to shoot its venom into his body. Just as Isis in her manifestation to Lucius uttered a multitude of the names she bore, so in the tabernacle of the gods did the great Majesty of Re cry out some of the multitudes of his names for the ears of 'the great enchantress'. In the end, when 'the Being whose name the gods know not' had promised that he would be searched through by Isis and that he would allow his name to come forth from his body and go into hers, she wrested it from him and through her magic spell caused the poison to die. The spell itself, as spoken by 'the great lady, the mistress of the gods', possessed its own efficacy, for by it Isis had acquired the name of the Almighty—his most important talisman—and so had made herself mistress of the earth. The legend concludes, therefore, with the injunction that the words were to be said over an image of Isis and of Horus.[46]

To know the true name and to utter it aloud was as important for the conjurer in addressing either the disease directly or its agent as it had been for Isis herself in her dealings with Re. We can see this attitude adopted by the speaker of the following spell (as he utters 'the great and wonderful names of the Great Deity'): 'I call upon thee, Lady Isis . . . Nemesis, Adrasteia, with thy many names and many forms, glorify me, as I have glorified the name of thy son "Horus".'[47] Black magic is here very evident. The spellbinder must take a piece of pitch and make sacrifice facing the moon. Isis is told: 'Thy kingdom resides in that which is utterly black.' The pitch black ink used in writing the magic spell well matches the substance chosen for the ritual offering and the moonlight wherein Isis dwells only enhances the weirdness of the scene.

Such an incantation as this, though spoken in the name of the Lady of Healing, would probably have made little appeal to the medical practitioner at Philippi, 'Moses' the Jew. But in Isiacism there was plenty of room both for doctors trained in the scientific techniques of Greek medicine and for wizards and quacks, claiming divine authority for their practices. Nor must we forget that even in the Christian dispensation the petitioner may indulge in similar formulas as he calls on the Divine names.[48]

In the Graeco-Roman world 'wisdom' (*sophia*) became a very popular term among both pagan and Judaeo-Christian theologians. For Plutarch, Isis herself was both 'wise' and 'philosophic.[49] *Sophia* was one of the key words in the heretical Gnosticism which Catholicism strongly attacked and in which Isis was at work. An Isiac priestess at Athens bore the name, probably in religion.[50] A very important bridge between paganism and Christianity was the speculative system of the Hellenizing Jew Philo of Alexandria and in it the cornerstone was 'Holy Wisdom' (*Hagia Sophia*), Mother of the divine Logos, rightly identified with Isis, Isis-Sophia could be thought to produce Harpocrates as the Logos.[51] When we consider the appearances of *sophia* generally in the copious Greek literature of the centuries that followed Alexander, we must be struck with its Museum outlines. It is a development from the therapeutic language used there[52] and indeed is another name for the Mage Isis who in one way or another identifies herself with Sophia.[53] In the Museum under her inspiration there flourished all the arts and sciences of the ancient world, particularly the subjects related to medicine in its various aspects as they were studied by her pastophors. A characteristic product of the *Wisdom Literature* is the pseudepigraphical work of 'Solomon'. In the section where the anonymous writer pays tribute to Alexandrian science, we are told that wisdom, 'she that is the artificer of all things', has instructed mankind in the natures of living things as well as in the diversities of plants and the virtues of roots. This wisdom, *Sophia*, undoubtedly represents *Isis Medica*.[54]

The rigidly drawn theology of the early Christian church was fringed with many heresies. None of these gave greater trouble than the Gnostic cosmologies, in which *wisdom* and *power*— *sophia* and *dynamis*—were indispensable notions. The ostensible founder of Gnosticism, Simon the Samaritan Mage who in the canonical *Acts of the Apostles* was commonly heeded as 'the Great Power of God', was wonderfully impressed by the greater wisdom and power of the orthodox Christian who beat his own sorcery by casting out unclean spirits.[55] When the Samaritans referred to this mage as 'the *power* of God called great' they were talking the language of Isiacism. One of the Gnostic sects, the Peratae, are specifically stated by the Christian historian of heresies, Hippolytus, to have worshipped Isis as 'ruler of the twelve hours of the day' and as 'the right-hand *power* of God'.[56] We also learn about the same sect that they use in their theology (*sophia*) of Father and Serpent Son (each with three *dynameis*) analogies from medical science. They appeal to the anatomy of the brain, to the pineal gland, to the spinal marrow, to blood-vessels and to arteries.[57] Clearly the Peratae are diligent students of Isiac medicine as it was pursued in the University of Alexandria.

The prowess of Isis in the field of pharmocology was recognized throughout the Graeco-Roman world. She is described as pouring out for her son Horus first the sweet draught of ambrosia, the elixir of life, and as having anointed her holy scriptures with the drug of immortality. Her name was given to a drug which won universal praise, according to the medical writer Galen, because it could staunch wounds, cure headaches, and was good for lesions, ulcers, fractures and bites of every kind.[58] Here emblematically we have portrayed the omniscience of the goddess in drug-lore. Long after the fall of pagan civilization Isis still maintained her botanical reputation (*Pl. 70*).[59]

A belief in the dream as a divine sign was certainly not peculiar to the religion of Isis: we need only remember what Socrates has to say on this subject in the *Phaedo*. The Graeco-Roman world regarded Isis as responsible for divination.[60] What is so striking in the therapy that Isis promises to perform is the need of faith and the sureness of hope on the side of those who patiently await the indubitable dream which will bring them health. In pagan literature, as of course in the Bible,[61] men take decisions after being divinely 'warned in a dream'. Isis demands delay: her believers must not be too eager for the promised salvation. The task of the professional soothsayer was therefore no light one. Lucius when told in a dream to undergo his second Isiac degree could not at first understand why, and it took the priest some time to convince him that this was a genuine order of the goddess. Such cases must have been common enough. When it was a question of restoration to full health the sufferer would need very little persuasion to wait. The history of Egyptian religion in its post-Alexandrian development indicates that those to whom visions came obeyed without hesitation. Thus Ptolemy I was prompted by a dream to send for a statue of Sarapis. For a similar reason Seleucus IV caused an image of Isis to be fetched from Memphis to Antioch.[62] We may remember Vespasian with the blind. His reputed power of healing accords with the ancient tradition of Isis and the eye of Horus[63] To the modern mind such behaviour may seem the mark of naïve credulity. If so, then pagan and Christian alike suffered from a blind trust in dreams. Each had his own soothsayers.[64]

The temples of Isis and her divine colleagues were adorned with *ex-voto* offerings left there by those who had been healed in body or who had escaped some calamity. At Pompeii in the Iseum was the figure of a large hand with open palm. Elsewhere there were votive paintings in gratitude for rescue from shipwreck.[65] Representations of ears suggest the dedicant's recognition that Isis is the goddess who listens to petitions.[66] The carvings of footprints such as can be seen at Delos and Beneventum probably symbolize the fact that the pilgrim has trodden in the path of the goddess. He could think of himself as 'in step' and 'foot to foot' with Sarapis.[67] As in Catholic churches of both eastern and western rites, so in the temples of the Egyptian gods *ex-voto* limbs, hands and other parts of the human body were dedicated symbolically. According to Clement of Alexandria the ears and eyes made out of precious material indicated that the deity sees and hears everything.[68] But the ordinary believer, less philosophically minded, doubtless looked on them as objects of sympathetic magic.

CHAPTER XV

THE GUARDIAN GUIDE
AND HERALD

IN THE *Pyramid Texts* the god Anubis, though not a member of
the Ennead of Heliopolis, is important as guardian of Osiris and
guide for the dead. He leads Osiris from the gods who belong to
the earth to those who are in heaven. He comes to meet the dead
as herald reporting from the horizon.[1] In the picturesque language
of ancient Egypt he is described as Counter of Hearts and First of
the Westerners. When the revitalized king arises as Anubis, the
gods of the Ennead tremble before him.[2] He can command that
the dead shall come in as a star. Wearing his mask down to his
neck, he is unmistakable of face. He can be linked with Thoth.[3]
In the rite of the Preservation of the Body, whereas Thoth heals
the limbs through the magic of his spells, Anubis washes the
entrails, prevents the corpse from rotting, and along with Horus
directs the embalmment.[4] We may be sure that when 'the
physicians embalmed Israel' on the instructions of Joseph, as
recorded in the *Old Testament*,[5] they carried out their forty days
ceremony in strict agreement with the embalmment ritual of
Cynopolis, the Egyptian centre for the worship of Anubis. Like
his companion god of the dead, Wepwawet, Anubis allies himself
to Osiris. He is related to have joined Osiris on his world tour and
when the good king suffered death to have assisted Isis and
Nephthys in the search for the dismembered limbs.[6]

As a god of the dead, and more specifically of funeral rites,
Anubis of Egypt naturally underwent identification with Hermes
of Greece. Each, of course, had his own ethnological characteristics. Hermes was never considered by the Greeks to be Lord of
the Mummy Wrappings. Anubis with the head of jackal or dog

ill-suited the Arcadian background which was the scene for the birth of Hermes, typically Greek in his baby prank of stealing the cattle of Apollo. Yet the conflation of Hermes the Conductor of Souls (*Psychopompus*) with the Nile god who ushered the dead into the presence of Osiris was inevitable when Egyptian religion received Greek interpretation.

The name *Hermanubis* marked the full acceptance of an assimilation which entailed the usual suppression of incompatible elements. When for example the Hermanubist 'convocation' of those who held the holy vessels at Thessalonica in the performance of the Egyptian religion walked in procession under the name of a god who was only half-Greek (*mixhellen*)[7] they doubtless held in their hands the *kyrekeion*, the herald's wand of Hermes, but wore on their skulls the dog's head mask of Anubis (*Pl. 46*).[8] In at least one other respect they were unmistakably Greek. For in accordance with a funerary practice of Greece which the dying Socrates asked his friends to fulfil at the shrine of Asclepius, they offered up a cock with white feathers,[9] which Anubis in Egypt never sought.

From the time of the Middle and the New Kingdom the role of Anubis (as of Isis herself) becomes increasingly important in the resurrection of Osiris. Re sends Anubis down from heaven to carry out the obsequies of the murdered god. The mummy is skilfully bound up so that it may not undergo corruption through contact with the air. This explains why Anubis is represented as superintending embalmments and as receiving the mummies at the entrance to the tomb.[10] In the tradition revealed to us by Plutarch Anubis is the nephew of Isis and is her cynocephalous guardian. As well as possessing his infernal, chthonic qualities he is portrayed at the beginning of a hymn in his honour from Kios in Bithynia as 'immortal Anubis, king of all the gods in heaven'. He belongs to Olympus as well as to the lower world: which is why, according to Plutarch, he is fashioned with the face of a dog, which can use its eyes equally well by night and by day.[11] Anubis, with his mask of jackal or dog, also has the palm of victory in his hand. It is he who thus symbolizes the victory of life over death. It is he who leads the dead to their resurrection.

Honoured with the name of 'guide' the Hellenistic Anubis is the
familiar attendant of Isis and her bodyguard[12] in the journey
beyond the tomb. He retains his dog-like features. He guards the
swamps of the North and opens the path of rebirth. He teaches
Isis the way in her search for Osiris' body and in her longing to
rear Horus.[13]

The order of precedence in the hierarchy of the Alexandrian
sodality termed 'Isis and the fellow-temple gods' (*synnaoi theoi*)
strongly supports the view that whatever the theological aims of
Ptolemy Soter, Manetho and Timotheus were at the outset, the
pattern of a family triad—father, mother and son—was not the
standard arrangement. It has been pointed out by Roussel, whose
epigraphical studies at Delos have added so much to our knowledge of the Alexandrian cult, that Anubis there is repeatedly
invoked with Sarapis and Isis whereas the son of Isis—Harpocrates/
Horus—is either missing or put in the fourth position after
Anubis.[14] To the evidence from Delos can be joined that from
other sites. In the temple at Thera, looking directly across the
Mediterranean towards Alexandria, there are seats for Sarapis,
Isis and Anubis, but not for Harpocrates. In Priene and Eretria
Harpocrates does indeed appear, but only as number four.

The important position occupied by Anubis is all the more
surprising when we remember that the general policy of Ptolemy
in his theological reformation was to get rid of whatever in
Egyptian religion was repugnant and monstrous to Greek eyes.
Isis, like her consort and her son, was regularly exhibited with
human features. Anubis seldom lost the face of a dog. His divine
colleagues uttered the same speech as the men and women who
besought their help. Anubis howled like a jackal and barked like
a hound. Virgil makes his readers vividly aware of this aspect of
Alexandrian religion when he alludes to Cleopatra summoning
her squadrons with her Isiac timbrel to the Battle of Actium—
opposed to the Roman gods Neptune, Venus and Minerva with
their weapons 'stand the beastly shapes of gods of every kind, and
Anubis the barker'.[15] This is, of course, the view of the Augustan
court poet whose unsympathetic approach is determined by
political considerations.[16] But other references in Latin literature

conclusively reveal that for educated minds the dog of Egypt was either a laughing-stock or an object of utter contempt. Juvenal thinks of the priest of Anubis as himself scoffing at the wailing people.[17] The latter doubtless treated the priest in his dog's mask with the same scant respect as they saw him walking past them at the head of the street procession, a startling and shocking sight.[18] Anubis could appear to Lucius the Isiac convert a really 'fearful herald'. Another view was held in a poem assigned to the third century Christian Cyprian. How can a man who has been a member of the Roman senate sink so low as to go around with a rattle in his hand and a dog's mask over his face?[19] Still, monstrous as this pagan god remained, he has not been without a Christian successor. In the Eastern Orthodox Church, how-ever discreetly concealed, there exists a cynocephalous Saint Christopher, who, in the manner of Anubis, acts as superhuman ferryman for the traveller.[20]

Animals never rose to positions of eminence in the anthropo-morphic mythology of Greece. Those who called themselves Hermanubists met a difficulty which not even the most ingenious 'Greek interpretation' could resolve. If Anubis acted as watchdog of Hades then he must be the same as the Greek Cerberus. Such would have been the Roman way of understanding the verse of Statius: 'Why the Lethaean doorkeeper guards the Pharian altar.'[21] Anubis is equivalent to Cerberus and the shrine over which he watches is that of *Isis Pharia*. But Anubis was also Hellenized as *Hermes Psychopompus*. Accordingly, as he shared identity with Egyptian Anubis, Hermes the Greek conductor to Hades was fantastically telescoped into Hades' watchdog Cerberus. The problem might have been solved if the prehistoric Wepwawet had retained his independence in Egyptian religion and had been important in the Alexandrian cult: but of this there is no evidence. The funerary rite known as the Opening of the Mouth was presided over by Anubis and in Egypt the priest who performed the ceremony was masked as a jackal.[22] The Greek writer Dio-dorus well indicates the nature of the problems involved in Hellenizing Anubis when he states: 'Among the Egyptians according to the ancient rite *Hermes Psychopompus* brings up the body of Apis and hands it over to one who wears the head of Cerberus.'[23]

Hermes with an animal head made no appeal to the Greek critic. Lucian writes sarcastically about it after an allusion to the fable of the arrival of Io in Egypt. 'She has now crossed the sea and swum ashore. Do you see she no longer walks about on all fours but Hermes has stood her up now and made her an altogether lovely woman? . . . But what has Hermes done to transform himself and alter his face from a young man's to that of a dog'?[24] The implication here is clear. An Io who has lost her bovine features and become an anthropomorphic Isis is welcome, but not a cynocephalous Hermes. Lucian, because to him a dog seemed an unclean and contemptible creature,[25] could not accept Hermanubis. To convert the messenger of Zeus into a dog was an insult to Greek intelligence and to the view that the measure of all things was man. In his native Egypt Anubis might rank as a great god. That very Greek philosopher, Socrates, well aware of Anubis' existence might admit his power and even 'swear by the dog', but to a man with Lucian's background the combination of Anubis with Hermes was a preposterous barbarism.[26]

Why then did Anubis with a face which was generally repulsive so often take a seat next to Isis and Sarapis? First, he was not merely the traditional Egyptian god of the dead but also of the resurrection of the dead. Secondly, Hellenistic theology if it turned a blind eye to the hound's muzzle and ears could find in the figure of Anubis a *numen tremendum*, a mystery which the speculative Plutarch could state thus: 'Some hold Anubis to be Kronos, generating all things out of himself and conceiving all things inside himself.' To the believer who scratched his own *credo* about AD 100 on a rock near Ptolemais, dog or no dog, Anubis was God Almighty: 'Zeus, Sarapis and Helios-Hermanubis are one.'[27] He linked the darkness of the underworld with the sun in the sky. In the ritual of the Isiac mystery, again, Hermanubis was the indispensable herald. At the moment when the initiate trod the very threshold of death this was the god who stood with *kyrekeion* in hand to lend support. The strongest reason, however, for his hierarchical importance in the Alexandrian cult was his indefatigable assistance to Isis herself. He it was who had fully shared with Isis in the sorrows, the mourning and the search for the body of Osiris. He had also proudly found for her the son she had lost.[28] He was Isis' mainstay and Osiris' bodyguard. On the expedition which led Osiris all over the world—like Alexander the Great as the mighty civilizer—Anubis joined up as a soldier, wearing his own dog-skin helmet, along with Macedon/Wepwawet.[29] The help Anubis gave Isis was well symbolized by the figure of the hound above which her image rode on the gable of her temple in Rome (*Pl. 42*). Nor would her public processions have been conducted in due form without an Anubis to march at the head with wand and palm, 'the go-between of gods on high and underground' and the harbinger by whom Isis was ushered in (*Pl. 38*).[30]

In the first century of the Christian era the name of Anubis acquired a notoriety at Rome which the Jewish historian Josephus discusses, as being a contemporary event, along with his single reference to the Crucifixion of Jesus, 'doer of wonderful works'.[31] The nobly born Paulina, who was a devout worshipper of Isis, was induced by the oldest priest in her temple to spend a night there. Bribed by her lover Mundus, the priest adopted this ruse so that Mundus himself might play the role of Anubis,[32] said to have been good enough to fall in love with the lady, who was to sup and lie with him. When darkness came and all the lights were put out, Mundus hidden in the inmost part of the shrine was able to enjoy his illicit 'wedding night' because Paulina, a lady whose chastity was unimpeachable and whose husband had consented, believed like some character out of Boccaccio that sexual intercourse could take place between a human and a divine partner. The Emperor Tiberius awarded the priesthood of Isis the condign punishment of crucifixion, besides destroying her temple and statue.

The facts here are reliably reported. Clearly at about the time when another Crucifixion is described as having occurred on Mount Calvary the Egyptian religion of Isis and Anubis was the concern of people of the highest rank in the capital of the Empire, even of the Emperor himself. It is no less evident that in the minds of some, if not all, of those who professed the religion where the phallus was not disguised, the idea of sacred prostitution in the temple precincts was accepted without question. The surrender of chastity was indeed as much a part of worship in Egypt as in the Greek mysteries. Whether in the cult of Isis incidents such as that of the seduction of Paulina by the libertine Mundus were common is a matter of conjecture. The assignations made at the Isea in Rome and Pompeii suggest that in this respect the goddess was as easy-going as other Egyptian divinities—Ammon as well as Hathor and Bast and perhaps Min and Ptah. Long before Paulina had ostensibly been promised 'sacred wedlock' (*hieros gamos*) it was not uncommon for the queen regnant, as the Egyptian annals show, to be visited by the chief of the male gods.[33] Sexual licence in the guise of divine worship appeared inoffensive to human morality. In Egypt as well as in Greece it was by no means unusual for a god to possess 'holy courtesans' (*hierodouloi*) whose attitude, like Paulina's, was that of utter willingness.[34]

The nature of the Isiac ritual, both inside the temple during the celebration of the mysteries and outside in the public processions, suggests that even when evidence is lacking, as at Philippi, the dog-headed herald must have held a place side by side with Isis. The archaeologist may be doubtful because the name of Anubis has not so far been discovered in the Roman colony where Isis reigned supreme, had her own priest, and received adoration in a series of five chapels which are still extant. But we must remember that not far away at Thessalonica the god Hermanubis had his faithful supporters. Among his worshippers, 'those who stepped into his precinct' (*sekobatai*), the names of three who held chief office (*prostatai*) have come down to us as Pontonius, Helenus and Cassius.[35] Across the Aegean along the coast of Asia Minor Anubis was held in honour: in Chios, in Smyrna with its associa-tion of *Synanoubiastai*, and in Cios in the Propontis where the hymn of invocation to Anubis has been discovered. That Anubis was familiar to the citizens of Philippi is strongly suggested by the fact that the deserter Volusius, after his proscription by the triumvirs, found his way into the Republican camp by acting as a mendi-cant Isiac priest and walking about the main streets with a dog's mask on his head.[36] A soldier in wartime with his life at stake must surely choose camouflage in keeping with the local landscape. How could Volusius have hoped to escape detection if those he met had never known about Anubis?

For the Christian critic, Tertullian, at the end of the second century, what the world owed to Egypt was superstition and a travesty of truths told in the Bible. The triad he knew comprised Sarapis, Isis and Anubis. Sarapis was the Old Testament 'saint', the soothsayer Joseph who expounded dreams to Pharaoh. Beneath his right hand, we are told, the Egyptians 'placed the sacred dog'. They added Isis, 'Pharia', whose name shows she is Pharaoh's daughter. Since, however, their religion contained both zoomorphic and anthropomorphic elements, 'they combined each of the two ideas in the single figure of Anubis'. Tertullian summed it up as a despicable religion in which the worshipper is led like a slave by the greedy throat and filthy habits of a dog.[37]

It is odd that Anubis should be scorned in this way. It is true his two emblematic creatures, the jackal and the dog, were in the ancient world notorious scavengers. But one of the main functions of Anubis was to release the human body at death from the uncleanness that possessed it. He embalmed it and perfumed it with myrrh.[38] He wrapped it with linen swaddling bands and received it at the door of the tomb.[39] Anubis in ancient Egypt was not the filthy dog of Tertullian's imagination but the august Lord of the Cleansing Room and of *T3-dsr*, 'the Holy Land,' *i.e.* the Necropolis. As Lord of the Divine Hall he stood beside Isis, Mistress of the Mountains.[40] In the crucial weighing of the souls of the dead it was he who ushered them in to be tried before Osiris and examined the tongue of the great balance.[41] Considered cosmologically, in the words of Plutarch, Anubis shared both in 'Nephthys'—what is below the earth and invisible—and in 'Isis'— what is above the earth and visible, and so his name was applied to the curving horizon which makes contact with each of them.[42]

A letter still extant and ostensibly sent by the archpriest Manetho to Ptolemy II contains a very early reference in 'Greek interpretation' to Hermes Trismegistus. The uncouth style suggests that this is an authentic document: its writer is more at home in hieroglyphics and communicates with the king and with his colleague Timotheus in a language foreign to him. The letter leaves no doubt that in the important theological discussions of the early Ptolemaic period a paramount position was assigned to Hermes, regarded as the Egyptian Thoth or Theuth. The influence of the theology of Hermopolis is evident. Hermes is called 'the founding father' of the divine family.[43] He is obviously identified with the universal Demiurge whose sacred animal was either the ibis or the dog-headed ape and whose figure does not exactly fit the tidy theological arrangement of Isis and her 'fellow-temple gods'. In the inscriptions witnessing to the popularity of the Alexandrian cult the god whom the Greeks renamed Hermes and the Romans Mercury appears as Anubis. Yet in the literary sources Hermes is constantly equated with Thoth. Already in Herodotus we find the city where the ibis of Thoth was adored called 'the city of Hermes'.[44] The mythographer Nicander of the second century BC, in telling the story of what happened when the Greek gods were pursued by Typhon and 'fled' to Egypt, specifies the metamorphosis of Artemis into a cat, but makes no mention of Hermes changing into a dog. Instead, he informs us that Hermes became an ibis.[45] The transformation of Greece's Messenger of the Gods into Thoth was in fact very common and not surprising. Thoth like Anubis had few problems (apart from the headpiece) when he was cast for the role of Hermes. Hermes was one who knew all the magic arts, as his wand betokened, and was a god with perfect wisdom. So too was Thoth, a god who like Isis herself could be invoked as a healer.[46] Thoth was the civilizer who had invented all the arts and sciences and had bestowed on Egypt its hieroglyphics and its literature. Hermes had a similar reputation. Each of them was devoted to music. Each was a spokesman for the gods to men, who adored each as their general benefactor.

In Egyptian mythology Thoth shared some functions with Anubis. He appeared at the Great Assize of the Dead. He assisted Horus' mother in her trouble, saying to her 'Fear not, Isis'. He was the gods' herald traversing the sky.[47] From the standpoint of 'Greek interpretation', therefore, it was not difficult for Hermes

to Egyptianize himself now as Anubis and now as Thoth and to
wear the mask now of a jackal or dog and now of an ibis or
baboon. When Hermes was thus depicted, a son of the Nile in
the likeness of an African creature, he did not lose his Greek
identity. His conversion into Thoth presented at least one problem:
Hermes delighted in sly dealing and even lies whereas Thoth was a
god of truth and justice. As usual, however, such inconvenient
anomalies were overcome by theological subterfuge. The Roman
Cicero enumerates five types of Egyptian Mercury, the fifth in
the list being Thoth/Theuth.[48] Clearly, if such splitting of the
complicated personality of Hermes/Mercury could be so elabor-
ately pursued, then his transformation and idealization as Thoth
suffered no stumbling block. The way was open for Hermes to
receive infinite power: thrice most great, *Trismegistus*.[49]

Although each was identified with Hermes, both Thoth and
Anubis maintained their individuality. Thus in the Iseum at
Pompeii there have been found representations both of a large
ibis, symbolizing Thoth, and of a priest wearing the jackal's
head of Anubis.[50] Although Thoth is not specifically one of 'the
fellow-temple gods' as Anubis, is, he fulfills a very important role
in the Isiacism of the imperial age. Egyptian Hermes—*Trismegistus*
—is the *mage* by whom Isis has been taught, the Thoth who is
himself the Word of God, the Logos by whom all things have
been created. When Hermes becomes the god who in Egypt was
despatched by the Aton and the Ennead to heal Horus for his
mother Isis, and when he is described by Plutarch as giving Isis
her bovine head,[51] he enjoys a prestige hardly lower than that of
Zeus/Sarapis. This can be detected even in Judaeo-Christian
literature. It is claimed for the patriarch Moses that he founded
Thoth's city Hermopolis and in it consecrated the ibis, this
being a bird which destroys creatures harmful to mankind.[52]
Hermes, we know, could receive the attribute *evangelos*, the
'messenger of glad tidings', a title equally suitable to each of the
Egyptian gods whose names he took.[53] The significance of such
facts appears when in the New Testament the people of Lycaonia
are told 'the message of glad tidings' preached by the Christian
missionary whom they proceed to deify as Hermes 'because he

leads the talking'. Here we meet the typical Graeco-Roman Hermes/Mercury. Whatever his past may have been, he is now true of voice like Thoth and watchful of justice like Anubis and Isis herself. Hermes/Thoth, *Trismegistus*, is indeed inseparable from Isis 'the wise', regarded as his daughter and pupil, and described both as 'prior to the Muses at Hermopolis', where he has invented writing and music, and as 'Justice'.[54]

In the philosophizing of later paganism Hermes *Trismegistus* in association with Isis and Asclepius becomes a remarkably transcendent figure. Hermes in the shape of Anubis literally guides the Isiac initiate. Hermes when identified with Thoth figurately guides the minds of men into all truth. Under this aspect he has infinite power, as befits his Egyptian descent. To men he grants understanding (*nous*), rational utterance (*logos*) and knowledge (*gnosis*) and by filling them with the vision of himself he 'deifies' them. His worshippers can invoke him with as much enthusiasm as they would Isis: 'O life of human life, O light of all knowledge, O womb pregnant with the father's planting.' We need not wonder that the 'Asclepius' to whom Hermes *Trismegistus* speaks hears it all from a shrine of Egypt.[55]

Whereas Hermes/Thoth was the object of the philosopher's devotion, Hermes/Anubis was as real and familiar a figure to anybody professing the Isiac faith as an undertaker in Christian communities. Outside Egypt Anubis could hardly ever fulfil his vocation as an embalmer in the Egyptian sense.[56] But he could still receive offerings for the dead. The priest who attended funeral rites would put on the dog's-head helmet to disguise himself and like Volusius collect the money payable to Anubis.[57] A specimen of such a mask has survived. We can see openings for the priest's shoulders and under the animal's muzzle are two holes for the human eyes.[58]

Other features of Anubis worship indicate how well it fitted into the general religious pattern. Lucian tells about the Egyptian embalmer who sits down and has a meal and a drink with the corpse.[59] In Rome the Emperor Commodus was so much addicted to Isiacism that he carried an image of Anubis in the procession. We are also told that with the head of it he soundly smote the heads of the Isiac priests.[60] Among miracles recorded for the edification of believers by the freedman of the Emperor Hadrian, Phlegon, is the birth of a baby with an 'Anubis head' in the first century.[61]

To answer the phenomenological question how significant a forerunner was the Family of Mother, Husband, Babe as we look at Egyptian religion in the light of the Christian dispensation cannot here be undertaken. Undoubtedly 'John the Forerunner' (*Prodromos*) always accompanies the Panagia/Theotokos, as any iconostasis can show us in an Orthodox Church.[62] The figure of Anubis 'holder of the keys' which is found in the Hellenistic period may also have its significance as we consider palaeo-Christianity. Certainly at the time when Christian theology was still seeking to establish itself in face of such competitors as that of Egypt, men did not hesitate to combine in one setting the guardian gods of the Nile and the Jewish angels who make their appearance in the New Testament. Two gems have survived in which we observe this happening.[63] On the one Thoth is found in company with Sabaoth-Michael. On the other can be seen Anubis in Roman dress standing to the left with palm and pouch, and on the right the archangel Gabriel-Sabaoth. In an age when men were groping around for theological truth and the Christian Church was as yet not much more than a name, it was natural enough for those who needed divine support to draw on all the help they could obtain. An amulet which displayed Judaeo-Christian angels side by side with Egyptian gods on guard indubitably possessed its own manifold efficacy.

CHAPTER XVI

THE YOUNG KING AND LORD OF ALL

AMONG THE EXOTIC fashions of male society in the middle of the first century AD was the wearing of an Egyptian signet ring. This we learn from the Younger Pliny: Harpocrates (*Hr-p3-ḥrd*) was among the gods whose miniatures were then in vogue.[1] Here is the clear proof that Horus the son of Isis, the infant described in one of the *Pyramid Texts* as 'the young one with his finger in his mouth',[2] was a favourite figure of paganism in the time of Christ. The theological eminence achieved at this date by the god who is variously called the Younger Horus, Harsiesis ('Horus the son of Isis'), Horapollo and Harpocrates is brought out in the Oxyrhynchus *Litany* in which the identification with Apollo is attributed to Isis herself: she has 'established Horus Apollo to be everywhere the youthful lord of the whole world'.[3] It is through his mother that he has been made immortal and enthroned as his father's successor. The view here stated marks a Ptolemaic development. Horus no longer remains confined to the Nile valley as an Osiris reincarnate in the body of a new Pharaoh. Isis may boast that she is 'mother of Horus the king' but the kingdom he now enjoys has done away with national barriers and he has become a world-wide ruler. His empire renders him great in the manner of Alexander and of Augustus Caesar. In the *Litany* he bears the same name as the first of the Ptolemies: *Soter*, 'Saviour'. For those who accept his sway certain words uttered by Isis at the birth of Horus in Egypt have ecumenical validity: 'He shall rule over this earth. . . . He will be your master, this god who is but an embryo'.[4]

Harpocrates (the 'Young Child Horus') in a divine triad

where the family's driving force is maternal love is not in himself a strong starter in what, under a monotheistic impulse, becomes a kind of race to decide which of the three shall claim control of the world. In the last days of paganism the power of the Son of Isis grows as the cosmopolitan faiths of Egypt, Persia and Palestine converge. Horus is now the radiant Sun, Horus Apollo, and as we are told by the writer to whom he eponymously gives the name of Horapollo his solar power is symbolized by lions, which like the Sun are fiery-eyed, round-faced and radiant-maned,[5] being placed underneath his throne, an imaginative touch reminiscent of the lion couchant of Saint Mark.

On the island of Euboea in the central area of Greece the cult of the Alexandrian gods was well established by the beginning of the Christian era, as is evident from inscriptions and from the Iseum excavated at Eretria.[6] At the important cross-channel city of Chalcis has been found a stele on which is inscribed an aretalogy of 'Karpokrates'. This stele is datable to the third century AD and, like the aretalogies of Isis discovered not far away in the Cyclades at Andros and Ios, clearly emanates from the Memphite source discussed earlier. Harpocrates in this his own *Magnificat* shows his sense of power. He is still as in Egypt the God of Time. He boasts himself to be the son of Sarapis and Isis, but also states his lineage is of Demeter and Kore, Bacchus and Iacchus. His functions are clearly those of a fertility god concerned like Demeter with food and like Bacchus with wine. The spelling, therefore, of his name on the stele unusual though it is can be held to confirm his status as Lord of the Crops (*karpoi*).[7] This, however, is not the only striking feature. From Horapollo we learn that Horus is identical with the Sun (*i.e.* Apollo) because (by false Greek derivation) he is 'ruler of the *hours*'. Other sources reveal the identity of Horus/Harpocrates with Cronos—'Father Time'— whose sickle he sometimes holds. He is the Horus reborn each year on 6 January and equated with Aeon—Eternity. In the stele inscription Harpocrates describes himself as 'the totality of time' and as the one who 'thinks of the years beforehand.' We can infer, therefore, that in the theology of the inscription on the stele Harpocrates is regarded both as a young child and as 'Old

Father Time'. But the precise functions fulfilled by Harpocrates in relation to his own declared parents Sarapis and Isis and his coalescence with the Sun God Apollo remain unmentioned. From the language of his *Magnificat* it would be hard to imagine the Harpocrates whom Hellenistic artists delight to portray with infant body and a finger to his lips (*Pls. 20, 52*). On the other hand, however, Harpocrates has some resemblance to Apollo's sister, Artemis, who bore the epiclesis of Amarusia at the neighbouring town of Eretria, a cult centre of Isis also. Harpocrates hunts all kinds of animals and is a dweller on the mountain, along the seashore and by the stream.[8]

We must not suppose, however, that he has overlooked his own Egyptian origins. In his role of Cronos he copies his mother, who was known at Qurnah as 'Lady of Eternity' and who, by identification with the goddess Meresger of the mountains west of Thebes, received such titles as 'the god's mother, the Lady of Heaven, the Lady of all gods'.[9] The stele shows him in the manner of Isis dispensing to doctors all the drugs they need to save life. He has fabricated the sistrum for Isis' use. Like Isis he has fostered religion by having been first to build the gods their shrines and palaces. No mention is made of Horus' falcon features. Harpocrates does state, however, that his appearance is horned. Understood literally, this makes him copy Isis/Hathor. Regarded symbolically, the horns bring him into line with an earlier cosmocrator, Alexander.[10]

Important details about Harpocrates are to be found in Plutarch. In telling the Osirian legend Plutarch uses the name Horus for Isis' son until he has almost finished when he states: 'Isis when Osiris had mated with her after his death became by him the mother of one untimely born and weak in his nether limbs, Harpocrates.'[11] Later on the divine nativity is alluded to again when Plutarch is urging his readers to give the story a cosmological interpretation instead of tiresomely alleging that theology can be summed up in the seasonal changes of Egypt. The burial of Osiris and the birth of Harpocrates mean far more than the sowing of the seed in the earth, the growth of the crops and the sprouting of the plants, and the marshes of the Delta and the lotus of the Nile.[12] Obviously Plutarch is familiar with the portraiture of Harpocrates such as meets us at Pompeii: the infant god holding the horn of plenty in his hand and wearing a lotus in his hair.

In the Graeco-Roman world the birth month of solar divinities was December. The fourth century calendar of Philocalus specifies 25 December as the festival of 'the Sun Invincible', *Sol Invictus*, whose cult dominated the pagan world in the final stages whether the heliolatrous association was reckoned to be with the name of Apollo, of Mithras, of Sarapis or of Horus/Harpocrates.[13] The nativity of Harpocrates is very clearly put by Plutarch in the latter half of December: it occurs about the time of the winter solstice, and must be interpreted within its solar context.

The sequence of events in the story of the dead king Osiris and his successor is briefly this. Isis discovers that she is pregnant on the 6th day of Phaophi, *i.e.* 3 October. She arises glad of heart that she holds inside her body the divine seed of her brother and that she is raising up the form of the god in the egg. On herself she fastens an amulet. The search instituted by Isis for the recovery of the missing members of Osiris' body lasts until the 7th day of Athyr, *i.e.* 3 November. A period of time must now be allowed for the embalmment. The mummified body is at last entombed 21 December. Isis brings forth her child two days later, 23 December being in the Egyptian calendar the date of the simultaneous burial and rebirth of the Sun God. Of cardinal importance for the chronology of the whole tale is the winter solstice.[14]

Plutarch, who hankers after a theology of revelation, admits that the Nativity as described in Egyptian mythology can be understood non-supernaturally. People can read into it a kind of weather religion, a theology of the changing seasons and of repeatedly observed and familiar phenomena. A possible view is that the babe Harpocrates 'was born imperfect and premature among flowers and plants that shot up before their time'. Offerings are accordingly made to him of early-growing lentils as first-fruits. Here, as in the inscription from Chalcis, we see Harpocrates represented as one who is Lord of Crops. He is honoured by his worshippers with an annual spring bean-feast.

For Herodotus the Egyptian Horus the Younger is linked with the Greek Apollo and affiliated to Dionysus and Demeter. Osiris' son Horus, 'whom the Greeks call Apollo', was the last king to rule Egypt.[15] Herodotus is following the traditional view of the young heir of his dead father ruling with solar power in heaven and with fructifying force in earth. Horus wears the *pschent* or double crown of Upper and Lower Egypt, the historical reminder of pre-Dynastic penetration of the one by the other, and the theological symbol of his joint power over the Sky and the Underworld.[16] The Beloved and indeed Only Begotten Son of the Father, the Omnipotent Child, he has under his control the circuit of the solar disk and so assumes the lotus which itself is the emblem of the rising Sun. In his chthonic capacity in the manner of his mother Isis he gives all herbs and the abundance of the ground. He is a god of seeds and manages the wood of the plants and all vegetables. True to his Egyptian ancestry Harpocrates is Lord both of Sun and Crops.

The Horus who sits on the walls of the Egyptian temple at Edfu in his name of the falcon, who wears the victor's crown of the Justified Son of Isis and Osiris, and who boasts, 'I am Horus whom Isis has brought forth and whose protection was guaranteed in the egg',[17] acquires non-Egyptian features when he crosses the sea to take up his abode at Delos. Here he becomes not only Hellenic Apollo, but also Heracles. As a result, no doubt, of the identification of Aphrodite and Isis, whose conjoint names were applied to the deified Arsinoe II, Horus in his infant manifestation is transformed into Aphrodite's son, Eros or 'Love'.[18] A dedication has been found at Delos to Eros/Harpocrates/Apollo. The same view is indicated by Plutarch when he states that 'the Egyptians hold that the Sun is Eros'.[19] At Delos in Hellenistic times references to Apollo and Eros imply Horus/Harpocrates. The infant types of Apollo and Heracles, like Eros, have the same significance. On one of the Delian statuettes of Apollo known as *Apolloniscoi* can be seen the Egyptian emblem of a falcon on the god's right thumb.[20]

The archaeological evidence from Pompeii reveals that in Italy as well as in Greece Harpocrates was transfigured. Horus certainly appears with the head of a falcon. But the usual treatment of Isis' son is thoroughly Hellenic. He can don the wings of Eros, anticipating the angel-iconography of Christianity, and in his left hand carry the cornucopia of Bacchus. He possesses the quiver of Apollo and the fawnskin of Dionysus. In the scene in which Isis is portrayed receiving Io from Greece on the banks of the Nile the figure of Harpocrates is visible as a naked infant, sitting at his mother's side cross-legged with finger to his lips (Pl. 27). In another scene where Isis reveals herself in all her majesty as mistress of the stars, a young god on horseback is advancing with diadem and halo about his head and a double axe in his left hand. Here, doubtless, we are invited to discover the youthful solar deity going forth to meet and overcome his implacable enemy Seth-Typhon.[21]

A story related by Plutarch about the conflict between Horus and Seth is that the latter escaped capture by turning himself into a crocodile, represented as the type of what is base and harmful (cf. Pl. 51). From Plutarch, too, we learn that Horus was supposed to have replied to his father's question, what he thought the most suitable animal for a man going out to battle, with the surprising answer 'a horse', and not 'a lion'. Whereas the representation of Horus as a cavalier is not characteristic of his native Egypt, he becomes so in the art of imperial times, Harpocrates-Helios appearing at Pompeii on horseback.[22] A work in the Louvre known as the 'Horus St Georges', perhaps of the fourth century, depicts a man with the head of a hawk running his spear through a crocodile, on which the horse he rides is trampling. If the group is really from Bawit, in the desert 200 miles southwest of Cairo, then the provenance supports the view that the legend of Horus has influenced Christian iconography.[23]

Two of Christendom's most celebrated military saints, George and Michael, had to win the fight against a dragon. Michael's was waged at the time when 'a woman . . . travailing in birth' fled into the wilderness, and was caused by her serpent persecutor 'to be carried away of the flood' (potamophoretos, an epithet appropriate to Isis). For the great dragon, 'that old serpent called the Devil, and Satan', and for Michael the battlefield was heaven.

But the same dragon, when he 'was cast out into the earth' turned his attack from the celestial hero to 'the woman' who had previously been encompassed with the Sun and the Moon but was now a terrestrial mother with her baby boy. Moreover, the dragon was *pyrrhous* in colour: and Plutarch thrice applies the same epithet to the complexion of Seth-Typhon.

Exactly what Christological interpretation is to be put on these mythical features does not now concern us, although their occurrence in the *Apocalypse*, itself the last of the canonical books in the Bible, is certainly 'a great wonder'. The passage inspired patristic writers to indulge in speculations about the Virgin Mary and the Second Eve. Its very nature, however, leads us back to Egypt. The Jewish Christian view here boldly inserted would hardly have arisen without pagan interest at Alexandria in the tradition of the pregnant Isis fleeing into the marshes of the Delta to escape Seth, and of Horus/Harpocrates triumphing over his foe.[24]

In considering the struggle between Horus and Seth as it is told in Egyptian texts we must concede that Seth is not always represented as evil, for he can co-operate with Horus, nor is the crocodile invariably an evil beast. Harpocrates can be exhibited as half man and half crocodile.[25] From the Neoplatonist Porphyry we learn that the Egyptian symbol for the Sun was 'a man going in a bark which rested on a crocodile'.[26] Clement of Alexandria obviously looks with favour on the image of 'the Sun on the crocodile'. He tells us this means the Sun in passing through the moist air generates time.[27] Nevertheless, in the period during which Christianity was establishing itself as a world religion the figure of Horus/Harpocrates in conjunction with that of a crocodile typified the triumph of good over evil, exactly the same as the victory over the dragon by the saintly combatants Michael and George.

Convincing examples can be found of the influence on Christian iconography of the figure of Horus/Harpocrates, both in his mother's company and on his own. The most obvious parallels appear when we compare the ways in which the sacred Mother and Child of Egypt are portrayed and the types of the Theotokos/

Madonna together with the infant Jesus in Byzantine and Italian ecclesiastical art (*Pl. 69*). The Panagia *Galactotrophousa*, Madonna *Lactans*, has some of the qualities of Isis *Kourotrophos*, the Mother suckling Horus. An Egyptian origin has been proposed for the *Hodegetria* and the *Deesis* types.[28] When we think of Isis as 'the Lady Mother' who claimed through her suffering to sympathize with suffering humanity[29] it is natural to remember the Theotokos *Eleousa*, a pattern which has in fact been studied on an ivory from a Coptic atelier at Alexandria and found to show traces of Isiac influence.[30]

In the Church of Osios David, called also the Latomou Monastery, at Thessalonica, a city in which the priest of Isis sacrificed to Horus-Apollo-Harpocrates,[31] can be seen a fine early Byzantine mosaic of Christ as a beardless boy, rediscovered for Christian eyes some forty years ago. Here 'the eternal youth of Emmanuel the promised son' in conjunction with the supporting figures of a lion with human face and an ox must be explained as of Egyptian derivation. Parallels are to be discovered in representations in a church at Bawit and on the wall of a crypt at Alexandria. It is significant that in one of the ecclesiastical legends a monk named Senouphios who had been living 'in the mountains of Nitria' was bidden by divine command to go 'to the monastery called Latomou at Thessalonica'.[32] Such stories as this imply that the ecclesiastical art of Byzantium which is so well represented at Thessalonica and Mount Athos was under a special debt to Egypt. It has been authoritatively stated that 'Hellenistic Egypt exerted a deep influence on Byzantium'.[33] The historians of ecclesiastical pictorial art need to bear in mind that the holy pair of Mother and Son had been in vogue for many centuries in the temples of Egypt before the genius of Christendom developed fresh treatments of an age-old subject. They must likewise remember that the proto-Christian handling of Emmanuel, the radiantly youthful Son of God with nimbus around his head and hand raised in imperial benediction, was not without parallel in the later iconography of Horus/Harpocrates, just as the emperor's outstretched right hand presupposes Sarapis-Sol.[34]

The fusion of Horus with Judaeo-Christian figures can be exemplified on Gnostic gems from Egypt. On one of these the deity Iao[35] (to be connected no doubt with the Iah of the Pentateuch) is seen standing on a crocodile. In his left hand he holds the sacred staff and the *crux ansata* in his right. Two birds and two scorpions appear and over his head is the scarabaeus, representing the Eternal Spirit. On the bevelled edge of the gem are inscribed the angelic names Michael, Uriel, Suriel and Gabriel.[36] Although the god fulfils the function of Horus yet he wears the ibis head of Thoth and is ithyphallic.[37] On another gem a divine figure treads on the back of a crocodile. Around the head is a nimbus and over the head is held a fish in the left hand, while the right hand is raised as if in prayer or blessing. Although a fish might seem a sacred symbol of Isis since she had once supposedly been rescued by one out of trouble, and the fisherman has a role in her worship, yet in this setting it seems to be the normal anagrammatic device of Christianity. As another example of assimilation between Horus and Christ may be cited a bas-relief on the wall of an early Egyptian church belonging to the Memnonium at Abydos. In it Christ is portrayed sitting on his throne with the horned disk of Horus and holding a modification of the staff or crook of Osiris.[38]

In the theology and art of Gnosticism Horus and Christ could easily be blended. One of the Gnostic sects indeed labelled itself 'Carpocratian' and in general they propounded cosmologies in terms of 'Aeons', the final and perfect Aeon being Jesus Christ. Those who bore the name Peratae in their astrological theories recognized the rule of Isis and Osiris over the hours, which Horus as the God of Time created. The Valentinian Gnostics can plausibly be said to have evolved a doctrine in which Isis fulfils the role of Sophia and Horus/Harpocrates that of Logos. As to the term Aeon, we learn from Epiphanius, who produced his massive anti-heretical treatise at the end of the fourth century, that among the pagans at Alexandria Horus/Harpocrates was the Aeon *par excellence*. Aeon/Horus was born of the Virgin Isis on 6 January.[39] Clearly in the Gnosticism which fringed Christian orthodoxy Horus and Christ could merge.

Harpocrates, the young king and solar pantocrator of imperial times, is as much the child of Isis as the Horus of the *Pyramid Texts*, but the treatment of the maternal aspect is less crude.[40] The Isis who laid hold of her breasts for her son (*Pls. 55–57*), and the Horus who was informed, 'Thy milk belongs to thee, which is in the breasts of thy mother', are sketched in the *Hermetic Literature* as sharing in mystical knowledge expressed in the manner of Platonic myth and concentrated on reincarnation. Like a schoolmistress Isis gives her child a lesson in Mediterranean geography. Her allusion to Egypt as 'our ancestors' most hallowed land' which 'lies in the centre of the world' finds a parallel elsewhere in Hermetic thought where a passage forecasts the decay of Egyptian religion: 'O Egypt, Egypt, thy cults will only survive in legends disbelieved by posterity, and thy words only in inscriptions carved on stones.'[41] The purpose, however, of the colloquy between Mother and Son is to impart 'knowledge' (*gnosis*) about God and the planetary spirits (*cosmocratores*) which haunt the Universe: to this esoteric wisdom Isis possesses the key.

The Hermetic handling of Egyptian mythology indicates the theosophical subtleties to which the names of Thoth and Imouthes, Isis and Horus gave rise. Such speculative blossomings from the land of the Nile, strange though they sometimes were, caused pious minds no offence. It had been fostered by the eclectic theology of Alexandria as we meet it in the writings of Philo the Hellenizing Jew.[42] The tendency was to get rid of the coarser elements in the religious tradition in favour of an allegorical and spiritual reinterpretation. It was in fact a development of the theological reformation begun by Ptolemy, Manetho and Timotheus.

We see the results of this reappraisal of Egypt's holy scriptures in Plutarch. Just as the Gnostic Marcion was repelled by what seemed to him the evil God of the Old Testament, so Plutarch detested certain hoary incidents in the Osirian legend: for example, the severing of the limbs of the murdered god and the beheading of Isis by her son. Such ideas about the blessed and imperishable nature of divine beings 'must be spat out for the mouth to be cleansed'.[43] As though he were echoing the condemnation of

scandalous myth voiced by Plato in the *Republic,* Plutarch brands
as detestable those whose theology violates the moral code and
Greek ethics. Yet the moralist of Chaeronea was well aware that
however much the primitive crudities were kept out of sight they
were inextricably embedded in the cult he so much admired.
The epithet 'Bull of Thy Mother' as applied to Horus may
establish that mother-incest was one of the themes of the traditional story.[44] Nor was there much need for a Greek to suffer a
puritanical shock. For he had only to remember in his own
mythology the incestuous tale of Oedipus.

At first sight sex when practised within the first of the forbidden
degrees of kindred might seem revolting. But so intimate was the
relation within the family triad of Osiris, Isis and Horus that the
term incest lost its validity. Plutarch himself provides us with a
clue to the understanding of the divine family's interdependence.
This can be demonstrated geometrically. If we construct a right-
angled triangle with its sides measuring three, four and five
units, then the first will represent Osiris as the origin, being the
upright, the second Isis as the recipient, being the base, and the
third Horus as the perfect product, being the hypotenuse.[45]

The importance of Horus as Creator of 'hours, times and
seasons', accepted by Plutarch and the later Neoplatonist Porphyry as the consequence of an indulgence in a false etymology, is stressed by Macrobius at the end of the fourth
century AD. Among the Egyptians, he explains, 'Apollo the Sun
is called Horus. From him the twenty-four hours which make
up the day and night have derived their name. Moreover, the
four seasons which complete the year's cycle are termed "hours".
In their desire to make a dedication specifically to the Sun himself
the Egyptians have fashioned a figure whose head is shaven except
for the hair remaining on the right side. The retention of this
hair teaches that in our world the Sun is never covered up. The
hair which has been removed bears witness through the roots
which stay that even when we do not see this heavenly body
it still possesses the property of coming forth again like hair.'[46]

In the Graeco-Roman world the hair style of boys was as
obvious a token of Horus/Harpocrates as the ring worn by men.

From various portraits of children and adolescent boys discovered in different countries—Egypt, Syria, France, Eleusis in Greece and Ostia in Italy—we can still study the so-called Horus Lock.[47] The religious significance was doubtless that of a preliminary dedication to the service of Isis and her associated deities. Lucian in the second century AD writes about a young boy clad in spotless linen with his hair fastened behind on either side of his forehead, and categorically adds that all boys of free birth in Egypt braid their hair until they reach puberty.[48] Whether Lucian's generalization is accepted or not for Egypt, the archaeological evidence belonging to a period of five centuries (from the first BC to the fourth AD) suggests that many a boyish head in the Mediterranean world witnessed to the fact a child had been hallowed as 'a son of Isis', and had undergone adoption into her religious service.[49] The styles vary. We see the very short thick clump over one ear. Sometimes there are curls on one side of the head, short or long, loose or tight. The locks may be plaited. The paintings may show several locks with the ends clubbed into a round bulbous knob, tied with ribbons which are left hanging. We observe the forebear of the pig's tail and of the pony-tail. The head may be shaven all but the lock, in Red Indian fashion. In a statuette in London we find Harpocrates himself wearing his own hair style and clad with the wings of Eros (*Pl. 20, and cf. Pl. 51*).[50]

From a Christian source we learn about a festival of Horus/Harpocrates at Buto at which young and old joined in with the utmost hilarity. Mention is made of toys and porridge, of wheaten cakes and boiling kettle, and intercessions for health and release from sufferings.[51] Here we may feel ourselves almost on the spree at a fun fair. To Christian eyes such riotous behaviour hardly suggested a god whom his worshippers could adore as saviour and lord of all the world.

CHAPTER XVII

THE GODDESS DARLING OF
ROMAN EMPERORS

ONLY THREE YEARS after Cleopatra had sat in the robes of Isis
on her golden throne at Alexandria and had been proclaimed
Queen of Kings and ruler over Rome's eastern provinces, the
menacing *uraeus* crown of Egypt vanished. The queen who had
demanded adoration as 'the new Isis' and her Roman husband
were crushed once for all at Actium in 31 BC and the Augustan
Principate was brought into being. In vain did Cleopatra 'summon
her troops with the sistrum of her ancestors'.[1] In vain did 'the
animal-shaped gods and the barking Anubis skirmish with
Neptune, Venus and Minerva'. Egypt fell. The political strength
of the kingdom of the Pharaohs could never be regained. The
prophecy of Book III of the *Sibylline Oracles*, which has been
plausibly referred to Cleopatra, that the world's 'mistress' and
incarnation of Isis should bring forth Alexander Helios,[2] a king
with the Sun as his father, was seen to be meaningless when
defeat in battle had driven the so-called goddess to make her
sacred serpents the means of her own death. She herself might
exclaim, 'I have immortal longings in me'. The world, now led by
Augustus, knew she was dead.[3]

In the capital of the world empire established by Augustus
the religion so ardently professed by the Nile's final sovereign
had for long been familiar. During the Republican period its
career had been chequered. When the Empire emerged the cult
of Isis became a thriving influence, which no political pressure
could stop.[4] Already in the time of the dictator Sulla at the
beginning of the first century BC an Isiac guild of Pastophori had
been founded in Rome.[5] In 58 BC altars to Isis on the Capitol

were destroyed by the consuls Piso and Gabinius and when the Senate had voted for the destruction of the Iseum and the Sarapeum and no workmen had the courage to lay hands upon those sacred edifices the consul L. Aemilius Paulus in 50 BC took off his toga, seized an axe and drove it through the temple doors.[6]

In the year 43, the young Octavian, with Antony and Lepidus, perhaps seeking popularity, decreed that a new temple should be built for Sarapis and Isis.[7] Fifteen years later, as Augustus Caesar, he refused to have Egyptian shrines within the sacred central area of Rome known as the 'pomerium'.[8] Seven years passed. Then we find him again forbidding the cults, 'which were now renewing their way into the city', to be practised anywhere in the suburbs less than a mile from the city centre.[9] Clearly the official policy was antagonistic: the heart of the empire had to be kept as far as could be untainted. Far away, however, on the outskirts of that same empire at Philae Augustus could be portrayed as the Beloved of Ptah and Isis offering the latter such gifts as wine and myrrh.[10]

Tiberius, who was also shown by Philae's artists as a worshipper of Isis with gazelles and geese, mirror and rattle, curbed the Egyptian rites (as he did the Jewish) in his capital by making those who practised them burn their robes and all the other religious appurtenances.[11] Yet he was apparently thought of as tolerant of the Nile gods, for an inscription shows him making his memorial to the Great Isis and he is represented in AD 23 sacrificing to Hathor, Horus and Isis.[12] The scandal of Mundus masquerading as a priest of Anubis belongs to the ensuing period, when the Emperor is said to have thrown the statue of Isis into the Tiber, and to have shown no mercy on the whole priesthood.

Gaius (Caligula), unlike Tiberius, fostered the cult of the emperor. His accession to the principate was termed his Manifestation or *Epiphany* and when he planned to set up his colossal statue in the Temple at Jerusalem it was to be called by the dual name of Neos Gaius and Zeus *Epiphanes*.[13] The mysteries with which Gaius linked the deification of the emperor have been shown to be Isiac in character.[14] On the Palatine this sovereign

built himself a Palace of Isis—*Aula Isiaca*—from the remains of
which can still be seen a fresco symbolizing through the mythology
of Psyche and Eros the Isiac mystery of redemption and illustrating the theme of living water.[15] Gaius followed the example of
the Egyptian Pharaohs by marrying his own sister Drusilla and
listened in true Isiac style to an Egyptian soothsayer who forecast
the emperor's death on the very day it happened. Gaius first gave
the Isiac cult state recognition, and had an Egyptian obelisk
brought to Italy.[16]

Although Claudius was the foe of religious rites found in
Britain 'he endeavoured to transplant the Eleusinian Mysteries
from Attica to Rome'. Isis by this time had become closely linked
with Demeter. The affinities were by then taken for granted.
Claudius therefore must have been more tolerant of Isiacs than
he was of Druids. Offerings to Isis were made by people of
importance during his reign, a military tribune who served under
him in Britain held an Egyptian life priesthood and a priest of
Isis dedicated a marble tablet for the Empress Agrippina.[18] Nero,
although interested in the Eleusinian Mysteries, was rude enough,
we learn, to urinate on the Syrian goddess, which indicates his
attitude to exotic cults in general.

During the reign of Galba and of the other two short-lived
emperors, Otho and Vitellius, Isis first appears on the provincial
coinage of Alexandria on the reverse of a bronze diobol, and
she was frequently depicted in her various aspects during the
reigns of Hadrian and Antoninus Pius. In the imperial series of
Rome her temple is shown as a reverse type on some of the bronze
coins of Vespasian (*Pl. 42*).[19] Afterwards she appears very
sporadically under Hadrian and Antoninus Pius, notably in the
guise of Isis Sothis (*Pls. 63, 64*), and later is represented in her
maternal aspect nursing Horus on a denarius of Julia Domna
(*Pl. 57*). She does not become really prominent in the imperial
series until the late Roman Empire (*Pls. 62, 65, 66*).

Otho is recorded to have taken part openly in the rites of Isis
only half a century after the death of Augustus. Truly the wheel
had come full circle. Suetonius tells us, at second-hand but
with plausibility, that this ephemeral emperor often celebrated the

46 Statue of a priest of Anubis, wearing the jackal's head mask of the cult. On his left arm he carries the herald's wand (*caduceus*) of Hermes/ Mercury, which identifies Anubis with that god

47–50 An Isiac altar from Rome. Its four sides are carved with a kneeling offerant, the Apis bull, a worshipper crowning himself with roses (*cf.* Apuleius *Met.* XI, 12) and two priests, one holding an open scroll, the other a lighted torch

51–53 Late representations of Horus/Harpocrates. *Above*, a *cippus* of Horus (a small magical stele) shows him as a boy with the side-lock of youth, standing on two crocodiles and holding various noxious reptiles. Above his head is the mask of the god Bes and around him are magical hieroglyphic texts. *Above, right*, a bronze figure of Harpocrates seated on a lotus flower, from Mainz. He holds a cornucopia in his right hand and wears a version of the Double Crown of Egypt. *Right*, one face of an Isiac altar from Rome, showing a figure of Harpocrates, a cornucopia in his left arm and right forefinger to his lips, standing in a car drawn by two hippopotami

54–59 Isis and her cult on Greek Imperial and Roman coins. Naturally, she appears more frequently on the Greek Imperial coins of Alexandria. She is shown here, on reverse types: alone; seated and suckling Horus; enthroned within her temple at Alexandria; sitting on a ship's prow; being greeted by Sarapis; and standing holding her sistrum and situla

60–67 Isis Pharia holding a billowing sail; similarly standing before
the Pharos at Alexandria, and then in the prow of a ship; Isis Sothis
seated side-saddle on a running dog, holding a cornucopia and her
sceptre; another version but on a medallion where she holds a sistrum;
seated Isis holding a ship in her right hand; the goddess in a *tensa*; and
a standing figure of Anubis

68 A detail from a late fourth century AD Greek papyrus referring to the Christian destruction of the Sarapeum at Alexandria. On the left the Emperor Theodosius stands on a pedestal enshrining a bust of Sarapis and, on the right, a monk is seen hurling a stone at the Sarapeum represented below him

69 A Coptic stele, from the Fayum, showing the mother and child – the basic iconography of Isis and Horus/Mary and Jesus

70, 71 Isiacism in a Christian setting. *Above*, Isis as Divine Engrafter identified in mediaeval legend with B.V.M. *Below*, Pinturicchio's painting of the Apis Bull in Procession, Room of Saints, Appartamento Borgia, Vatican

72 Another of Pinturicchio's paintings of the Procession of the Apis Bull from the Appartamento Borgia. This emphasizes the 'Egyptianism' of Pope Alexander VI (1492–1503); Pinturicchio's subject was familiar in the first century AD to the Roman Emperor Titus

ceremonies of the goddess in full public view, wearing the appropriate linen vestments. When Titus and Vespasian had besieged and stormed Jerusalem and had brought their campaign against the stubborn Jews to an end with the destruction of the Temple, they thought it meet and right to usher in their official triumph at Rome keeping vigil on the eve within the Iseum.

Vespasian at Alexandria was called on to perform miracles in the name of Sarapis. The god was already renowned at the end of the fourth century BC for having restored sight to Demetrius of Phalerum, who afterwards composed hymns in his praise.[20] When two men came to Vespasian to be healed, the first blind, the second with a withered hand in consequence of visions during the night, they wished him to moisten the one's cheeks and eyes with his spittle and to tread on the other's hand with his feet. When Vespasian inquired of the medical experts whether these ailments could be cured he was assured that in the one case the sight had not completely gone and in the other if healing pressure were applied to the joints of the hand then its use would come back to it. Accordingly, with a smile, Vespasian did as he had been asked and won a reputation as a wonder-worker which, according to one of our two sources, the Alexandrians much resented.[21]

There seems no doubt that by the time of Vespasian the link which afterwards became strongly marked between the imperial and Isiac cults had been achieved; even in the reign of Claudius we find an inscription with a prayer to the emperor in conjunction with Isis.[22] But Vespasian himself was known for his sense of humour and probably thought with less gravity about contemporary religion than his august rank officially required. A man who could joke on the day of his death, 'Dear me, I fancy I'm turning into a god', must sometimes have poked fun at the cult of the emperor. The words that Juvenal was soon afterwards to write would have met with his wholehearted approval about the adoration of the crocodile, the ibis, and the long-tailed ape on the part of those who professed the faith of Egypt.[23] Vespasian's official admission of the importance of the cult in Rome is indicated by his willingness to spend the night before his triumph in the Iseum. His son Titus, so briefly his successor, is recorded to have been there too, and before that to have taken a prominent part at the consecration of the Apis bull in Memphis, where he certainly got to know 'the wonted ceremonial of the ancient religion'[24] and saw the living image of Isis' husband, the Divine Calf, borne in a golden stall on a state-barge into the Temple of Ptah. Titus like his father had first-hand experience of cult procedure in Egypt.[25]

Titus' younger brother and successor Domitian, like the aedile M. Volusius a century earlier, found it useful early in his life during military operations to disguise himself in the garb of a follower of Isis. Thus he was able to escape from the temple on the Capitol where he had hidden and cross the Tiber into safety.[26] Perhaps as a token of thanksgiving to the goddess to whom he owed his life and who had verily been his helper in time of trouble he rebuilt her temple in the Campus Martius at Rome.[27] The Iseum at Beneventum, from which rich finds have come to light, was either founded by him or reconstructed and enlarged in the year 88. Here he can still be studied as a Pharaoh in Egyptian dress and here in the centre of the cortile of the museum are the obelisks with their fulsome flattery: 'O King live for ever!' and 'Domitian living for ever!' The same Pharaonic and oriental conception is revealed in the formula adopted at the beginning of one of the acclamations directed to himself as 'Our Lord and our God'.[28] All this clearly demonstrates how much more seriously Domitian took Egyptian religion than his father had done. He thought of himself as the incarnation of Isis' consort Sarapis, for whom as for her and the companion deities he was ready to build sumptuously.

During the earlier years of the Roman Empire the cultural background of the sovereign could be that of Alexandrian religion. The Stoic philosopher Chaeremon, a well-known writer on the civilization of Egypt,[29] and sometime Alexandria's librarian at the Sarapeum, became tutor to Nero, whose religious education, however, was quite abortive. Chaeremon had another pupil named Dionysius, who followed in the footsteps of his teacher to become the palace secretary and librarian in the reign of Trajan. Under the next sovereign, Hadrian, the same offices were held by another expert in the lore of the Alexandrian Museum, the Isiac 'pope' Julius Vestinus.[30]

Trajan, when he was on the point of invading Parthia, showed proper regard for the contemporary solar religion by consulting an oracle at Heliopolis in Syria (now Baalbek) which was traditionally linked with Egypt: the god whose help he sought was *Sol Invictus*, a blend of Syrian Baal, Egyptian Amun-Re-Sarapis, and Greek Apollo-Horus-Helios.[31] In a bas-relief on his triumphal arch in Rome, Trajan appears before Isis and Horus presenting them with a votive offering of wine. With his personal secretary, Dionysius, the emperor at any time could have discussed the topics of Alexandrian religion. It was with his absent friend and panegyrist the Younger Pliny that Trajan corresponded about what must have seemed in many ways a similar faith. Its followers, he learnt, came together sometimes before sunrise and sang hymns antiphonally in praise of the divine founder of the cult. Trajan never dreamt that posterity would deem his gift of wine to Isis and Horus about as odd as Pliny and he found the stubborn refusal of the Christians to bow the knee before the image of the deified emperor.[32]

Trajan's successor Hadrian wandered as waywardly in his religious speculations and far as he did in his tours of the empire.[33] Apart from his connection with the expert Vestinus he had close personal knowledge of Egypt, where indeed his favourite Antinous perished by a mysterious death, allegedly ritual, in the waters of the Nile.[34] Hadrian in truth thought the Egyptians as fickle in their faith as posterity is apt to find him. In a letter to the consul Servianus the emperor says he has learnt this himself and provides examples. In Egypt those who worship Sarapis are Christians and those who call themselves Christ's bishops ('overseers') are addicted to Sarapis. Jewish rabbis, Samaritans and Christian priests in Egypt become astrologers and soothsayers. The visiting archbishop is obliged to worship Sarapis by some and by others Christ.[35]

From such forthright remarks as these we might imagine Hadrian floundered amid the welter of beliefs which abounded in his domains, especially along the Nile. What his reactions would have been to the unswerving devotion to Isis in the novel which Apuleius was to write soon after the end of his reign must be pure speculation. Temperamentally an Isiac, Hadrian had something in common with Vespasian. On his deathbed he could talk agnostically and plaintively to his soul as his little wanderer about to disappear down into the cold bleak spots of the world below and never again to crack a joke. He lacked the vision of Lucius to behold the tender and benign Egyptian goddess shedding light upon those in the shadow of death and giving the comfort of her brightness to her Stygian realm.[36] Yet Hadrian in his official capacity actively encouraged the expansion of Alexandrian religion. For example, after his conquest of Palestine he established the cult of Sarapis on the holy mountain of Samaria called Gerizim and erected a temple in honour of Isis at Petra. A temple of Isis at Cyrene was dedicated 'for Hadrian's health'.[37] In his villa at Tibur he built copies of many famous places in the empire including Canopus, where Isis and Sarapis were held in high honour. On an Adventus coin of Hadrian we see the divine pair, while on a bronze drachma piece of Alexandria the emperor stands, wreathed with laurel, in the Sarapeum and is presented with the globe, the token of his rank as cosmocrator, by Zeus/ Sarapis with sceptre in hand.[38] Other Alexandrian coins of his reign display Isis with lotus flower on head, sitting on a dog and holding a sistrum and spear, as well as Hadrian's reception at Alexandria by Sarapis with modius and Isis with lotus and sistrum, who offer the hand of welcome to the emperor and his wife Sabina.[39] The Alexandrian coins, from their date letters, fix this event in year 15 of his reign.

Numismatic witness to the continuing importance of Isis in the period of the Antonines is not lacking. On a coin of Antoninus Pius, Isis is portrayed sitting on her dog and holding her sistrum (*Pl. 63*). We see her on the coinage of Marcus Aurelius where she unites with her usual emblems a peacock and a lion.[40] As *Pelagia* she has a veil flying above her head, behind her a light-house (like a modern Britannia) and in front of her a ship with mast and sail.[41]

With the accession of Commodus the prevailing heliolatrous cults which had spread from eastern countries including Egypt led to the official assumption by the Roman emperor of the titles *felix* and *invictus*.[42] Commodus himself is reported to have been so much attached to the rites of Isis that he shaved his head bare, carried a dummy Anubis in procession, and stopped at the proper points in order to hymn her praises. As *Sol Invictus* and indeed Mithras, the emperor was not guilty of any cult inconsistency in worshipping Isis. Lucius, we may remember, was conducted after his initiation into her mysteries by the High Priest 'Mithras' within the full view of all the uninitiated wearing the palm of victory 'with leaves sticking out like the rays of the sun'.

The sun disk of Akhenaten, the nimbus of the deified Roman emperor,[43] and the halo of the Christian saint all belong to the same line of thought: it is the theory that what is divine and kingly is fringed, so to speak, with an aura of sanctity. The same conception is encountered in the philosophy of Plotinus, who came from Alexandria to settle in Rome half a century after Commodus, and who utilizes the theory of light irradiated as an incorporeal energy by the Sun with undiminished giving as an analogy for his metaphysical doctrine of emanation. When Commodus took the title of 'the Invincible' he was entering into a deliberate association with Helios/Apollo/Sarapis,[44] with Mithras, and with the goddess whose tokens he carried in procession, in whose temple 'the Sun's face' could be dedicated, and who said of herself, 'I am in the rays of the Sun'.[45]

At the beginning of the third century the reigning emperor, Septimius Severus, iconographically assimilated to Sarapis, is said to have visited such sites as Alexandria and Memphis touring the Sarapeum and the Pyramids and to have sought to gain whatever hidden knowledge books and temples in Egypt afforded.[46] It was during the reign of his successor Caracalla, called *Philosarapis*, that a new peak of interest in Egyptian religion was reached. In Ptolemaic style he called himself Lord, the Universe's Saviour and the World's Creator.[47] Admittedly this sovereign grumbled because Sarapis could heal neither his body nor his mind. Yet he gave the rites of Isis greater importance in

Rome, celebrating them with deeper reverence than hitherto. He built her various sanctuaries on a lavish scale, as he did for Sarapis and in his Baths for Mithras.[48] On a coin, where lively imagination is displayed, Isis welcomes Caracalla in the year 215 to Egypt[49] and on another, which is likewise a direct record of his visit to Alexandria the goddess, who holds the sistrum, presents two corn-ears to the emperor, who stands in military uniform, holding a spear in the style of Harpocrates and trampling on a crocodile.[50] Caracalla's mother, Julia Domna, is also brought by the mint of Rome into direct link with Isis, who is exhibited wearing a peaked head-dress, standing with her foot on a ship's prow and suckling her young child Horus (Pl. 57). Clearly it is a reign where Isis enjoys the warmest imperial patronage: on the coinage with the effigy of the empress she is styled in accordance with her reputation of Good Luck as Saeculi Felicitas: 'Our age's Happiness'.[51]

For the next few years a loss of devotion to the Egyptian cult on the part of the emperors may be inferred from the absence of numismatic evidence: on coins of Greek provenance there is a gap in representations of Isis between Caracalla and Decius. Sarapis Cosmocrator seems to have undergone actual attack by Mithras.[52] According to the Historia Augusta the eccentric Heliogabalus, despite his addiction to the sun cult of Emesa and Syrian Astarte, brought Egyptian serpents to Rome. These serpents, called 'Good Demons' (Agathodaemones) were symbols of Apollo-Horus-Harpocrates.[53] Along with them came hippo-potami, a crocodile and a rhinoceros. The next monarch, Alexander Severus, who provided himself with a kind of all-risk religious insurance policy in embellishing his private chapel with figures of Christ and Abraham along with Orpheus, is stated to have supplied additional statues to grace the public temples of Isis and Sarapis.[54] The century, however, which saw Alexandrian philosophy conveyed to Rome and transmuted into Neoplaton-ism by the genius of Plotinus under the patronage of emperor and empress,[55] does not offer much testimony of a continually maintained imperial interest in Isis and her temple partners. The cult still appealed to the people and the philosophers.

With Diocletian the situation changed. This emperor had first-hand experience of military operations in Egypt. For months he had besieged Alexandria. He had imposed terms on the Nobatae and the Blemmyes, perfervid worshippers of Isis, and had caused altars to be erected at Philae for the combined worship of the Egyptian and the Roman deities. Showing the other side of his character he had caused Egyptian text-books of chemistry to be gathered up and burnt. Here was an emperor who took Egypt seriously. Whereas in the days of the newly established Principate Virgil could envisage Anubis and Isis contending at Actium against Roman Neptune, on the coins of Diocletian a truce between the Roman and Egyptian divinities was openly declared. The obverse of one coin exhibited the sovereign robed with the mantle of Jupiter and wearing the radiate crown. On the reverse was Neptune with his foot on a ship's prow and trident and dolphin in his hand. Opposite to him stood Isis with sistrum and sacred vessel. Like the altars at Philae the two sides of Diocletian's coin symbolized the contemporary phenomenon of religious syncretism.[56]

Galerius who assumed the title of Augustus when Diocletian abdicated and divided the imperial power with Constantius, Maximinus and Severus, but for the swift rise of Constantine, would have made Thessalonica the Byzantium of the eastern empire. We have numismatic evidence that he followed the official policy of Diocletian in promulgating the blend of Graeco-Roman and Egyptian religion. For the first time in the coin series with the imperial bust Isis appears.[57] On the reliefs of the great Arch of Galerius at Thessalonica which still survive, though now much worn through time's decay, the scene is occupied by Isis and Sarapis in the company of the Dioscuri, as protectors of the tetrarchy.[58] How was Galerius Maximian to forecast the official repudiation of paganism by Constantine his successor?

The adoption of Christianity as the religion of the state is not reflected in Constantine's coinage. Whereas coin-types with unequivocal Christian subjects await discovery those with Isis (and sometimes Anubis) in traditional postures number nearly twenty.[59] Admittedly the effigy of the emperor on the obverse is of more consequence for his subjects than that of any divinity on the reverse: the presence of Isis (like that of Britannia on a twentieth-century penny) could be regarded as due to a wistful nostalgia for a vanished past. What is really surprising, however, is the persistence of Isis as a numismatic figure till late in the fourth century (*Pls. 62, 65, 66*), well after the Roman empire had been officially baptized with the outward sign of the cross. The characteristic features have certainly not become Palestinian, but remain essentially Egyptian: the *kourotrophos* Isis, the recumbent Nile, the Sphinx, Anubis with his palm-branch and *kyrekeion*, Isis *Pelagia* with her seated dog,[60] with her sistrum, with her hands on the sail. All this implies that the power of the Egyptian cult was not suddenly broken. The Nile is still with us. We see the boat, the sail and the rudder of the Isiac Voyage. Our instrument of music is the sistrum, not the harp. Our holy creatures are the sphinx and the dog, not the lamb or the dove of the New Covenant.

It was in the year 331 that Constantine issued an edict for the destruction of pagan temples. From what Rufinus tells us this action marked the beginning but not the completion of paganism's discomfiture: 'The worship of idols which had started on Constantine's initiative to undergo a persisting neglect and breakdown fell to ruins in the reign of Theodosius.'[61] Constantine did not scruple to cause the so-called 'Nile Cubit' to be brought out of the Sarapeum at Alexandria and transferred to a Christian Church.[62] Theodoretus states that although Constantine forbade sacrifices to 'demons' utterly yet he did not actually pull down the shrines but only caused them 'not to be trodden on' (in the word used there lurks an apparently studied ambiguity).[63] Julian, when he is extolling their champion Sarapis to the citizens of Alexandria, reminds them it was Constantine 'of most blessed memory' who brought soldiers 'into the holy city' to occupy the most hallowed temple in Egypt.[64]

Yet the actual destruction of the Sarapeum did not take place for another half century. Certainly in the reign of the first Christian emperor the followers of Isis and Sarapis could not expect their cult to receive any such state support as it had enjoyed in the time of Caracalla *Philosarapis*. But the cult was not to be stamped out by an imperial edict overnight. And if the emperor was 'converted to' the Palestinian faith then the pagan *temples* might also be 'converted to' the *rites* of the faith. We are specifically informed that Constantine 'was the first to enact a law that the shrines of idols should be handed over to those people who were dedicated to Christ.'[65]

The Theodosian Law which ordered the closing of 'all fanes, temples and shrines of the pagans' was not passed until AD 426. The coins leave us in no doubt at all that Isis and her temple colleagues retain their symbolic prominence well after Christianity's triumph as the empire's law-established religion. The large number of anonymous specimens on which the gods of Egypt preside were all struck in the mint at Rome[66] and have a direct connection with the others which show the same gods on the reverse with the imperial portrait on the obverse. Isis is always prominent. Thus we observe her as goddess of the sea. She reclines on the ground, leaning on an urn, out of which flows water in abundant waves. The upper part of her body is undraped and in her hair are reeds. In both hands she holds the horn of plenty. Again, we can meet the standard-bearer of the Isiac procession. He walks with what appears to be the image of a cow on the top of a pole. On a third type Isis is seen coming in a carriage drawn by two sphinxes. Below her is Harpocrates with a cornucopia and still further down is the Sothis-dog running to the right and lifting up his irradiated head.[67]

Before the final overthrow and outlawing of such pagan rivals as the Isiac cult, the legalized Christian Church suffered a blow which threatened for a time to dash all its hopes. Julian in daring to withstand those who to him were 'apostates' earned this name as one who had abandoned religious truth. On the coins of his reign his policy is expressed with all the force of pagan emblems. He means to revert to what he embraces as the old and the true. The emblems of long ago are revived.[68] On one coin he is portrayed in the company of the she wolf of Rome suckling her twins, and with Anubis on the reverse. On another Isis suckles Horus. She assumes other poses also. She sits on the back of the Sothis-dog, she stands facing her sister Nephthys, each crowned with the *uraeus*, and she is drawn in her *tensa* now by a pair of sphinxes and now of mules (*Pl. 66*) The empress Helena is also represented in the habiliments of Isis and Julian and she are figured as Sarapis and consort.[69] Julian Cosmocrator 'held worthy to rule the world by all the gods, especially mighty Sarapis',[70] rejoiced as much in being styled 'priest' as 'king' and was devoted to Sarapis' paredros, 'Maiden Consort, Isis, Queen of all Egypt'.[71] He caused the 'Nile Cubit' to be returned to the Sarapeum. He reopened the pagan temples. He revived the purificatory rites of Isis.[72] But all his love of Isis, the goddess of polytheism, failed to change the course of history. For the triumphant Church the bitter hostility of Julian was just a temporary setback.

CHAPTER XVIII

XENOPHON'S ISIAC ROMANCE

THE *Ephesiaca* of the novelist Xenophon is a typical Isiac romance of imperial times. The plot is built on a deeply religious basis. The heroine Anthia undergoes adventures reminiscent of Isis. At all times Artemis and Isis are treated as two aspects of a single divinity. The novel in the form in which it has come down to us shows a hand, not necessarily of the novelist himself, which feels the influence of the heliolatry characteristic of the age and visible in similar works written by Achilles Tatius, Heliodorus and others.[1]

Anthia, probably the leading priestess (*hiereia*) at Ephesus and herself *worshipped* at the outset as Artemis, informs the reader that her father 'dedicated her to Isis until her wedding day'. It is at the nocturnal festival of Artemis-Isis that the marriage is solemnized in a rite which is also an initiation. Anthia and her lover Habrokomes[2] are involved in sea voyages during which the Greek and Egyptian elements of the story are skilfully interwoven. Before she sets out for Egypt Anthia at Ephesus invokes the aid of her city's patroness Artemis, yet when she has arrived in the temple at Memphis she offers thanksgiving to Isis as the goddess who has kept her pure and to whom she is dedicated. The two lovers seek guidance of the Sun God, Colophonian Apollo, in his sanctuary just outside Ephesus. The oracle bids them to make gifts at the end of their trials and tribulations to 'holy Isis on the banks of the River Nile'. Their Isiac Odyssey takes them to such well-known cult centres as Rhodes,[3] Tarsus and Alexandria.

Both Artemis and Isis are specialists in the salvation of the troubled when all likely means of rescue seem to have failed:[4] and for their miraculous aid there is plenty of room when the wanderers are faced (like the Christian Paul of Tarsus) with perils of waters, perils of robbers, weariness and painfulness.[5] Anthia having been buried alive is brought back out of the grave and Habrokomes is rescued by the River Nile from dying first by crucifixion and then at the stake. The novel in its present form concludes with the offering by the two lovers of a list of all their hardships to the goddess of Ephesus, plainly identified with Egyptian Isis.

As the Artemision of Ephesus was plundered by the Goths in AD 263 the novel of Xenophon, where the sanctuary still stands in all its greatness, must have been composed before that year. Perhaps we should date it to the reign of Gordian III, when a political twinning or 'concord' (*homonoia*) between Ephesus and Alexandria resulted in the minting of coins on which can be seen Isis combined with one or other of her Egyptian associates together with Artemis.[6] In the parallel work entitled *Aethiopica* by Heliodorus we learn that 'Whatever can be heard or told about Egypt is most alluring to Greek ears'.[7] In those days the land of the pyramids and the Sarapeum provided story tellers with as much inspiration as it has in much more recent times. Then the Holy City was either Alexandria or Memphis—and holiness meant Isis, whose name in truth was one to be conjured with in the writing of romances.

About the author Xenophon nothing of a biographical nature is known. He was obviously a child of his age, an age when the emperor himself (as witness Heliogabalus) could be a Sun-worshipper. He did not hesitate to equate Artemis and Isis. The phallic aspect of Isiacism was utterly alien to his mind. Instead, he upheld the ideal of chastity, and the band of 'virgins' whose leader was Anthia must have seemed like Artemisian ancestors of Christian nuns. In the service of Isis lay perfect freedom; Habrokomes even when a slave could still feel himself Stoic-wise to be at liberty: 'They have power over my body but the soul I have is free.' To seek was in the end to find, as the example of Isis herself had proved. The festival procession of the Ephesian goddess was the occasion for match-making and to kindle lovers' torments Eros could lend a hand with all his potent philtres. But in marriage there was always a price to be paid (as witness Isis herself) and the oracle of Apollo at Colophon (speaking also

as the voice of Horus/Harpocrates/Eros) made clear to Habrokomes, Anthia and their relatives that 'the marriage chamber is the
death chamber' (*taphos thalamos*).[8] Only Isis in her august majesty
could rescue the pair, which was the reason for their abasement
before the altar of her temple at Rhodes.

Anthia is portrayed as a blooming girl of fourteen, whom her
fellow citizens at Ephesus could mistake for Artemis herself.
Her fair hair, for the most part untressed (in the manner of Isis
Lysikomos),[9] floated in the wind, as she went about like the goddess
with swift glances from eyes that girlishly bright put the fear of
Artemis the chaste into the mind of the beholder. Her tunic was
befittingly divine in colour, of purple, and tucked up to the knee.
She was clad in a fawn skin, she carried quiver, bow and arrows
and she was attended by hounds. Anthia evidently looked to the
Ephesians the young virgin severely beautiful like a nun[10] and
not the fertility goddess with bosom full of nipples whose statue
was so striking an ornament of their temple. Hers were the looks
of chastity and not of human fecundity.

It is to Artemis naturally that the Ephesian populace sacrifice
and pray before the wedded pair set out on their voyage to
Egypt. When, therefore, Anthia and Habrokomes have symbolically dedicated in the Temple of the Sun at Rhodes a golden suit
of armour inscribing it with their names as 'citizens of hallowed
Ephesus' and Habrokomes has had a dream soon afterwards about
a grim superhuman female figure in a scarlet robe setting their
ship on fire, we need not suppose this must be exclusively Artemis
herself. The truth is that the divine figure partakes of the character
both of the Ephesian and of the Egyptian. This can be deduced
from what is afterwards said by Anthia in a mention of Isis,
'If you ravish a female who is hallowed to this goddess, she will
show anger and her punishment will be terrible'.

Artemis and Isis have interchangeable roles. The Greek goddess
could take merciless vengeance on such offenders as Actaeon and
Agamemnon. Isis, according to a popular story, gave help to the
citizens of Rhodes when Mithridates fetched up a military appli-
ance called a *sambuke* against that part of the wall where her temple
was, and her apparition seemed to send forth a great burst of

fire for its destruction.[11] In the mind of our novelist there was no incompatibility between the Greek goddess who as Orthia saw that Spartan boys should be whipped and the Egyptian who could chastise men and women in the guise of Divine Anger or Nemesis.

From another author of an Isis romance, Achilles Tatius, we obtain specific details about betrothals in Graeco-Roman days. 'At Alexandria,' he tells us, 'lovers meet at the Iseum and are in the habit of calling upon the goddess to witness that they have plighted troth.'[12] Perhaps the girl would wear the white linen dress of Isis for the occasion: a man sends a letter to inform his beloved that this is the dress which so much attracts him as he thinks of all her charms.[13]

The high price set on chastity and avoidance of promiscuity is unmistakably linked by Xenophon with the cult of Isis. Whatever moral looseness there may have been in such Italian centres of Isiac worship as Rome and Pompeii, in the whole of the *Ephesiaca* (not to mention the romances by Achilles Tatius and Heliodorus) the name of the Egyptian goddess marks sexual purity both before and after marriage. For Xenophon Isis and Artemis stand firmly together. The cult of the virgin Artemis when considered entirely by itself reminds us at once of Catholic devotion to the Panaghia/Madonna in the nunnery.[14] Charicles in Heliodorus is forbidden to marry but must remain her whole life a virgin, devoting herself to Artemis as a minister of the sanctuary—*zacoros*, a title belonging to Isiacism as well.[15] For followers of Isis perpetual virginity was not obligatory, although the Christian Tertullian knows of such cases.[16] On the other hand, a girl like Anthia vowed her chastity to Isis until her wedding day.

After this, under the authority of the same goddess (as we can easily see from Xenophon), the ideal of the married couple could be summed up in a liturgical phrase they were never to hear used: 'till death us do part'. Anthia when she had passed by Alexandria and reached Memphis went into the Temple of Isis to utter the following prayer: 'Greatest of the gods, I who am considered to be thine have remained unblemished till this day and have kept

my marriage with Habrokomes free from defilement. . . . Do
thou then either save me in my misery and restore me to my living
Habrokomes or else, if it be absolutely fated that we should meet
separate deaths, let me remain pure for him when dead.'

At a later stage in the development of the plot Anthia renews
her entreaty for help in the Iseum at Memphis and begs 'the
Mistress of Egypt' to save her again as before. Then when her
tormentor has taken an oath not to molest her Anthia goes to the
sanctuary of Apis and prostrates herself before the Holy Calf of
Egypt. To a modern reader this may seem almost like a work of
supererogation. To the mind of the ancient follower of Isis
Anthia's behaviour would not have been surprising. Certainly
Anthia was doing more than the Emperor Augustus was ready to
do, when he sarcastically remarked he worshipped gods not bulls,
but she was in good company with Titus who had worn a diadem
when he attended the Apis consecration.[17] Anthia lived in an age
when the Sacred Calf of Memphis was yet one more manifestation
of the Sun. He was the living image of the soul of Osiris. Well
established in Hellenistic tradition as the Divine Physician,[18]
Apis was the animal emblem of Sarapis, the approximate though
not the exact equivalent in Egyptian religion to the Lamb in
Christianity, a god to be venerated for his excellent kindness,
in Anthia's view, as well as for his mercy towards all strangers.
It was not an accident that Anthia at Memphis went first to Isis
and then to Apis. Isis was popularly considered to have instructed
the Egyptians to worship the Sacred Calf. The priests of Apis
also would have been congenial to her. For on the evidence
of a Christian writer they were renowned, like those of Magna
Mater and Isis, for the purity of their lives, although, in the worship of the Apis, female chastity was liable to be disregarded.[19]

In sending Anthia at Memphis from Isis to Apis, our novelist
brings out the importance of another link in the mythological
complex out of which his story is woven. Already the Apis bull at
Memphis was identified by Herodotus with Epaphus,[20] the son
of Zeus and Io, whom he obviously regarded as Isis in the statement: 'The image of Isis being that of a woman has the horns of
a cow, like Io as the Greeks depict her.'[21] The Ovidian phrase

'Cow of Memphis' well conveys the Graeco-Roman assimilation
of Io and Isis.[22] Diodorus could seriously suggest that 'the
birth of Isis was transferred by the Greeks to Argos in their myth
about the transfiguration of Io into the shape of a cow'.[23] Usually,
however, as in the Pompeian treatment of the theme, Io was
imagined to have made her way from Greece to Egypt, not Isis
from Egypt to Greece. After wanderings that took her around the
shores of the Aegean and the Black Sea the daughter of Inachus
found rest at last on the banks of the Nile, becoming Isis/Hathor
and evidently, according to 'Greek interpretation', mother of the
Apis Bull as Epaphus.[24]

It was not the bovine-featured Io with whom the writer
Xenophon was specifically concerned, but underlying the plot of
his novel (as indeed in other Isiac romances of the period) the
myth of Io can be traced as a kind of *leit-motiv*, receiving a stress
here and a stress there. At the very beginning we meet Anthia
performing the duties of a priestess so admirably that she is
honoured by her associates as being herself godlike. Io is treated
in the same manner as priestess of Hera. The father of Anthia
consults the oracle of Apollo at Colophon concerning his
daughter's future. Inachus goes to the Pythian Apollo at Delphi
about Io. Io craves to be freed from her sufferings instead of
lingering for death. So does Anthia. Io is promised the Nile with
his hallowed sweet-tasting waters. Apollo's oracle makes clear
to Anthia that she will have to make sacrifice to hallowed Isis
on the banks of the Nile, when she has reached Egypt.[25]

The wanderings of Io assume two aspects. Like Isis she goes
in search of her son Epaphus, making her way right through
Syria. She herself is searched for by Triptolemus and his companions who on her disappearance at Tyre roam through the
region north of it including Cilicia and while on their quest for
her found Antioch and Tarsus.[26] In Xenophon's novel Anthia
finds herself much against her will in the company of a brigand
at Tarsus and at the same moment Habrokomes sets out to pass
northwards through Cilicia in the hope of finding Anthia if he
roams far enough. Another significant resemblance between
the legendary Io and the fictional Anthia is the part played by

Phoenician pirates in their capture. All the parallels provide cumulative proof that Xenophon was one of the novelists to be influenced by the Io legend. Without it he would have been lost for his plot. And all the time, of course, Xenophon keeps well to the fore that the haven of rest for his pair of lovers is not the holy city of the Pharos at the mouth of the Nile but Ephesus in Asia Minor.

The modern scholar, Merkelbach, who has done much to help us to understand how such romances as the *Ephesiaca* were influenced by the mysteries of Isis, well remarks that its heroine Anthia is the representative of Artemis and Isis jointly and that unless the religious meaning of each separate episode is grasped such love stories as this one must remain unintelligible. In other words, what we are dealing with is a species of sacred writing, a *hieros logos*, and the ordinary canons of literary criticism are not always relevant. For instance, when Anthia and Habrokomes had been married they could expect to live happily ever after: 'Their life was all one holiday.' So it would have been but for Apollo's prophecy and but for the hand of fate. Again, as Kerényi has observed, the behaviour of Anthia on the bridal night has to be judged by a cult criterion. We are told that she took the initiative. 'She fastened her lips to his with a kiss, and through the lips all the thoughts that were in their minds were transmitted from one soul to the other.' The active partner is Anthia. In her actions she copies Isis at the time when she embraced the dead Osiris. We may almost regard Anthia and her newly-wed husband as puppets in the religious drama of the Marriage and Death Chamber.[27]

In Isiac circles along the coast of Asia Minor, where by the third century AD the Egyptian cult had been firmly established, Xenophon's romance no doubt proved popular. The author's conflation of Artemis and Isis could rouse no objection. In fact, as an inscription from Ephesus belonging to the reign of Antoninus Pius indicates, the city and its Greek goddess could be coupled with the names of the Egyptian queen of heaven and the Roman prince of earth.[28] The dedicant, a certain Cominia Junia, would have found themes to her liking in the story of Anthia and

Habrokomes, a story she might even have recommended to those whom her dedication names as being the gatherers of the city's fishing tolls.

At the beginning of the last book of the *Ephesiaca* a very strange episode with an obviously ritual interest is introduced. At Syracuse we meet a fisherman named Aegialeus ('Long-shoreman'). Whereas to the mind of an ancient Isiac the scene would have appeared to display exemplary piety, the modern reader must find it gruesome to be told that the old fisherman has embalmed the body of his dead wife Thelxinoe ('The Heart Charmer') and lives with the mummy beside him. 'I talk with her,' he informs Habrokomes, 'as if she were alive, I lie down with her, and I have my meals with her. Whenever I return tired out after fishing, the sight of her comforts me.' Earlier Greek literature can provide somewhat similar parallels when a bereft husband consoles himself with an image which he keeps near him.[29] But here we have Aegialeus asserting not merely that he has mummified Thelxinoe 'in the Egyptian manner of embalm-ment', but also that he is constantly kissing her and staying with her. Once more we must bear in mind that this is not just a secular tale. As Merkelbach has emphasized,[30] the passage contains unmistakable Isiac symbolism. When Aegialeus narrates the past and mentions the all-night festival at Sparta (where both Artemis and Isis were worshipped), the making of a lovers' covenant, and the cutting off of Thelxinoe's locks of hair, Habrokomes (with a name suggesting that hair luxuriated on his head) is listening to incidents which combine together to create a short Isiac parable.

After this we are not surprised that the young man shares for a time in the fisherman's calling. Here, too, an allegorical meaning is perceptible. For the faithful follower of Isis the fish is taken out of the water just as the initiate is removed from the water in which he has been ceremonially dipped. Such is the significance, no doubt, of the fisherman character seen by Lucius in the Isiac procession at Cenchreae walking with some fish-hooks in his hands. In the Pompeian 'Adoration of Osiris' Mummy' a fisher-man can be seen. Nor should we forget that according to one legend a fish saved Isis from her trouble (*Pl. 25*).[31]

In the Christian era the ancient Egyptian practice of mummification was falling into disuse: either it was done badly in Egypt or it was not done at all. Outside the Nile valley Osiris and Anubis, of course, were well known. But although an example of mummification outside Egypt has been found[32] the physical embalmment of the body of Osiris by Anubis did not automatically travel overseas with the cult.[33] Nevertheless, as one of the frescoes from the Iseum at Pompeii shows us, the symbolic resurrection of the dead god by raising his mummy from the horizontal to the vertical position was regarded as of cardinal importance in the Isiac ritual (Pl. 25).[34] Moreover, in the realm of religious practice age-old customs die hard, and this is especially true of those in vogue along the Nile.

On the evidence of one of Christianity's most stalwart champions, Saint Athanasius, we can be certain that even in the fourth century Egyptian Christians delighted to swathe the bodies of martyrs in linen bands and instead of inhumation 'to place them on biers and to preserve them in their homes, thinking that in this way they were doing honour to the departed'.[35] The statement is reliable, and it is confirmed by the discovery of mummies which are undoubtedly Christian.[36] Needless to say, this heathen practice was frowned on by the Church. It is noteworthy, however, that St Anthony in the same passage should have left instructions that the place of his own burial should be kept secret so that the same treatment of immortality by mummification should not be meted out to him.

Habrokomes in the course of his adventures in Egypt is bound and delivered up to the governor to be crucified. He feels himself to be innocent of all offence and is therefore struck speechless with surprise. The governor without ordering detailed investigation sends him away to the banks of the Nile for crucifixion. There Habrokomes is raised up on the cross, his hands and feet bound with cords. He turns his gaze to the Sun and then entreats the River Nile. The Nile God listens to his prayer and performs a miracle. The cross is undermined and tumbles down. Habrokomes drops into the river and is carried safely away to the Nile Estuary, only to be re-arrested immediately.

In this crucifixion scene Merkelbach has discovered further telling evidence of Isiac allegory. The episode illustrates the value of a trust in the divine power to save from a situation which seems hopeless. To gain one's life one must endure 'voluntary death' (*voluntaria mors*). Habrokomes is required to repeat the experience of Osiris, whose mummified body was borne away by the Nile unharmed. To this we may add that the author of the New Testament *Apocalypse* (11, 8) is certain to have been thinking of such a scene when he makes the otherwise inexplicable reference to Egypt, 'where also our Lord was crucified'.

If for a moment we ignore the religious message of Xenophon's romance we can regard it as belonging in spirit though not in form to the same *genre* as Homer's *Odyssey*, Apollonius' *Argonautica*, and at a much later stage, of course, in the history of European literature Malory's *Morte d'Arthur*. Habrokomes and Anthia in their misadventures have nothing to learn even from Odysseus. To adapt some words of a writer about dreams and what they mean, and to apply the same to what happens in waking life, the significance of Isis with her temple colleagues was the advent of troubles, dangers, threats and crises, and afterwards unexpected salvation from them.[37] The two lovers in the *Ephesiaca* certainly could claim to have had such experience as this. Then, like the Greek Argonauts or the exiled Trojans under Aeneas, Habrokomes and Anthia went on a quest and found each other again after long search. To compare the late pagan *Ephesiaca* with the medieval *Morte d'Arthur* may itself seem a dangerous adventure. Yet the two works exhibit the same tone in the treatment of love. The courtly love or romantic *courtesy* which is one of the main themes in medieval minstrelsy, albeit the ostensible product of Christian ethics, derives its descent from the affection mutually displayed by man and woman in such Greek romances as the *Ephesiaca*, which may fairly claim to be one of *Morte d'Arthur*'s more distant ancestors.

Merkelbach and Kerényi before him have forced scholars to re-examine the Greek writers of romances known (somewhat unfortunately) as *Scriptores Erotici* in the light of the mysteries of Isis. Isiac symbolism exists abundantly in this field, whatever importance we give to it. Xenophon is not just a story-teller. He has a didactic and indeed a religious aim. His tale is that of the salvation of human lives through faith in divine powers that do intervene. The Isis of Xenophon is the Isis of Plutarch, 'training us to endure unbroken and hard worship in the sanctuary with the aim of knowing Him who is First, and Lord, and there for us to understand, and whom she exhorts us to seek—for He is there along with her and joined to her. Moreover, the name of her sanctuary clearly implies knowledge and understanding of reality. . . .'[38] The writer of the *Ephesiaca* would have concurred wholeheartedly with the view shortly afterwards expressed in the *Essay on Isis and Osiris* that 'He who is really an Isiac is one who searches with his mind those things that are shown forth and done in the name of these gods considering their metaphysical truth'.[39] Just as in the New Testament the purpose is to set forth the Gospel, the *Good News*, and to proclaim the *Mighty Works* of Christ's *Messengers* (the *Acts of the Apostles*) so in the literature of Isiacism of which the *Ephesiaca* is a fair specimen the implied aim is to prove the redemptive power of faith.

The biggest drawback for Xenophon and the other authors of *Erotica*, from the standpoint of the comparative study of religion, is the baffling polytheism. Nowhere are we told explicitly that Artemis and Isis are in unity. An ancient reader, of course, would not need to be apprised of the fact that Isis was the goddess of myriad names. When therefore he came across a reference to 'Samos the *hallowed* island of Hera' he might at once think of Isis who, as the Oxyrhynchus *Litany* states, received this as her own special title on that island. But even the contemporary pagan mind might well have boggled before the prospect of reconciling the Apis Bull with the virginal Artemis. Anthia might plausibly wed Habrokomes after a spate of hardships and become one with him. To arrange a happy marriage between Greek and Egyptian mythology was harder. There were so many difficulties because of the partners' different upbringing and it always remained a patched-up union. Paganism had so many ill-assorted denizens in its pantheon that not even Isis with all her magic arts could cure this chronic ailment.

Some of the ablest minds in later antiquity turned to the healing monotheism of Judaeo-Christianity just because it swept clean away the heterogeneous crowd of Olympus and the Nile, over whom Isis *Panthea*[40] had come to preside, and looked simply at the eternal problem of theism: the relation between God and Man. How much more scope, for instance, did the Christian revelation offer Origen, named though he was 'Son of Horus', than the polytheistic tangle of contemporary paganism!

The last five chapters of the *Ephesiaca* illustrate the unresolved theological incongruities. First Anthia invokes the Sun God, Helios (Apollo, Horus, Sarapis) at Rhodes: he is 'the Overseer of all mankind'. Then the people of Rhodes cry out 'Great is Isis' and declare 'We give thee thanks, goddess most great, for our salvation'.[41] Lastly Habrokomes and Anthia repair to the Temple of Artemis at Ephesus to utter their thanksgivings and to render their vows to her. The three cults, though closely linked, are distinct, and the three deities who are named are not specifically correlated in the version which we have. What is in fact lacking wherever we look in this piously contrived adventure story is an integrated theology. In the religion of Isis beliefs were very loosely bound and it was left to Christianity to hold church councils for the formulation of creeds.

CHAPTER XIX

THE PAULINE VIEW

OCTAVIAN, THE BITTER FOE of the last of the Pharaohs Cleopatra, when spurring his Roman troops into battle at Actium, is reported in the manner of the Persian emperor Cambyses and the Greek poet Anaxandrides to have uttered the gibe: 'The Egyptians worship reptiles and animals as gods, and bestow upon their own bodies by embalmment the glory of immortality.'[1] In the Pauline *Epistle to the Romans* (1, 23) a condemnation of pagans in general for their alleged folly, impiety and unrighteousness contains the remark couched in similar terms that they 'have changed the glory of immortal God by copying him in the image of mortal man and of birds, quadrupeds and reptiles'. We need only recall to mind the hawk of Horus and ibis of Thoth, the jackal of Anubis, his dog and the cat of Bast, or the cobra of Edjo and crocodile of Sobek, all notorious as sacred animals in the land of the Nile, to infer that the main target of attack at this point in the *Epistle* is Egyptian religion. If that is granted, then the question cannot be avoided how well the writer knew the cult and the aretalogical doctrine, the ritual and the mysteries of Isis.

What information we have about Christianity's first great missionary is derived from the New Testament.[2] In contemporary pagan literature Paul has preserved complete anonymity. From this source we obtain even less help for facts about 'Paul of Tarsus' than for 'Xenophon of Ephesus'. For the orthodox reader, however, the biographical validity of the *Acts*[3] and the *Epistles* must remain unquestioned, the latter indeed being treated as genuinely autobiographical. Such is the standpoint to be adopted here. On the evidence, then, of the New Testament there are grounds for believing Paul to have come into contact with the Isiac faith. We need only to consider his missionary voyages (*Fig. 3*).

Paul's position in the *Acts* is interesting. He is unmentioned till a quarter of the narrative has been told: but from then onwards he is the dominant figure. He is the undisputed Apostle to the Gentiles, Herald to the Heathen, and it is not by accident that when the Lycaonians, amazed at the mighty deed he has wrought, propose his apotheosis, they call him Hermes as the leader in the preaching of the Good News.[4]

Like every other religious leader in history Paul was a child of his times, 'a complete member of the Greek world'[5] where his preaching tours took him. Nobody now doubts his familiarity with the terminology and perhaps the actual practices of the mystery faiths. Like the Founder of the religion he proclaims, Paul uses *mystery* both singular and plural whenever it suits his purpose: in connection with knowledge (*gnosis*) and wisdom (*sophia*)[6] with the Christian revelation and resurrection and once along with the technical name for *stewards* at the Sarapeum.[7] He boasts that he has been '*initiated* in every possible thing—the full and the empty stomach, having more than enough and being without. Through him who gives me the *power* (*i.e. dynamis*) I can do all things.'[8] Not only could Paul *do* all things: he could also *become* all things to all men, a description which to the eye of the vigilant reader in the Graeco-Roman world would invite comparison with the power attributed to Isis *Myrionymus*, a title she bore in Cilicia, the province of Paul's birth.[9] He could introduce Greeks into the Jewish temple and call himself (in the passage already cited from his *Epistle to the Romans*) a borrower both from them and from 'the barbarians'. To the Greeks (as to his own fellow Jews) he could preach the gospel that Christ was the Power (*dynamis*) and Wisdom (*sophia*) of God.

Accepting, then, what the New Testament tells us as historically reliable, we find that the boy Saul was born at Tarsus.[10] Here he presumably grew up, though he may well have been taken for his Rabbinic education to Jerusalem later on. Tarsus (like a dozen more cities of Asia Minor to be visited by Paul later on as a missionary), was acquainted with the worship of Isis. The archaeological remains, such as a figure of the goddess or of a minister with sistrum and high peaked head-dress, Hellenistic and Roman pottery with the Isis palmette symbol, and examples of Isis conflated with Fortune and Victory, all suggest the cult's local prevalence.[11] It was at Tarsus 'upon the river of Cydnus' that Cleopatra 'first met Mark Antony': and there as afterwards at Alexandria she perhaps

> In the habiliments of the goddess Isis
> That day appeared.

Cleopatra, whose Egyptian-style barge and Isis-like person, in the words of Shakespeare, 'beggared all description', would have been for long a thrilling topic of conversation in the city on the Cydnus where the little Jewish boy Saul spent his childhood.

We may plausibly treat *Acts*[12] as the second volume of a single work written by the Third Evangelist, whose apologetic purpose is to present what he obviously holds to be a good case for the defence of Christianity.[13] Of the truth of the supernatural *doings* (the 'mighty works') and the *teachings* he is absolutely sure. Conditioned as he is by the contemporary climate of opinion, he is respectful towards dreams as a guide to deeds—what in the religion of Isis played so important a part as oneiromancy, and what is also accepted by the First Evangelist in the story of the Flight of the Holy Family into Egypt. At Damascus both Paul and his helpmate Ananias are led by visions. In the Troad a vision comes to the apostle by night. At once he obeys the call and is shown bringing the Christian gospel from Asia into Europe. While at Corinth he is encouraged in a vision not to be afraid. Without ignoring obvious parallels in the Old Testament, we may notice the resemblances in Egyptian religion, where traditionally the priest was granted the vision of God and His secrets and 'only those could enter the sanctuary whom Isis herself had deigned to summon through visions in their sleep'.[14]

Saul is said to have been smitten on his journey to Damascus with loss of sight for three days. His conversion and baptism resulted directly from his recovering it. We may notice that later in the book the sorcerer Barjesus ('Jesusson') is punished by the irate Saul (here first given his Graeco-Roman name) with the same kind of temporary blindness. Current belief ascribed to Isis the power to blind men who provoked her wrath and afterwards restore to them their sight.[15] So a character in Juvenal can exclaim: 'Let Isis with her angry sistrum strike my eyes.'[16] Her consort Sarapis was associated with her in curing blindness, as we observe in the case of Demetrius of Phaleron, writing hymns of praise to the God who had given him back his vision. Whether asleep or awake, men trusted Isis and Sarapis to bestow on them the power of vision.

Paul's greatest achievement, of course, was to have spread the Good News from its native Palestine northwards and westwards. His missionary tours took him away from Jerusalem and the land where the Gospel had first been preached. Both in Palestine and in Syria,[17] as in Asia Minor on which so much of Paul's apostolic zeal was concentrated, the cult of female deities was deep-rooted and very old. If Paul had visited Samaria or Byblos on a conversion campaign he would have felt the presence of Egyptian religion. In Samaria, where it was Paul's missionary predecessor Philip who proclaimed Christianity, it would appear from an ivory plaque that the cult of Isis-Nephthys was known even during the reign of Ahab and Jezebel (c. 860 BC). There also in the third century BC a dedication was made to Sarapis and Isis. A prayer of a Greek and his family shows Isis equated with the local Mother Goddess.[18]

Caesarea, originally called Strato's Tower, was Samaria's great sea-port and like coastal towns to the south (Rhinocolura, Raphia, Gaza and Ascalon) and to the north (Dora, Ptolemais and Tripolis) according to the Oxyrhynchus *Litany* was acquainted with Isis.[19] It was at Caesarea that Peter, not Paul, preached the new faith of Christ when bidden to do so in an Egyptian-sounding and zoological dream. There Paul landed and there he was brought to stay in Philip's house. Thither he was sent from Jerusalem to be tried before Felix and to plead before Festus and Agrippa. Coins prove that the Oxyrhynchus *Litany* is not mistaken in linking 'Strato's Tower' with Isis.[20] From Caesarea Paul in due course took ship to another Isiac sea-port, Italian Puteoli. Caesarea of Samaria gave Paul plenty of opportunity to contemplate the power of the goddess he was to meet again at Puteoli when he reached there (as Renan imaginatively writes)[21] to preach Christ crucified after landing from his Alexandrian ship with the name *Dioscuri* written on her side. As the apostle looked about him he saw the signs of an oriental faith encountered again and again on his journeys through Cyprus, Asia Minor, the Aegean, Macedonia and Achaia.

It has been remarked by a distinguished twentieth century theologian that 'the streets along which Paul wandered had been trodden before him by the apostles of Isis, the God of Jewry and the Great Mother'.[22] We do well to consider that as Paul travelled around he was actually *meeting* the professors of these other faiths. In the middle of the first century AD Isiacism, far from being dead, was in the ascendant. Plutarch slightly later was writing that all men possess Isis and her associated gods and are familiar with them. Just as at the philosophical level on Mars' Hill in Athens the missionary of Christ's Resurrection had to combat the incredulous Epicureans and Stoics, so he had to face in the Troad Isis-Athena wearing the lotus he could have seen on the sceptre of his own Baal at Tarsus, in Cyprus Isis-Aphrodite (the Venus of Paphos invoked by Horace), and Isis-Artemis at Ephesus with her 'marines'.[23]

Before his conversion Paul is portrayed as having been implacably hostile towards the 'Hellenist' Stephen. Significantly Stephen was full of *power* and *wisdom* and did wondrous deeds, and in his apologia made his appeal to Moses as one who had been trained in all the *wisdom* of the Egyptians and who was powerful in words and deeds. The Hellenism of Stephen, for which he was to suffer martyrdom, seems to have been characterized by Egyptianizing views, views which to Paul were at that time detestable.[24]

Paul may have disliked Egypt and its theology. But towards the end of his career in Palestine he was himself mistaken for an Egyptian, and indeed for a false prophet who in the time of Felix had planned an attack on Roman-occupied Jerusalem from the Mount of Olives.[25] Paul lived in an environment strongly influenced by religious ideas from Egypt.

As though to justify the title of his book the writer of *Acts* (19, 11) tells about the 'mighty works, not accidental,' which 'God wrought by the hands of Paul'. Among these were miracles of healing through the medium of the apostle's personal belongings such as handkerchiefs, and exorcisms of diseases in the name of 'the Lord Jesus'. All such acts, 'mighty deeds', of Paul surpassed the conjuring tricks of the sorcerers. The passage can be paralleled in the Egyptian-Greek magical literature, where traditionally Isis the divine was mistress and where her name had a sorceress's virtue.

As time went on Paul was led to preach not to the Jews but to 'the heathen': both at Antioch and at Corinth he declared this to be his intention.[26] The cities he is recorded to have visited after forming this decision at Pisidian Antioch were generally familiar with the Egyptian religion. Sarapis was known at Iconium and Isis in the Troad. On Samothrace, where Paul called on his way to Neapolis (Cavalla), [27] she was termed 'bovine-faced'. The scene at Philippi by the riverside with women at their prayer meeting might suggest a devotion to Isis Regina.[28] When the apostle went on from Philippi to Thessalonica he passed through Amphipolis and Apollonia. Near the door of a church at Amphipolis was found a dedication to Sarapis, Isis and Philip V of Macedon.[29] At Apollonia (or alternatively Anthemus) a certain Gaius Olbius dedicated a thank-offering to Sarapis, Isis and Anubis.[30] In the large cities he next visited the gods of Egypt were prominent. Mention has previously been made of the Sarapeum at Thessalonica, the cult of Isis Lochia at Beroia, and the ascendancy of Isis in the intellectual atmosphere of Athens. At Corinth the goddess had two temples, and Sarapis one. He was worshipped as the God of Canopus, and she both as 'Egyptian' and as 'Pelagian'.[31] At Cenchreae, the scene of the first 'Pauline tonsure',[32] Isis shared her authority with Aphrodite, Poseidon and Asclepius.[33] On the second missionary journey, therefore, Paul was directing his sermons to a pagan audience well used to the preaching of the ministers of Isis with their own 'way of salvation'.

The sermon attacking the idolatry shown by the Ephesians[34] towards the Great Goddess Artemis has not survived in detail.

We need not doubt that Paul had taken the measure of the female deities of whose influence he had had long experience, especially Artemis and Isis, and that his condemnation was as scathing as it sounds on the lips of the silversmith Demetrius, even though the town clerk is represented as repudiating the charge of 'blasphemy against our goddess'. Paul could tell that here was a dangerous rival. At Ephesus, as has been well remarked, the conflation of Alexandrian doctrine and local cults which had lasted for some generations competed with nascent Christianity and imperilled its very existence.[35] Paul and his silversmith opponent agreed in one thing: the Great Goddess was not merely Ephesian nor Asian, but ecumenical. In Paul's eyes Artemis resembled Isis *polyonymous*.

The last chapters of *Acts* list certain places that Paul visited before his departure for Italy. All four Greek places there named— Samos and Chios, Cnidus and Crete—as well as Myra in Lycia are connected with Isis in the Oxyrhynchus *Litany*.[36] Clearly Paul's missionary tours ended as they had begun. For on his first journey he had started out from Antioch on the Orontes, where the cult of Isis had been brought from Memphis,[37] and had preached in Cyprus at Salamis and Paphos, all three named in consecutive lines of the *Litany*. The evidence is unimpeachable that the places where Paul preached cultivated the faith of Isis.

Without embarking on the complicated questions of the autobiographical value of the various *Letters*[38] attributed to Paul in the Canon of the New Testament and the wider one as to how the Canon itself was determined, we shall for convenience regard the *Letters* as offering a useful background against which to judge the impact made by such religions as Isiacism on the mind of a proselytizing apologist like the converted Jew of Tarsus. To its existence he was not blind. The *Letters* which go under his name witness proto-Christianity's awareness of the crafty competitor. To search there for the 'Pauline view' of the rival faith may be a novel undertaking: yet the task is not hopeless but rewarding.

In the canonical arrangement of the *Epistles* we find *Romans* placed first and at its beginning the candid acknowledgment that the writer is indebted to paganism, both Greek and non-Greek. Two key terms of his theology are divine *power* and *salvation*. Immediately afterwards comes the outburst against anthropomorphism and zoolatry. That the object of attack here is Egyptian religion is confirmed by Augustine who, in commenting on the passage, remarks that no idolatry is more profound and more superstitious than that of Egypt.[39] Even the non-Christian Plutarch shares the same view when he declares that in their apotheosis of animals the Egyptians have made their religious services look utterly ridiculous and a complete mockery, besides opening the door to atheism and a rationalism which is itself bestial.[40] To lampoon the beliefs of the Nile, petrified survivals from the dynasties of long ago, was a favourite pastime of Christian critics. The intelligent pagans who could cheerfully accept Greek anthropomorphism were yet troubled with the ibis and the hawk, the dung-beetle of Khepre the young Sun God, the cow, the dog and the cat which seemed to overshadow the bright shape of Isis. In the *Ethiopica* of Heliodorus the *prophetes* Kalasiris from the Iseum at Memphis meets Greeks at Delphi and explains to them the reasons for animal deifications among the Egyptians.[41] The Pauline criticism of those who like the Isiacs 'worshipped and served the creature' followed a stereotyped pattern. The weakness was obvious and the censure telling.

Later in *Romans* (Chapter 13) mention is made of the 'higher powers' to which 'every soul' must be in subjection. Admittedly the straightforward interpretation of the passage is that the Christian must show obedience to the existing authorities of the Roman Empire. But another meaning is also possible. We have only to look at the *Epistle to the Ephesians* (3, 10) to observe that in the 'Pauline correspondence' through the ruling forces and powers in heaven is manifested 'the wisdom [*sophia*] of God in all its multiplicity' (phraseology which would appeal to any reader whose background was Isiac). Although any Christian writer would spurn the thought of emperor worship there is the possibility of ideas seeping through from that source, for the existence of a close link between the cult of the Roman emperor and that of Isis seems very clear.[42]

Christian writers are ostensibly unsympathetic towards the astrological and zodiacal systems which are revealed to us by such writers as Celsus, Hermes Trismegistus and Firmicus Maternus. An Egyptian planetary theology cited by Chaeremon embraces Decans, Horoscopi and 'Mighty Rulers', and in speculations of this kind, as we know from the heresy of the Gnostic Peratae, the Overall Rulers of Night and Day are respectively Osiris and Isis.[43] When therefore towards the end of *Ephesians* we meet 'powers', which are in this case wicked, they belong to the same order of being as what we have already encountered. They are the 'rulers and powers' which in *Colossians* Christ has triumphantly despoiled.[44] Of particular interest is the term *cosmocrator*,[45] which strongly suggests Isiacism. A similar treatment of the cosmic forces created by the fertile imagination of Egyptian astrologers can be detected in the Pauline use of the term 'elements' in *Galatians* and *Colossians*. When the Lucius of Apuleius with the help of Isis *triumphs over his destiny* and is then *borne through all the elements*, he is portrayed as mastering exactly those 'rulers and powers' of *Ephesians* and 'beggarly elements' of *Galatians*[46] which the Pauline treatment so strongly disparages. In *Colossians* mention is made about deliverance from the power of darkness. In the *Hymn* from Cyme, Isis says about herself: 'I release those who are in chains.' Pauline soteriology can be easily paralleled in Isiacism and is based on the same theory, that certain cosmic forces exist in the heavens—'spiritual wickedness in high places'— which nevertheless are not finally invincible.[47]

Allied to this idea of triumphant salvation is the belief in religion as a source of joy and peace in the performance of the will of God: 'In la sua volontade è nostra pace.' This is strikingly illustrated in the final chapter of *Romans* where we are told: 'The God of peace shall bruise Satan under your feet.' Isis was specially venerated as 'the Queen of Peace'. Lucius begs her to grant him 'rest on his way' (*pausa*) and peace. He also sings of her as bruising Hell: 'Thou dost tread down Tartarus.'

The triad of Christian virtues, Faith, Hope and Love, so eloquently praised in *Corinthians*, is introduced in such a way as to suggest that the writer of what is obviously an aretalogy is

3 The Near East with the route of St Paul's journeys. Isiac find-spots and localities attributed on literary and numismatic evidence marked by ●; Isiac finds of pre-Christian date by ■

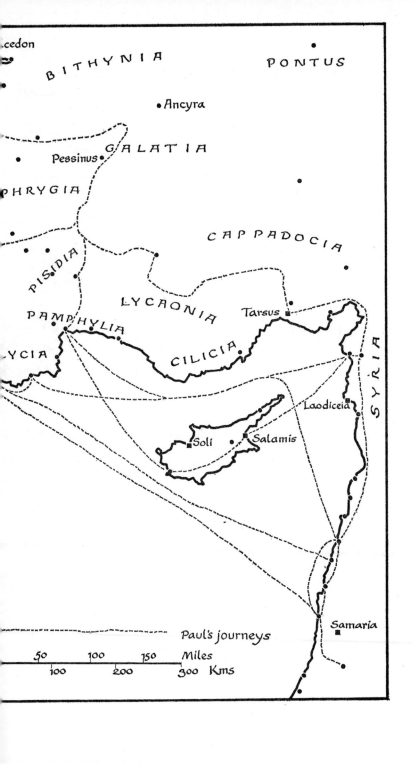

.cedon

BITHYNIA

PONTUS

•Ancyra

GALATIA

Pessinus•

PHRYGIA

CAPPADOCIA

PIS.IDIA

LYCAONIA

PAMPHYLIA   Tarsus

YCIA   CILICIA   SYRIA

Laodiceia

•Soli   ■Salamis

Samaria

- - - - - - - - - - Paul's journeys

50   100   150   Miles
100   200   300 Kms

taking a close look at contemporary cults. He mentions the gift of tongues, a gift on which much stress is laid in the New Testament. The followers of Isis held that she controlled the various tongues, 'dialects', that prevailed in the world. The words, 'I am become as sounding brass, or a tinkling cymbal' can hardly be appreciated unless we remember how Isis the Moon is addressed: 'Shaking thy cymbals thou dost renew midwinter with thy sistrum'[48]—'the sistrum to be heard in Egypt'—'the sorrowing waters of the Nile with its sounding brass.'[49] The 'Love' (*agape*) which is the crowning virtue throughout the passage is apparently not restricted to Christianity. According to the received text of the Oxyrhynchus *Litany*, *agape* is a cult name for Isis, who in Egyptian tradition as old as the *Pyramid Texts* personifies tenderness, compassion and divine love. The 'prophecies' which 'shall be nullified' are surely not what had been foretold in the Old Testament but rather the soothsaying of current Isiacism in which an important part was occupied by the 'dream expert' (*oneirocrites*) and the 'prophet'.[50] The Isiac 'prophet' has to know the Holy Scriptures of his religion (indeed, 'all mysteries')—and this is the 'knowledge' (*gnosis*) which we are again told in an emphatic repetition 'shall be nullified'. The religious beliefs which in the writer's view are going to be 'unemployed and out of work' are clearly not those inspired by Jesus Christ but those of the heathen Isis and Hermes Trismegistus.

The virtue of Faith in its Christian context is inseparable from Love: 'love believes everything'. Religious belief of this kind was not unknown to the followers of Isis. Lucius tells us that he was 'diligent in holy devotion to the genuine religion because of his complete faith'.[51] Through faith men of the noblest birth were led to practise incubation in the Sarapeum at Canopus. The vision of Isis was granted to those who invoked her name 'in faith'.[52] Just as the Pauline *Epistle* encouraged Timothy to go on in pure conscience and not give up, holding the mystery of the faith, so Isis ordered: 'Believe what is true: believe. Do not give up. If your conscience is pure you can be of good courage.'[53]

The Christian virtue of Hope deserves to be studied against the background of the cult of *Spes Bona* (*Agathe Elpis*) which is only one example of the Graeco-Roman deification of abstract ideas, *Fides Augusta* ('faith in the Emperor and loyalty to him')[54] being another. As can be seen from *Thessalonians*, Hope when linked with Faith and Love means 'Hope of Salvation'. For Paul, Christ is the saviour: for those who believe in the religion of Alexandria 'Isis and Sarapis, the greatest of the gods' are likewise 'saviours'. The Pauline 'helmet, the hope of salvation' would have allured the mind of Lucius as he waded into the water at Cenchreae 'in the hope of salvation' after his sevenfold baptism.[55]

Scholars who choose to treat the Pauline *Epistles* as being primarily documents for internal consumption by those already converted to Christianity, as spontaneous 'letters', have ignored the protreptic purpose of the writer. The language and even the names reveal an awareness of what would interest contemporary pagan readers. The same consideration applies when we examine the narrative in *Acts*. Such names as Paul and Apollos (born at Alexandria) have the right sound. For any potential convert from Isiacism to Christianity the names of Timotheus Epaphroditus and Silvanus arouse immediate attention. Was not a Timotheus responsible in the days of the early Ptolemies for 'Greek interpretation'? Was there not an Isiac priest named Epaphroditus at Athens?[56] And was not Silvanus the woodland deity worshipped side by side with Isis at Philippi as also he was at Ostia?[57] The references to ships are equally telling. The centurion found 'a ship of Alexandria sailing into Italy'—on a voyage which as we have earlier indicated must have been undertaken on many occasions when the religion of Isis was one of the exports. From Malta another Alexandrian boat took Paul to Puteoli. Her name was that of the Heavenly Twins 'made Saviours by Isis'—the *Dioscuri*. Earlier in *Acts* a proper name is used of a woman 'full of good works' as a Greek equivalent for the Hebrew form. It is 'Dorcas', a name borne by an Isiac dedicant and specifically applied to the gazelle regarded as 'the plaything of Isis'. The reader is never able to forget the pagan world for long.

The Christian community to whom *Philippians* was ostensibly addressed could hardly have been unaware of the Roman colony's

'Queen Victoria'—Isis *Regina, Victrix*. For non-Christians there the countless names of the goddess must have been among her main attractions. She could indeed herself be 'the First Name'.[58] The writer of the *Epistle* therefore may well have had her much in mind when he proclaimed that God had given Jesus a name above all others,[59] at which every knee must bow, in heaven, in earth and under the earth. We must genuflect to *Jesus* not *Isis*.

The 'devout Greeks' at Thessalonica whom Paul converted would have eagerly compared their abandoned cults with the new gospel, and the two *Letters* sent to them would have been studied from the same standpoint. Words reminiscent of Egyptian worship as practised in the local Sarapeum would be marked. For instance, 'thanksgiving to God' (*eucharistia*) and 'God's churches' (*ecclesiae*) would recall the dedicatory formula *eucharisterion* and the architectural term *ecclesiasterion* (the inner sanctuary).[60] Having perhaps adored the divine mother who sheltered all idols under her polytheistic wings, they would treat as a plain reference to her forsaken cult the declaration that they had been converted to monotheism from idolatry to become servants of the living and true God. A reader of *Thessalonians II* would be struck in particular by the 'mystery of iniquity' and of the Anomos to be destroyed 'by the epiphany of the Lord's coming'. Here modern New Testament scholars have detected an allusion to the intended desecration of the Temple at Jerusalem by Caligula (Gaius), represented in a colossal statue as a hybrid ruler Neos Gaius and Zeus *Epiphanes*. The contemporary reader might have observed undertones of the local Cabiric and Isiac mysteries, which are plausibly linked with the cult of the Emperor.

Clearly the Pauline view of Isiacism was penetratingly critical. Paul's world was a patriarchy, his religion was Christological and monotheistic, and God was found in fashion as a man. Isis was female, Isis was the champion of idolatry, and Isis was the lover of the Nile menagerie. And yet the Pauline and the Isiac faith had at least one common characteristic. Each swept aside racial and social distinctions. 'There is neither Greek nor Jew . . . Barbarian, Scythian, bond nor free: but Christ is all, and in all.'[61] Change *Christ* to *Isis*—and the words are still true.[62]

CHAPTER XX

THE GREAT FORERUNNER

LESS THAN FOUR HUNDRED years ago Bruno suffered a martyr's death by fire. Excommunicated by an obscurantist ecclesiasticism he went to the stake for his beliefs. He was convinced that the wisdom and magic-born religion of ancient Egypt excelled the fanatical theology that burnt dissident thinkers as heretics. For him the Biblical record was on a par with the Greek myths. Refusing to retract his teachings, he met his doom dauntlessly, for he had less cause than his judges to fear the verdict of history and could snap his fingers at them in warning.[1] Giordano Bruno, the unfrocked monk, perished on 16 February 1600, for his intransigent denial that Christianity was unique.

Bruno's influence before this had doubtless led to the inclusion of Pinturicchio's astonishing frescoes at the Sistine Chapel in the Room of the Saints. Commissioned by the man who became Pope in the year that Columbus discovered the New World, they include some astonishing novelties or rather mythological borrowings from Ancient Egypt. Here we can still gaze at Io, the Greek cow, turning in to Egyptian Isis, at the Apis Bull, identified with the Bull of the Borgias, at Apis Bulls worshipping the cross of Christendom, and at Moses, Hermes Trismegistus and Isis in a single group[2] (*Pls. 71, 72*). The German Cardinal Nicholas of Cusa might teach an Egyptianizing mysticism and die in his bed. The Italian Cardinal Cesio might garnish his Roman villa with a marble bust of Isis *Victrix* and still escape excommunication. Bold in his theory of the infinite Universe and Worlds,[3] stubborn in his behaviour and passionately unswerving in his devotion to Egypt, Bruno in the end was sacrificed to the flames:

Such load of wrongs religion could induce.

The destruction of the Alexandrian Sarapeum[4] bears witness that the theological ideas of Egypt were dreaded by Christians even more in the fourth century than at the beginning of the seventeenth when Bruno became the Inquisition's burnt offering. The obvious foe of the Church in its early ecumenical struggles was the cult of Isis and her temple companions. This is made clear even before the deathblow which paganism received from Theodosius. For Eusebius makes mention of the Egyptian faith and declares (somewhat mistakenly) that by his day the land of the Nile had been 'freed from this disease'.[5]

To find good in the ideas and usages symbolized by Isis is not unknown in modern times.[6] But though the path lies open it does not allure many. We think it odd to look again far back into our own Mediterranean past for possible truth in the Alexandrian Sarapeum and to risk our reputation by siding with Hypatia, Eunapius and Bruno. To belong to the losing side carries small hope of reward. Heresy hunting, we remember, was more than just a funny game for Bruno.

Today at least in England martyrdom in the name of religion is not the rule. Good luck (called in the Graeco-Roman world Isis *Fortuna* or Isityche) can bestow the blessings of birth and education during the twentieth century in the free world of western Europe, where the debt to a civilization long ago Christianized must be readily granted by those who deal with religious origins. Protestant Christianity has itself fostered intellectual curiosity without an utter rejection of the faith handed down —*fides quaerens intellectum* is its motto and truth its only goal. In the Pauline *Epistle* opposition is voiced to knowledge, 'science', *gnosis*.[7] If this is indeed the attitude of orthodox Christendom then the prospects for its survival as one of the great powers for good seem bleak. It must surely welcome freedom to think, especially about its own origins. Otherwise it loses its meaning.

We live at a time when ever-fresh knowledge is looming up over an ever-widening horizon, when hitherto accepted 'facts' have to be re-examined again and again, and when hidden truth has to be searched out and found as in the old Isiac parable. Our theories need to be modified and even scrapped in the light of

negative instances. We need the intellectual colloquy of Athens
and Alexandria, and nowhere more urgently than in the field of
religious experience. What the western world today upholds as
the inveterate tradition of its own formative Christianity gains
in value when correlated with even earlier tradition. A principle
in all our thinking must be the conviction that theological
speculations have never arisen *in vacuo*. It is a platitude that the
pantheon of Greece and Rome did not suddenly fall down flat
like the walls of Jericho. What is not so well understood is how
this classical polytheism before it was finally assaulted by the
Church had undergone a manifold foreign infiltration in which
one of the strongest influences was Egyptian. It was no accident
that the heathen stronghold attacked and destroyed by the
emperor in 391 was Egypt's Sarapeum (*Pl. 68*).

To attempt to follow the path of Isis down the long centuries
is a fascinating but complicated task. The picture changes.
Even in the *Pyramid Texts* the references to Isis are many and
varied. To an Egyptian of the earliest Dynasties parts of the
aretalogy in the Oxyrhynchus *Litany* might have seemed very
strange. The one constant factor is the goddess' name. When
full attention has been given to the rich sources which survive
from antiquity—temple buildings and obelisks, coins and gems,
inscriptions[8] and statues, literary passages in prose and verse,[9]
papyri and other records—and when the views of modern and
earlier commentators have been weighed up and carefully sifted,
the question remains open how deeply bent on Isis at any given
moment were the minds and hearts of ordinary men and women
in the last centuries of the pagan world. Certainly the mention
of the name of Isis and her temple associates at a particular site,
or some find there, is presumptive evidence of its being a cult
centre, though at times the link may seem slender. On the other
hand, silence never rules out the absence of a cult which claimed
to be ecumenical. The sceptic may contend that in the Oxyrhynchus *Litany* the fine-sounding catalogue of place-names discloses
aliases: the local divinity has been fused with Isis *in the mind of the
aretalogist* and the epicleses therefore are not her own genuine
cult titles. In the absence of the statistics which modern opinion

polls undertake to gather, there is no obvious way of finding out the size of Isis' following at specific times and places.[10] We can but guess the relative importance of Philae and Rome, Thessalonica and Beneventum, Delos and Ostia, Alexandria and Puteoli. We have no guidance as to the formality of membership or the regulation of laical and sacerdotal duties. A deeply centralized hierarchical organization such as marks the Roman Catholic Church seems never to have arisen.

In Hopfner's invaluable collection of the literary sources, *Isis* needs more pages of the Index than any other name. A brief glance at her attributes as there listed reveals her sharing titles with the Blessed Virgin whom Catholic Christianity has ever revered as Mother of God. Some of these resemblances may be set aside as once as commonplace. Yet so many are the parallels that an unprejudiced mind must be struck with the thought that cumulatively the portraits are alike. Indeed, one of the standard encyclopedias of classical mythology specifically deals with 'Isis identified with the Virgin Mary'.[11]

Let us observe a few of the resemblances. Isis and Osiris, as we have so often seen, are mythologically interfused. In the language of the Roman Church the Blessed Virgin Mary is 'sister and spouse of God: sister of Christ'. Christian writers identify Sarapis with Joseph and then make Isis 'wife of Joseph'. Like her heathen forebear the Catholic Madonna wears a diadem. She too is linked with agricultural fertility being termed 'the fresh tuft', 'the earth', and 'the cornucopia of all our goods'. She can be the 'form' of heaven and earth and of all created things. She can be called 'fructificatio' as well as a young heifer (*iuvenca, iuvencula*). 'Africa' and even 'Alexandria' can be her title. The Blessed Virgin is 'the power that heals the world' (*medicina mundi*). She is 'the lofty Pharos of light', 'Pelagus'.[12] Like Isis she is the protectress of sailors (*salvatrix*) who when saved from shipwreck bring her their thank-offerings. Like the pagan goddess she can take such names as *Inventrix* and *Justitia*. As Isis with Anthia so the Blessed Virgin Mary guards the maiden's chastity. Like Isis she may be likened to a deer, a swallow and the moon.[13] She can be identified with the Roman goddesses Juno, Minerva,

Venus and Diana, and with the god Mercury. She can be identified with the Nile and the *situla*, can be termed 'God's bride' (*Nympha Dei*) as Isis was of Sarapis.[14] Like her great forerunner the Blessed Virgin Mary has been known as 'she whose praises are innumerable' (*myria*),[15] as 'Nurse' and 'Nature', as 'the goddess of all goddesses', and as 'the great first principle (*elementum*) in which the "elements" (*elementa*) are all specifically contained'. All these epicleses can be found in the Marian aretalogy published at Cologne in 1710 by Hippolytus Marraccius.[16] Latin patrology has been well culled by this enthusiast.

The *Akathist Hymn* of the Greek Orthodox Church supplies us with similar results. 'The Maiden', like her pagan predecessor, is *mystis* ('she who initiates') and 'cornland making the tilth of mercies to sprout'. Her flower is that of Isis, 'the unfading rose'. As Mother of God she is described as 'the heifer who has brought forth the spotless calf'.[17] Assuredly the Panagia has 'quenched the fever of polytheism'. Yet she is acclaimed in the style of Isis as the Lady who is herself 'a chariot in the form of fire'. Just like Isis Pharia as the personification of rest and haven of safety at Alexandria[18] so the Panagia is invoked: 'Be thou our haven and anchorage on the sea of our troubles.' Through the Panagia's agency diseases are exorcized and 'the hosts of the spirits in the air are worsted'. Perhaps the most significant parallels in the *Akathist Hymn* are the expressions: 'Throne of the King' and 'Mistress of the World'. Like Isis also the Panagia is identified with the ray of the Sun.[19]

The examples quoted of Marian epicleses in Latin and Greek are enough to prove the continuity of the aretalogical tradition. The Egyptian goddess who was equally 'the Great Virgin' (*ḥwnt*) and 'Mother of the God'[20] was the object of the very same praises bestowed upon her successor. Mary, Virgin Mother of Jesus, could gradually (and silently) replace the Graeco-Roman Isis-Sophia.[21] Historians generally, and specifically those who trace the development of religious ideas, need to avoid the trap of confusing chronological order with cause and effect: *post hoc ergo propter hoc*. On the other hand, the veneration (*hyperdulia*) of the Blessed Virgin Mary was certainly introduced at about the same time as Theodosius ordered the destruction of the pagan temples, including the Sarapeum and other shrines of the Egyptian gods. Here, we may think, lies a reason for the absorption of elements, ideas and usages from the old religion into the new. The take-over in Egypt itself would have been easy. The question has been well put: 'Can we seriously believe that a Christian Coptic priest would have succeeded in changing the general conception of the Nubian, who in Mary the Theotokos could only reverse what he had for centuries worshipped in his Lady Isis?'[22]

Long after the cult of pagan Isis had been officially stamped out by Theodosius her figure survived in some very remarkable ways. Christine de Pisan in the fourteenth century, following a legend which is obviously old, links 'Ysys, the which is a planter' (*Pl. 70*) with 'the blissyd Concepcion off Jhesu Cryst by 'e Holy Gost in the Blyssyd Virgyne Marie'.[23] As Baltrušaitis (a self-confessed Egyptomane) has recently indicated, the etymology of *Paris* could be derived (however mistakenly) from *Isis*—'une citée située emprès Ysis'. Colour was added to this specious derivation by the fact that a certain famous idol of hers had been long preserved inside St Germain des Pres whence it had been removed and smashed to smithereens on the orders of the ecclesiastic Bretonneau.[24] However fanciful the etymology, the breakage of the idol showed history repeating itself. In ancient Rome Tiberius had smashed Isis. Bretonneau did the same to her in Paris. Her violent end proves her dreaded power.

Because the transition from the paganism for which the name of Isis stood was a stealthy and insensibly prolonged blending, rather than a sudden disruption, statues like the one in Paris might stay inside Christian churches without arousing comment.[25] Images of Isis could become 'black Madonnas'.[26] Even more striking, however, was the readiness to build the churches themselves at or near to the sites of Isea. Augustine clarifies this practice. Temples, idols and groves, he states, are turned over not to private individuals but to the glory of God.[27] So also Pope Gregory informs the Abbot Mellitus on his departure for Britain that temples are to be purified from devil-worship and dedicated to the God of Christianity. It is his hope that the people, seeing that their hallowed shrines are not destroyed, will abandon idolatry and resort to these places as before.[28] The policy of ecclesiastical authority was clearly as far as possible to conserve and not to pull down what was there (*Pl. 19*).

When a temple was actually destroyed the spoil of demolished stone and brick could be re-employed on the spot. Thus at Saqqara in Egypt a Christian settlement could be built on the site of a temple erected by Nectanebo.[29] The church, dome and, later on, the spire betokened the triumph of the cross on the very plot of ground once hallowed to the now outcast demon. Such was Cyril's procedure at Menouthis.[30] Above the sacred edifice of the old faith now there arose that of the new, literally as well as figuratively, on top of it.[31] But the fact chiefly stressed by the new dispensation was not sudden change but the maintenance of services as before. For the take-over was not to mean an utter break with the past.

A geographically wide range of churches numbering nearly fifty can be cited for inscriptions in honour of the Egyptian gods.[32] The interest differs from church to church. Thus at Philae the West Coptic Church of St Mary stands close to the temenos wall of the Great Iseum.[33] In the Church of St John the Divine on Ios (*Fig. 2*) the writer in 1965 examined the stele (upside down) behind the iconostasis and saw for himself that in this building, where the priest had just invoked the Panagia as 'Mistress of the World', Isis still stood hidden but obstinately alive, uttering her own praises to prying eyes. In Athens the Old Metropolis with its Isis-sounding nickname *Gorgoepekoos*[34] (not to mention *Hagia Dynamis*—'Holy Power'—only a few steps away) is probably the direct successor of an Iseum associated with Isis-Eileithyia.[35] 'Isis Bringer of the Crops' has come to light in the Church of Ara Coeli in Rome. Here too is Santa Maria Navicella, with its Isiac-looking model of the boat as a conspicuous landmark outside, marking the site, no doubt, of the ancient Iseum Metellinum on top of the Caelian Hill. Among many pagan remains beneath St Peter's is the epitaph in memory of Primitiva Flavia, 'chaste worshipper of Isis'.[36]

The reader may now well ask how much Christianity owes on the ceremonial side to the cult of Isis. To find the answer let us for a moment consider the case of Bruno. Bruno, who came to hold that the cross had been borrowed by the Christians from the Egyptians, would be proud to know that the familiar black cassock and white surplice were worn in the service of Isis. Passiontide and Holy Week would perhaps make a man of his temperament search for comparisons outside the faith he as yet professed. The use of the *crotalus*, or rattle, certainly heard by him at church on a Maundy Thursday, [37] could have made him think of the same instrument as used by women worshippers of Bast as well as of Isis' own timbrel or *sistrum*.[38]

On Good Friday Bruno would have taken part in the 'Stations of the Cross'. Heretical ideas at last drove out all belief in revelation. But before this he would often have uttered the *Ave Maria* or have stood in silent ecstasy like his ancient forebears in front of holy sculptures of 'the Lady'. In his monastic days Bruno would have fasted like the ancient priests of Isis, confessing his sins and doing penance. Many a time, like the Egyptians with their *Amun*,[39] he would have uttered the Christian Amen. He would know the import of holy water. With the keenness of his critical mind Bruno would perhaps have found the non-vernacular language of the Latin Mass surprisingly like the mystical hieroglyphics which, for all his growing enthusiasm towards whatever came forth from Egypt, he himself would never read and understand as his ancient predecessors had done but would revere with the stupefaction born of the Renaissance. The debt of Roman Catholicism to Egyptian religion would have seemed a considerable one to Bruno.

In the Eastern Orthodox Church where tradition is the inveterate watchword, few Protestant eyes will be blind to the powerful influence of pre-Christian ideas. We need not look very far, for example, for parallels with what we find in the Egyptian cult. The dominant figure in Orthodox belief is the Panagia-Theotokos, the All Holy Mother of God. She greets us with her gaze of grief wherever we go, even at Athos where no other female presence is tolerated and where the mysterious usages during the night hours make us remember the Cabiri and Isis. As the goddess of Egypt revealed herself to Lucius, so to a devout Greek today the Blessed Virgin appears as Queen of Heaven, merciful to those in distress, succouring women in labour, a light to those in death, a divine face with never-failing love and pity written upon it. Her hallowed ikon draws kisses from the faithful. The present writer has witnessed the ikon of the Panagia at Castoria in northern Greece transported (like the statue of Isis at Philae) a short way over the water on the Feast of the Koemesis to the chapel at the near-by Mavyrotissa, here to be exposed for eight days beneath a plane tree and venerated before its restoration to its habitual home, the Metropolis Church.[40]

In the Cyclades before the arrival of Christianity the fusion had been achieved between Isis and 'triune Artemis'. On the islands of Delos, Syros, Andros and Tenos (the special haunt of the thaumaturgic Panagia today with her immemorial *panseptos* ikon) the Egyptian cult was well established before the end of the Christian era, side by side with those of the Hellenic Dionysus and Demeter, Poseidon and the Dioscuri, and the Cabiri.[41] On Syros, where an Iseum was erected at considerable expense by a certain tribunician Claudius Secundus,[42] the rocks along the shore still bear inscriptions (*Grammata* being their name) scrawled there to the Saviour God Sarapis,[43] and in the view of one local historian the deities regarded as the city's 'protectors' ($\pi o\lambda\iota o\hat{\upsilon}\chi o\iota$ $\theta\epsilon o\acute{\iota}$) just as before the advent of Christianity were the Cabiri and Isis.[44]

The very capital of the Eastern Empire with its architectural miracle of Hagia Sophia, the Church of the Hallowed Wisdom, was entrusted by Constantine to the Blessed Virgin Mary's keeping. The continuity of tradition was not broken. In pre-Christian times Byzantium was strongly linked with such female characters as Io and 'torch-bearing Hekate' and the *Navigium Isidis* began along its shores.[45] Before the cathedral was started and completed by Justinian's two architects, each with the same theophoric name Isidorus,[46] the goddess Isis-Sophia was not a complete stranger in the city which Constantine and his successors were to make great.[47]

Other features of Orthodox usage already noted as reminders of Egyptian religious practice are the retrieving of the holy cross from the sea at the Piraeus on the Feast of Lights (the same day as that on which 'all Egyptians draw water') and the preceding Eve's *hagiasmos* in the village of Greece.[48] Even with imprecations a thread (even if somewhat tenuous) can be discovered between ancient and modern Greek behaviour. The Athenians of old were wont to swear 'by Isis'. One of the commonest oaths today (wherever Greek is spoken, of course) is 'by the Panagia'.[49]

One striking resemblance between the earlier Egyptian religion and what followed it is the holy mother on her throne with her babe. Theologically and iconographically the likeness exists.[50] Herein lies the significance of the story told in the First Gospel about the Flight into Egypt, especially if this is looked at as a Gospel written for the Church of Alexandria.[51] Strict Catholic orthodoxy understandably rejects as legendary the tale, part of the Coptic Church's heritage, that Jesus was indeed a child of Egypt. This takes us from a flight out of Palestine to an actual birth in Egypt. On this view the Christian Nativity occurred in the Fayum at Ahnas, Heracleopolis Magna, the cult centre of the ram-headed god Arsaphes whom an ancient authority was ready to regard as a son of Isis, herself powerful in the locality.[52] (*Cf. Pl. 69.*)

Other uncanonical stories claim Egypt as the land where the Founder of Christianity lived his early years. At Hermopolis, a city, according to one Jewish enthusiast, founded by Moses and connected not only with Thoth but with Isis also,[53] Jesus celebrated his first Mass.[54] Another odd tale is this. St Mary of Egypt, 'Our Lady, holy and pure virgin, Mother of God', on archangel Gabriel's bidding took her son to dwell in the Fayum. Known to his brothers as 'son of sorrow' the child bore the name *Aour*, which reminds us of Horus the son of Isis, or as the Egyptians called him *Ḥr*.[55]

We may notice another tradition about Christ. Clement of Alexandria reproduces a saying from 'The Gospel according to the Egyptians'.[56] Christ's words are interesting and in such a context they are almost certainly directed against the current worship of Isis: 'I have come to destroy the works of the female.' Here surely is the Christ who is specifically concerned in the canonical Gospels to outshine 'the queen of the south' on her visit to Palestine in search of *sophia*.[57] His prophecy is clear. His own wisdom will in the end be found to be superior to hers.

Egyptomania in greater or less degree has been experienced by a strange assortment of authors. In ancient times among the Greeks were Herodotus and Plato, the philosophers Chaeremon and Plutarch, Diodorus and Aelian, the novelists Xenophon and Heliodorus. In more recent times we have had Bruno the apostate and the contemporary Isiac Baltrušaitis. The nineteenth century Egyptology of England could claim as one, who took as his theme the Horus myth in its bearing on Christianity, an enthusiastic writer named W. R. Cooper. His words are still true: 'The works of art, the ideas, the expressions, and the heresies of the first four centuries of the Christian era cannot be well studied without a right comprehension of the nature and influence of the Horus myth. We cannot ignore these facts. We have as Christians no reason to be afraid of them.'[58] To this may be fairly added but one thing else. Without his mother Isis the child Horus could not have existed. It is in the light of this fact of Egyptian mythology that we must regard emergent Christianity's struggle, so bitterly fought at Alexandria, against what was then its most stubborn and insidious foe.

Between *Isis* and *Jesus* as names confusion could arise. Thus a Christian mage is to be witnessed exorcizing physical ills from the body of a child, but uttering an Isiac formula according to the *hieros logos* which Isis would employ in addressing Horus: 'Let every sickness, suffering and pain cease at once. It is I who speak, the Lord Jesus, giver of healing.'[59] An Arabic source instructs us about a beautiful maiden: 'She has two ears of corn in the hand and sits on a throne. . . . She protects a small child . . . called by some Īsū.'[60] In the Graeco-Roman world the figure of Jesus could be represented holding the *ankh*. The old and the new had to come to terms. In the Nubian Temple of Wadi Sebua the figure of the Apostle Peter was plastered over Amun, and Ramesses II now appears to worship him.[61] At Philippi the features of Isis received as a lateral stamp the emblems of the supplanting faith, the cross and dove, each of which, nevertheless, could bring to mind the Isiac past.[62]

To hold that the Egyptian goddess Isis was the forerunner of Catholicism's Mary, Mother of God, is to raise the question of the uniqueness of Christianity. Both in the ancient world and in these latter days the argument has been advanced that humanity was being *prepared* for a dispensation never previously known. In support of this view fathers of the Church such as Clement of Alexandria and Eusebius wrote learnedly. It has also been a stock feature of modern Christian apologetics, for it has the strongest scriptural warrant. The Incarnation means that a particular man who was the Divine Logos took flesh at a particular time and in a particular place.

Herein for the Catholic abides truth. To him has come the qualitatively unique revelation; a rival creed that does not accept this doctrine is false. The faith 'once for all handed down to those who are holy'[63] can hardly be tolerant of any system which threatens its validity.

The time has come for Christian churches to acknowledge that the roots of the 'new' religion they exist to uphold were abundantly watered not just by the Jordan but also by the Nile, and that one of their holy cities long ago was Alexandria. Even when the cause of the monks and the bishops had triumphed the distinction between *ankh* and cross was blurred, and the Sanctus bell still tinkled like the Isiac sistrum.[64] Holy aspersions were practised as in the past. Alexandrian Greeks were seen by a Christian monk still worshipping animals in the sixth century.[65] Palaeo-Christian hagiography is a storehouse of names from Egypt's ostensibly outworn cult. Besides Anuph (Anub, Nub), Harpocras and Harpocration (each found twice) the Church uneasily accommodates the 'Horus-born' theologian Origen (condemned at one of its Councils for heresy)[66] as well as sixteen Serapions. From Isis herself stem such Christian names as Ision and Paesis, to say nothing of over forty Isidores.[67]

No loftier ideal can be imagined than what Plutarch, the Graeco-Roman world's enthusiast for Isis, tells us about her religion. She imparts an appetite for truth and a love for wisdom and knowledge.[68] In our own age of scientific advance and inter-planetary travel, when millions grope in search of a reasoned faith, all of the contemporary religious creeds would do well to pursue the same goal.

For Bruno the most acceptable theology was what had arisen in ancient Egypt. Were he alive today he would surely be glad with mingled scientific and religious delight that the sacred planet of his Lady, Isis Myrionymos, had been trodden by human feet. Now, he would tell us, the Infinite Universe is one step nearer knowledge.

Bruno's was an Egyptianizing religion. Our western world today needs such a critical mind for a comparative study of the faiths of Isis and Jesus. Certainly the resemblances exist. A modern Bruno could contend that the cult of Isis exerted a major and even a formative influence on the religion which followed. Bruno reborn might well remind us that the very Inquisition which had burnt him had done nothing to stop Pope Alexander VI from openly welcoming Isis as a cult figure in the Vatican. Had not Bruno seen her sitting on the back of an ass in a painting of the Borgia Apartments?[69] (Pls. 71, 72).

For countless numbers of men and women in the Graeco-Roman world Isis remained what she had been in the Black Land of the Pharaohs: Mistress of the Word in the Beginning, Mistress of Eternity, Source of grace and truth, Resurrection and Life, the Supreme Deity as Maker of Monarchs and Mother of the God. Many centuries before the Christian Era Isis had been revered in the Nile valley as the Unique and the Incomparable. So she for long remained, creating as she had always done, her own beauty and perfection. Lady of the House of Life, Shelter of the Living and of the Dead.[70] We do well, therefore, to see her steadily and to see her whole—Isis, the great ruler of the Graeco-Roman world, ever active and magical with her gifts of knowledge, power and wisdom, the eternal mainspring of men's deepest faith, hope and love.

ABBREVIATIONS

ABSA	*Annals of the British School at Athens*
AC	*L'Antiquité Classique*
AE	*Ἀρχαιολογικὴ Ἐφημερίς*
AJA	*American Journal of Archaeology*
AJSL	*American Journal of Semitic Languages and Literature*
APA	*Abhandlungen der preussischen Akademie (Phil.-hist. Klasse)*
Apul.	Apuleius, *Metamorphoses*, Book XI
BCH	*Bulletin de Correspondance hellénique*
BD	*Book of the Dead*, ed. E. A. W. Budge, London, 1898
BIAFO	*Bulletin de l'Institut français d'Archéologie orientale*
CAH	*Cambridge Ancient History* (1956)
CE	Roussel, P. *Les cultes égyptiens à Delos*. Paris and Nancy, 1915–16
CIG	*Corpus Inscriptionum Graecarum*
CIL	*Corpus Inscriptionum Latinarum*
CIMRM	*Corpus Inscriptionum et Monumentorum Religionis Mithriacae* (ed. Vermaseren) 1956–60
Dio C.	Dio Cassius
Diod. S.	Diodorus Siculus, *Geography*
ERE	*Encyclopaedia of Religion and Ethics* (ed. Hastings)
FHG	*Fragmenta Historicorum Graecorum*. C. Müller, Paris, 1841–70
FRA	*Fontes Historiae Religionis Aegyptiacae* (ed. Hopfner) 1922
Her.	Herodotus, *Histories*
HTR	*Harvard Theological Review*
JEA	*Journal of Egyptian Archaeology*
JHS	*Journal of Hellenic Studies*
JNES	*Journal of Near Eastern Studies*
JRS	*Journal of Roman Studies*
JTS	*Journal of Theological Studies*
JWCI	*Journal of the Warburg and Courtauld Institutes*
NSA	*Notizie degli Scavi di Antichità*
OGIS	*Orientis Graeci Inscriptiones Selectae*, ed. Dittenberger
OL	*Oxyrhynchus Litany* (Papyri Oxyrhynchi 1380; Pt. XI, pp. 190–220)
PCPS	*Proceedings of the Cambridge Philological Society*
PEFQ	*Palestine Exploration Fund Quarterly*
PG	*Patrologia Graeca*
PGM	*Papyri Graeci Magici*, ed. Preisendanz, Leipzig, Berlin, 1928–31
PL	*Patrologia Latina*
Plut.	Plutarch, *De Iside et Osiride*

PT	*Pyramid Texts*, ed. K. Sethe, Berlin, 1908
PW	*Philologische Wochenschrift*
RA	*Revue Archéologique*
RHR	*Revue de l'Histoire des Religions*
RMA	Merkelbach, R. *Roman und Mysterium in der Antike.* Berlin, 1962
SEG	*Supplementum Epigraphicum Graecum*
SS	*Salomonis Sapientia*, ed. H. B. Swete, Cambridge, 1907
TTT	Tran Tam Tinh. *Le culte d'Isis à Pompeii.* Paris, 1964
UPZ	*Urkunden der Ptolemäerzeit* (ed. Wilcken), 1922
VS	*Sylloge Inscriptionum Religionis Isiacae et Sarapiacae*, ed. S. Vidman, Berlin 1969
YCS	*Yale Classical Studies*
ZÄS	*Zeitschrift für ägyptische Sprache und Altertumskunde*

NOTES

CHAPTER I

1 See Münster, 203–8. *Cf. infra*, p. 281.

2 The name ⬭ 𓆓 𓊖 *Kmt* shows this. *Cf. Plut.* 33: *FRA* 237, 2. Her. 2, 12.

3 Paus. 8, 24, 6: *FRA* 337, 30.

4 See the 'Nile Aretalogy' (not later than the XIXth Dynasty) in Erman, 146.

5 Paus. 10, 33, 10: *FRA* 340, 11. *Cf. PT* 1944 + 2: the *w3g* festival came to the uplands as Osiris. See further Bonneau, 361*ff*.

6 For Isis as the Throne see *PT* 1154a and Anthes, *JNES* 18, 197. For Isis as 'king-maker' by suckling the Horus babe with her milk, *cf.* Porter-Moss, IV, 263 (IX–X Dyn.) and the discussion in Münster, 10; 73–4; 137–45. For the name *Aset* see H. Grapow in *ZÄS* 46, 107–8. For fanciful Greek etymologies *cf.* Witt, *PCPS* 192, 50, 4.

7 See Münster, 203 for this and other refs. and Bergman, 280.

8 The early Queen Isis obviously suffered physical death, and she seems identified in the mind of Augustine with the goddess: *De Civ. D.*, 18, 37: *FRA* 646, 32.

9 For this important aspect *cf.* Münster, 71*ff*.

10 For Isis as *hwn* in the *Hymn to Osiris* see Münster, 193. *Cf. infra* p. 143.

11 *Cf.* Münster, Chap. D, Sect. XIX, 'Isis-Sothis', p. 153. Also

Roscher, 434.

12 Ptolemy III ordained a pan-Egyptian festival on the day when the star of Isis rises, New Year's Day for the sacred scribes (*OGIS* 56).

13 *Timaeus* 22b: *FRA* 45, 19.

14 *Cf. PT* 1973b. For the Woman of Sorrow, *PT* 1926; *BD* 110.

15 See Dennis, 16.

16 *Legg.* 657: *FRA* 46, 28. Plato's debt to Egypt is stressed by Ammianus 22, 16 (22): *FRA* 553, 34. The story Strabo tells (17, 806: *FRA* 159, 5) of Plato's 13 years in Egypt (along with Eudoxus) is apocryphal.

17 Nilsson, *Hist.* 10–11, contrasts the absence of Semitic and Babylonian influences with the active interplay between Cretan and Egyptian religion proved by sistrum and ankh being both found in Cretan art.

18 Her. 2, 59: *FRA* 13, 34.

19 *Cf.* Münster, 29 (for the north wind) and 11 (for the loneliness of Isis: *cf. infra*, p. 160).

20 Isis sailed in one (*Plut.* 18: *FRA* 229, 8) and papyrus flowers decked the gods' statues (Pliny, *Natural History*, 13, 11, 71: *FRA* 194, 39).

21 *PT* 655a. *Cf. BD* 1. Besides quality quantity was important: *PT* 474c.

22 *Cf. PT* 291b; 1061b.

23 Her. 1, 140: *FRA* 5, 19.

24 Lucian, *De Sacrif.* 15: *FRA* 310, 15.

25 Both Thoth and Anubis could be

princes in the Court of Justice: *PT* 1713c. The importance of *Ma'et* for the Memphitic theology of Isiac hymnography is demonstrated by Bergman, 178ff. For Isis-Dikaiosune *cf.* Roscher, 460.

26 *PT* 39c. The *Pyramid Texts* go back to at least the twenty-second century BC. Very much later Isis herself is styled 'Ruler of the Pyramids' (Bergman, 244, n. 2).

27 We must remember the Apis Bull, however, as the very incarnation of Osiris—

'in Memphian grove or green
Trampling the unshower'd grass
with lowings loud.'

The Apis Bull in later times was identified specifically with Ptah in whose temple at Memphis he was enthroned. *Cf.* Bergman, 253ff. Like Isis he could be appealed to for mercy by the suppliant (Xen. *Ephesiaca*, 5, 4: *FRA* 453, 35).

28 See n. 8 *supra* and Ch. V.

29 *Cf. PT* 589a, 767a, 1002c, 1748a.

30 *Plut.* 12: *FRA* 226, 6.

31 *PT* 3c, 2089a. *Cf.* also her 'rejoicing through love' in *PT* 1635b.

32 For details of the Iseum see Porter-Moss, IV, 40–2. *Cf.* Münster, 158.

33 Christian writers include Joseph's father-in-law and Moses among their number. *Cf.* Hopfner's Index, *FRA* 874–5.

34 Nephthys like Isis is a mourning bird in *PT* 1255c.d. and 1280b. *Cf.* Münster, 148. In Hellenistic times Nephthys is named at Athens in company with Osiris (*VS* 14) but she is generally ousted by Isis.

35 'Vom Kult der Isis im Alten Reich wissen wir kaum etwas', Münster, 159. But note (*ibid* 189) the rejection of Bonnet's view that Isis was simply the Paredros of Osiris.

36 *PT* 1214b. See Münster, 78 (for the jubilation at the birth of Horus 'my beloved son'), and 6 (for the purificatory incense).

37 See Münster, 192–5. Dennis, 35.

38 *Cf. PGM* 36, 134ff. 'Isis cried out with a loud voice and the earth quaked', on which A. A. Barb, *JWCI* 29 (1966), p. 15, n. 14. But (as Münster points out, p. 4) she could be jubilant along with Anubis when Horus had avenged Osiris his father.

39 John Lewis ('Mother Worship in Egypt', *Jour. Manch. Eg. Or. Soc.*, 1924, 58) well writes about 'the chastity of her character', as others have done. It is significant also that Isis is identified with the Graeco-Roman goddess of Hearth and Home (Hestia-Vesta) *e.g.* in *VS* 88, 199, 513, *OL* 22, 73, and that Isis-Nemesis punishes homosexual love (*RMA* 102). But the erotic side appears also: *cf. infra*, p. 85.

40 See Münster, 198.

41 Dio C. 50, 4: *FRA* 374, 25. Antony doubled the parts of Osiris and Dionysus.

42 A. H. Gardiner in *JEA* 24, 165.

43 *Cf. infra*, p. 100.

44 *OGIS* 695. *Cf. infra*, Chapter IX.

45 *Cf. infra*, p. 121ff.

46 *PT* 939a. *Cf.* 1472a.

47 *OL* 208.

48 In his essay *Isis*, 193.

49 See Lafaye, 148, Dill, 582. For *militia sacra* see *HTR* 20, 536. *RMA* 121, 126, 183. Apollonius, the priest who emigrated from Memphis to Delos in the first half of the third century BC, was guided perhaps more by mercenary motives (*cf. CE* 246) than by proselytizing zeal. *Cf.* also Wessetsky, *Aegyptische Kulte*, 56.

50 Seneca, *De Vita Beata* 26: *FRA* 177, 22. We may compare the Scala Santa in Rome today. That Seneca was thinking of Isis is clear from his mention of the sistrum, and the linen-clad old man with lamp in hand at noon.

51 The important monograph by G. Grimm has come to hand too late for the full benefit of its scholarship to be felt in the present study. Grimm's verdict on the statement in Tacitus (*Germ.* 9: *FRA* 289, 16) *pars Sueborum et Isidi sacrificat* is convincing: either Isis as such was unknown to the Suebi, or the cult was brought to them by sea. (*op. cit.* 98).

52 *PT* 1655b. Absentees from this *Ur-pantheon* are Horus, Ptah and Bast.

53 Among later practitioners of the art are known to have been Alexarchus, Anticleides, Hermaeus and Mnaseas, to say nothing of Plutarch himself.

54 See Tertull., *De Baptismo* 5: *FRA* 381, 21-2. Cf. *infra*, p. 164.

55 *Pap. Ebers* 2. For the thaumaturgic aspect of Isis see Roscher 540.

56 Roeder 90. Cf. Ch. XIV, n. 26.

57 See Münster 72; Apul. ch. 21: *FRA* 325, 28. Cf. in the New Testament, *Matt.* 16, 18; *Romans* 16, 20. See further Witt, *Studia Patr.*, VIII, 137.

58 Cf. *infra*, p. 121. Of ancient Egyptian lineage is the phrase, *the god in all his names.* In the *Oxyrhynchus Litany* Isis is *polymorphos* and *polyonymos* (9. 101). In the second century AD her specially apt title, *myrionymos*, is widely prevalent. It is cited by Plutarch (Plut. 53: *FRA* 246, 21) and is found in inscriptions of Cilicia (the province of Paul's birth), Minturnae in Latium, Cisalpine Gaul, Pannonia, Dacia, Germany (at Cologne), and Northern France (at Soissons): *VS* 351, 505, 639, 656, 692, 698, 721, 749. It was also in vogue in Egypt and elsewhere in North Africa (*e.g.* at Cyrene, *VS* 808). See further Bell, 16. *Isis* embraces all other divine names and so is above them all: *cf. infra*, p. 268.

59 See 'Cyprian', *Carm.* 4, 36: *FRA* 441, 31. The ex-consul now a minister of Isis is heard confessing: 'I have sinned; Goddess, forgive me; I have turned back.' See further Ovid, *Ex Ponto* 1, 1, 50: *FRA* 153, 35; Juvenal 6, 535: *FRA* 281, 24.

60 She was as obviously a divinity for women as Mithras was for men (*cf.* Tarn, 359). Isis was 'the ornament of womankind, and affectionate' (*OL* 131) and 'she made women to be loved by men' (*Ios Hymn* 29). An altar was dedicated (near Grenoble) to 'Isis the Mother' (*VS* 741). See further Roscher, 491-3.

61 See *TTT* 53; 16, n. 6 (for the emancipation of slaves in her honour). At Valencia in Spain she was worshipped by 'the Fellowship of Homeborn Slaves' (*VS* 762). Jesus was also the Friend of the Slave: *cf.* New Testament, *Philipp.* 2, 7; *I Tim.* 6, 1.

62 Mithras, however, excluded women, whose special advocate Isis always remained. For links between the two deities see *CIMRM* I, 356 (the Lararium with Isis-Fortuna affording access into the lower chamber or crypt, the Mithraeum proper); 634 (Cybele, Astarte, Isis joining Mithras). Among cities where Isis/Sarapis and Mithras were both found were Memphis and Alexandria, six in Asia, six in Greece (including Athens, Thessalonica and Philippi), eight in Dacia and Moesia, two in Thrace, ten in Pannonia and Dalmatia, seven in Noricum and Cisalpine Gaul, eight in Italy (including Rome), four in Gaul, four in Germany, two in Britain (London and York), four in Spain and six in North Africa. Geographically this is a spread from Lat. 25 to Lat. 55 and from Long. 41 E to Long. 8 W. See *infra*, p. 137.

63 Her. 2, 186: *FRA* 42, 34.

64 Plut. 15: *FRA* 227, 34. Thus also sat Demeter, Homer, *Hymn* 5, 98.

65 Varro (*Antiqu.* 18, 3: *FRA* 82, 6) knows of a tradition that Isis had travelled as queen from Ethiopia into Egypt. Arnobius (*adv. Gentes* 1, 36) writes of Isis as 'tanned by the sunshine of Ethiopia' and from other references (*FRA* 140, 23, 165, 34 and 278, 13) it is clear that Egypt could merge in men's minds into Ethiopia, Meroe then ranking as the special home of the goddess. See F. Snowden, 'Ethiopians and the Isiac Worship', *AC* 25, 1956.

66 Isis as 'the Year' was important for the Renaissance. See Giehlow, 175, and his illustration fol. 4, no. 3. Panofsky (in his *Albrecht Dürer* II, 101) criticizing Giehlow for ascribing this to Dürer points out that the artist's own squatting Isis has been replaced by the figure of a Mary Annunciate.

67 Ramesses II is acclaimed in a hymn as 'Hawk that did enter the royal ring [the cartouche], born of Isis—Horus', Erman, 272. A statue of this Pharaoh was set up in the Iseum at Rome: Porter-Moss, VII, 413.

68 'Isis belongs to Greece', Plut. 2: *FRA* 220, 8.

CHAPTER II

1 Dio C. 51, 16: *FRA* 375, 6. The same attitude had been shown by an earlier potentate, the Persian Cambyses, when he smote the Apis Bull (Her. 2, 29: *FRA* 40, 37). *Cf.* also Lucian's revulsion at the sacred ibis, ape, goat and cat: *Deor. Concil.* 10 and *Imagin.* 11 (*FRA* 316, 3 and 311, 37). *Cf. infra* p. 255.

2 See Buhl, in *JNES* VI, 80–97, and E. O. James, *The Tree of Life*, Leiden, 1966.

3 Statius, *Silvae*, 3, 2, 113: *FRA* 209, 24.

4 It was sacred to Nut and Isis: Budge, *Gods* II, 107 and Bonneau, 228.

5 Plut. 68: *FRA* 254, 19.

6 Sozomenus *Eccles. Hist.* 5, 21: *FRA* 661, 9. A modern painting by Edwin Long (now at Bournemouth) shows 'a gorgeous procession' headed by Isis and Horus and in the centre 'a tired donkey bearing a woman and child', E. L. Butcher, 1, 12.

7 As early as the twelfth century BC reference is made to 'plants of Isis'— probably papyrus tufts (Bonneau, 397). *Cf. infra*, p. 273.

8 A theological development was that Isis became the Mother even of Re: see Münster, 84, 94.

9 See *infra* Ch. I, n. 42. See also Bergman, 290.

10 The basis is what Plutarch tells us (Plut. 12: *FRA* 225ff.)

11 Diod. S. I, 21: *FRA* 101, 28.

12 *Ibid.* I, 83: *FRA* 125, 37.

13 Porphyry (ap. Eus. *Praep. Ev.* 3, 12, 6): *FRA* 471, 41.

14 Of obviously great importance for the future of Isiac studies are the discoveries now being made at Saqqara by Professor Walter Emery in the Mausoleum of the Sacred Baboon and the Baboon Galleries, pointing to the worship of Thoth in the area of Memphis, and his association with the great Imhotep, vizier of Zoser, side by side with the cult of Isis as the mother of the sacred bull Apis. In front of Sector C is an Iseum.

15 Diod. S. I, 21 fin.: *FRA* 101, 32.

16 Bérard (*Syria* 1952, 1–43) argues persuasively that Epaphus and his descendants were not purely legendary but figures of history identifiable with the Hyksos.

17 Nicander (*Metam. ap. Antonin. Liberal.* 28): *FRA* 81, 19.

18 Her. 2, 60: *FRA* 13, 39. The sistrum, traditionally associated with Hathor (*e.g.* at her Dendera temple) for its apotropaeic value was held in late antiquity to have been invented by Isis (Isidor. Hisp. *Etymolog.* 3, 22: *FRA* 723, 20) and handmade for her by her son Harpocrates (*VS* 88, 4).

19 See Emery, *JEA* 55, 34. Herodotus (2, 153; *FRA* 34, 35) identifies the Apis with Epaphus. For the rejection of this Greek identification by the Egyptians, see Aelian, 11, 10: *FRA* 423, 8.

20 Diod. S. 1, 11: *FRA* 93, 34. Note also the representation on the altar at Scarbantia in Pannonia (*VS* 664).

21 Ovid, *Metamorphoses* 4, 689: *FRA* 152, 2.

22 This is the carefully considered view of Bonnet. For the ancient Diod. S., on the other hand, Isis had as her sacred animals the cow and the dog. *Cf. infra*, p. 169. For the bird, the cow, the serpent and the hippopotamus, *cf.* Münster, 201–3.

23 For the milk of life as the source of immortality, *cf.* Bergman, 147, 2. *Cf. infra* pp. 63, 167–8. The hieroglyphs for 'milk' and 'make' are remarkably similar.

24 The pair are found together in *PT* 164a, 577a, 584a and b, 610c, 628a. They make Osiris hale.

25 Rufin., *Historia eccles.*, 11, 29; Socrates, *Eccles. historia*, 5, 17; Sozomenus, *Eccles. historia*, 7, 15: *FRA* 631, 1; 659, 15; 662, 31.

26 See Horapollo 1, 8: *FRA* 579, 30.

27 In the eyes of the Christian this was emblematic of the Blessed Virgin's immaculate conception: Rufin, *Comm. in Symbol. Apostolor.*, 11 (*PL* 21): *FRA* 624, 16. For the phoenix in Isiacism see *RMA* 130. At

Pompeii in the Adoration of the Mummy of Osiris can be seen on the top of the sarcophagus a phoenix with outstretched wings (*TTT* 142, Pl. X, no. 2), here Plate 25.

28 Statius, *Silvae* 3, 2, 101: *FRA* 209, 12.

29 One Christian tradition held that in the absence of Moses on Sinai the Jews made the Golden Calf in the likeness of the Apis (Pseudo-Clement, *Recognit.* I, 35; Mythographus Vaticanus I, 79—*FRA* 565, 1; 638, 30).

30 Artapanus ap. Euseb. *Praep. Ev.* 9, 27, 32: *FRA* 279, 1. According to the non-Christian Strabo (16, 760: *FRA* 154, 19) Moses 'an Egyptian priest' propounded a monotheism devoid of theriolatry at Mount Casius.

31 Old Testament, *Deuter.* 33, 27.

32 Mayassis (17) points out that in a vignette in *BD* Isis is seen standing at the prow of the Solar Bark, stretching out her wings and reciting her incantations.

33 Aelian, 10, 23: *FRA* 420, 15. Io could be termed *damalis* (Lucian, *Dialogi Marini* 7: *FRA* 309, 26) on arriving in Egypt to be deified as Isis: a name applied in the *Akathist Hymn* to the Virgin Mary.

34 Pliny, *Nat. Hist.* 10, 33: *FRA* 194, 6.

35 Plut. 63: *FRA* 252, 22.

36 *TTT* 181–5.

37 Dio C. 79, 10: *FRA* 378, 6. This cult symbol links Isis with Artemis.

38 *Cf. e.g.* Marucchi, who considers it very probable that the artist conceived the cult of Fortuna as emanating from the very ancient one of Isis: the artistic interpretation being that Isis is responsible for the fertility of the plains. See further *Bull. Commun.* 1895, 31. Rostovtzeff, 318. Marion E. Blake, *Mem. Amer. Acad. Rome*, VIII, 140–1. At Praeneste Isis appears

CHAPTER III

on Syrian bowls wearing over her forehead a winged disk of the sun. The linking of Isis with Tyche (Fortuna) can be seen for example at Rhodes, Rome and Lyon (*VS* 180, 412, 745). At Pompeii miniatures of the conflated goddess were worn by women about their necks (*TTT* 112) and several statues of Isis-Fortuna have been discovered (*ibid.* 154–60). Isis-Tyche-Protogeneia appears on Delos (*CE* 119, 120, 148). Isityche and Eros are joined (*VS* 634). *Cf.* Rusch, 44 and *infra*, pp. 86 and 163. I think those scholars who (like Tschudin) identify the Palestrina Primigenia with Isis-Tyche are right (and Vidman wrong, *VS* 528). The Nilotic panorama (especially the emphasis on Alexandria and Memphis) so brilliantly achieved on the Palestrina mosaic entitles it to be set for comparison with Nilotic scenes in early Christian churches both in Cyrenaica and in Palestine. Crowfoot (*Early Churches in Palestine*, London, 1941), making no reference to Palestrina, illustrates a mosaic in the Church of SS Peter and Paul at Gerasa (Pl. XVIIIb) which he labels 'a topographical picture of Alexandria and Memphis' and having reproduced another (Pl. XII) from the Church of the Loaves and Fishes at Tabgha on the Sea of Galilee with details reminiscent of Palestrina (pp. 122ff.) and one from the Church of St John Baptist at Gerasa with indications of Pharos, Canopus and Memphis (129) he appositely writes (130): 'Memphis was a place of no particular ecclesiastical importance, and this leads me to question whether there is any special religious significance to be attached to these pictures of Egyptian cities.'

1 Diod. S. 1, 11 and Plut. 10: *FRA* 93, 20 and 224, 28. In *OL* 129 Isis herself is likewise termed 'many-eyed'.

2 Plut. 12: *FRA* 226, 7.

3 Translated by R. O. Faulkner in *Mélanges Maspero*, I, 338–41.

4 Diod. S. I, 25: *FRA* 104, 33.

5 About a hundred metres from the Lion of Chaeronea and only a few miles from the Delphic Omphalos, the Mecca of Greek religion, was found the sepulchral stele (early third century AD) mentioning the 'most holy priestess Flavia Lanica, Hieraphoros during the whole of her life to Isis' (*VS* 62). Delphic Clea tended Isis.

6 See Vandier, 48–9. A. H. Gardiner, *Chester Beatty*, Pap. 1.

7 Diod. S. i, 27: *FRA* 106, 16.

8 Her. 2, 61: *FRA* 14, 14ff. *Cf.* also 2, 132: *FRA* 27, 29: we are told, 'The one for whom they beat their breasts it is impious to name.'

9 Diod. S. I, 14: *FRA* 96, 8. For breast-smiting, *cf.* Lact. *Divin. Instit.* 1, 21; *FRA* 489, 1. The priests profess to be copying Isis herself.

10 Firm. Matern. *De Errore profan. rel.* 2, 3: *FRA* 519, 12.

11 Lucan, *Phars.* 8, 833: *FRA* 186, 16. Plutarch (25: *FRA* 232, 8ff.) finds likewise the attribution of human suffering to Osiris and Isis a theological stumbling-block. A statue showing Isis herself mourning Osiris (Isis Taposiris, as in *OL* 67) has been found at Faesulae (*VS* 564).

12 See (1) Plut. 14: *FRA* 227, 16 (Diod. S. 1, 87: *FRA* 128, 29); (2) Plut. 18: *FRA* 229, 11 (Diod. S. 1, 21: *FRA* 101, 16); (3) Plut. 15: *FRA* 227, 25.

13 *Cf.* Sethe, *ZÄS* 45, 10–11; *AJSL* 55, 337–59 (for the Hyksos); Jidejain, N., *Byblos through the Ages*, Beirut,

1968; Montet, 287. *Dawn of Civiliza-tion*, ed. S. Piggott, p. 151. *Cf. infra*, pp. 109 and 166.

14 Already in the residence of Ramesses II Astarte had a special temple. A tale about her (Erman, 169) throws a certain light on the way the goddess was brought to Egypt from abroad and specifies 'the tribute of the sea'. Plutarch (Plut. 15: *FRA* 228,3) treats Isis and Astarte as having been made fast friends at Byblos.

15 Diod. S. 1, 25: *FRA* 104, 32.

16 *PT* 628b. Isis and Nephthys restore him.

17 *PT* 628c.

18 *PT* 1652b regards Atum Khoprer as rising like this *bennu* bird.

19 So Griffiths, 104—followed by Münster, 6. Recently it has been well contended by Faulkner (*JEA* 54, 40-44) that the first sentence of the *PT* Spell (148) here in question implies that the pregnancy of Isis was brought about by a flash of lightning.

20 Porph. *ap.* Euseb. *Praep. Evang.* 3, 11, 51: *FRA* 471, 8. *Cf.* Münster 198-200.

21 *Gospel of Philip* (translated from the Coptic text by R. M. Wilson, London, 1962), 107, 10.

22 Published in *RA*, 1847.

23 Even at Akhenaten's Amarna Isis could make the claim, which to Münster seems remarkable (187), that she was 'Mistress of Heaven' and that Egypt's new capital or its necropolis was *her city*.

24 Apul. Ch. 25: *FRA* 327, 33.

CHAPTER IV

1 We should give special attention to the astronomer Eudoxus (*fl.* 360-50) often named by Plutarch. He may have exerted a strongly Egypt-ianizing influence at Athens.

2 Paus. 9, 16, 1: *FRA* 338, 5. For Ammon-Osiris *cf.* Diod. S. 1, 25: *FRA* 104, 37. Isis could be treated as Ammon's mother (Münster, 134). For the sacerdotal utterance of his name (like the Biblical Amen: *e.g. Revel.* 3, 14) *cf. infra*, p. 275.

3 Pindar, *Pyth.* 4, 14ff.: *FRA* 3, 30.

4 Strabo 17, 813: *FRA* 163, 14.

5 Arrian, *Anab.* 3, 1, 4: *FRA* 296, 25; Pseud. Callisthenes 1, 34: *FRA* 410, 19 ('after his arrival at Memphis the Egyptians set him on the throne as an Egyptian King in the Throne Chamber of the Temple of Ptah'). See the discussion of this *enthronismos* in Bergman, 92.

6 Clem. Alex., *Stromat.* 4, 54, 2: *FRA* 367, 40 ff.

7 For Isis Pharia, *cf. infra*, p. 55, p. 70. Philip of Salonica wrote a poem in her honour (Baege, 160) telling of the gifts to her of spikenard and frankincense for having saved Damis from shipwreck. For the symbolism of the Lighthouse of Alexandria see *RMA* 136.

8 The Osiris-Isis relationship. Oddly enough Minucius Felix (*Octav.* 31: *FRA* 296, 20) lumps Athenians with Egyptians as legalizing it.

9 *CE* p. 262.

10 Diod. S. 1, 25: *FRA* 105, 24.

11 So F. H. Schwarz, *Herophilus und Erasistratus* (1826), 21: Ptolemy broke the superstition and gave clinical anatomists the inestimable benefit of being able to dissect human bodies. *Cf.* Aulus Gell. *Noct. Att.* 10, 10. *Cf. infra*, p. 190.

12 John Chrysost., *adv. Iud.* (*PG* 48), 1, 6: *FRA* 611, 35, tells the story, not always accepted, that Ptolemy Philadelphus 'deposited' a copy of the Septuagint in the Sarapeum.

13 Julian Apost., *Orat.*, 1, 45: *FRA* 538, 1ff.

14 *Cf.* the joke of Aristophanes

(*Acharnians*, 530) about 'Pericles the Olympian'.

15 For the Apollo-Horos-Harpocrates identification see *VS* 421, 496. See also *ibid.* 114, 116 and *CE* 18, 193, 196.

16 The named statue of him found at Carthage (*VS* 776) indicates that he was still remembered in the second century AD.

17 This summary of the Ptolemaic reformation is based on Bonnet. The iconographical development is discussed by *TTT* 77 under the three aspects: Pharaonic, Alexandrian-Roman and Egyptianizing (from the reign of Hadrian). Discussion of such archaeological problems lies outside the scope of the present work.

18 For the identification of Sarapis with the Patriarch Joseph see Goodenough, II, 283: It 'was persistent within Judaism itself'. *Ibid.* 284: 'Isis as nursing mother of the Universe was obviously a figure very attractive to Jews. Gnostic Jews brought her in by identifying her with Eve.' Goodenough also calls attention to Philo's implicit identification of Sarah and Rebekka with Isis and (*ibid.* 286) discusses the association between Isis, Artemis and the angel Gabriel. *See also HF* 341, 23.

19 Macrob. Saturn. 1, 20, 17: *FRA* 597, 39. We must also remember the Memphitic Lord of Life Osiris-Ptah (Bergman, 255, 3).

20 See P. M. Fraser, in *Opuscula Atheniensia*, 1960 and 1967. Like him I have spelt the divine name as Sarapis. The Romans liked Serapis.

21 The Christian Origen at the end of the second century, writing rhetorically but knowledgeably, declares that the cult of Sarapis has only recently started—'yesterday and the day before'. *Contra Cels.* 5, 37: *FRA* 439, 38.

22 Clem. Alex., *Protrep.*, 4, 48, 1–3: *FRA* 367, 11. The epithet given—'the so-called *achiropoeetos*'—is shared between the Alexandrian religion and Christianity: *cf.* in the New Testament, *Mark* 14, 58; *Cor.* 2, 5, 1: *Col.* 2, 11. Also *Acts* 7, 48. *Cf. infra*, p. 189.

23 The Patriarch Joseph underwent earthly as well as heavenly identification with Egyptian cult names. 'Sarapis' suggested the false etymology 'child of Sarah' (Firmicus Matern., De *errore prof. rel.*, 13, 2: *FRA* 520, 27)—as Isis Pharia suggested 'Pharaoh's daughter' (Tert. *Apol.* 2, 8: *FRA* 380, 38). Joseph was then regarded as a 'priest of Osiris', (*Excerptum chronogr.*, p. 175, J. A. Cramer: *FRA* 743, 37). See further, Epiph., *Her.* 3, 2, 24: *FRA* 608, 5, for Isis-Thermuthis as Pharaoh's daughter who reared Moses. Christian writers are concerned to discover links between Judaism and Egyptian religion.

24 A temple in his honour was built at York towards the end of the second century AD by a certain Claudius Hieronymianus, Commander of the Sixth Legion (*VS* 750).

25 *Cf. infra*, pp. 55 and 68. For the steady ascendancy of Isis, see Leclant (*Bull. Fac. Lett. Strasb.*, 1959, 306) and *TTT* 84. But *cf. infra* Ch. VI, n. 5.

26 Julian, *Orat.*, 4, 135: *FRA* 538, 15. See also, *VS* 769, where Sarapis is equated with the Jewish Jahweh. See further *Pap. Ox.* 1382.

27 His fertility role is revealed by an inscription from Cyprus (*VS* 355) where a temple was founded to Priapus at the behest of Sarapis.

28 Strabo, 17, 801: *FRA* 156, 13. *Cf. infra*, p. 135. For incubation, *infra*, p. 191.

29 Jul., *Ep.*, 51: *FRA* 540, 15.

30 Phlegon, *Epist. ap. Vopisc.*

(*Saturnin.*), 8: *FRA* 280, 15.

31 For Sarapis as himself prince consort at Pompeii see *TTT* 68. *Cf. RA* 1970, 55ff. for *confrontation*. Isis precedes Osiris in Plutarch's essay title and is named in front of Sarapis in the following inscriptions of Vidman's *Sylloge:* (pre-Christian period), 5, 87, 105; and (in the imperial age) 257 (Chios), 272 (Halicarnassus), 273 (Bargylia), 290 (Priene), 295 (Tralles), 302 (Ephesus), 531 (Nomentum), 540 (Ostia), 595 (Veleia—Sarapis as 'Osiris'), 697 (Potaissa), 785 (Lambaesis) and 803 (Cyrene).

32 Ovid, *Ars Amat.* 3, 635: *FRA* 151, 6. For Isis Pharia see p. 47 *supra* and *cf. TTT* 99, n. 3, *VS* 358 and 403, besides Ovid, *Amores Am.* 2, 13, 7 and Met. 9, 773 (*FRA* 150, 4; 152, 21). For the ship 'Isopharia' see *VS* 171.

CHAPTER V

1 Peek, *Cyme* 22–4; *Ios* 19–21.
2 Plutarch, however, favours the idea of a house of mourning: Plut. 20 (*FRA* 230, 26). For the opposite view *cf. infra*, p. 166.
3 Mayassis stresses that this means Isis' own bosom (*Mystères et initations de l'Egypte ancienne* 111. Athens, 1957).
4 See Porter-Moss, VI, 106: V, 125. It was at Dendera that Nut brought forth Isis in the shape of a black and rose-coloured female. Bergman (280–1) discusses Isis the Magician as 'older than her Mother'.
5 *Cf.* Kees *Priestertum*, 147–8. For Isis at Coptos see further Münster, 171–3, 189. *Cf. supra* Ch. I, n. 35.
6 Her. 2, 176: *FRA* 38, 26.
7 Lucian, *adv. indoct.* 14, *De Syria dea* 7: *FRA* 314, 13, 315, 10; Pliny,

Nat Hist. 5, 10, 51: *FRA* 167.
8 Juv. 6, 526: *FRA* 281, 15. *Cf.* for the view the inhabitants of Meroe took of Isis, Diod. S. 3, 9: *FRA* 140, 23, and (for the fetching of water from the Nile) the practice among devout Christians of securing Jordan water.
9 Dio. C. 79, 10: *FRA* 378, 6. *Cf. infra*, p. 241. A figure of Isis Sothis has been found at Savaria (*VS* 663). For the gable *cf. VS* 533a, 713.
10 Porter-Moss, VII, 235.
11 Chassinat, *BIFAO* 1903, 154.
12 See Junker, cited by Bleeker, *Numen Suppl.* IX, 52.
13 A Sacred Scribe (*cf. infra*, p. 93) with the theophoric name Arnuphis offered an altar to Thea Epiphanes, *i.e.* Isis (*VS* 613).
14 Priscus, *fr.* 21: *FRA* 653, 4.
15 Exhaustively studied by Junker-Winter: *Das Kloster am Isisberg. Das Geburthaus.* Vol. 66, *Öst. Akad. Wiss. Phil. Hist. Kl. Dankschr.* 1965.
16 The miracle of her bestowing the Milk of Life is well discussed by Bergman, 147. For the Blessed Virgin Mary's miraculous milk, *cf. ERE* 8, 637b.
17 See *infra*, p. 279.
18 See Rusch, 44.
19 Diod. S. 1, 22: *FRA* 102, 10.
20 *Cf. supra*, Ch. I, n. 8.
21 Diod. S. 1, 22: *FRA* 102, 1.
22 Roussel ably dealt with Delos half a century ago. Vidman (in his *Sylloge*) has gathered an impressive collection of Isiac and Sarapiac inscriptions from the Greek mainland (1–134), Asia Minor (267–351), the Cyclades save Delos (135–58), the Sporades (173–266) and Crete and Cyprus (159–172, 352–5).
23 Paus. 7, 26, 3: *FRA* 336, 38.
24 Paus. 2, 4, 7: *FRA* 333, 15.
25 Paus. 3, 18, 2: *FRA* 334, 33.
26 *VS* 62.

CHAPTER VI

27 Paus. 10, 32, 17: *FRA* 340, 5.

28 See Roscher *s.v.* 'Meleagrides' (2586): Artemis transformed Meleager's sister into guinea hens.

29 *OL* 99.

30 Diod. S. 1, 13: *FRA* 95, 34.

31 Picard (*RHR* 95, 220ff.) has proved untenable Foucart's theory that Demeter is an imported and Hellenized Isis of the XVIIIth Dynasty. For the 'Grave of Isis' where a small statue of the goddess in Egyptian faience was discovered see *AE* 1898, 31. *Cf.* also *ibid.* 1885, 169; 1889, 171. For Attica *cf. Hesperia*, 34, 125ff.

32 *VS* 450.

33 Note that the priestess of Isis who served her at Megalopolis (*VS* 42) held the theophoric name of Dionysia.

34 *Timaeus* 21e: *FRA* 45, 13.

35 A copy of it was kept on his work desk by Beethoven.

36 Sterling Dow, in *HTR* 1937, 231. For the Iseum *cf. SEG* 24, 230.

37 *Cf. infra*, p. 260.

38 *OL* 84.

39 At Thessalonica (Tod, *ABSA* 23, 87–8) such names as Isis, Eisias and even Coprias are taken by female worshippers: and the theophoric 'Isias' even appears in an inscription found in the Monastery of Lavra on Mount Athos [Demitsas, Μακεδονία, p. 639, no. 776 (33)] as it does at Apollo's Delphi: *Griech. dialekt. Inschr.* 2178.

40 *Cf.* Pelekides, 7ff. In the Museum (cat. no. 908, not given in *VS*) the Temple of Isis of Memphis is dedicated to 'the City'.

41 See Brady, 42.

42 See *CE* 82 and 132.

1 See *VS* 552 (dated AD 201) for a typical (though late) Portus Ostiae dedication to Isis Adrastia by a certain priest of Sarapis, Superintendent of the Alexandrian Mission.

2 *Cf. supra*, p. 47. We must remember the Pharos harbour was the only safe anchorage for miles along the Mediterranean coast: Diod. S. 1, 31, 2. For the recently found colossal red granite statue of Isis Pharia in the Bay see *Egypt Travel Magazine*, 1967, 146.

3 Seneca, *Ep.* 77, 1.

4 *OL* 235 (accepting Chapouthier's restoration). Herodotus (2, 50: *FRA* 12, 15) writes categorically that, like Poseidon's, their name 'is unknown in Egypt'. But in the Graeco-Roman cult of Isis the Dioscuri ('the Saviours') were acceptable: see *VS* 313, 335, 336; *CE* 110. Also Chapouthier, 248–62. The Greek 'sons of thunder' (*cf.* Mark 3, 17, and Peake's note *ad loc.*) had had a long and venerable history in Greek religion (*cf.* Nilsson, pp. 34, 124) before their recognized eminence as tutelary divinities of sailors linked them with the Alexandrian divinities.

5 For 'Isim Giminianam' see *CIL* 14, 2028 and *cf.* note 1, *VS* 549. For the name '*Isis*' twice on a ship's prow see Lucian, *Navig.* 5: *FRA* 314, 21ff. *Cf.* also *VS* 171 (from Crete) for 'navis parasemo Isopharia', where the adjective is the same as that found in *Acts* 28, 11, for the ship 'of Alexandria' with the name 'Dioscuri' which conveyed Paul from Malta to Syracuse. *Cf. CIL* X, 3640, cited by C. G. Starr, p. 102, n. 81. Roman sailors liked names after Serapis (*ibid.* 87).

6 For inscriptions see *VS* 502 (Capua: 'una quae es omnia'), 503 (Ager Falernus), 505 (Minturnae: 'myrionymos'), 511 (Tarracina), and

538 (Syracuse: 'Restorer of Salvation').

7 An Italian Campanian gem of the third century BC shows Isis Victoria with palm branch in hand (Vandebeek, 71).

8 As we shall see (*infra*, p. 154) the link between Isis and Ptah (transformed into Hephaestus and Vulcan) was very close at Memphis. At Ostia the cordiality of relations between Isis and Vulcan is evident in the imperial age; the Pontifex of Vulcan gave permission for dedications to the Egyptian gods: *VS* 550, 536.

9 Unhappily these murals (as is pointed out by *TTT* 8, n. 1) even when they have not deteriorated are no longer in their proper architectural setting.

10 Isis appears with Mars in *VS* 538, with Poseidon *ibid*. 713 (as also on coins: see *infra* 239) and Sarapis is identified with Neptune in *VS* 770 (as he is implicitly by Aristides, *Orat.* 45, 23: *FRA* 305, 6).

11 L. Pacilius Taurus was simultaneously priest of the Great Mother, the Syrian Goddess, and Isis (*VS* 467).

12 By the age of Hadrian Egyptian themes were familiar in works of art found not far from Rome itself. Not to mention the Palestrina mosaic (*supra*, p. 44), a relief found at Ariccia shows two pigmies dancing in a bark on the Nile. See *NSA* 1919, 110, where a contrast is drawn between the religious indulgence of the ancient Romans and the attitude of the monks of Athos or the Anglo-Saxon Quakers.

13 See *OL* 100, 106, 116. *CE* 112, 132. *VS* 467.

14 Cf. *infra*, p. 137.

15 See Nonnus, *Dionys.* 40, 399: *FRA* 603, 25.

16 *TTT* 68.

17 For Isis Augusta see *VS*, where in the Index more than thirty examples are cited. For the 'august hair style' see *TTT* 73.

18 *VS* 534. Cf. *ibid*. 67, 423, 664. *CE* 201 (Bubastis and oneirocrites).

19 *VS* 535. He is named (*ibid*. 418) fourth in the list—after Sol-Sarapis, Bacchus and Mercury. Silvanus (giver of the theophoric name to the 'Silas' who is mentioned in the Pauline Epistles) was one of the divine triad (the others are Apollo and Diana) worshipped by the Roman army. (Domaszewski, 53) and was a readily accommodating deity (like Isis herself): *cf.* Festugière in *Comptes rendus de l'Academie des Inscriptions*, 1923, 277. The worshippers of 'holy Silvanus' honoured him on a lofty crag near the Theatre of Philippi (Demitsas, 937).

20 See *TTT*, Ch. IV. The debt must here be acknowledged to the archaeological researches both of *TTT* and of C. M. Dawson (Romano-Campanian Landscape Painting, *YCS* 9, 1944).

21 See *TTT* 79, 147. Pl. XIV, fig. 1.

22 Listed *TTT*, pp. 181-5.

23 Ingeniously re-imagined by Brion, 36.

24 *TTT* 30.

25 Details are drawn from *TTT* 33.

26 *TTT* 34. *CE* 90. The view here stated is shared by Lanciani, L. R. Taylor and Squarciapino.

27 *TTT*, 134. Pl. XIV, 2.

28 Cf. *infra*, 161.

29 *TTT* 147, Pl. XIX, fig. 1.

30 For Panthea, *TTT* 77, 83. Cf. *infra* p. 254.

31 Bread is still the object of Christendom's daily prayer, in spite of Tertullian's jibe directed at Isiacism 'a matter of the belly' (*De Corona* 7: *FRA* 381, 16). See *John VI*.

32 See *TTT* 57. In Caria a dedication was made to Heracles in con-

junction with the Egyptian gods: *VS* 292.

33 *TTT* 142, Pl. X, fig. 2.

34 Cooper (39) contends that the Egyptian counterpart of Priapus, Khnum ('Khem') was not worshipped with similarly obscene rites.

35 Epiphan., *Ancorat.* 104: *FRA* 605, 33. The whole passage is bitterly hostile. (See Merkelbach's comment: *RMA* 167).

36 Admitted by *TTT* himself, 115.

37 *VS* 353.

38 For the Egyptian 'maypole', *cf.* Hippol., *Ref. Haer.* 5, 7, 27: *FRA* 435, 22.

39 *CE* 291. The uterus ('tet') emblem of Isis is discussed by Barb, *JWCI* 16, 200. See also Bonner, 83. The fertility aspect of the cult of the Virgin in Christianity must not be overlooked: see Briffault, 3, 206. (The erotic imagery of *Salutations to the Blessed Virgin Mary* (trans. Budge) is on a par with that in the *Song of Solomon*.)

40 Regarded as Io she could be said to make 'many women what she was to Jupiter' (Ovid, *Ars Amator.* 1, 78: *FRA* 150, 29).

41 Minuc. Felix. (*Octav.* 25: *FRA* 295, 25) generalizes about pagan (especially Egyptian) religion: sexual licence is rife at the altar and in the temple.

42 Ovid, *Am.* 2, 2, 25: *FRA* 149, 31. *TTT* remarks (117): 'Isiacism contained a purer and loftier morality than classical Roman religion.' The facts are against him: *e.g.* the statue of Priapus in the Iseum displayed by Schefold, *Vergessenes Pompeii*, Berne, 1962 Pl. 152.

43 *CE* 119, 120.

44 *Cf. supra*, Ch. II, n. 38.

45 The Roman found it hard to believe the two rivers could mix: 'Cum Tiberi Nilo gratia nulla fuit.' Propertius, 2, 33, 20.

46 Marucchi (*NSA* 1904, 130) remarks 'the attitude of prostration is noteworthy, shown by the priestess perhaps at the moment of presenting a table of sacred offerings'. Humility, he suggests, is characteristic not of the free Greeks and Romans but of the orientals. In earliest Egyptian religion (*PT* 460a) the two souls are said to genuflect like Isis and Nephthys at the sunrise: see Sethe and his illustrations, *Sitz. Ber. Berl. Akad.*, 1928, 272.

47 For the 'impressed human feet' see *CE* 115 and references in Vidman's Index archaeologicus (*VS* pp. 358–9) to pes humanus, plantae pedum, and soleae.

48 For illustrations see Leipoldt, figs. 57, 58; Marucchi, 122 and 126; Grimm, pl. 27. *Cf.* also *RMA* 43.

49 So Marucchi. *Cf.* also Iversen, 53–5, and C. D'Onofrio, *Gli Obelisci di Roma*, 1965. For the fifteen obelisks still standing in Rome (though not all in their original positions), see E. Nash, *Pictorial Dictionary of Ancient Rome*, II, 1968, 130–62 (148–52 for the four from the Iseum in the Campus Martius).

50 Amm. 17, 4, 12; 4, 18; Pliny, *Nat. Hist.* 36, 9: *FRA* 548, 32, 546, 6, 198, 6.

51 *Hermes Tris. ap. Stob. Fl.* I, p. 407 W.: *FRA* 393, 38.

52 Pignorii, L. *Patavini Mensa Isiaca*, Amsterdam, 1669; Iversen, 85, 158.

CHAPTER VII

1 For the priest as διάδοχος ὁρασείας see Bonnet, 606. Chaeremon (ap. Psell. *BCH* 204: *FRA* 781, 37) mentions the Egyptian ritual of anointing the eyes for 'autopsy'.

2 For the power (*dynamis*) of Isis *cf*. *infra*, p. 187.

3 Diod. S. 1, 88: *FRA* 129, 30. The Egyptian god here referred to is the Ram of Mendes usually identified with the Greek Pan (see Budge, *Gods*, II, 353).

4 Artapanus ap. Eus. *PE* 9, 18, 1; 23, 2: *FRA* 276, 5, 10.

5 Vitr. 8, *pref*.: *FRA* 154, 12. Besides kneeling down and raising their hands, the priests of Isis may have closed their eyes in prayer: 'Speak [the incantation] then open the eyes,' *PGM* 1, 4, 624.

6 Epigraphical and papyrological examples are found at a later date: and the word occurs in the Septuagint. We may contrast the history of this term with that of *mysterion*.

7 Plut. *Sup*. 13: *FRA* 787, 2.

8 Arist. *Met*. 1, 1: *FRA* 54, 12.

9 Plut. 10: *FRA* 224, 9.

10 DL 3, 8: *FRA* 431, 28.

11 Plut. 6: *FRA* 222, 5. Porph. ap. Eus. *Praep. Evang*. 4, 23, 3: *FRA* 474, 10 (where the Egyptian priests are said to cleanse the temple of evil spirits).

12 Tert. *Cast*. 13: 381, 23.

13 In the words of Kipling the priest 'can talk with kings'.

14 Apul. Ch. 17: *FRA* 323, 42.

15 See pp. 23 (*supra*) and 137 (*infra*) and *cf*. *VS* 438, 439, 698.

16 See p. 22. Botti (109) discusses the λοῦτρον at the Alexandrian Iseum.

17 See the words of Chaeremon (in Porph. *Abst*. 4: *FRA* 180, 9ff.).

18 Origen declares that the Christians derived the habit of circumcision from Egypt (not from the Jews): *Cels*. 1. 22: *FRA* 352, 7. The reason for the practice, according to Herodotus (2, 37), was hygienic: *FRA* 7, 14.

19 Her., *loc. cit*.: *FRA* 7, 16.

20 On festal days he could wear a special richly jewelled crown: *VS* 524.

21 Porph., *loc. cit*.: *FRA* 181, 27.

22 Lucius used to await the daily opening 'apprehensive and wonder-struck', Apul. Ch. 20: *FRA* 324, 32.

23 For the singing of the hymn the Paeanists of Sarapis (*VS* 384) would have doubtless been available. The Hymn to the Rising Horus (*PT* 573) can be studied in Erman, 12.

24 The Isiac acclamation 'Awake Thou' was γρηγόρι (*VS* 620—where a certain assimilation of Isis and Diana can be detected; 586—'Memphi, glegori!'; 593—'gregori'). The verb is fairly common in the New Testament.

25 Porph., *Abst*. 4, 8: *FRA* 467, 16.

26 Epiph., *Her*. 1, 38: *FRA* 607, 11.

27 For the use of incense in the Egyptian cult see *CE* 81, 187, 286, 1.

28 For the linen robe on which the 'holy saga' was portrayed see *VS* 313. *Cf*. *infra*, p. 183. For the sable shroud see Plut. 52: *FRA* 246, 12.

29 See *VS* 524 and 761. For the vulture's feathers Ael. 10, 22: *FRA* 419, 41. *Cf*. *PO* 66.

30 Apul. Helm 280, 6 and 22.

31 They were placed before the temple with lustral water in them.

32 Apul. Ch. 23: *FRA* 326, 15. Lucius was in fact conducted to the bathing pool (conveniently near) and washed very clean all over (still an ass) after a prayer for divine mercy had been uttered.

33 See *VS* 459–63—all sepulchral formulae from Rome. *Cf*. also the New Testament type of kindly gift, 'a cup of cold water' (*Matthew* 10, 42). For 'Osiris called water' see Hippol., *Refut*. 5, 7, 23: *FRA* 435, 15.

34 Chaerem. ap. Porph., *Abstin.* 4, 8: *FRA* 182, 7. *Cf. infra* Ch. XIII, n. 2.

35 Tib. I, 3, 31: *FRA* 147, 21. For 'the saying of Lauds' see *VS* 390 (an inscription found in a Roman monastery): *Laus Isidis. Crede et noli deficere. Cf. infra*, p. 264.

36 This is implied by the scene in the Herculaneum frescoes: see *TTT* 101, and Pl. XXIII.

37 Prop. 3, 31, 1: *FRA* 148, 25.

38 *Cf. infra*, p. 122. For the Lychnapsia as the birthday of Isis see M. S. Salem, *JRS* 27 (1937), 165–7.

39 See *Rep.* 327a, with the scholion.

40 See *infra*, p. 167.

41 See Lafaye, p. 132ff.

42 Some twenty references are given in *VS* p. 348. The title, *scoparius* (*ibid.* 517), conveys the same meaning. The presence of animals about the temple buildings obviously entailed even greater care in sweeping up than is the case in a Christian church.

43 See *VS* 556 for *kameineutae*, a term which, as Vidman and Cagnat (*ad. loc.*) suggest, must refer to the fire on the hearth.

44 For 'interpreters of dreams' see the references in *VS* (p. 348) to *CE*, and to 'somnia' in *FRA* Index, p. 916. *Cf. infra*, p. 257. The belief in the sending of dreams by the god was common enough in ancient religion. We see it in Homer (*cf.* Nilsson, *Hist.* 131) and in the Old Testament.

45 See *CE* 269–70. For the *canephori cf. VS* 8 and references on p. 347 *s.v.* The scholiast on Aristoph., *Acharn.* 242, establishes that the baskets carried by these ministers, like the modern Greek κανίσκια (Lawson, 487), were receptacles for 'the firstlings'. For *paeanistae cf. VS* 384.

46 For *pastophori* see Diod. S. 1, 29: *FRA* 107, 27. They are there dis-

tinguished from the (higher ranking) priests and are declared exemplars of the Athenian Heralds (*Kerykes*). Apuleius knows the name. Lucius meets one called Asinius Marcellus (Chap. 27: *FRA* 328, 26) and the guild of the order is said to have been founded in the Sullan age (*ibid.* Chap. 30: *FRA* 329, 33). See also *VS* 433 with note. Hopfner (cited *VS* 16 n.) identifies the *pastophori* with the *hieraphori* (for the name, and for *hagiophori, bomophori* and *hierophori*, see *VS* 16 and 150 n.). A female minister of Dionysus, simultaneously 'pastophor of holy Isis of the Nile', was buried in a sarcophagus at Rome: see *VS* 433 with note.

47 Just as he was also taught the Hymn: *Herm. Trism. ap. Stob. W.*, p. 407 (*FRA* 394, 23).

48 Clem. Alex., *Strom.* 6, 4, 35, 3: *FRA* 372, 21.

49 *TTT* 92. Note *Arnuphis*, *VS* 613.

50 For the way of holding the vase see Levi, I, 289, n. 10. For the rank of 'prophet' see *VS* 384, where the Prophet Embes is 'Father' in the religious order of the Paeanists of Roman Jupiter, great Heliosarapis. *Cf.* further *FRA* p. 894 Index *s.v.* The Prophet's office demanded deep education. *Cf. infra*, p. 93.

51 *CIG* 4946.

52 See D. J. Chitty's *The Desert a City*, Oxford, 1966. Choukas (p. 173) showing greater perspicacity than others who have written books about Athos and its roots remarks 'Christian monasticism was born on Egyptian soil'. The Isiac's 'unbroken and stiff acts of worship' (Plut. 2: *FRA* 220, 14) can be paralleled, of course, in the monasteries of Athos where, incidentally, the author's interest in the whole question of Isiacism was first awakened.

53 Chaer. *ap.* Porph., *Abst.* 4, 7:

FRA 181, 32.

54 The writer is not squeamish, for he mentions the occasional problem of seminal emission which the celibate priest encounters while asleep: *loc. cit. FRA* 181, 26, 28.

55 Eun. *VS* 41-5: *FRA* 639, 24. 640, 22.

56 According to Herodotus in the Egyptian religion of his day there was no place for women priests in the service of either gods or goddesses (2, 35: *FRA* 6, 37), but in the Graeco-Roman world women could obviously serve in the priesthood of Isis. See *TTT* 96 and Pl. XVIII, fig. 2. The priestess Marcia is known at Cyrene (*VS* 807). Statues of priestesses have survived from the Iseum at Beneventum (*cf. supra*, p. 86). The fringed scarf worn by a priestess is shown by Leipoldt, fig. 51.

57 See *CE*, p. 267. Also no. 110, where the sequence is Sarapis, Isis, Apollo, Artemis and the Dioscuri. A follower of the Egyptian gods was named Dioscoros: *VS* 799.

58 A modern parallel may be suggested: nowadays a 'Governor' represents the Greek state on Mount Athos, which, however, is a theocratic community under the jurisdiction of the Patriarchate at Constantinople.

59 *CE* 138-42.

60 *CE* 268.

61 *CE* 269.

62 *CE* 270. But we must not forget the specific mention of an *aretalogue*, Maiistas. *Cf. infra*, Ch. VII, n. 19.

63 *Cf. infra*, p. 194.

64 For the *Melanephoroi*, *cf.* Plut. 52: *FRA* 246, 13 and *VS* 75. 426.

65 Val. Max. 7, 3, 8: *FRA* 170, 16; Appian *Bell. Civ.* 4, 47: *FRA* 342, 9. *Cf. infra*, p. 204.

66 Tert. *De Ienun.* 2: *FRA* 381, 30.

67 Rusch 53. So also at Heliopolis

(Plut. 6: *FRA* 222, 1) wine was not brought into the shrine, although it was not absolutely forbidden if drunk in small amounts.

68 Plut. 221, 26. The various food taboos are to be seen from the Index of *FRA*, p. 900, col. 2. The eating of pork once a year at the full moon (Plut. 8: *FRA* 223, 11) seems to be a typically Greek custom. The sacrifice of living pigs belonged to the Thesmophoria of Demeter (Nilsson, *Hist.* 91) and in the Greek villages today the pig is ritually slaughtered with the sign of the cross made over it on Christmas Eve.

69 See Isocrates, *Busiris* 9, 22: *FRA* 49, 11 (the Egyptian priests enjoy 'the greatest health and the longest life'); Lucian, *Long.* 4 (210): *FRA* 314, 15 (an example of longevity is afforded by the so-called 'sacred scribes').

70 The wand is technically *kerykeion* (*caduceus*). The 'altars of help' (*auxilia* is found in an inscription *VS* 591) were doubtless carried by *bomophori* (*VS* 315) and appear to have some link with the otherwise obscure *ergasteria* (*VS* 477). *Cf. infra*, p. 167.

71 The rose as the flower of Aphrodite is appropriate to Isis, identified with 'Venus, quae primis rerum exordiis sexuum diversitatem generato Amore sociasti'. Isis is the Rose-breasted Lady in Nubia: *CIG* 5115.

72 Seneca, *Nat. Quaest.* 4a, 2, 7: *FRA* 178, 13.

73 See *JRS* 27, 165; Bonneau, 403.

74 See Roscher, 429, for analogies between Isiac and Catholic procession. See *infra*, p. 183.

CHAPTER VIII

1 His 'holy hymns' are mentioned by Plutarch (Plut. 52: *FRA* 245, 24).
2 For Isis Pelagia see *BCH* 85, 435; 87, 301. She was worshipped as such especially at Corinth (Paus. 2, 4, 7: *FRA* 333, 17). *Cf.* the inscriptions from there and Lesbos, Caria, Rome and Spain: *VS* 34, 259, 274, 396 and 764. See further *CE* 67 and *TTT* 99. *Cf. supra* p. 65, *infra* pp. 124, 240. Isis Pelagia is named in *VS* 274 between Anubis and Isis Bubastis. She is found on coins at Ephesus (Drexler, 87). The whole question of Isis as Goddess of the Sea has been handled by Roscher, 474–90. The question is complex. Even Artemis Pelagia may be influential (*cf.* Witt, *PCPS loc. cit.*, p. 56). A part may have been played by Io-Isis travelling over the sea. *Cf* Lucian, *Dial. Mar.* 7: *FRA* 309, 27: 'She will be ruler over sailors, and our mistress.'
3 *Cf. infra*, p. 154. Münster, 184, points out that at Memphis, where by the time of the New Kingdom Isis had achieved independence from Osiris, she was worshipped as Goddess of the Dead along with Hathor, the male deity being invoked as Ptah-Sokar-Osiris.
4 The connection between Isis and the Apis Bull and the latter's entry for enthronement into the Temple of Ptah have been well treated by Bergman, 251–5. (Note also that at Chalcis in Euboea—*VS* 84—Apis is substituted for Horus-Harpocrates, appearing as the fourth of the divine names after Sarapis, Isis and Anubis.)
5 Pausanias (1, 42, 18: *FRA* 332, 4) contrasts the Sarapea at Alexandria and Memphis. The former is the most famous, the latter the most

ancient. At Memphis the ancient Osiris-Apis (equated with Ptah) maintained his nationality, Apis statues being found from the XVIIIth to the XXVIth Dynasties. See Vandebeek, 35.
6 *Andros, Hymn* 3.
7 Ovid, *Ars Amat.* 3, 393 : *FRA* 151, 2.
8 Ovid, *Amores* 2, 13, 8 : *FRA* 150, 5.
9 See Levy I, 163ff.
10 *CE* 247.
11 Bergman has recently (especially pp. 297–300) laid stress on the Memphitic source. He points out that so far from there being anything anomalous in the Isis Hymn's connection with Ptah's Temple (276) there were inside the Temple statues equal in size of both the god himself and Isis, with the infant Horus at her breast.
12 See Weinreich, *PW* 1922, 797.
13 On a tombstele of the XVIIIth Dynasty. Text by Chabas, *RA* 14, 307. Translation in Erman, 141.
14 From Cyril Aldred's translation in his *Akhenaten*, London, 1968, pp. 187–9.
15 Apul., Ch. 25: *FRA* 327, 23.
16 See Peek, 145. Unto Isis 'one hymn is sung on land and on board seafaring ships'. Peterson (192, 1) brings out the importance of Isis' catholicity: the Universe praises her in complete unity.
17 *Cf. infra*, p. 112.
18 *First Peter* 2, 9. *Cf. Acts* 2, 11.
19 At Delos aretalogues did the same before this date. We know the names of Maiistas (*supra*, p. 97), Pyrgias and Ptolemaeus (*CE* 60, 119).
20 Diod. S. 1, 27: *FRA* 106, 18. The prefatory phrasing is significant: 'I am not unaware that certain of the authorities represent,' etc.
21 Two works of special importance for the subject which have been published within the last decade are

Dieter Müller's *Ägypten und die griechischen Isisaretalogien*, *APA* 53 (1961) and J. Bergman's *Ich bin Isis*, *Acta Universitatis Upsaliensis*, *Hist. Relig.* 3 (1968).

22 *Cf.* Bergman, 178.

23 *Cf. PT* 1140c ('the breath of Isis the Great'). As Bonneau observes (287) already in Egypt Isis is 'mistress of the Etesian winds'. As I have elsewhere remarked (*PCPS* 192, p. 56, n. 5) just as in Apuleius (Chap. 5: *FRA* 320, 13) the winter gales abate and the storm-tossed waves subside through the power of Isis, even so in the New Testament the winds and sea obey the marvellous Lord.

24 In the age of Alexander Severus Isis appears with situla as a member in a group of maritime figures (*VS* 713). Her head is on the left and Amphitrite's on the right, with those of Sarapis, Asclepius, Hygeia and Neptune in the centre.

25 The author's style and subject matter suggest comparison with Catullus 64. The inspiration of Callimachus is therefore possible.

26 *PT* 1271a, 1272 a: in their 'evil coming'. They unite to guard: *ibid.*, 1265a–b. *Cf. infra*, p. 206ff.

27 As by Aristides the Rhetor.

28 Plut. 52: *FRA* 246, 13. The epithet μελανόστολος is applied to Isis herself: Kaibel, *Epigr. Gr.* 1023, 3. See further Roscher, 469.

29 Montet, 287. Greek Imperial coins of Byblos show Isis Pharia with Claudius and Elagabalus (*Greek Coins*, *Phoenicia*, G. F. Hill, pp. 99 and 107). *Cf. supra*, p. 43.

30 See *PEFQ* 26, 132: 57, 7. *VS* 368. (G. F. Hill's identification of the Petra in *OL* 91 with Wadi Musa is accepted.)

31 *Cf. TTT*, Pl. XIV, pl. 1. Isis appears at Ascalon on a coin of Alexander Severus (*Greek Coins*, Palestine, G. F. Hill).

32 See *PEFQ* 21, 82. *CE* 82. *Cf. infra*, p. 131. Roscher 500. For a similar (amazingly 'Papal') conflation, *cf. JWCI* 29 (1966), p. 232, n. 41.

33 *VS* 502, *Te tibi una quae es omnia* is the beginning of the Isis dedication found in the Church at Capua called S Maria Capua Vetere.

CHAPTER IX

1 Other Greek philosophers, of course, had shown discontent with current theology, *e.g.* Plato in the *Republic*. Antisthenes also, the founder of Cynicism, rebutted popular polytheism well before Christianity with the monotheistic *credo*, 'In nature there is only one God' (Philodemus, *Piety* 7).

2 *Cf. supra*, p. 22.

3 Plut. 53: *FRA* 246, 19. Other Platonists were to regard Isis as the World Soul: *cf.* Mayassis, 90ff.

4 *Cf. supra*, p. 23. Notice the depth of religious feeling shown by Lucius in Apul., Ch. 2: *FRA* 318, 33–8.

5 It is applied in the Greek Orthodox Church to the Theotokos. See Canticle Six for the Mattins of the Entry of the Theotokos, 21 November (Mother Mary and Kallistos Ware, 182.)

6 Apul., Ch. 5: *FRA* 320, 1–10. With the long-delayed last words, 'Queen Isis', the Egyptian-born cult states its ecumenical creed: Isis is uttering her catholic claim, *urbi et orbi*. See Bergman, pp. 299–300.

7 *Cf. VS* 15 and 757. The nocturnal liturgies celebrated at the monasteries of Mt Athos have some of the characteristics of the ancient Isiac and Cabiric Mysteries.

8 Late belief (Horap. 1, 12 and *cf.*

the 'Ineffable Mistress' of *Orphica*, Hymn 42, 1: *FRA* 581, 7 and 533, 34) could hold Athena-Mises, male-female, as daughter of Isis.

9 Diod. S. 1, 29: *FRA* 107, 27.

10 Sterling Dow in *HTR* 1937, 232: 'Isis and all the other foreign deities . . . remained a metic'.

11 *OL* 102. See *VS* 373 : the Roman priest (fanaticus) serves Isis and Bellona. *Cf*. Apul. 6: *HF* 320, 6. See further Bergman, 103. *Cf*. *infra*, p. 183, for the opposite view—Isis the goddess of peace.

12 See *VS* 413, 474, 479, 588, 660 and 743.

13 Severan marble plan, Nash 510.

14 Joh. Lyd. 4, 57: *FRA* 699, 19. The 'Good Angel' (*Agathodaemon*) is Horus-Eros: *cf*. *RMA* 124, 1. The same power is asked to intercede for suppliants with 'the Lady Isis': Bell, 66. It could be a name 'in religion' (*VS* 603). *Cf*. *infra*, p. 238, n. 53.

15 But Harder (on *VS* 88, 10) points out that Apollo himself could have horns and Nilsson (*Hist*. 27) that Athena could transform herself into a bird.

16 So Vandebeek, 140.

17 Her. 2, 41: *FRA* 8, 35ff., mentions both Isis and 'Aphrodite' (*i.e.* Hathor) in discussing the sacred cow.

18 *TTT* 140 supports Isis-Hathor.

19 *Cf*. *supra*, p. 100.

20 *Cf*. *supra*, p. 30.

21 Her. 2, 112: *FRA* 24, 16. For Isis as Astarte (Saviour and Aphrodite), see *CE* 194.

22 See Roscher, 494-7.

23 Vandebeek, 82.

24 *Ibid*., 38, 88, 98.

25 *Ibid*., 128-30. *RMA* 12, 93, 103, 125, 288.

26 *Anubis Hymn* 6, Mesomedes *Hymn* 9. Horace (*Odes* 3, 29, 9: *FRA* 147, 2) recognizes the Isis-Aphrodite

identification: the goddess haunts Cyprus and Memphis.

27 Gérard de Nerval seems to identify the Venus of Lucretius with Isis: *cf*. *supra*, p. 20.

28 Paulina (*supra*, p. 67) was initiated as an Isiac priestess in the Eleusinian rites of Demeter and Kore.

29 Diod. S. 1, 13 *fin*.: *FRA* 95, 35. For Isis-Demeter see Roscher, 443-8.

30 *Cf*. *VS* 379 and 724 for 'Isis frugifera'. *Cf*.*VS*165 πλουτοδότειρα.

31 Lucan 8, 832: *FRA* 186, 15.

32 Plut. 64: *FRA* 253, 6.

33 In a sense Isis and Osiris were bound (like Siamese twins) insepar-ably together by Eros: Plut. 12: *FRA* 226, 7

34 *Cf*. *supra*, p. 20.

35 *OL* 231. Note the ecumenical claims throughout the *Litany*: 20, 24, 93, 121, 125, 137, 171, 177, 183, 201, 231, 244, 268. See further Vandebeek, 136.

36 See Roscher, 545ff., for Isis Nemesis (Fortuna).

37 For Isis Panthea see Roscher, 546; *TTT* 77, 83-4, pl. XX, 2 (p. 90). For Sarapis Pantheus, *VS* 753, 777.

38 Her. 2, 50, Diod. S. 1, 15: *FRA* 12, 16; 96, 28.

39 For Isis as Hera and Regina see Roscher 512-14. The identification with Hera is recognized by Diod. S. 1, 25 (*FRA* 104, 34), Apul., Ch. 5 (*FRA* 320, 6), *OL* 32 ('in the Sais') and the sister-wife relation (Isis-Osiris, Hera-Zeus) is basic in the theology of the Isiac mysteries (*RMA* 31-2). For Isis Regina nearly thirty inscriptions can be cited by Vidman, five of them from a convent obvi-ously built over an Iseum at the corner of *Borgo dei Greci* in Florence.

40 Inscriptions show Isis as 'the Great Mother, holding all' (*CE* 50a) and even Pantocartor (*VS* 42). In *OL* she is Dynastis (34, 41, 57, 97). As consort of Sarapis she is also Juno the consort of Jupiter: on a statue from the Aventine Hill in Rome (*VS* 391) she is linked with Juno Dolichena (pl. 33). Note also that at Locri there seems to have been a funeral college of 'Sarapis and Juno' (*VS* 481a).

41 For all these attributes see Vandebeek, 139. *Cf. infra*, p. 150.

42 Diod. S. 1, 15: *FRA* 96, 41. *Cyme Hymn* 23-4.

CHAPTER X

1 See Briffault, III, 180: 'The All-Mother is older than the All-Father. Ishtar and Isis were the universal mother long before any sky-god or tribal male deity had evolved into universal fatherhood.' Briffault's picture of Isis in her Egyptian setting is here out of focus. His main point, however, is valid. (But see Kees, *Aegypten*, 16, for the Pantheistic Osiris in the reign of Ramesses IV.)

2 For the possibility of a link between religion in Crete and in Egypt see *supra*, p. 16.

3 See J. Mellaart, *Catal Hüyük, A Neolithic Town in Anatolia*, London, 1967, p. 181: 'Statues of a female deity far outnumber those of a male deity.' See also Graillot, 8.

4 According to Pliny (*Nat. Hist.* 2, 8: *FRA* 189,8) the planet Venus was also popularly known as Juno, or Isis, or the Mother of the Gods. *Cf. VS* 543, where the priest ministers to Isis of Ostia and to the Mother of the Gods with her temple over the Tiber.

5 Coins (Drexler 229) show Isis was worshipped there.

6 A single priest (*VS* 467) ministered simultaneously to the Great Mother, to the Syrian Goddess, and to Isis. Late in the fourth century AD 390 (*VS*

447) a priest of Isis dedicated an altar to the Great Mother of the Gods on Ida and to Attis.

7 *Cf.* Apul., Ch. 5: *FRA* 320,2. 4 *Phryges Pessinuntiam deum matrem . . . Cretes sagittiferi Dictynnam Dianam* (*i.e.* the Magna Mater at Dicte). We should note her Egyptian claim of Sovereign Supreme Divinity as Mother of the God/the Gods: *cf.* Bergman, 274.

8 *CE* p. 112.

9 *VS* 467 (Brindisi), 543 (Ostia) and 579 (Falerii).

10 *PT* 1272a.

11 *Cf. supra*, p. 19. Note 'Isis the Mother' in *VS* 741.

12 Isis made her son Horus so, and can even bear the title herself: *supra*, p. 129.

13 *Jerem.* 44, 1, 17, 19.

14 These cakes were doubtless similar to the ancient *panspermia* employed in the ancient Greek cults of the crops and the dead (*cf.* Nilsson, 300-1) and the κόλλυβα in the Orthodox Church even today (the present writer has partaken of them in a church at Ios and notes with interest that an Isiac priest (*VS* 307) was Κολλυβᾶς). They resembled also the firstlings carried at the Isiac festivals (Diod. S. 1, 14: *FRA* 96, 13) doubtless in the baskets by the order of women known as *canephori*: *cf. supra*, p. 93. Further for κόλλυβα: Rodd, 199. Lawson, 487, 535. The pagan custom was maintained by the Collyridians condemned for their heresy of cake offerings to Mary 'the heiress of ancient deities' (Lucius, 521). Briffault (III, 181, n. 9) cites the case of St Augustine's mother who brought her *panspermia* to church until told it was unchristian.

15 See Bergman, 98, with his notes.

16 See Plut. 27; *FRA* 232, 38.

17 See Graillot, 206. For Aristides

(*Sacr. Or.* 3, 46: *FRA* 307, 38) 'light from Isis and other untold benefits portending salvation' was accompanied by a visitation the same night by Sarapis and Asclepius. 'Isis as Saviour Goddess' has been sympathetically treated by C. J. Bleeker in *The Saviour God*, ed. S. G. F. Brandon (London, 1963). *Cf.* also *Matthew*, 1, 21.

18 Apul. 278, 2, *ed.* Helm. *Cf. RMA* 148, 174. *Regnare servire* is a cardinal principle of Christianity. *Cf. Matt.* 11, 29–30.

19 Diod. S. 1, 25: *FRA* 105, 9

20 *Cf. infra.*, p. 258.

21 Discussed by Bleeker, p. 2. Bergman (202) stresses the same point.

22 Kyri̲a Eleison well conveys their cry of supplication. See the citation (Witt, *Studia Patr. VIII*, 126) from the Louvre Pap. 81, 24, and *cf.* also Ovid, *Met.* 9, 700: *FRA* 152, 13 (*dea sum auxiliaris opemque exorata fero*). For Isis, Saviour of the Hungry, *cf.* W. Spiegelberg, in *ZÄS*, 53, 1917, 34.

23 See *CAH* 12, 210.ʹ

24 See *VS* 47, 412, 34, 359; *CE* 99, 189, 194. Ears by themselves are important in Isiac portraiture (*cf. VS* 28 and the ears featured in the Palestrina Mosaic, producing a surrealist effect). At Lyon (*VS* 744) a dedicant named Edias offered Isis the image of a human ear. See also Witt, *Studia. Patr.* VIII, 143, nn. 5, 6.

25 Arist. *Or.* 49: *FRA* 308, 34. The same person is doubtless the Aristides of a dedication which has been preserved (*VS* 316).

26 Vitr. *De Archit.* 30: *FRA* 154, 3.

27 *TTT* 56, 83, 105. *Cf.* pp. *supra* 123, *infra* 238, and *CE* 11.

28 *TTT* 149.

29 For Baltis *cf.* Cumont, *RE* s.v. For Atargatis *OL* 100. For Jupiter Dolichenus (and Juno Dolichena) *cf.*

supra, Ch. IX, n. 40. In a relief discussed *VS* 392, Jupiter Dolichenus stands (left) on the bull, Juno Dolichena (right) on the hind, and Sarapis and Isis (in the middle) face Dolichenus (Pl. 33). For Zeus, Sarapis and Iao see *VS* 769.

30 Apul., Ch. 22; *FRA* 325, 41. *Cf. supra*, p. 23. A certain 'Mithres' (a manumitted slave of 'Augustus' at the end of the third century AD—*VS* 388) made offering to Sarapis. One and the same man Ulpius Egnatius Faventinus (in the late inscription of AD 376, *VS* 457) is a 'father' in Mithraism and an Isiac priest. The word 'pater' in the inscription to Isis Myrionymos from Potaissa (*VS* 698) is probably the Mithraic title.

31 See *VS* 487, 488.

32 *VS* 751a. We may also notice the dedication (*VS* 540) of shops or taverns (*tabernae*) to Isis and Sarapis, a dedication found piquantly enough in the mud of the Tiber, whither Tiberius caused the idol of Isis to be thrown.

33 Porph., *Vit. Plot.* 10: *FRA* 469, 25.

34 Statius, *Silvae* 3, 2, 101: *FRA* 209, 12. For the Isis-Io assimilation see Roscher, 439–40 and *TTT* 81 (where the actual identification is considered not to be pre-Hellenistic —but this is implicit in Her. 2, 41: *FRA* 8, 39, as appears from Wiedemann's note *ad loc.*).

35 Plut. 43: *FRA* 243, 1. For Isis-Selene see Roscher, 437–8.

36 Apul., Ch. 3: *FRA* 319, 8.

37 *PT* 1248a. *Cf.* Clark, 92. But a less crude interpretation of the story of Shu's creating the world is that the process is an exhalation of breath. *Cf.* Faulkner in *JEA* 54, 40.

38 *VS* 39.

CHAPTER XI

1 OL 102. Note *ibid.*, 78–9, Isis and Leto.

2 An inscription has been found on Mount Athos of some importance in such a locality for the study of links between the veneration of the Panagia and what preceded it. Just as at Athens a certain Epaphroditus dedicated ears to Isis (*VS* 28) so at Athos (*Tò* "*Aγιον* "*Oρos*, Andreas the Monk, 1969, Thessalonica, p. 28) one Nevris offered a large ear sculptured in marble to Artemis Agrotera.

3 For Artemis as Mistress of Wild Animals see Nilsson, 28, and Guthrie, W. K. C., *The Greeks and their Gods*, London, 1968, 99ff.

4 Call., *In Dianam*. Note in l. 7 *πολυωνομίη* Callimachus does indeed know Isis (*FRA* 63, 25; 64, 2) but there is nothing to prove that he specifically linked her with Artemis.

5 *Pap. Eg. Brit. Mus.* 10. 188 (cited by Morenz, S.) For the idea of 'Juno' as the Virgin *cf.* Apul. 131, 8 Helm. See Budge, *Gods*, I, 293. See also *supra*, p. 15.

6 Prop., 5, 5, 34: *FRA* 149, 25. Separate beds were then the rule (Tibul., 1, 3, 26; Ovid, *Amores* 3, 9, 34; Juven., 6, 535; *FRA* 147, 16. 150, 19. 281, 24.)

7 Prop., 3, 31, 1: *FRA* 148, 25.

8 Rufin., *Eccl. Hist.* 9, 23: *FRA* 627, 6. *Cf. supra*, pp. 89–90.

9 Prop., 2, 28, 60–61 (not included in *FRA* despite the obvious allusion to Isis-Io):

Munera Dianae debita redde choros,
Redde etiam excubias divae nunc ante
    iuvencae.

10 *Cf. infra*, p. 243.

11 *Cf. supra*, p. 66.

12 OL 84. 91.

13 CE 179.

14 See Lazarides, p. 41, as well as his useful bibliography, pp. 57–8. Personal exploration by the author both here and elsewhere on Greek soil (*e.g.* Thera) confirms the view that here at least (in contrast with Roman practice as stated by Vitruvius—*cf. supra*, p. 136) the Egyptian gods could literally top Greece's mountains. *Cf.* OL 130, '*εν' Ολύμπῳ*.

15 *VS* 107. Unlike the stele preserving the egotist Hymn of Isis in the Church of John Theologos at Ios, this 'fine marble dedicatory plaque' which Cormack found in 1936 serving as the Holy Table in the Church of Saint George at Beroea has now been removed to the local museum (here *Pl. 15*).

16 See Her. 2, 156: *FRA* 35, 29— followed by Athenag., *Suppl.* 28: *FRA* 344, 24.

17 Her., *loc. cit.*: *FRA* 768, 9; Paus. 8, 37: *FRA* 337, 38.

18 See Nicander, *Metam.* ap. Antonin. Liberal. 28: *FRA* 81, 23.

19 Juv., 15, 7: *FRA* 282, 27.

20 *VS* 690.

21 Plut., 52 *ad fin.*: *FRA* 246, 11.

22 Wessely, *Neue griech. Zauberpap.*, 1893, 498.

23 Plut., *Anton.* 54: *FRA* 271, 24; Dio C. 50, 25: *FRA* 374, 34.

24 *SEG* 18, 698.

25 *Andros Hymn*, 37.

26 For a Selene Dolorosa with traces of horns found near the Golden Gate see Macridy and Casson's article in *Archaeologia* 81 (1931), p. 80. For the Byzantine connections of Io and Hekate see Preger 3, 9. Isis, 'polyonymos among the Thracians' (OL 101) could be easily equated with Artemis polyonymos, well represented at Byzantium (*cf.* Preger, *loc. cit.* 32, 51, 70). *Cf.* Ach. Tat. 8, 18. Paganism afforded good precedent for Constantine to entrust his city to the Blessed Virgin's keeping. He was quite ready to give an idol of a pagan goddess a new Christian look, for he brought an archaic Magna Mater to Byzantium (Zosimus 2, 31) and by altering one or two features he changed Πότνια Θηρῶν into Mater Orans (see Chapouthier, p. 344). *Cf.* also *St Sophia* and Isis-Sophia.

27 The 'Great Name' was shared by Isis (and Artemis) with Sarapis: see *VS* 357, where the note indicates that the formula was not narrowly restricted. What was typical of the name of both Artemis and Isis was the impulse it gave the worshipper to shout it aloud. *Cf. RMA* 151, and *infra*, p. 254.

28 Drexler (78-94) gives references for the appearance of Isis on Ephesian coins of dates 91, 88, 87, 82 and 68 B.C. For *homonoia cf. infra* p. 244.

29 Apul., Ch. 2: *FRA* 318, 26. For the *neocorus* of Isis see *VS* 247 (Cos) and 277 (Mylasa in Caria).

30 Macrob., *Saturn.* 1, 20: *FRA* 598, 7.

31 Costorius the Italian, identifying his local goddess at Tibur, Albula, with ecumenical Isis, offered her a statue of Diana: *VS* 530.

32 Iambl., in *Nicom. arith. intr.*, p. 13: *FRA* 511, 20.

33 *Cf. RMA* 240.

34 Heliod., *Aethiop.* 5, 21: not included in *FRA*.

35 *Cf. supra*, p. 129.

36 For the Boscoreale patera see J. M. C. Toynbee, *The Hadrianic School*, Cambridge, 1934, p. 12. We may at once agree that here the personification is probably of Africa (or Alexandria). But in the light of similar treatment at Pompeii (*cf. TTT* 73) the further identification with Isis, goddess of Africa (and Alexandria), cannot be ruled out. We see the emblems of divinities associated with her: the stars and pilei of

the Dioscuri, the bust of Helios, the eagle of Zeus-Ammon, the club of Hercules, besides the symbols of Asclepius, Hephaestus and Ares. See also Goodenough II, 236, for Isis with star and crescent joining Artemis with bow, arrows and moon.

37 Schefold, *VP* 30, n. 50 (*cf.* also 102). *Cf. Cronachi di Arch.* Catania, 1963, 2, 64.

38 See *TTT* 82. Dawson (*YCS* 9, 1944, 90, no. 23a) suggests that it is probably Athena. He disregards Artemis, although he specifies three huntsmen and two dogs, animals sacred to her as goddess of the chase. He also points out the presence of the *vannus mystica*, an emblem of Isis (for this *cf.* Apul., Ch. 10: *FRA* 322, 23-4).

39 *TTT* 107 and 72.

40 *Cf. RMA* 31.

CHAPTER XII

1 See C. J. Bleeker 'Initiation in Ancient Egypt' in *Numen, Supplem.* 10, 49-58.

2 Isis could receive the Greek epithet *orgia*: this is evident from exhibit 986 in the Museum at Thessalonica (omitted in *VS*). Isis being the inventress *par excellence* was the foundress of her own special mysteries (*cf.* Clark, 147).

3 *Cf. supra*, p. 103.

4 Minuc. Fel., *Octav.* 22: *FRA* 295, 7. Bonnet holds that this is a late development in the Osirian saga.

5 The discussion by Hatch (*Hibbert Lectures*, 1888) about the influence of the mysteries upon Christian usages (Lecture X) is still valuable for an understanding of the relevance of earlier cults and religious practices for emerging Christianity. The Orphic enigma, 'I fell, a kid, into the milk', has been analysed by such able scholars as Jane Harrison and W. K. C. Guthrie. In the Eleusinian mysteries two main ideas were purification and personal piety. The ancient Phrygian Mystery of the Mother (Magna Mater, Cybele) and the Dying Youth (Attis) flourished during the formative years of Christianity.

6 For the third century Christian Hippolytus (*Refut. Haeres.* 5, 7, 22: *FRA* 435, 9) next to the Phrygians the Egyptians had the oldest mysteries and initiations in the world. About the mysteries of Mithras he is silent.

7 *Cf.* Apul., Ch. 28: *FRA* 328, 41, *nocturnis orgiis inlustratus.* Lucian (*De Syria dea* 6-7: *FRA* 315, 3, and 315, 13) links the *orgia* of Adonis with 'Aphrodite of Byblus'.

8 *Matth.* 13, 11.

9 See Hatch, *op. cit.* 298.

10 For 'rebirth' in Isiacism see *RMA* 12, 187. The importance in Christianity is evident from *John* 3, 3.

11 Plut. 3: *FRA* 220, 26.

12 Her. 2, 171: *FRA* 37, 10. *Cf.* Diod. S. 1, 27. *FRA* 107, 13: 'The priests have received exact information as one of the ineffable secrets.'

13 See Roscher 461-2.

14 Plut. 27: *FRA* 232, 34.

15 *SEG* 8, 548, 20.

16 *OL* 107, 112.

17 *OL* 111. So is Sophia in *Ss.* 8, 4. *Cf. infra* Ch. XIV, n. 54.

18 Edson (*HTR* 41, 199) well remarks that by the Roman period the Cabiri had been conflated with the Dioscuri, who were important for the Egyptian cult (*cf. supra*, p. 96).

19 For this view *cf.* Hemberg, 27. Already in Herodotus the Cabiric mysteries, celebrated at Samothrace by Pelasgians, were memorable (2, 51). Aeschylus is known to have

written a play with the title *Cabiri*. Some interesting facts are brought to light by Lucius, 223. *Cf. ERE* VII, 628-32.

20 An Isis inscription has been found there (*VS* 263).

21 Her. 3, 37: *FRA* 41, 21.

22 Sandman, 219. *Cf.* also Bergman, 257: The Prophet of Isis, Lady of Semenmaa't, is also Prophet of the (other) gods in the Temple of Semenmaa't.

23 *OL* 2. The Temple was a very memorable sight according to Herodotus, 2, 99: *FRA* 22, 14. *Cf. supra*, p. 102, n. 11.

24 Already in the New Kingdom Ptah symbolized Memphis: one who longed for Memphis could say (Erman, 205) 'Come to me, Ptah, to take me to Memphis.' At Saqqara (*cf.* n. 18, *supra*) the incarnation of Ptah, the Apis, had Isis as his Mother, with her own precinct. See Budge, *Gods*, II, 196 and see Bergman, 255, n. 1.

25 Bergman, 254, n. 6.

26 *Ibid.* 289. Her fusion with Sekhmet, Bast, Hathor and Ma'et led to this.

27 Cic. *Nat. Deor.* 3, 22 (55): *FRA* 87, 36 (*Phthas, ut Aegyptii appellant, quem custodem esse Aegypti volunt*); Diod. S. 1, 13: *FRA* 95, 24.

28 See Witt, *Balkan Studies*, 1970, on 'The Egyptian Cults in Macedonia between Alexander and Galerius'.

29 See Istrus of Cyrene ap. Clem. Al., *Str.* 1, 21, 106: *FRA* 77, 25.

30 For the 'Instructions in Wisdom' of Ptahhotep see Erman, 54. The excavations of Professor W. B. Emery at Saqqara in the Temple of Nectanebo (a very important Pharaoh for the history of Isiacism) have created a stir among Egyptologists with the hope that soon Imhotep's tomb may be revealed. Already the link there has been demonstrated between Isis (in various guises, e.g. nursing her baby Harpocrates, squatting on one leg to support him with her knee raised up so that he can lean upon it), Ptah himself, the Apis Bull, and Imhotep-Thoth, (the mummies of whose sacred animals the ibis and baboon, are features of the galleries).

31 Ox. Pap. 1381, 200. In 1. 187 he is named 'discoverer of this scripture, Asclepius, greatest of gods'.

32 Paus. 2, 27, 6; Hermes Trismeg. ap. Stobaem 1, 49, 467 W and Core Cosm. 1, 49, 387 W: FRA 333, 28; FRA 389, 26 and 390, 5.

33 The words that inspired the music are as follows:

Heil sei Euch Geweihten! Ihr dranget durch die Nacht.
Dank sei Dir, Osiris und Isis, gebracht.
Es siegte die Stärke und krönet zum Lohn
Die Schönheit und Weisheit mit ewiger Kron.

See also Iversen, 122 and Baltrušaitis, Ch. II.

34 The triad are named on a bronze situla found in the Aegean, and belonging to a date between the XXIInd and XXVIth Dynasties: see Pendlebury, 92.

35 See Sandman, 247.

36 Diod. S. 1, 22; FRA 102, 3.

37 OL 248, followed at once with the invocation 'Thou at Memphis'. Mesomedes Hymn 9. The New Kingdom Isis was 'the fiery (serpent)', Münster, 109.

38 The 'certum signum' of Apul. 27: FRA 328, 20 may easily have been as important for the ancient Isiac as the formula in VS 364 (see the translations quoted of Jalabert, Guarducci and Catharina Fisher).

39 To take a name 'in religion' was as obvious a practice for the dedicated

pagan as it has been in Catholicism. For theophoric names cf. infra, p. 256, n. 855. For 'father' in Mithraism, cf. supra, nn. 15, p. 91 and 30, p. 137.

40 Apul., Ch. 23: FRA 326, 28. A simulated death such as Lucius' words imply offers a point of resemblance between Isiac and Mithraic initiation.

41 Proserpine (Persephone) was identifiable with Isis: Plutarch quotes the earlier Archemachus and Heraclides Ponticus as holding this view (Plut. 27: FRA 233, 7).

42 See Bleeker, Numen, Suppl. 10, 55, with the references to ZÄS 57 (1922) 27, 35.

43 Apul., Ch. 24: FRA 327, 15. It was a kind of 'birthday party' (festissimus natalis). The Isiac cult meal, Merkelbach suggests (RMA 124), could be 'a communion breakfast' (Ach. Tat. 2, 33). More pertinent to the banqueting aspect of Egyptian religion is Ox. Pap. I, 110: 'Chaeremon invites you to dine tomorrow in the Sarapeum at the table of Lord Sarapis.'

44 For the Egyptian Mysteries of 'the Sufferings of Osiris' see Her. 2, 171: FRA 37, 10. For the Egyptian tradition of Isis as mainspring of the mysteries, temples and statues (Cyme Hymn 22-4), see Bergman, 161. She it is, the kindly goddess, who is active in the fulfilment of 'all for her brother' in the mystery drama, and she it is who is besought to save her son.

45 Guthrie remarks on the cost of such ceremonies.

46 The watchword of Plotinian mysticism. Bergman well observes that to Isis was specifically applied the epithet, 'the only one', 'the unique'. Cf. supra, p. 14, n. 1. Born and bred in Egypt, Plotinus with his mystical temperament could hardly have failed to know this.

47 Cf. *RMA* 296, n. 1. See Plotinus, *Enn.* 5, 1, 6; 1, 6, 9; 4, 3, 11.

48 *Ibid.*, 1, 6, 7: 'Stripping ourselves of clothes before going up naked.' Cf. *RMA* 318.

49 Cf. *supra*, p. 22, n. 54.

50 Apul., Ch. 1: *FRA* 318, 14. The parallel with 2 *Kings* 5, 14, where Naaman dipped himself seven times in Jordan, is very striking. See Tarn, 347 for the 'persistent' seven, *e.g.* stoles of Isis.

51 See Doro Levi in *Berytus*, 1942 ('*Mors voluntaria*'). Cf. the Astrologer depicted by *TTT*, Pl. IV, no. 2. Cf. *supra*, p. 83.

52 Well treated by Levy, *loc. cit.*, 19–55.

53 Her. 2, 61; Diod. S. 1, 21: *FRA* 14, 18; 100, 31.

54 Cf. also what Pausanias says about the priests at Phlious in the Peloponnese: the statues of 'Dionysus' and 'Apollo' (*i.e.* Osiris and Horus) could be viewed by laymen, but that of Isis only by priests (2, 13, 7: *FRA* 333, 25).

55 The epithet ἑπτάστολος used here is the one (*VS* 254) mistakenly declared by Vidman to be ἅπαξ λεγόμενον: Hipp. 5, 7, 23: *FRA* 435, 14.

56 For a second century inscription starting with *heuresi* see *VS* 501.

57 Cf. Milton's well known
'In vain with timbrell'd anthems dark
The sable-stoléd sorcerers bear his worshipt ark.'

58 See Pascher, 59.

59 See Chapter XIX, *infra*.

60 See *VS* 453 for the Isiac priestess wearing just such a mantle.

61 Apul., ed. Helm, 288, 1.

62 Apul., Ch. 24: *FRA* 244; 377, 9.

63 Cf. *supra*, p. 22, n. 54, *RMA* 23, 200. In the Iseum at Eretria there was a baptismal chamber: Papadakis, 129.

64 This is '*le mot juste*'. Cf. *infra*' p. 268.

65 The meal at the Sarapeum seems to have been proverbial. See *Tert. Ap.* 39: *FRA* 379, 30. Cf. also *VS* 48, 120 (a 'table' dedicated to Isis at Philippi), 265, 275, 720 (the *cline* found in Cologne Cathedral and dedicated to Heliosarapis). At Delos 'tables' were offered, especially to Chrēstē Isis (*CE* 20, 99).

CHAPTER XIII

1 Hipp., *Her.* 5, 7, 23: *FRA* 435, 15. Cf. Origen *Cels.* 5, 38: *FRA* 439, 44. For Plutarch the Nile is 'the effluence of Osiris', (*Quaes. Conv.* 8, 8, 2: *FRA* 263, 39) but his 'power' could be located also in the Moon (Plut. 43: *FRA* 242, 39).

2 See *VS* 459–63 (all from Rome) and 778 (from Carthage). The *PT* 22a, 'This cold water of yours, Osiris', anticipates by many centuries the text in the New Testament, *Matt.* 10, 42.

3 Priscus, fr. 21: *FRA* 653, 2ff.

4 Her. II, 58: *FRA* 13, 24.

5 See Desroches-Noblecourt, 139. Cf. further Bonneau, 396, for the Festival of the Nile inundation.

6 *PT* 1347b.

7 The 'Advent of Isis' from Phoenicia to Egypt was on 2 January. See Plut. 50: *FRA* 244, 32.

8 Lucian, *Syr. D.* 2: *FRA* 315, 4. For a very early reference to 'the mysterious city, Byblos by name' and 'their goddess' see the composition belonging to the reign of Ramesses II, Erman, 229. Cf. *supra*, p. 43, n. 14.

9 Here we are confronted by the overjoyed Isis of the Oxyrhynchus *Litany* (127: 'the glad face in Lethe') instead of the one who mourns with her sister Nephthys (*cf. supra*, p. 59). The Festival of Rejoicing (*Charmosuna*) which is mentioned by Plutarch (Plut. 29: *FRA* 234, 17) is attested at Cius in Bithynia, provenance of one version of the Isis aretalogy, as well as at Tomi (Constanza) on the Black Sea, where it may have cheered the celebrated and enforced immigrant Ovid, a poet not unacquainted with the vagaries of Isis at Rome: *VS* 324, 704. For similar celebrations in Egypt see Magie, *AJA* 1953, 176, n. 132. See also Bergman, 141ff. for 'Das Freudemotiv'. Isis in the Graeco-Roman world could be considered (like Apollo) as 'Leader of the Muses' and 'Yielder of Victory in the Games' (*OL* 62. 78).

10 Merkelbach (*RMA* 108) treats the fisher in Isiacism as the spiritual father of the cult. The fisherman figure is well-known in the worship of Orpheus, and is of cardinal importance in the Christian gospel (*cf. Mark* 1, 16–20).

11 The spiritual exhilaration may be fairly likened to that of the modern Salvationist, for whom the *militia sacra* is as gladsome an experience as it was for the ancient Lucius.

12 *Cf.* New Testament, *Rev.* 7, 13.

13 *Cf. infra*, p. 264.

14 Their function is here the same as that of the lay orders *hieraphori* etc. named in *VS* pp. 346–7. *Cf. supra*, p. 93, n. 46.

15 The lamp is like that from Puteoli with *EΥΠΛΟΙΑ* inscribed across its 'deck' (here *Pl.* 37).

16 The *Lychnapsia*, the Isiac Festival of Lamps or glowing *Candlemas*, has its place in the Roman Calendar on 12 August (*FRA* 525). In Egypt the equivalent *Lychnokaia* took place in honour of Neith of the Saite nome (Her. II, 62. *Cf.* also Jul., *Orat.* 11, 267; Choricus Gaz., *Laud. Marc.*, 1,

100: *FRA* 14, 24; 543, 18; 696, 4). *Cf.* also the female lamplighter of Isis-Aphrodite at Athens, *VS* 16 (*cf.* 291, 798). Heliodorus (*Aeth.* 1, 18: *FRA* 455, 1) writes about Thyamis' dream in which 'the Iseum at Memphis seemed ablaze with flambeaux'.

17 See Roscher, 461.

18 *Cf. supra*, p. 150. For the 'uterus emblem' see Barb, *JWCI* 16, 200.

19 See Budge, *Gods*, II, 266, and *VS* 662.

20 A late mythographer states, 'Isis is represented as having crossed the sea in the likeness of a cow, since she did so in a ship with a picture of a cow on it.' (Myth. Vatic. II, 89: *FRA* 728, 16ff.) Herodotus (2, 41: *FRA* 8, 37) specifies cows as 'sacred to Isis'. *Cf. supra*, p. 30.

21 For these nautical details I am indebted to my friend, Mr R. F. G. Hanbury of Southgate.

22 *Cf. CE* 194: 'To Isis, Saviour, Astarte, Aphrodite, Euploea, Epekoos.' For Euploia, see *TTT* 99, n. 2. *RMA* 140, 330, 332; for Aphrodite-Euploea, *CIG* 4443; Pausan. 1, 1, 3.

23 *Acts* 18, 18. Whether the tonsure was originally a token of grief or not, it seemed to Herodotus that the Egyptian priests shaved their whole body to avoid polluting holy things (Her. 2, 37: *FRA* 7, 16). It is noteworthy that the bearded Hebrew Joseph shaved himself before entering the presence of the Egyptian Pharaoh (*Genesis* 41, 14).

24 See Scranton's article 'Glass Pictures from the Sea', in *Archaeology* 20, 163. One who has seen these underwater excavations more than once must congratulate the archaeologist on the ingenious use of the most up-to-date scientific equipment in this worthwhile quest for Isiac remains at Cenchreae.

25 The 'captain' (ναύαρχος) is in inscriptions: *VS* 130, 428, 500.
26 *VS* 80. Presumably for reasons of space Vidman's list is much attenuated. All the names quoted are found, of course, in the complete transcription—*CIG* 12, Supp. 557. For παίδευσις as a form of address *cf.* Lid. Sc. *Lexicon*. Isis herself was a Nurse or Educator (*VS* 371) and her followers dedicated schools in honour of the cult (*VS* 525. 557).
27 *VS* 302 (*Latinus* is a better reading than *Laginus*).
28 Johannes Lydus, *De Mens.* 4, 45: *FRA* 698, 26.
29 Yet according to Plutarch (32: *FRA* 236, 8), 'Pilots because they get their living from the sea are not spoken to by Egyptian priests'.
30 *Cf. infra*, p. 241.
31 Veget., *Epit. rei mil* 4, 39: *FRA* 590, 27 (cited by Alföldi, 47).
32 *VS* 562 (=Εὐθηνία *infra*, Ch. XX, n. 19).
33 Plut. 39: *FRA* 240, 17.
34 Levi (1, 38, 7) well remarks, 'The Isiac ceremonies of November, the solemn Isia, seems to have had more importance in the West than the spring festivals of this goddess' as suggested in the Antioch 'Calendar'.
35 See Alföldi, 52ff.
36 *Ibid.* 61, no. 20.
37 The latest epigraphical reference to an existing Isiac cult appears to be one on an altar in Rome (dated AD 390). Here Rufius Volusianus appears as a follower of the Mother of the Gods and Attis, whereas his mother was a priestess of Isis (*VS* 447). When the heathen rites were finally attacked and subdued in 391 the only two cults which were endangering Christianity on the numismatic evidence, in the view of Alföldi (40), were those of the Magna Mater and Isis.
38 See Hyg. *Fab.* 277: *FRA* 349, 36.

39 See Rufin *Eccl. Hist.* 30, 11: *FRA* 631, 10ff.
40 See Socr., *Eccl. Hist.* 1, 18: *FRA* 657, 32.
41 Diod. S. 1, 51: *FRA* 113, 1ff.
42 *VS* 727; 400, *Isidi et Osiri mansionem aedificavimus. Cf.* the similar priesthood in Orelli 2244; *CIL* 6, 348.
43 Spart. *Carac.* 9: *FRA* 556, 34.
44 Apul., Ch. 2: 318, 35. *Cf. supra*, p. 123.
45 Yet *cf. supra*, n. 29.
46 See Alföldi, 57, *cf.* Černý, 140. But G. Grimm (106) is critical of Alföldi's theory.
47 Ciaceri, 268. *Cf. VS* p. 238. For the Veil of Isis *cf. supra*, 91. Quibell (482) has suggested a pre-Christian survival of Isis in a Mohammedan funeral procession: the woman tugging her yellow hair 'surely was Isis'. Rather more evidence than this is needed to prove his case.
48 From Alexei Dmitrievsky, *Opisanie Liturgitseskich Rukopisej*, Kiev, 1895–1917, 11, 685. The congregational response is "Ανω, "Ανω, Νεῖλε.
49 In the Liturgy of St John Chrysostom it is not difficult to find expressions which are reminders of the religion supplanted by Christianity: ἐλέησον, Σοφία, τὰς θύρας (sic) "Ανωσχῶμεν τὰς καρδίας, Δύναμις (as the Deacon's monosyllabic interjection).

CHAPTER XIV

1 Orig., *Cels.* 1, 28: *FRA* 352, 10.
2 The Marianites, condemned in the fifth century for worshipping Mary as a goddess (Briffault, III, 183) followed this tradition.
3 Sophr., *Laud. Cyr.* 26: *FRA* 732,

28. The epiclesis of Isis at Menouthis, according to *OL* 63, was 'Truth'. Isis of Menouthis was in favour at Ostia: *VS* 403, 556a.

4 Jouguet (434) is therefore mistaken in supposing that 'a very prosperous Iseum existed at Menouthis at the *end* [my italics] of the fifth century'.

5 Eunapius (*Vit. Soph. Aedes.* 45: *FRA* 640, 33ff.) roundly condemns it all as a sham.

6 Sophr., *Laud. Cyr.* 29: *FRA* 733, 18. Aristides (*Or.* 45, 33: *FRA* 306, 32) pays tribute to Sarapis for bringing sailors safe to harbour.

7 Isis was she who arose in the beginning (as) magician. *Cf.* Bergman, 283, and Münster, 207–8. The ἐνάρχως of *VS* 293 may resemble *John* 1, 1. *Cf.* also *Primitiva* (*VS* 451).

8 *Pap. Ebers*, ed. Joachim, p. 2.

9 *PT* 610c, 628a, 1280b.

10 Roeder, 95.

11 Diod. S. (1, 20: *FRA* 100, 28) joins Isis and 'Hermes' in the revealing of mysteries 'magnifying the divine power'.

12 *FHG*, p. 512: *FRA* 74, 17.

13 In *Hermes Tris.* (466, 17ff.: *FRA* 389, 20) Isis tells Horus that he and she, along with Osiris, are thus associated with 'Hermes' and 'Asclepius'.

14 *Cf.* Chaeremon, *BCH* 1, 129: *FRA* 183, 40—181, 1, for the secret *sophia* of Egypt. The God of Israel (*Exod.* 7, 11) is represented as telling Moses about the skill of Pharaoh's 'wise men'.

15 For the Christian treatment of the Nile rising see Bonneau, 423. For *Kraftglaube* in pagan religion see Nilsson, *Geschichte* 2, 534ff.

16 *VS* 541. This seems clearly a name 'in religion'. *Cf. infra*, p. 256.

17 Sozom. 7, 15: *FRA* 662, 9, *Eccl. Hist.*

18 See Justin Martyr, *Apol.* 1, 30, dealing with the objection to the divinity of Jesus: 'What prevents him from having produced the "powers" so-called through the skill of a *mage?*' In the New Testament (*Luke* 2, 52) the adolescence of Jesus was characterized by an increase in *sophia*. Bruno was condemned by the Catholic Church for holding *inter alia* that 'Christ was not God but merely an unusually skilful magician'. See *infra.*, p. 269.

19 *1 Cor.* 1, 24. The use of *dynamis* (and *charis*) in acclamations to Anubis as an expression (on amulets) conveying best wishes for the wearer is attested: Bonner, 49 and 177.

20 *Legacy of Egypt*, 185. Glanville, S. R. K.

21 Doresse, 15. *Acts*, Ch. 6, 8; 8, 10, 13.

22 *Acts* 7, 22.

23 Artap. *ap.* Eus. *Praep. Evang.*, 9, 27, 30: *FRA* 278, 30.

24 *Ephes.* 6, 12.

25 See Doresse *Secret Books*. By greater *sophia* and greater *dynamis* Philip convinced Simon he was the true *mage* with unclean spirits.

26 *Cf.* n. 8 *supra*. For Isis 'useful in magic', *cf. Pap. Edwin Smith*, 47, Westendorf.

27 *Kore Kosmou*, 407 W: *FRA* 394. 16. At the end of the Chalcis aretalogy of 'Karpocrates' (*VS* 88) Isis' son himself claims to have given physicians all life-saving cures through drugs.

28 Names that have the like ring are 'therapy' in Hippocrates (*Art.* 80) and '*therapeutae*' (worshippers in the cult of Isis and Sarapis) in *VS* 307. The Ionic ἴησις of Hippocrates ('healing') is not unlike the name of the goddess Isis herself.

29 Diod. S. 1, 25: *FRA* 105, 7. For the 'goddess who manifests her power'—*Thea Epiphanes*—see *VS* 613.

30 *FRA* 59, 1—it was still being sung in the time of Diog. Laer. (5, 5).

31 Aristid., *Sacr. Or.* 3, 48: 308, 17.

32 See *supra*, p. 53, n. 22. The importance of the epithet at Thessalonica in Christian circles is shown by the name of the ancient church there.

33 Rufin, *Eccl. Hist.* 11, 23: 627, 5. The name was adopted for the side rooms of the palaeo-Christian church (*Ap. Const.* 2, 57).

34 *Cf. supra*, p. 49.

35 Cited (from *CIG* 5900) by Dill, 568, n. 2.

36 Rufin, *Eccl. Hist.* 11, 26: *FRA* 629, 20.

37 *CE* 1, 13–14. *Cf. Matt.* 2, 12, 22.

38 Cited by C. Sudhoff, *Studien zur Geschichte der Medizin* (Leipzig, 1909), 5/6, 226.

39 Josephus, *Ant.* 18, 4, 74, and *Bell. Iud.* 7, 5, 4: *FRA* 216, 9. 41.

40 Arist, *Or.* 49, 46: 307, 39. For the identification of Sarapis with Asclepius, as god of healing, see Tacitus, *Hist.* 4, 84: *FRA* 288, 11.

41 Johannes Lydus, *De Mens.*, 4, 45: *FRA* 698, 31.

42 Paus. 2, 27, 6: *FRA* 333, 28. *Cf. VS* 769a, a dedication to 'Aesculapius, Salus, Serapis and Isis'. *Cf.* also *VS* 740.

43 See *BCH* 53, 87. It is not quite correct to state that Isis is named in *all* the surviving inscriptions: *cf. VS* 123, 124.

44 *Cf. RHR* 86, 172.

45 *VS* 121 (of the second or third century AD).

46 Budge, *Legends*, 42.

47 *PGM II* 7, 501. The 'curious parallel' in New Testament, *John* 17, 1, is mentioned by A. E. Brooke in Peake.

48 Exorcisms are performed on the Eve of Epiphany: the *Kalikantzaros* is 'cast out' by the twig of

vasilikos and the holy water for the *agiasmos*. *Cf. infra*, p. 278, Lawson, 197.

49 Plut. 2: *FRA* 229, 6.

50 Her father's name *Agapetos* suggests that *agape* and its derivative adjective may have been significant in Isiacism (*cf.* Witt *JTS* 19 (NS), pt. 1, 209). *Cf.* the Isiac name *Am(a) bilis, VS* 645. Leopoldt (Pl. 50) displays the mantle with fringe and Isiac knot, the situla and sistrum. He holds that wearing the robe confers divinity (*cf.* the case of Anthia, *infra*, p. 243).

51 See Pascher, 61. 'Isis religion is the corner stone in the βασιλικὴ ὁδός of Philo', *ibid.* 101. For Philo, Sophia-Isis is simultaneously 'virginal as the earth' and 'wife of God' as being an 'androgynous reality', Philo, *Cherub*, 49.

52 *Cf. supra*, p. 97.

53 See Torhoudt, *Een onbekend gnostisch systeem* (Louvain, 1942), 5.

54 *SS.* 7, 20. The botanic wisdom here is that of Isis: *cf. supra* p. 26, *infra*, p. 273. The *Sophia* of this apocryphal book, shown to be Isiac by W. L. Knox, *JTS* 38, 230–37, influenced the thinking of Bruno the Egyptomane (*cf. infra*, Ch. XX). Long before Bruno the African Augustine had allowed the existence of Egyptian 'wisdom' and had acknowledged Isis as being responsible for it as the inventress of 'letters' (Augustine, *De Civ. Dei* 18, 37: *FRA* 646, 32).

55 *Acts* 8, 10, 13. *Cf. supra*, p. 188.

56 Hippol., *Her.* 5, 14, 6–7: *FRA* 436. 18ff. *Cf.* Doresse, *Secret Books*, 273–4.

57 Hippol., *Her.* 5, 17, 11–12.

58 *Kore Kosmou*, p. 385, 13–15: *FRA* 389, 31. Gal. vol. 13, Kühn, v, 773: *FRA* 362, 4. The vaunted κῦφι, a compound incense used as an antidote and for a variety of medicinal purposes (cf. Plut. 52. 80; Aristid, Or. 47, 26) was prepared by the Egyptian priests according to a most elaborate prescription: cf. FRA pp. 203 and 783-4.

59 Cf. supra, p. 26, and infra, p. 274. The leaf and fruit of the persea tree, reputed in ancient Egypt to be a panacea (Theoph. Conf. Chron., p. 49 de B.: FRA 742, 36) was sacred to Isis, but so were other trees such as the sycamore.

60 The gift was conferred on children (Plut. 14: FRA 227, 14) and the sportive element may have had some importance. On the other hand we may recall the New Testament saying 'Thou hast hid these things from the wise and prudent, and hast revealed them unto babes' (Matt. 11, 25).

61 Cf. in the Old Testament, Gen., Chs. 20. 31. 37. 40. 41; I Kings 3. Dreams are warning signs in the New Testament both at the Nativity and at the Crucifixion (Matt. 2. 27, 19). See also Acts 9. 10. 16. As a literary device the dream has a long history— and we may remember the dream ascribed by Plato to Socrates in the Phaedo.

62 Plut. 28: FRA 233, 10; Liban., Or. 11, 111: FRA 542, 26 (but the early date is suspected by Roussel, followed by Downey, 91).

63 See Münster, 14-15: Isis heals Horus' eye and enables him to open it. Cf. infra, pp. 277ff.

64 For the trust placed in dreams in the Greek Orthodox Church cf. Lawson, 300ff.

65 Tib. 1, 3, 28: FRA 147, 18.

66 Cf. VS 28, where Epaphroditus dedicates such ears. Cf. supra, p. 142, n. 2.

67 The 'Dromos' or Way was as deeply symbolic in the Egyptian religion as the Way in the New Testament. Strabo quotes Calli-

machus (17, 1, 805: FRA 158, 8): 'This is the sacred way of Anubis.' In the Old Museum at Thessalonica is an inscription (no. 999) to which my attention was called by Professor Cormack but which does not appear in VS: δρόμον 'Οσείριδι. For 'steps' and 'position of feet' cf. supra, p. 158, n. 38. Further references in VS 61, note.

68 Strom 5, 7, 42, 2: FRA 371, 19.

CHAPTER XV

1 PT 1676a.

2 Ibid., 794a.

3 Ibid., 2150c. As Thoth the King rules heaven, so Anubis the house.

4 Roeder, 301. Cf. Clark, 134-5.

5 Gen., 50, 2.

6 Plut. 14: FRA 227, 22. The legend that he assisted Isis in her search for her lost son (Min. Fel. Octav. 22: FRA 295, 7) as Bonnet has pointed out is a late accretion.

7 Porph. ap. Eus. Praep. Evang. 3, 11, 43: FRA 470, 9.

8 Like the ex-consul, minister of Isis in ps. Cypr. 4, 32: FRA 441, 27.

9 Plut. 61: FRA 251, 7 (white to supernal Anubis, yellow to Herma-nubis). See VS 543: on the front of a marble altar are a priest of Cybele, a cockerel, a lotus and a phallus, and the dedication is made to the infernal gods by a priest ministering jointly to Isis and the Mother of the Gods. In the inventory of the Anubeum at Delos a cockerel in bronze is mentioned: CE, p. 231. A cockerel is offered at Athens to the funerary Nephthys and Osiris: VS 14.

10 Budge, Gods II, 262.

11 The Hymn from Kios in VS 325. See for Plut. 44: FRA 243, 19. For Lucian (Vit. Auct. 16: FRA 310, 27ff.) Anubis is either Sirius in heaven, or

Cerberus in hell.

12 For 'guide' see *CE* 49, and for 'bodyguard' Diod. S. 1, 87: *FRA* 128, 32.

13 Budge, *Gods* II, 264. *Cf.* Münster, 54ff.

14 *CE* p. 278. See also *TTT* 87.

15 *Aen.* 8, 698: *FRA* 92, 18.

16 *Cf. infra*, p. 223.

17 Juv. 6, 534: *FRA* 281, 23.

18 For 'priests of Anubis' see *VS* 536, 538, 734, 742 (*Anuboforus*).

19 *Cf. supra* n. 8.

20 The question of iconographical influence is debatable. Saintyves argues for it, but is challenged by Klauser *Reallexicon Ant. Christ*, Stuttgart, 1950, vol. I, 484 (the thesis 'ist in gar keiner Hinsicht verifizierbar') and by Schwartz (*Museon* 1954, 93–8). *Cf.* also Trencsényi-Waldapfel, *Unters. Rel. Gesch.* Amsterdam, 1966, 421: Saintyves has to admit 'dass wir eine Anubis-Darstellung, mit einem Kind, das er trägt, überhaupt nicht kennen'. It is a fact, as any visitor to the Byzantine Museum in Athens can see for himself, that Christopher for Eastern Catholicism can be represented with a dog's head. For a *Coptic* cynocephelus *demon*, *cf. Theo. Quartalschr.* 94, 598.

21 Stat., *Silv.* 3, 2, 112: *FRA* 209, 23.

22 *Cf.* Budge, *From Fetish* . . . 214.

23 Diod. S. 1, 96: *FRA* 135, 39.

24 Lucian, *D. Mar.* 7: *FRA* 309, 36.

25 It is worth noting that Christianity, unlike Isiacism, gave the dog a bad name: *Matt.* 7, 6; *Phil.* 3, 2; *Rev.* 22, 15 (associated with sorcery).

26 Lucian, *Vit. Auct.* 16: *FRA* 310, 23.

27 Cited by Milne, *JHS* 21, 278.

28 *Cf.* n. 6, *supra*.

29 Diod. S. 1, 18: *FRA* 98, 25.

30 Apul., Ch. 11: *FRA* 322, 26. A priest could conjointly officiate as

minister to Isis and Anubis (*VS* 538).

31 Lafaye dismisses the story as apocryphal. *Cf.* Dill, 566.

32 Anubis is exhibited on an altar in Spain with ibis and palm. The dedication was made by an (Isiac) priestess to Isis the patroness of young women.

33 Her. 1, 182: *FRA* 5, 25. See further *ERE* 675–6, and for the priestesses of 'Zeus' (*i.e.* Zeus-Ammon or Osiris) at Thebes, *cf.* Strabo, 17, 816: *FRA* 165, 5.

34 The term *hierodulia* does not of course connote temple prostitution. T. Abidius Trophimianus of *VS* 375, a *hierodule* 'in every office' was surely not a pimp.

35 *VS* 110. Another interesting name in this connection is that of the Prophet and Father of the August Gods at Rome, *Embes* (*VS* 384).

36 *Cf. supra*, p. 97, n. 65.

37 *Ad Nation.* 2, 8: *FRA* 381, 2.

38 Myrrh was important in the Egyptian cult. In a magical acclamation of the fourth century AD (*Pap. Mag. Osl.* 1, 338) it is invoked thus: 'Thou hast burnt the godless Typhon, hast fought on the side of Horus, hast protected Anubis, and hast shown the way for Isis.'

39 See *BD* Vignette I.

40 *Cf.* Bonnet, 43; Clark, 136.

41 See n. 10 *supra*.

42 Plut. 44: *FRA* 243, 15.

43 *FHG*, p. 512: *FRA* 74, 21.

44 Her. 2, 67: *FRA* 16, 24.

45 Nic., *Met. ap. Ant. Lib.* 28: *FRA* 81, 22.

46 *PT* 830a (*cf.* 610c, 628a).

47 *PT* 130d.

48 *Nat. Deor.*, 3, 16, 56: *FRA* 88, 1ff. He 'is said to have fled for refuge to Egypt because he had slain the Argos', etc.

49 Thoth and Hermes Trismegistus were identified at Saqqara as early as the second century BC (*JEA* 54,199ff.).

50 *TTT* 136. Pl. V, no. 3.

51 Plut. 19: *FRA* 230, 1.

52 Artap. *ap.* Eus. *Praep. Evang.* 9, 27, 9: *FRA* 277, 27.

53 Hesychius *Lex. s.v.* characterizes Hermes as Εὐάγγελος. An Isiac dedicant of the same name is known at Lyon: *VS* 745.

54 For the association of Isis with the Greek Muses see *OL* 62 and Plut. 3: *FRA* 220, 24. For the association between Thoth and Ma'et see Bergman, 176: the Pharaoh in his role as Thoth is Lord of Ma'et (Justice).

55 *Ascl.* 41: *FRA* 622-23.

56 But see *infra*, p. 251, n. 32.

57 See *supra*, p. 97, n. 65; p. 205, n. 36.

58 In the Roemer-Pelizaeus Museum, Hildesheim. Roeder, *Denkm. Peliz. Mus.* 127.

59 Lucian, *Luct.* 21: *FRA* 312, 43. Lucian writes from personal knowledge.

60 Lafaye disbelieves it. *Cf. supra*, p. 182.

61 *Cf. supra*, p. 54.

62 A certain phonetic likeness is observable in the (important) genitive case: Ioannou and Anoubidos. Both 'John' and 'Peter' are hagiographically linked with Anubis: for Anubis as Holder of the Keys see Roeder's Index. *Cf.* for the importance of the genitive, Lawson, 44.

63 Leipoldt, fig. 79. Bonner, 31. 239.

CHAPTER XVI

1 Pliny, *Nat. Hist.* 33, 3: *FRA* 196, 35.

2 *PT* 663c, 664a.

3 *OL* 209. At Amphipolis and Philippi the close Macedonian link between Isis and Horus-Apollo-Harpocrates is evident: *VS* 116 and

114 (note the double theophoric name, Isidorus-Apolla).

4 Cited by Clark, 214.

5 Horapollo 1, 17: *FRA* 583, 15ff.

6 *VS* 73-88.

7 Already in the *Amon Mose Hymn*, Horus, son of Osiris and Isis, is the Corn God (Roeder 25). *Karpocrates* is the result of false etymology (see Harder in *APA* 1943) and so the comment by Bonnet (146) that the spelling is 'unnecessarily confusing' misses the point. *Karpocrates* was an important name in Gnosticism: see Clem., *Strom.* III, ii.

8 *VS* 88, 10.

9 See Bonnet 578. Porter-Moss, 4, 163. *Cf.* Münster, 105. See also *BD* 42.

10 Harder observes that the epithet 'horned' is not absolutely excluded for Greek Apollo. The horns were assigned to representations of Alexander after his death.

11 Plut. 19 fin.: *FRA* 230, 5.

12 Plut. 66: *FRA* 253, 29ff.

13 For Sarapis identified with Helios see *VS* 266, 288, 331.

14 Plut. 65: *FRA* 253, 22ff. For the chronology see Hopfner's edition of Plut., 2, 291ff. Note the mystery about the place of birth (Kees, *Aegypten*, no. 41) and the loneliness of Isis (*supra*, pp. 14 and 160). *Cf.* Her. 2, 156: *FRA* 35, 27.

15 Her. 2, 144: *FRA* 31, 21ff.

16 A *pschent* was found at Cagliari in Sardinia with a dedication by a certain A. Vitellius Urbanus, and near to it a statue of Isis (*VS* 519).

17 Cited by Drioton, 66. *Cf.* Roeder, 205; Clark, 213-17.

18 Plut., *Amat.* 19: *FRA* 264, 28.

19 Plut., *loc. cit. Cf. RMA* 21.

20 *CE* 278.

21 See *TTT* Pl. XVII.

22 See *TTT* 80, with the reference to Plut. 19: *FRA* 229, 27ff.

23 See Roscher, 431-2. In the figure

of Horus in the Christian catacombs of Alexandria trampling on crocodiles, serpents and the lion he sees the evidence that the son of Isis is an influence on the iconographical treatment of the Madonna's Child. *Cf. infra*, p. 278.

24 Bousset's *Excurs.* Ch. 12, discusses the Greek, Egyptian and Jewish ingredients in the mythology. Commenting on this chapter, Charles admits it is full of features which could not have been the original creation of either a Jew or a Christian. The chapter is the basis for the view of Mary as the Second Eve: *cf. Blessed Virgin Mary*, Mascall and Box, Appendix. It is also important for the Holy Grail Legend (*cf.* Hagen, 70).

25 *RMA* 11, 3.

26 Porph. *ap.* Eus. *PE* 3, 11, 48: *FRA* 470, 27ff.

27 *Strom.* 5, 7, 41, 3: *FRA* 371, 9.

28 So Dalton, 673: 'The resemblance is so strong as to be almost convincing.' See also p. 643.

29 Scullard, 374.

30 Wessel in *Atti VI Congresso Intern. Arch. Christ.* (1962-5), 212.

31 *VS* 116. In *VS* 117 Harpocrates even ranks before Isis and Sarapis.

32 Papadopoulos-Kerameus (1909), *Varia sacra Graeca*, 110. Cited Witt, *Greece the Beloved*, 143, n. 1.

33 Diehl, I, 83. *Cf. infra* p. 278.

34 L'Orange, 147.

35 Iao is identified with Sarapis in *VS* 769 and with Abrasax-Dynamis of the Gnostics (Bonner, 134).

36 Bonner, 224.

37 Cooper, fig. 6, and p. 45.

38 Cooper, fig. 3, and p. 43.

39 See *RMA* p. 20, n. 4; p. 32, n. 1.

40 *Cf.* the allegorizing treatment adopted by Asclepiades as reported by Damascius: *FRA* 691, 1ff.

41 *Asclepius* 90: *FRA* 620, 26ff.

42 The Jewish population in Alexandria was very large in his day. A typical representative of the liberalizing Judaism of the Diaspora, Philo may be accepted as reliable in his estimate that the Jews at Alexandria numbered over a million (*cf.* Bergman, 62, 1).

43 Plut. 20: *FRA* 230, 13.

44 See Griffiths, 91-2 (as well as his discussion (p. 14) about the entry of Horus into the Osirian myth).

45 Plut. 56: *FRA* 248, 11.

46 Macrob. 1, 21: *FRA* 598 24ff. The false etymology of *horae* from *Horus* is characteristic of Graeco-Roman writers on the Egyptian cult. Plutarch errs in the same way.

47 See V. von Gonzenbach's recent monograph.

48 *Navig.* 3: *FRA* 314, 18.

49 A child taken from his parents by untimely death could be considered 'Son of Isis': he had won immortality as Horus-Harpocrates. The title is held by a sixteen year old boy 'by immortal ordinance handed over to Death' (*VS* 585). *Cf. infra* Ch. XX, n. 5.

50 Note also *VS* 747, where a boy at Sens in France wore the Horus lock, carried a hammer, and had his left foot unshod.

51 Epiph., *Ex. Fid.* 3, 2, 11: *FRA* 608, 17ff.

CHAPTER XVII

1 Virg., *Aen.* 8, 696: *FRA* 92, 17. See also Manilius 1, 915 (not included in *FRA*) *Atque ipsa Isiaco certarunt fulmina sistro.*

2 Dio C. 50, 25: *FRA* 374, 35.

3 Shakespeare, *Ant. Cl.* V, 2: Hor., *Od.* 1, 37, 49 uses the long-delayed 'morte' with telling effect.

4 See *TTT* 19ff. and the monograph by Tschudin.

5 Apul., Ch. 29 *fin.*: *FRA* 329, 36.

6 Val. Max., *Mem.* 1, 4: *FRA* 170, 5.

7 Dio C. 47, 15: *FRA* 374, 20.

8 See the discussion by Ilse Becker (*Das Altertum* 11, 1965, 40ff.) of Octavian's attitude towards the Egyptian gods. At Alexandria, Macrobius states (1, 7: *FRA* 595, 15ff.): 'The Egyptians as they were not allowed by their religion to appease their gods with animals and blood-sacrifices but only with incense placed the temples *extra pomerium.*'

9 An altar found (rather piquantly) in the bed of the Tiber (*VS* 401) gives a composite dedication (datable to the very beginning of the Christian era) in which Isis is sandwiched into a lowly place between the minor native deities Ops and Pietas.

10 *Cf. supra*, p. 63 and Junker and Winter, pp. 323, 345, 359.

11 Suet., *Tib.* 36: *FRA* 292, 15.

12 *AZ* 38, 124ff.; *SEG* 8, 654.

13 A sacred scribe named theophorically Arnuphis hailing from Egypt dedicated an altar in Cisalpine Gaul to Isis as Θεὰ Ἐπιφανής (*VS* 613).

14 Köberlein (25) has called attention to the important part played by the Dioscuri. From Gaius Caligula's reign an Iseum existed beneath the Domus Flavia (cf. *VS* 388).

15 For Biblical parallels *cf. Jerem.* 2, 13; *John* 4, 10–11; 7, 36; *Rev.* 7, 17.

16 For the soothsayer *cf.* Dio C. 59, 29: *FRA* 375, 21. For the 'great obelisk transported from Egypt' see Sueton., *Claud.* 20: *FRA* 292, 31. Claudius used the ship that transported it as a harbour breakwater.

17 *Cf.* the offering by M. Aedius Amerimnus (*VS* 402). The famous soldier doctor, C. Stertimius Xenophon, a strong polytheist and a priest of Isis and Sarapis (*VS* 249) served under Claudius in Britain as a military tribune. *Cf.* Dill, 566.

18 *Cf. VS* 707 for the dedication at Tomi on behalf of Agrippina, wife of Claudius and mother of Nero. Nero was at first bent on initiation but was scared away (Hatch, 285).

19 See also the inscription from the Iseum Campense (*VS* 382). An overall count of coin-types on which Isis is portrayed at Alexandria reveals double figures for only Hadrian (20) and Antoninus Pius (28). See further R. S. Poole, *Brit. Mus. Catalogue, Greek Coins, Alexandria*, 1892: Index, p. 378 *s.v.* Isis. For Vespasian, Mattingly, *Brit. Mus. Catalogue Coins Roman Empire*, II (1930) pp. xlix and 123.

20 *Cf. supra*, p. 189, n. 30.

21 Dio C. 56, 8: *FRA* 375, 39.

22 The freedman (*supra, n.* 17) who made an offering to *Isis Invicta* in AD 51 did so at Rome, and was connected with M. Acilius Aviola, consul in AD 54. A coin of Byblos shows Claudius with Isis Pharia (G. F. Hill, *Brit. Mus. Catalogue, Greek Coins, Phoenicia*, p. 99).

23 Juv., 15, 1ff: *FRA* 282, 21ff.

24 Suet. *Tit.* 5 (*FRA* 293, 22): 'he wore the diadem'.

25 For the importance of the Crowning of the Apis in the Temple of Ptah at Memphis and of Isis as the 'King-maker' see Bergman, 92ff., 121ff ('Isis und die Königsideologie'). *Cf. supra*, pp. 15 and 46.

26 Suet., *Domit.* 1: 293, 28.

27 Eutrop. 7, 23, 5: *FRA* 555, 14.

28 *JEA* 1961, pp. 80 and 91.

29 The writing of 'books on Egypt' (*Aigyptiaka*) was a popular literary pastime. *Cf. FRA*, pp. 53, 60, 65, 80, 91 and 167 (Aristagoras, Hecataeus, Manetho, Lyceas, Lysimachus and Thrasyllus). Leo of Pella, who was specially interested in the Isis-Demeter identification, wrote

a work on Egyptian theology (*FRA* 59, 11).

30 *Cf. supra*, p. 190.

31 Macrob. 1, 23, 10: *FRA* 600, 2ff.

32 Trajan is reputed to have persecuted the Christians. In Jerusalem itself a dedication was made for the Emperor's health and safety to Jupiter-Sarapis by the corps of the Third Cyrenaic Legion (*VS* 362).

33 *CAH* 11, 321.

34 Like Osiris in one of the *Pyramid Texts* (615). For the link between the cult of Antinous and that of the Egyptian gods see *RMA* 134 *et al.*

35 *Cf. supra*, p. 54.

36 For Hadrian's religious eclecticism *cf. CAH* 11, 321 and 324.

37 *VS* 804.

38 *JEA* 1961, 129. For Hadrian's *Adventus* coin: Mattingly, H. *Brit. Mus. Catalogue Roman Empire*, III, 489.

39 A dedication was made in AD 142-3 on behalf of Hadrian and his children to Sarapis and Isis in Arabia (*VS* 366).

40 An altar was consecrated to 'holy Isis' for the safe return of Marcus Aurelius (*VS* 535). A statue of Isis was offered at Phaene south of Damascus for the safety and victory of 'the liege Lords' (*VS* 360). The emergence of the imperial title of *cosmocrator* (*cf. infra*, p. 263) can be traced to the favour shown towards Isis and Sarapis (see Vandebeek, 71, n. 3).

41 Her effigy, like Britannia's on the pence of successive British monarchs in modern times, indicates the realm's dependence on the freedom of the sea. Isis, shown as a maritime deity with her lighthouse, brings the Mediterranean into the hands of the Roman emperor (*cf. Pls. 60-2, 65*).

42 See *JEA* 1961, 122.

43 *Cf. ibid.* 130: Caracalla's head is surrounded with the rays of the Sun: *Sol in suo clipeo.*

44 For Heliosarapis etc. *cf. VS* 331, 280, 332.

45 *Ios Hymn*, 44. For 'the Sun's face' (*caput Solis*) *cf. VS* 524 and note.

46 Spart., *Sever.* 17: *FRA* 556, 8. A dedication to 'Queen Isis' of *c.* AD 200 was found near the Navicella Church in Rome (rightly linked by Lafaye with the Iseum between the Porta Esquilina and the Porta Coelomontana) for the safety of Septimius Severus (*VS* 370). *Cf.* also *VS* 556 (Severus Alexander) and 560 (perhaps Caracalla). The constant formula is 'for the safety' [salvation].

47 *JEA* 1961, 130.

48 Vidman (*VS* 805) is doubtless right that for Caracalla was built an Iseum at Cyrene. See further F. Cumont, *Relig. Orient.*, Paris 1929, 233, n. 8.

49 See H. Mattingly and E. A. Sydenham, *Roman Imperial Coinage*, London, 1936 IV, i, pp. 88, 249.

50 *Ibid.* no. 257.

51 *Ibid.* nos. 577, 645, 865. Note also the Sarapean acclamation (very fitting for Modern Greek conversation!), καλὴν τὴν ἡμέραν (*VS* 363: *cf.* 458).

52 Harder (*APA* 1943, 53) follows Drexler's view that the break lasted until Decius and Gallienus. On an inscription belonging to the Mithreum in the Baths of Caracalla (*VS* 389) the name of Mithras was added during the third century to the acclamation 'One Zeus Sarapis Helios' (for the names conjoined with Hermanubis *cf.* Peterson, 238). *Cf. supra* p. 202.

53 For Heliogabalus' *agathodaemones* see Lampr., *Heliog.* 28: *FRA* 557, 7). A priest (*neocorus*) who dedicated the *Hymn from Cyrene* to Isis and Sarapis (*VS* 803) held the theophoric name 'Agathos Daemon.' *Cf. supra*, p. 123.

54 Lamprid., *Sever.* 26: *FRA* 557, 11.

55 For a thanksgiving dedication from Egypt in the reign of Gallienus to Isis and her associated deities see *OGIS* 717.

56 In a sculpture of the reign of Alexander Severus from Ostia (*VS* 713) Isis is named in conjunction with Poseidon.

57 *Numismatica*, 6, 97–98.

58 Alföldi, 49. For Isis in association with the Dioscuri see Chapouthier, 248–62.

59 See Burckhardt, 425. Alföldi, 60–2.

60 *Cf. supra*, p. 61.

61 Rufin. *EH* 11, 19: *FRA* 626, 1.

62 Socr. *EH* 1, 18: *FRA* 657, 30ff.

63 Theodor. *EH* 5, 21: *FRA* 667, 21ff.

64 Jul. *Ep.* 10: *FRA* 539, 41ff.

65 Theoph. Conf. *Chron.* p. 16: *FRA* 742, 24.

66 Alföldi, 15.

67 *Ibid.* 71ff. *Cf. infra*, p. 179.

68 So Geffcken, *Kaiser Julianus*, 88.

69 Geffcken, *ibid.*

70 *Ep.* 10, *FRA* 539, 37–39. See *JEA* 1961, 131. *Cf. infra*, p. 263.

71 *Ep.* 51: *FRA* 540, 15–17. For Isis as Ptah's *paredros* at Memphis *cf.* Bergman, 263; also *VS* 347.

72 Greg. Naz. *Or.* 5, 32; 34, 5: *FRA* 569, 20, 33.

CHAPTER XVIII

1 The Budé edition of the *Ephesiaca* by Dalmeyda is very useful and the discussion by Merkelbach (*RMA* 91) is illuminating.

2 Habrokomes is a name in Herodotus (a point overlooked by the present writer in *PCPS* 192, 52 n. 3).

3 At Rhodes Isis was 'the Great Goddess'—*VS* 173, n. *Cf. infra*, p. 254. Somewhat remarkably the inscriptions from Rhodes (*VS* 173–245) name Isis much less often than Sarapis, although Athena of Lindus and Artemis Kekoia find mention.

4 For Isis as the one *Dea ex Machina*, the rescuer when all other means have failed, see Lafaye, 76, Roscher, 539, and *RMA* 111–12. According to Diod. S. 1, 25: *FRA* 105, 9ff., it is Isis by herself who appearing in dreams affords unexpected help in the cure of illness. According to Artemidorus all four Egyptian deities—Sarapis, Isis, Anubis and Harpocrates—rescue unexpectedly (2, 39: *FRA* 357, 24ff.)

5 *2nd Cor.* 11, 26.

6 See Rusch, 73. Magie, *AJA*, 1953 173, n. 99.

7 Heliod. 2, 27: cited by Burckhardt, *Zt. Konst.*, 50, n. 36.

8 *Cf. RMA* 12, etc.

9 Philos. *Ep.* 16 (348/49): *FRA* 447, 33.

10 For 'the virgin priestess of the goddess at Memphis, holding the sistrum' see *VS* 789.

11 App. *Mithrid.* 27: *FRA* 341, 35.

12 Ach. Tat. 5, 14, 22: *FRA* 461, 30.

13 Philost., *Ep.* 60: *FRA* 447, 35.

14 *Cf. supra*, p. 245.

15 Heliod. 2, 33, 4. See *VS* 75 and 398. For ζακορεύων *VS* 3, etc. and for the use of the term in the cults generally *RE*, 16, 2, 2422.

16 Tert. *Cast.* 13: *FRA* 381, 23ff.: 'We know women devoted to the African Ceres [*i.e.* Isis], for whom of their own accord they grow old, forgoing marriage.'

17 See *supra*, p. 226.

18 Scano of Mytilene (a late fifth century author), *FHG* 4, fr. 5: *FRA* 48, 13 ('Apis being indigenous to Egypt introduced medicine before Io arrived there').

19 See Tert. *Ieiun.* 2: *FRA* 381, 31. It is from Diodorus (1, 85: *FRA* 127, 23), who is an unimpeachable source for the Augustan era, that we learn the women stand face to face with the Apis, raising their dress and showing him their private parts. Long before Diodorus' day Ramesses II had made provision for the 'holy women' (*hieroduli*) who served Ptah at Memphis: *ERE* 6, 676 (*cf. supra,* p. 204).

20 But Aelian, writing centuries later, states that the Egyptians repudiate this genealogy (11, 10: *FRA* 423, 8).

21 Her. 2, 41: 8, 37.

22 *Ars. Amat.* 3, 393: *FRA* 151, 2.

23 Diod. S. 1, 24: *FRA* 104, 29. For Isis-Io *cf. RE s.v.* Isis 2121. *Cf. supra,* pp. 83; 138, n. 34; 168.

24 Herodotus had hellenized 'Apis' as 'Epaphus', but about the half-divine and half-historical role of Epaphus there was not absolute agreement in the Graeco-Roman world. Some (*e.g.* Ovid, Apollodorus, Eusebius and other later writers) regarded him both as son of Io and founder of Memphis, and as Pharaoh. According to Mnaseas (quoted by Plutarch) he was Dionysus-Osiris. Aelian cites 'the Egyptians' as rejecting the affiliation of Epaphus to Io. In an important article (*Syria*, 1952, 1–43) Bérard argues that Epaphus was an historically real person and identifies him with the Hyksos Apophis. See also Van Seters, *The Hyksos* (London, 1966), 155.

25 1, 6, 1. Dalmeyda expresses surprise that this oracle is not mentioned again. But the fact of redaction must be allowed for. Moreover, Isis and Artemis fulfil interchangeable roles.

26 Strabo 14, 5, 12; 16, 2, 5.

27 The whole passage has been studied by Merkelbach, *RMA* 94.

28 See *VS* 301.

29 See Dalmeyda's note on 5, 1, 9.

30 *RMA* 108.

31 *TTT* Pl. X, fig. 2. F. J. Dolger, in his wide-ranging *IXΘΥΣ*, seems little interested in this (158, n. 3). Merkelbach (*RMA* 163) argues that the fisherman is a significant character in the Isiac mystery drama.

32 *Archaeologiai Ertesitö* 91 (1964), 176–91.

33 *Cf. CAH* 12, 427.

34 *Cf. TTT* 65.

35 Athan. *Vit Anton.* 90: *FRA* 561, 24.

36 *Cf.* F. H. Hallock, in *Egyptian Religion*, New York, vol. 2, 1934, p. 11.

37 *Cf. supra,* p. 243.

38 Plut. 2: *FRA* 220, 14ff.

39 Plut. 3: *FRA* 221, 1ff.

40 *Cf. supra,* pp. 72, 84, 123.

41 *Cf. supra,* n. 3.

CHAPTER XIX

1 *Cf. supra,* p. 25. For Anaxandrides (criticizing in the early fourth century) see Athen. 7, 299f.: *FRA* 52, 6ff., especially the line 'You worship the ox, but I sacrifice to the gods.' See also *SEG* 18, 698. *Cf.* further *FRA* Index p. 811, col. 2 *fin.* (animalium cultus) *deridetur vel condemnatur.* Clearly it was a stock gibe.

2 There, of course, he is stated to have come into contact with historical personages about whom we have information from other sources and to have visited places about which we know much: *cf. CAH* 11, 257.

3 *Ibid.* The work (with a title signifying 'mighty deeds') gives an account (from Chapter 13 onwards, after Peter's disappearance from the scene—*cf.* the significant 'what was become of Peter' in 12, 16—of Paul's 'complicated journeyings' through Asia Minor and the coastal towns of the Aegean. His preaching tours took him to what may fairly be called 'Isiac centres'.

4 *Acts* 14, 12. For *Hermes-Evangelos* cf. *supra*, p. 207.

5 Cf. E. B. Howell's interesting article in *Greece and Rome*, March, 1964, 'St. Paul and the Greek World'. But an important fact is not appreciated, namely that often the names borne by members of the Pauline circle are of a theophoric type found among the followers of the Egyptian cult. Whatever the explanation, we are entitled to assume that the class of person with whom Paul dealt was the same as that so commonly met with in the religion of Isis and her Temple Associates. Just as the Jew Saul adopted the name 'Paulos' (*Acts* 13, 9 —silently introduced) so in the Isiac faith a name could be adopted 'in religion', *e.g.* in *VS* 278 Theodorus the priest of Isis adopts the name of Eisiodorus(υἱοθεσία occurs at Rhodes very frequently). Examples are these: Apollos (*VS* 156), Artemas (347), Dionysius (171), Hermes (393, 448), and Silvanus (672). The Epaphras-Epaphroditus of the *Pauline Epistles* has the same name as an Isiac priest (*VS* 36: cf. 27, 28, 37, 533c and 657). The priests Jason son of Jason (*VS* 136) and Jason Aeneas (*VS* 279) recall the names Jason and Aeneas of *Acts* 17, 5; 9, 34. Other names worth mention here are Crescens (*VS* 382), Epaenetus (227), Eutychus (111d: cf. 462, 533h, 619, 550, 556), Onesimus (415, 419), Nymphe (594), Sosipatros (193), Theophilos (319, 491), and Tryphaena (641). Cumulatively the resemblance of names is striking.

6 In Heliodorus (3, 13: *FRA* 455, 41) Calasiris 'Prophet of Isis of

Memphis' virtually combines the two terms in the remark that the gods are infallibly known by the wise man: τὴν σοφοῦ γνῶσιν οὐκ ἂν ιαφύγοιεν.

7 *I Cor.* 4, 1. The οἰκόνομοι resemble in name those officers who kept bread bills at the Sarapeum (*UPZ* 56, 7).

8 *Phil.* 4, 12.

9 *VS* 351. Vidman dates it to 'the imperial age'.

10 Already in the fourth century BC Tarsus had a Baal with lotus-crowned sceptre. The appearance, therefore, in *Romans* 11, 4, of a Baal with the feminine article suggests Baltis, for whom see Ch. X, n. 29.

11 Over a century ago Barker (191) wrote about 'the prevalence of the Isiac worship' at Tarsus (cf. also p. 177, and Goldman, *Tarsus* I, 208). Drexler, although he gives examples of Isis on coins of Tarsus (216-25), is critical of Barker's exuberant remarks.

12 The 'Acts' (Πράξεις) have at least a nominal resemblance to the πράξεις ἐναργεῖς of Isis (Diod. S. 1, 25: *FRA* 105, 7).

13 Cf. *CAH* 11, 257.

14 Paus. 10, 32, 9: *FRA* 339, 12. For incubation cf. *supra*, pp. 192, 225-6. For dreams cf. *supra*, p. 93, and p. 196, n. 6. See further Bonnet *s.v.* 'Traum'. Christians at Gadara in the Holy Land practised the same kind of incubation, sitting all night amid the lamps and the incense (*PL* 72, 902: *mittuntur intus luminaria et incensum; et sedent in isto solio tota nocte: et dum soporati fuerint videt ille qui mundatus est aliquam visionem.*)

15 See Plut. 17; *FRA* 228, 25 and *CE* pp. 290-1. The BVM at the Athonite monastery of Docheiariou (*Athos*, Norwich-Sitwell-Costa, 154), 'reproved a negligent monastic butler for allowing the smoke of his candle to scorch her image, blinded him when he persisted, then later forgave him and restored his sight'. *Plus ça change plus c'est la même chose.*

16 Juv. 13, 93. *FRA* 282, 18. *Cf. VS* 464: sacrilege will arouse Isis' wrath.

17 See Roscher, 374-9 for Palestine, Syrophoenicia and Syria.

18 For Samaria generally *cf. PEFQ* 1933, 19: 1932, 17; 1962, 124. *VS* 361a. G. F. Hill (*Some Palestinian Cults*, London, 1912, 4) dealing with Samaria remarks, 'The cult of Sarapis, to judge from the coins, played a great part'. For Jerusalem *cf. Jerusalem*, H. Vincent and F. M. Abel, Paris 1914-26, pp. 695, 880, 888.

19 Hill (*op. cit.*) gives no such indication. He mentions only such goddesses as Athena, Hygieia, Ephesian Artemis, Astarte-Aphrodite and Atargatis (as well as Osiris in the reign of Antoninus Pius).

20 *Cf.* Drexler *s.v.* and *PEFQ* 1914, 195.

21 *Cf.* the apposite citation *TTT*, p. 1.

22 Deissmann, 133.

23 Drexler, 59. 379. *OL* 86. Hor., *Odes* 3, 29, 9: *FRA* 147, 2. Apul., Ch. 2: *FRA* 318, 26-7. For the 'marines' of Isis see *VS* 302 (Ephesus): ναυβατοῦντες is worth comparing with ἐμβατεύων of Coloss. 2, 18.

24 The narrative (*Acts* 7, 58) makes Paul connive with those who stoned the Hellenist.

25 Josephus, *Ant.* 20, 8, 6; *Bell.* 2, 13, 6.

26 *Acts* 13, 46; 18, 6.

27 *Cf. supra*, p. 68.

28 The woman Lydia from Thyateira came from a Lydian city which depicted on its coins Isis standing with sistrum and sceptre. (Drexler *s.v.*). Isis in an inscription is named 'Lydia' (*VS* 371).

29 *VS* 113.

30 *VS* 112.

31 Paus. 1, 4, 7: *FRA* 333, 15.

32 For tonsures see Otto, II, 256, n. 3.

33 Paus. 1, 2, 3: 333, 11-14.

34 Paul resided at Ephesus a long time: *cf. CAH* 11, 257.

35 See Miltner, 72. The term *Serapis*lehre is needlessly restrictive. What was so dangerous was the Ephesian devotion to the 'Great Divinity' Artemis-Isis (the divine *greatness* had been hymned already in the fifth century by the poet Timotheus, as Picard has pointed out). Ramsay, 129, connects the hyperdulia of the Blessed Virgin Mary at Ephesus with an Anatolian Virgin Mother, but is silent about an Artemis-Isis fusion.

36 Inscriptions for the four places: *VS* 159ff., 252-3, 256, 268.

37 See Liban. 11, 114: *FRA* 542, 26.

38 Their date, of course, is mid-first century: AD 50-64. *Cf. CAH* 11, 257.

39 *PL* 38, 1022.

40 Plut. 70: *FRA* 255, 8.

41 Heliod. 3, 13: *FRA* 455, 37ff. The *prophetes* speaks with highest authority (*cf. supra*, p. 94). For epigraphical references see *VS* 359, 383, 384, 434, 725.

42 So Alföldi (supported by Leclant), *Jahr. für Ant. und Christ.* 1965-6, 87.

43 *Cf. supra*, p. 195.

44 *Coloss.* 2, 15.

45 For Sarapis-Helios-Cosmocrator see *VS* 389, and the reference to astrology. *Cf. supra*, p. 237 and p. 242. For cosmocrator *cf. supra*, p. 241.

46 *Eph.* 6, 12; *Gal.* 4, 9. *Cf.* Pascher, 59. The 'elements' are obedient to Isis as she appears to Lucius (Apul., Ch. 25: *FRA* 327, 35).

47 *Eph., ibid.*

48 Buecheler-Riese, *Anth. Lat.* 723, 8 (Claudi. *De Luna*).

49 *Aerisoni lugentia flumina Nili,* Statius, *Theb.* 1, 265: *FRA* 784, 36. *Cf.* Ausonius *Ep.* 29, 22-23:

*Isiacos agitant Mareotica sistra
    tumultus
nec Dodonaei cessat tinnitus aeni.*

50 For the *prophetes* and the priest
wisdom, in the real sense, 'has
regard to things in the heavens
above' (Heliod. 3, 16: *FRA* 456,
32–34). *"Ἄνω πρὸς τὰ οὐράνια*
resembles *τὰ πνευματικὰ ἐν τοῖς
ἐπουρανίοις* in *Eph.* 6, 12.

51 Apul., Ch. 28: *FRA* 328, 41ff.
Cf. Ch. 23: *FRA* 326, 33. Also *Kore
Kosmou, FRA* 390, 6; Plut. 23; *FRA*
232, 3.

52 *OL* 152. Festugière (*Rev. bibl.* 41,
257–61) refers to this statement,
which he translates (cited Vandebeek, 136) as 'Those who invoke thee
in the true way, *i.e.* according to thy
true name.' This hardly does justice to
the fact of Isiac *faith. Tim.* 1, 3, 9; 2,
1, 3; 2, 2, 10, 53. *VS* 390.

54 For *fides Augusta* see Axtell, 21.
For *spes, ibid.* 18. For *Isityche* and *spes*
in juxtaposition see *VS* 528. *Cf.* also
RMA 267, n. 5. For Aristides (*Or.* 45,
33: *FRA* 306, 33) Sarapis appeared
miraculously to men when they were
past hope and faith.

55 See Witt, *Studia Patristica*, VIII,
136. *Elpis* appears as a name 'in
religion' in an Isiac inscription *VS*
347. At Philippi, even in post-Isiac
times, a dedicant could bear the
name *Elpidios* (*BCH* 60, 48).

56 *Cf. supra*, n. 5 and Ch. XVI, n. 49.

57 See *VS* 535. He appears at
Rome (*VS* 418) fourth after Sol-
Sarapis-Jupiter, Liber and Mercury.

58 *OL* 143.

59 *Phil.* 2, 9.

60 Epaphroditus, the stolist of Isis,
offered an *eucharisterion* (*VS* 27), like
Longus (*VS* 351), and Aurelius (with
theophoric name *Origen*) to Sarapis
and his divine associates (*VS* 802).
See further *VS* 132, 406 and 550. For
the *ecclesiasterion, TTT* 36.

61 *Coloss.* 3, 11. *Cf. Hymns Cyme*
(15) and *Ios* (12). Vandebeek (107)
well compares the Isiac view with a
passage from Akhenaten.

62 My view of Paul differs much
from that of Carl Clemen, *Der Isiskult
und das Neue Testament.*

CHAPTER XX

1 See Singer, 179. Schopp's 'gloating account' is cited of the death
scene on 8 February 1600. 'Bruno
with a threatening gesture addressed
the judges, "Perchance you who
pronounce my sentence are in greater
fear than I who receive it." ' A
Bernard Shaw might set this against
the brief mention by A. Pupi, in the
New Cath. Enc. 1967 (*s.v.*): 'Bruno's
speculative work was interrupted by
a tragic event. . . .'

2 See Yates, 115–16 and *cf.* 259 with
references. F. Saxl (*Lectures, Warburg,*
I, 184) holds the Pope was 'probably
within the limits of orthodoxy'.

3 The Third Dialogue is of special
interest (Singer, 317): the astral
dwellers when they lower their eyes
perceive 'this divinity that we call the
Earth, which hath been named Ceres,
figured as Isis, entitled Proserpine and
Diana, and is the same which is called
Lucina in the heaven', etc.

4 Gibbon was moved in particular
by the irreparable loss of the Library,
exciting 'the regret and indignation
of every spectator whose mind was
not totally darkened by religious
prejudice'.

5 *Praep. Evang.* 3, 5, 5. The word
'now' (ἤδη) implies the early fourth
century.

6 Esslie, *Le Renouvellement d'Isis*;
Baltrušaitis, *La Quête d'Isis. Introduction à l'Egyptomanie.*

7 *I Tim.* 6, 20. It is 'falsely so called'—*pseudonymous*.

8 Vidman's *Sylloge inscriptionum religionis Isiacae et Sarapiacae* came to hand opportunely. My debt to this important and long needed source-book is evident.

9 Theodor Hopfner's *Fontes Historiae Religionis Aegyptiacae (FRA)* although now half a century old is still indispensable. The bulk of my references are citations from either *FRA* or *VS*.

10 Della Corte (cited *TTT* 60) estimates the number of Isiacs at Pompeii as 10 per cent of the total population: 2000 out of 20,000.

11 Roscher's caption 'mit der Jungfrau Maria identificiert' raises a methodological problem.

12 *Cf. supra*, p. 100, for Isis Pelagia. Usener (xxiv) argues that Isis exerted influence on the legend of St Pelagia.

13 Briffault (III, 184) points out that the Blessed Virgin Mary controls the Moon and through this the stars and all the planets. In these respects again she functions as Isis.

14 For Isis as Kore Paredros of Sarapis *cf. supra*, p. 242. For Isis Nymphe *cf. VS* 111 d.

15 *Innumera propter innumerabilem seu infinitam laudationum copiam* (Joh. Damasc. *Orat. 4 Nativ. S. Virg.*). Seven entries appear for *omnia omnibus*, an expression suggestive of Isis. *Cf.* Witt, *PCPS* 192, p. 55.

16 His alphabetically arranged aretalogy gives the Praises of Mary (*innumera laudum encomia*) in eighteen books. Maria Myrionymos shares other names with Isis, *e.g.* Augusta, Aurora, Gubernatrix, and Primigenia (Primogenita). She can also be called Exorcista, Jupiter and Mars.

17 With greater fidelity to the New Testament she is a ewe with a lamb.

18 *Cf. supra*, pp. 47–70.

19 The Panagia is ἀκτὶς νοητοῦ 'Ηλίου. Isis is 'in the rays of the Sun' (*Cyme Hymn* 44–5) and *Solis ambagibus dispensans incerta lumina* (Apul. Ch. 2: *FRA* 318, 31–2). Christ is 'lamplighter of truth in Egypt' (λάμψας ἐν τῇ Αἰγύπτῳ φωτισμὸν ἀληθείας). See *PG* 92: 1337 A.B.D. 1341A. 1344C. 1345B. Notice too Εὐθηνία Isis was so named *Plenty*. See B. M. *Cat. Coins of Alexandria*, index; Levi I, 265; *OL* 135; *supra* Ch. XIII, n. 32.

20 *Cf. supra*, p. 15, n.10.

21 *Cf.* Tarn, 360.

22 Weber, 34. *Cf.* Budge, *Gods* II, 220–21.

23 Caxton's translation is given of no. 25 of *Les cent histoires de troye*, Paris 1499/1500: 'Ysis fait les plantes et tous les grains fructifier.' Christine de Pisan was born in 1364. *Cf. supra*, pp. 26, 195. For the link between Isis and Mary as Divine Engrafter *cf. JWCI* II, 68.

24 H. W. Müller, *Münchner Jahrb. bild. Kunst*, 1963, 35, cites the relevant passage from *Hist. Geneal. de la Maison des Briçonnet*, 1620. For the false etymology of *Paris* see Baltrušaitis, *op. cit.*

25 For the 'blending' *cf. ERE* 7, 436.

26 *Cf.* Tarn, *loc. cit.* Petrie, 138–9. But L. Bréhier (*Comptes rendus Acad. Inser.* 1935, 379) denies there is any evidence of affiliation with a black Ephesian Artemis, Demeter, Tanit or Isis, though he permits himself to mention Byzantium and Syria. Perhaps the St Germain idol was black!

27 *PL* 33, 185. *Cf.* Lawson, 46: In Greece are 'churches built with the material of the old temples or superimposed upon their foundation', which is 'evidence of a deliberate policy on the part of the Church'.

28 Bede, *Hist.* Ch. 30.

29 See Emery, *JEA* 55, 34.

30 *Cf. supra*, p. 186.

31 Examples can be found in Britain, *e.g.* at Lullingstone and at Stone near Faversham.

32 *VS* 20, 52, 65, 88, 89, 90, 101, 102, 107, 112, 113, 120, 127, 138, 145, 147, 158, 179, 264, 313, 352a, 362, 370, 374, 379, 384, 451, 502, 510, 513, 563, 586, 589, 592, 598, 623, 648, 718, 719, 720, 721, 767. *Cf.* 275-6, 283 317 (found near mosques).

33 'Still in the fifth century AD the church and temple at Philae were contiguous', *Jahrb. deutsch. Archaeol. Inst.* 54, 123.

34 *Cf. supra*, p. 136. Witt, *Studia Patristica* VIII, 143.

35 So Michel and Struck, *Ath. Mitteil.* 1906, 323-4: 'Unsere Kirche ... zwar als Ersatzbau für eine dem antiken Isis-Eileithyia-Kultus entsprechende Eleutherios-Tempel-Kirche, welche Personifikation neben der Panagia bis auf den heutigen Tag fortdauert.' See *supra*, p. 67.

36 *VS* 451. *Cf.* J. Toynbee and J. Ward Perkins, *The Shrine of St Peter* (London 1956), 82ff. Note 'Tomb of the Egyptians', *ibid.* 51.

37 So Fortescue, 308: 'A wooden clapper or rattle may be used instead of the bell.' The practice exists in the Ethiopian Church. *Cf.* B.M. Or. MS. 584, f. 232r.

38 *Cf. supra*, p. 29.

39 Plut. 9: *FRA* 224, 6-7.

40 The year was 1962. For the sake of exactitude the ikon was seen just after its transport to its temporary abode: *cf.* p. 85 of Witt, *Greece* ...

41 So Ampelas, Ἱστορία τῆς Νήσου Σύρου, p. 292. *Cf.* for the Egyptian gods *VS* 151-7, and *CE* passim. For the Tenos festivals of Poseidon in March and Dionysus in August see St Philippidis in Κυκλ. Ἡμερολ. 1928, 118-20.

42 *VS* 155. *Cf.* Stephanos, Ἐπιγρ.

Νήσου Σύρου, 42. Claudius was honoured by the Senate at Ephesus with a statue.

43 See Stephanus, *op. cit.* 78: *e.g.* Εὔπλοια τῷ Φιλοσέραπι τῷ Ἰουλιανῷ.

44 So Ampelas, *op. cit.* 292-3. He conjectures that Christianity was established there round about the fifth century. For coins from Syros in the British Museum see Roscher, 382. For the Egyptian gods as Πολιοοῦχοι Θεοί at Delos *cf. CE* 110.

45 *Cf. supra*, p. 178.

46 Isidorus of Miletus (active 532-7) and Isidorus the Younger (558-63).

47 Constantine is said by Zosimus (2, 31) to have set up pagan statues in the Hippodrome (to Apollo, Rhea and the Tyche of Rome). Although this is challenged by A. H. M. Jones there is surely nothing improbable in the statement. We know (Sozom. *Eccles. hist.* 2, 5: *FRA* 660, 7; Theodor., *Hist. eccles.* 5, 21, 1: *FRA* 667, 25) that the Emperor's habit was to conserve rather than to destroy. *Cf. supra*, Ch. XI, n. 26. In the same way Justinian, despite his suppression of the cult of Isis at Philae, is recorded by Procopius (*Bell. Pers.* 1, 19, 37: *FRA* 708, 16) to have ordered the temple statues to be sent to Byzantium.

48 *Cf. supra*, p. 194.

49 For the Athenian oath see Diod. S. 1, 29: *FRA* 107, 27-8. To swear 'by the dog' was a Socratic habit: and Socrates knew very well he was taking this oath in the name of 'the Egyptian god', *i.e.* Anubis (Gorg. 482b: *FRA* 44, 8). Perhaps the blasphemous Italian 'diocane' (said to be Tuscan) is to be traced back to the presence centuries ago of the dog-headed Anubis in Italy (*cf. VS* 599; Juv. 6, 534: *FRA* 281, 23).

50 Brandon, p. 297, has brought

the First Gospel into theological connection with Egypt, more particularly Alexandria. About the iconographical links scholars are not agreed. Snijder thirty years ago could find no connection (*cf.* Nilsson, *Geschichte* 2, 632, n. 1). But opinion nowadays has changed and it has been considered now possible, now probable, and sometimes even certain. Dalton, years ago one of Britain's foremost Byzantinologists, found the Hodegetria type of the Panagia 'very probably of Egyptian derivation' and the Deesis resemblance to the representation of Isis and Horus 'so strong as to be almost convincing' (p. 673). Bearing in mind with Diehl (*Manuel d'Art Byz.*, I, 83) that a deep influence was exerted by the art of Hellenistic Egypt on Byzantium, we must be struck (if we look without prejudice and with objective detachment) at the general iconographical similarity. Campbell Bonner (221 *et al.*) thinks the group of Isis with Horus on her lap 'probably had some effect'. Wellen (163-4) with like caution holds that the possibility of the Egyptian representation having more or less prompted the type of Panagia Galaktotrophusa is not altogether excluded. C. R. Morey (89, n. 145) states categorically, 'The Karanis fresco is an excellent example of Egyptian type of Isis suckling Horus, which affords a prototype of Christian Madonna.' Still more boldly H. W. Müller (in *Münchner Jahrb. bild. Kunst*, 1963, p. 34) writes about the artistic transformation of Isis and the infant Horus to the Virgin Mary with the child Jesus.

51 This is well argued by Brandon, *loc. cit.*

52 Aristo of Alexandria, quoted by Plutarch (*FRA* 177, 14ff.) *Cf. OL* 150.

53 Here (according to Plut. 3 : *FRA* 220, 24-5) Isis was known as Chief of the Muses (*cf. supra*, Ch. XIII, n. 9 *ad fin.*) and Justice.

54 Discussed by Doresse, *Hieroglyphes*, n. 71 on p. 27.

55 The tale is given by Amélineau, *Contes et Romans de l'Egypte chrétienne*, Paris, 1888.

56 *Strom.* 3, 63, 2. For Isis as foe, Münster 197.

57 *Matth.* 12, 42 and *Luke* 11, 31. *Cf. supra*, p. 61. We must not forget that in the Old Testament (*I Kings* 4, 30) King Solomon's wisdom ($\phi\rho\acute{o}\nu\eta\sigma\iota\varsigma$ in the *Septuagint*) surpassed that of other lands, including Egypt.

58 Cooper, 49.

59 Cited by Leipoldt and Morenz, 187.

60 See Boll, *Sphaera* p. 513 and *cf.* pp. 129, 224, 242.

61 Cooper, 43.

62 *Cf. supra*, p. 192.

63 *Jude*, 3, terms intelligible to an Isiac.

64 The Coptic and Ethiopian rites apparently offer close parallels to Isiacism, e.g. howling, dancing, liturgical fans and rattles (all dealt with by Fortescue).

65 Nonnus Monachus, *ad Greg. Orat. Jul.* 2, 32: *FRA* 717, 1ff.

66 In AD 553. Note *Horus* as a Saint.

67 See Smith and Wace, *Dict. Christ. Biog. s.vv.*, London, 1887.

68 Plut. 2: *FRA* 220, 1.

69 Yates, 115-6. 259. Another scene shows the Discovery of Osiris' Limbs: *Uxor eius membra discepta tandem invenit.*

70 See Münster, 207-8. *Supra*, p. 14 and Ch. X, n. 7.

BIBLIOGRAPHY

ALFÖLDI, A. *A Festival of Isis in Rome.* Budapest, 1937.

AXTELL, H. L. *The Deification of Abstract Ideas in Roman Literature and Inscriptions.* Chicago, 1907.

BAEGE, W. *De Macedonum Sacris,* Halle, 1913.

BALTRŠUAITIS, J. *La Quête d'Isis, Introduction à l'Egyptomanie. Essai sur la legende d'un myth.* Paris, 1967.

BARKER, W. B. *Lares and Penates.* London, 1853.

BELL, H. I. *Cults and Creeds in Graeco-Roman Egypt.* Liverpool, 1953.

BERGMAN, J. *Ich bin Isis (Acta Univ. Uppsal.: Historia Religionum 3).* Uppsala, 1968.

BONNEAU, D. *La Crue du Nil.* Paris, 1964.

BONNER, C. *Studies in Magical Amulets.* Ann Arbor and London, 1950.

BONNET, H. B. C. *Reallexikon der ägyptischen Religionsgeschichte.* Berlin, 1952.

BOTTI, G. *Fouilles à la Colonne Theodosienne (Bull. Soc. Arch. Alex.).* Vienna, 1897.

BOUSSET, W. *Die Offenbarung Johannis.* Göttingen, 1906.

BRADY, T. A. *The Reception of the Egyptian Cults by the Greeks.* Columbia, 1935.

BRANDON, S. G. F. *Jesus and the Zealots.* Manchester, 1967.

BRIFFAULT, R. *The Mothers.* London, 1927.

BRION, M. *Pompeii and Herculaneum.* London, 1960.

BUDGE, E. A. T. W. *The Book of the Dead.* London, 1898.

—— *The Gods of the Egyptians.* London, 1904.

—— *Legends of the Gods.* London, 1912.

—— *From Fetish to God in Ancient Egypt.* London, 1932.

BURCKHARDT, J. *Die Zeit Constantins des Grossen.* Berne, 1950.

BUTCHER (née FLOYER), E. L. *Story of the Church in Egypt.* London, 1897.

ČERNÝ, J. *Ancient Egyptian Religion.* London, 1952.

CHAPOUTHIER, F. *Les Dioscures au Service d'une Déesse.* Paris, 1935.

CHOUKAS, M. *Black Angels of Athos.* Brattleboro, Vermont, 1935.

CHRISTINE DE PISAN. *Les cent histoires de troye.* 1499/1500.

CIACERI, E. *Culti e Miti.* Catania, 1911.

CLARK, R. T. RUNDLE. *Myth and Symbol in Ancient Egypt.* London, 1959.

CLEMEN, K. *Der Isiskult und das Neue Testament. (Heinrici Festschrift: Neuetestamentliche Studien,* pp. 28–39). Leipzig, 1914.

COOPER, W. R. *The Horus Myth in its Relation to Christianity.* London, 1877.

DALTON, O. M. *Byzantine Art and Archaeology.* Oxford, 1911.

DAWSON, C. M. *Romano-Campanian Landscape Painting.* Yale, 1944.

DEISSMANN, G. A. *Paulus*. Tübingen, 1911.

DEMITSAS, M. G. Μακεδονία ἐν λίθοις φθεγγομένοις καὶ μνημείοις σωζομένοις. Athens, 1896.

DENNIS, J. T. *The Burden of Isis; being the laments of Isis and Nephthys*. London, 1910.

DESROCHES-NOBLECOURT, C. *Tutankhamen*. Harmondsworth, 1965.

DIEHL, Ch. *Manuel d'art byzantin*. Paris, 1925.

DILL, S. *Roman Society from Nero to Marcus Aurelius*. London and New York, 1904.

DOMASZEWSKI, A. VON *Die Rangordnung des römischen Heeres*. Bonn, 1908.

D'ONOFRIO, C. *Gli Obelischi di Roma*. Rome, 1965.

DORESSE, J. *Des Hieroglyphes à la croix*. Paris, 1960.

—— *The Secret Books of the Egyptian Gnostics*. London, 1960.

DOWNEY, R. E. G. *A History of Antioch in Syria*. Princeton, 1962.

DREXLER, W. *Der Isis- und Sarapis-Cultus in Kleinasien*. Vienna, 1889.

DRIOTON, E. *Le Théatre Egyptien*. Cairo, 1942.

ERMAN, A. (*transl.* by A. M. BLACKMAN). *The Literature of the Ancient Egyptians*. London, 1927.

FAULKNER, R. O. *The Ancient Egyptian Pyramid Texts*. Oxford, 1970.

FORTESCUE, A. K. *Ceremonies of the Roman Rite*. London, 1943.

GEFFCKEN, J. *Kaiser Julianus*. Leipzig, 1914.

GIEHLOW, K. Die Hieroglyphenkunde des Humanismus in der Allegorie der Renaissance (*Jahrb. Kunsthist. Sammlung*). Vienna, 1915.

GONZENBACH, V. VON *Untersuchung zu den Knabenweihen im Isiskult*. Bonn, 1957.

GOODENOUGH, E. R. *Jewish Symbols in the Graeco-Roman Period*. New York, 1953.

GRAILLOT, H. *Le Culte de Cybèle, mère des dieux*. Paris, 1912.

GRIFFITHS, J. GWYN *The Conflict of Horus and Seth*. Liverpool, 1960.

GRIMM, G. *Zeugnisse ägyptischer Religion und Kunstelemente im römischen Deutschland*. Leiden, 1969.

GUTHRIE, W. K. C. *Orpheus and Greek Religion*. London, 1950.

HAGEN, P. *Der Gral*. Strasbourg, 1900.

HATCH, E. *The Influence of Greek Ideas and Usages upon the Christian Church* (Hibbert Lectures). London, 1888.

HEMBERG, B. *Die Kabiren*. Uppsala, 1950.

HOPFNER, T. *Fontes Historiae Religionis Aegyptiacae*, Bonn, 1922.

IVERSEN, E. *The Myth of Egypt and its Hieroglyphs in European Tradition*. Copenhagen, 1961.

JAMES, E. O. *The Tree of Life*. Leiden, 1966.

JIDEJAIN, N. *Byblos through the Ages*. Beirut, 1968.

JOUGUET, P. (*ed.* HANOTAUX, G. A. A.) *Histoire de la Nation Egyptienne*, vol. 3. Paris, 1933.

JUNKER H. and WINTER, E. *Das Geburtshaus des Tempels der Isis in Philä.* Vienna, 1965.

KEES, H. *Das Priestertum im ägyptischen Staat.* Leiden, 1953.

—— *Aegypten (Religionsgeschichtes Lesebuch—10, ed. A. BERTHOLET).* Tübingen, 1928.

KÖBERLEIN, E. *Caligula und die ägyptische Kulte.* Meissenheim, 1962.

LAFAYE, G. *Histoire du culte des divinités d'Alexandrie.* Paris, 1884.

LAWSON, J. C. *Modern Greek Folklore and Ancient Greek Religion.* Cambridge, 1910.

LAZARIDES, D. I. *Οἱ Φίλιπποι.* [Guide to Philippi] Thessalonica, 1956.

LEIPOLDT, J. *Die Religionen in der Umwelt des Urchristentums,* 9-11 *(Bilderatlas zur Religionsgeschichte, ed. H. HAAS).* Leipzig, 1926.

LEIPOLDT, J. and MORENZ, S. *Heilige Schriften.* Leipzig, 1953.

LEVI, D. *Antioch Mosaic Pavements,* 2 vols. Princeton, 1947.

L'ORANGE, H. P. *Studies on the Iconography of Cosmic Kingship in the Ancient World.* Oslo, 1953.

LUCIUS, E. *Die Anfänge des Heiligenkults in der Christlichen Kirche.* Tübingen, 1904.

MARUCCHI, O. *Gli Obelischi egiziani di Roma.* Rome, 1898.

MASCALL, E. L. and BOX, H. S. (eds.) *The Blessed Virgin Mary: appendix.* London, 1963.

MAYASSIS, S. *Le Livre des Morts de l'Égypte ancienne est un livre d'initiation.* Athens, 1955.

MERKELBACH, R. *Roman und Mysterium in der Antike.* Berlin, 1962.

MILTNER, F. *Ephesos.* Vienna, 1958.

MONTET, P. *Byblos et l'Egypte.* Paris, 1928-29.

MORENZ, S. *Die Geschichte von Joseph dem Zimmermann.* Berlin, 1951.

MOREY, C. R. *Early Christian Art.* Princeton, 1942.

MOTHER MARY and WARE, KALLISTOS. *The Festal Menaion.* London, 1969.

MÜLLER, D. *Aegypten und die griechischen Isis-Aretalogien.* Berlin, 1961.

MÜNSTER, M. *Untersuchungen zur Göttin Isis.* Berlin, 1968.

NASH, E. *Pictorial Dictionary of Ancient Rome.* London, 1968.

NERVAL, G. DE *Les Filles du Feu.* Paris, 1888.

NILSSON, N. M. P. *A History of Greek Religion.* Oxford, 1925. *Geschichte der griechischen Religion.* Munich, 1949.

OTTO, W. G. A. *Priester und Tempel im hellenistischen Aegypten.* Leipzig and Berlin, 1905-1908.

PANOFSKY, E. *Albrecht Dürer.* Princeton, 1943.

PAPADAKIS, N. *'Αρχ. Δελτίον* I, 1915. Athens, 1915.

PAPADOPOULOS-KERAMEUS, A. I. *Varia Graeca Sacra.* St Petersburg, 1909.

PASCHER, J. *'Η Βασιλικὴ 'Οδός.* Paderborn, 1931.

PEAKE, A. S. *A Commentary on the Bible.* London, 1919.

PEEK, W. *Isishymnus von Andros, und verwandete Texte.* Berlin, 1930.

PELEKIDIS, S. 'Ἀπὸ τὴν Πολιτεία καὶ τὴν Κοινωια τῆς 'Αρχαίας Θεσσα λονίκης. Thessalonica, 1934.

PENDLEBURY, J. D. S. *Aegyptiaca: A Catalogue of Egyptian Objects in the Aegean Area.* Cambridge, 1930.

PETERSON, E. Εἷς Θεός. Göttingen, 1926.

PETRIE, W. M. FLINDERS *Egypt and Israel.* London, 1925.

PORTER, B. and MOSS, R. L. B. *Topographical Bibliography of Ancient Egyptian Hieroglyphic Texts, Reliefs and Paintings.* Oxford, 1927.

PREGER, T. *Scriptores Originum Constantinopolitan arum.* Leipzig 1901.

QUIBELL, J. E. (ed.) *Studies presented to F. Llewellyn Griffith.* London, 1932.

RAMSAY, W. M. *Pauline and other Studies.* London, 1906.

RODD, J. R. *The Customs and Lore of Modern Greece.* London, 1892.

ROEDER, G. *Urkunden zur Religion des alten Aegypten.* Jena, 1923.

—— *Die Denkmäler des Pelizaeus-Museums.* Berlin, 1921.

ROSCHER, W. H. *Ausführliches Lexikon für griechische und römische Mythologie* s.v. 'Isis'. Leipzig, 1882–1921.

ROSTOVTZEV, M. I. *The Social and Economic History of the Hellenistic World.* Oxford, 1941.

ROUSSEL, P. *Les cultes Egyptiens à Delos.* Paris and Nancy, 1915–16.

RUSCH, A. *De Sarapide et Iside in Graecia cultis.* Berlin, 1906.

SAINTYVES, P. (i.e. EMILE NOURRY) *S. Christophe, successeur d'Anubis, d'Hermès et d'Héraclès.* Paris, 1936.

SANDMAN, M. HOLMBERG *The God Ptah.* Lund, 1946.

SCHEFOLD, C. *Orient, Hellas und Rom.* Berne, 1949.

—— *Vergessenes Pompeji.* Munich, 1962.

SCULLARD, H. H. *From the Gracchi to Nero.* London, 1959.

SINGER, D. W. *Giordano Bruno, his Life and Thought.* New York, 1950.

SNIDJDER, G. A. S. *De forma matris cum infante sedentis.* Utrecht, 1920.

STARR, C. G. *The Roman Imperial Navy.* Ithaca, N.Y., 1941.

TARN, W. W. (ed. GRIFFITH, G. T.) *Hellenistic Civilisation.* London, 1952.

TRAM TAM TINH *Le Culte d'Isis à Pompéi.* Paris, 1964.

TSCHUDIN, P. F. *Isis in Rom.* Aarau, 1962.

TRENCSÉNYI-WALDAPFEL, I. *Untersuchungen zur Religionsgeschichte.* Amsterdam, 1966.

USENER, H. *Legenden der heiligen Pelagia.* Bonn, 1879.

VANDEBEEK, G. *De Interpretatio Graeca van de Isisfigur.* Louvain, 1946.

VANDIER, J. *La Religion Egyptienne²* Paris, 1949.

VIDMAN, S. *Sylloge Inscriptionum Religionis Isiacae et Sarapiacae.* Berlin, 1969.

WEBER, W. *Aegyptisch-griechische Götter im Hellenismus.* Groningen, 1912.

WELLEN, G. A. *Theotokos.* Utrecht, 1961.

WESSELY, C. *Neue griechischen Zauberpapyri.* Vienna, 1893.

WITT, R. E. *The Importance of Isis for the Fathers. Studia Patristica* VIII, 135–45. Berlin, 1966.

WITT, R. E. Isis-Hellas. *Proceedings of the Cambridge Philological Society*, 192, (NS). Cambridge, 1966.

—— The Use of Agape in P. OXY. 1380.(*JTS* XIX, Pt. 1, 209, NS). Oxford, 1968.

—— The Egyptian Cults in Macedonia. *Balkan Studies*. Thessalonica, 1970.

—— The Flight into Egypt. *Studia Patristica* XI, 100–6. Berlin, 1971.

—— *Greece the Beloved*. Thessalonica, 1965.

YATES, F. A. *Giordano Bruno and the Hermetic Tradition*. London, 1964.

SOURCES OF ILLUSTRATIONS

Mansell-Alinari, 1–11, 22, 23, 26–28, 30, 36, 44–46, 71, 72; Musée de l'Homme, Paris, 12; Dr Henri Riad, 13; French School of Archaeology, Athens, 14; Professor James Cormack, 15; American School of Classical Studies at Athens, 16, 17; Trustees of the British Museum, 18, 20, 38–40, 47–51, 53; Trustees of the London Museum, 21; Rheinisches Bildarchiv, 19; Deutsches Archäologisches Institut, Rome, 24, 25, 41; Edwin Smith, 29; Fototeca Unione, 33, 43; courtesy of the Editor, *Berytus*, 34, 35; Gabinetto Fotografico Nazionale, Rome, 37; John Webb (from coins in the British Museum), 42, 54–67; Staatliche Museen zu Berlin, 69; from originals in Thames and Hudson's archives, 31, 32, 68, 70.

INDEX